Carl Vinson

As a young boy at family gatherings, I knew Carl Vinson as "Uncle Carl" long before I realized that on Capitol Hill and at the Pentagon, he was known as "Mr. Chairman" and "Boss of the Pentagon." My time in Washington in 1962 and 1963, as a young lawyer working for the House Armed Services Committee, exposed me to an inside view of global security challenges, including the Cuban Missile Crisis. It also made a deep impression on me as to Chairman Vinson's strong and responsible exercise of Congressional power. I have a vivid recollection of accompanying Chairman Vinson when he testified before Chairman Richard Russell's Senate Armed Services Committee—two powerful committees, two powerful Chairmen, both from Georgia. Carl Vinson dedicated his life to America's strength, security and freedom. He also inspired me, and I am sure many others, to serve our nation in the U.S. Congress. Carl Vinson's story is, in large part, the story of America's national security in the 20th century. This important story is now being expertly told by author James Cook. The lessons of his leadership should be learned by the young leaders who must protect America in the 21st century.

—Sam Nunn, former U.S. Senator

Dr. James Cook has done a masterful job. This book will become the definitive study of Carl Vinson. Not only is it a highly readable portrait of this great American patriot, but it is also a clear and compelling chronicle of how this remarkable congressional leader from Georgia got great things done for his country at a crucial time in our history.

—U.S. Senator Zell Miller (D-GA)

Two men head the list of Americans responsible for our victory in WWII: Franklin Roosevelt and Carl Vinson. Much of the two-ocean Navy that won the war in the Atlantic and Pacific was built, against heavy odds, during the lean years before the war through Vinson's extraordinary vision and effort. This is his remarkable and beautifully-told story.

—R. James Woolsey
Director of Central Intelligence, 1993-95

Carl Vinson was a legend who served the people of Georgia and America in Congress for fifty years. His vision, leadership and determination transformed the Naval forces of the United States for World War II and challenges that followed. Dr. James Cook's book vividly portrays the essence of one our Nation's greatest public servants. All who love freedom owe Carl Vinson a profound debt of gratitude. His example of honor, courage and commitment live on in the magnificent aircraft carrier that bears his name, our Sailors and Marines who serve today.

—Gordon R. England, Secretary of the Navy

The rise of American military power is directly related to the persistence, courage and wisdom of Carl Vinson. It is impossible to understand the American military from 1922 to the Vietnam era without studying the impact of Carl Vinson as the most powerful House member on military affairs. James Cook has made a major contribution to understanding the history of American national security.

—Newt Gingrich

Carl Vinson was a man firmly rooted in his Georgia district but with a larger national and world vision. Dr. Cook quotes liberally from Vinson's own words to define the man: a protagonist for a strong defense not dependent upon other nations; a thoughtful planner with a long view of the needs of the armed forces; an implacable enemy of waste; a fierce defender of the separate authorities of each branch of government, a master of the political arts and a devoted friend of the United States Navy.

This excellent and well-researched biography defines a patriot whose words today are as timely as when they were first spoken or written. As a naval officer and former Vice Chairman of the Joint Chiefs of Staff, I learned much from this book.

—David E. Jeremiah, Admiral, U. S. Navy (ret.)

Professor Cook has produced a terrific biography of Carl Vinson which should be mandatory reading for anyone interested in the development of the U. S. Navy as a global force.

—B. R. Inman, Admiral, U. S. Navy (Ret.),
Professor, Lyndon B Johnson School of Public Affairs,
The University of Texas at Austin.

Dr. James Cook does a wonderful job of describing the life and work of the "Father of the two ocean navy." Carl Vinson spoke at my graduation ceremony from the U. S. Naval Academy in 1964, and I am pleased that we have this definitive book on all that he did for our national security.

—John H. Dalton, 70th Secretary of the Navy

Carl Vinson was a true American patriot whose remarkable vision and leadership built our modern military. Today, we stand on the shoulders of his tireless efforts to make our country stronger and our world safer. For more than fifty years, Vinson's devotion to Georgia and his dedication to public service earned him the admiration, affection, and respect not only of his colleagues in Congress but of a grateful nation as well. This well-documented account of Vinson's life is critical in keeping his spirit alive and honoring his legacy of outstanding service to our nation.

U.S. Senator Saxby Chambliss (R-GA)

United States Senate
John Warner
Virginia

As the current Chairman of the Senate Armed Services Committee and former Secretary of the Navy, I have dealt with the Congressional Committees on Defense over many years. I can speak with some knowledge about the histories of these committees and their distinguished chairmen.

No one stands above Carol Vinson who, as chairman of the House Armed Services Committee for twenty-nine years, created a two-ocean Navy and presided over the construction of ninety-two major warships through the Vinson-Trammel Act. Few can parallel his leadership and achievements in the half-century that he served the men and women of the Armed Services of the United States.

I believe one brief chapter of Naval history, in which I played a role as Secretary of the Navy, clearly memorializes his services.

During the war in Vietnam, Congress granted the Navy funds to build the third super-aircraft carrier. The First had been named for a sailor, Admiral Chester W. Nimitz, representing the generations of sailors who man our ships. The second named for President Eisenhower, symbolizing his role as Commander-In-Chief of the Armed Forces, as stated by the United States Constitution. The good fortune to name the third ship fell to me, as the Secretary of the Navy traditionally has this duty.

Having named one super-carrier to honor the men who sail them and another to honor the Presidents who direct their missions, I felt it appropriate to name one in honor of the third entity in this triumvirate—the Congress that authorizes and appropriates for their construction.

Because of my deep respect for Chairman Carl Vinson, I recommended to Secretary of Defense Melvin Laird that the long standing tradition of over 150 years, of naming warships only after deceased individuals be given an exception. To this day I recall seeing Secretary Laird's astonishment when I presented this idea, as he was a distinguished naval officer and veteran of World War II. He sternly said— "this idea can only sail forward if you have the blessing of the President." Later Secretary Laird and I joined President Nixon who himself, was a naval officer and well versed on the tradition of the Navy. Likewise, Secretary Laird served in the House of Representatives with Carl Vinson.

I still remember the President's reply—"Warner, I like the idea, lets float it. If it sails, it becomes your idea, if it sinks, it's your idea."

History records the rest of the story as the ship was named and all of the Navy rejoiced in this exception to tradition.

I am including a photograph of President Nixon, Carl Vinson, Secretary Melvin Laird and myself. The original proudly hangs in my Senate office.

March 5, 2004
John Warner

Carl Vinson

Patriarch of the Armed Forces

James F. Cook

Mercer University Press
Macon, Georgia

ISBN 0-86554-754-8
MUP/H566

© 2004 Mercer University Press
1400 Coleman Avenue
Macon, Georgia 31207

First Edition.

∞The paper used in this publication meets the minimum requirements
of American National Standard for Information Sciences—
Permanence of Paper for Printed Library Materials, ANSI Z39.48-
1992.

Library of Congress Cataloging-in-Publication Data

Cook, James F.
 Carl Vinson : patriarch of the Armed Forces / James F. Cook.— 1st ed.
   p. cm.
 Includes bibliographical references and index.
 ISBN 0-86554-754-8 (hardcover : alk. paper)
 1. Vinson, Carl, 1883–1981. 2. Legislators—United States—Biography. 3. United States.
Congress. House—Biography. 4. United States. Navy—History—20th century. 5. United
States—Armed Forces—History—20th century. I. Title.
 E748.V57C66 2004
 328.73'092—dc22

                                                              2004002828

Dedicated to

Lou and Neta Stockstill

Contents

Preface

In the 13 January 2002 issue of *Parade Magazine*, a reader from West Virginia, noting the prominent role the *USS Carl Vinson* was playing in fighting terrorism in the Middle East, asked: *Who was Carl Vinson?*[1] It was a valid question, for a whole generation now has grown up with no memory of the man for whom the nuclear carrier was named.

Carl Vinson was an old-fashioned American patriot who served fifty years in the United States House of Representatives. No one had ever served that long. No one had chaired a committee in the House as long as he had. And no one during that era that spanned nine presidents from Woodrow Wilson to Lyndon Johnson had exerted as much influence upon America's armed services. Known as the "Admiral" and the "Father of the Two-ocean Navy," he had labored long and hard to build up the navy in the 1920s and 1930s, a time when America was more committed to disarmament and isolationism than to preparing for war. As chairman of the House Naval Affairs Committee, he had achieved only modest success by the time the Japanese bombs fell on Pearl Harbor on 7 December 1941, but a foundation had been laid that enabled the United States to build the greatest fleet the world had ever seen and achieve victory in World War II. Some knowledgeable participants contend that his contribution to the war effort was as important in achieving the victory as the leadership of the president and the most outstanding generals. After the war, Vinson chaired the new Armed Services Committee whenever the Democrats controlled the House of Representatives (which was most of the time). Operating on the principle that "the paramount duty of government is self-preservation," he insisted

---

[1] Walter Scott, "Personality Parade," *Parade Magazine*, 13 January 2002, 2.

that "enemy capabilities—not dollars—must determine our defenses." A
loyal Democrat, he ran a bipartisan committee, and for many years
enjoyed the reputation of being the acknowledged congressional expert
on military affairs. Defying the Peter Principle, he was perfectly content
serving in the House as chairman of the Naval Affairs Committee and
later the Armed Services Committee, and never aspired to higher office.
When offered the position of secretary of war, his standard reply was,
"I'd rather run the military from here."

Recognized as one of the shrewdest political operators in
congressional history, he dominated his committee and steered countless
measures through the House of Representatives. Although forced to
compromise many times, he lost only three floor fights completely
during his entire career. His uncanny political skill earned him the
sobriquets the "Old Operator" and the "Georgia Swamp Fox."

One of the most powerful men in Washington when he retired,
Vinson also was one of the most eccentric. Throughout his lengthy
career, he abstained from alcohol, profanity, and womanizing—showing
a moderation rarely exhibited in Congress. Representing a landlocked
area of central Georgia, he became the champion of naval expansion, yet
rarely set foot on a warship. As chairman of the Armed Services
Committee, he was entitled to take jaunts all over the world at taxpayers'
expense, but he never did. When Congress adjourned, he headed to his
Baldwin County farm by train, for he never drove a car and feared flying.
In his two-story Milledgeville home, he refused to sleep on the second
floor for fear of fire. Although he spent most of his adult life in
Washington, DC, he maintained his distinctive Middle Georgia accent to
the end. He spoke in a loud and forceful manner, and often with humor.
He was fond of pithy sayings, such as, "I never take my shoes off till I
come to the creek"; "Our great need right now is to get the ox out of the
ditch, not spend a whole lot of time figuring out who pushed him in";
and "All the world's a stage, and there's no use hurrying to get to the
other side." His appearance belied his power and intellect. In his mature
and later years, when he was directing the American defense
establishment, he had the look of a small town sheriff or country lawyer
who would have been comfortable "chewing the fat" in a country store or
playing checkers with his neighbors. Always formally dressed, he wore

loose-fitting dark suits and bright ties, and he chewed tobacco and smoked cheap cigars all his life. As he aged, his hair receded, accentuating his forehead, and with glasses perched precariously on the end of his prominent nose, the genial old man became everyone's "Uncle Carl."

When he retired, he was a household figure, a beloved leader of Congress, and the recipient of practically every honor available to a civilian. Shortly after his retirement, a nuclear carrier was named for him—the first time a living person had been so honored. Members of Vinson's extended family, aware that a new generation was emerging with no memory of Uncle Carl, approached me about writing his biography. Emmett Hall pointed out that "if a man has done enough to have a nuclear carrier named for him, he ought to have his biography written." I agreed. Although several dissertations and theses had been written about aspects of his career, this is the first full biography. It attempts to answer the question: Who was Carl Vinson?

In this endeavor, the Vinson family has cooperated fully. Many family members granted interviews. I am especially indebted to Ed and Betty Vinson, Laura Vinson Northrop for her genealogical work on the Vinson family, and to Sam Nunn, who not only provided a helpful interview but also directed me to Lou and Neta Stockstill, whose letters and recollections were crucial sources for the last two chapters. Vinson's "grandson" Tillman Snead and his wife Karen graciously shared materials and personal memories. The unpublished thesis of Susan Landrum and the dissertations of Michael West, Calvin Enders, and Meredith Berg provided keen insights and directed me to useful sources. A work of this nature is dependent upon the assistance of many librarians. Mary Hargaden rendered valuable assistance with the Vinson Scrapbooks in Milledgeville, Susan Field directed me through the maze of federal documents at the University of Georgia, and Susan Vines of Floyd College kept me supplied with a steady stream of inter-library loan materials. To all of them I express my heartfelt thanks.

I also want to thank my proofreaders for providing sage advice, spotting embarrassing errors, and making my jumbled prose more readable. Among those who reviewed the entire manuscript were my wife Ida, Lea and Don Wilson, Tillman and Karen Snead, Dr. Raymond

Cook, Dr. Willard Gatewood, and Dr. Nancy Applegate. Finally, my thanks go to my technical advisor, Barbara Walden, who kept my computer operating properly, and to the staff of Mercer University Press for making this work possible.

James Cook

Carl Vinson

A Photograph Album

1. Edward Storey Vinson with his five sons. Back row, left to right, Carl, Edward Augustus, Morris; front row, left to right, Fred Louis, Edward Storey, and Wilbur Henry.

2. Edward and Annie Vinson, the parents of Carl Vinson.

3. Following his swearing-in as the youngest member of the U. S. House of Representatives in 1914, Vinson is shown leaving the White House after a call on President Woodrow Wilson.

4. Mary Greene Vinson at around age twenty. Photo taken in The Green Studio, New Philadelphia, Ohio.

5. A happy Representative Carl Vinson and his new bride Mary Greene Vinson leaving the Foundry Methodist Church, where they were married. The photo, taken by a Washington photographer, appeared in the *Atlanta Constitution* on April 10, 1921.

6. An early photo of the Vinson home at No. 4 Primrose Street, Chevy Chase, Maryland.

7. Representative Vinson, far right, was a member of President Calvin Coolidge's 1925 Aircraft Board, which blueprinted the future of U. S. commercial and military aviation. President Coolidge, wearing a light suit, is fifth from left; Dwight Morrow, who chaired the Board, stands third from left.

8. The Vinson home at 421 Montgomery Street in Milledgeville, before it was painted white by the Vinsons. The photo was taken between 1921 and 1934.

9. Sitting between President Franklin Roosevelt and Massachusetts Senator David Walsh, Vinson tours the selection site of what was to become the National Naval Medical Center in the District of Columbia suburb of Bethesda, Maryland.

10. The S. Robles caricature of Representative Vinson which appeared in the *Washington Post* on May 17, 1934.

11. Mary Vinson in the
late-1930s.

12. An aerial view of Congressman Vinson's farm, showing his
residence and home orchard in the center. Photo taken on October
9, 1939.

13. Senator David Walsh, chairman of the Senate Naval Affairs
Committee, and Representative Vinson, chairman of the House
Naval Affairs Committee, conversing after meeting with
President Franklin Roosevelt on June 12, 1940.

14. Till Snead and Paddy,
Mary Vinson's dog, circa
1940.

15. The wedding of Charles Tillman Snead, Jr. and Molly Steman Snead, with a Navy nurse Matron of Honor and Congressman Vinson as Best Man, in the chapel at Bethesda Naval Hospital on June 6, 1947.

16. Chairman Vinson presents a silver bowl to James Forrestal on March 29, 1949, as members of the House Armed Services Committee bade farewell to the retiring Secretary of Defense. In the center is Louis Johnson, who succeeded Forrestal.

17. By the time this photo was taken in 1950, Representative Vinson had served his state and nation more than forty years.

18. Two long-time friends, Speaker Sam Rayburn and Representative Vinson. Photo taken by Mark Kauffman for *Life Magazine* on April 6, 1951.

19. "Grandpa" Vinson (age 72) with "grandson" Tillman Snead (age 5) playing with "the spoils of Christmas" in 1955.

20. Congressman Vinson opposed the full-scale reorganization of the Department of Defense proposed by President Dwight Eisenhower in 1958.

21. Chairman Vinson listens to General George C. Marshall, a former secretary of state and secretary of defense, at a committee hearing in January 1959.

22. From left to right, Army Chief of Staff General George H. Decker, Air Force Chief of Staff General Thomas D. White, ten-year-old Tillman Snead, Representative Vinson, Chief of Naval Operations Admiral Arleigh Burke, and Marine Corps Commandant General David M. Shoup, at a luncheon in the Capitol honoring Congressman Vinson on February 25, 1961.

23. Congressman Vinson introducing Tillman Snead to Secretary of Defense Robert McNamara at a luncheon honoring Vinson in the Old Supreme Court chamber of the Capitol on February 25, 1961.

24. Congresman Vinson and Lou Stockstill engaged in a one-on-one in February 1961 in the old House Armed Services Committee chambers of the Cannon House Office Building. Stockstill was then Congressional Editor of the venerable *Army Navy Air Force Journal*. As a newsman, he covered Vinson and the Armed Services Committee for seventeen years, ultimately taking over the editorial helm of the *Journal*.

25. Chairman Vinson presiding over the House Armed Services Committee near the end of his congressional career.

26. Left to right, Representative Phil Landrum, Senator Richard Russell, Representative Vinson, Secretary of Defense Robert McNamara, and Representative Mendel Rivers at Vinson's eightieth birthday luncheon at the Capitol on November 18, 1963.

27. Representative Vinson meeting with Senator Richard Russell and President Lyndon Johnson on March 20, 1964.

28. Retiring Congressman Vinson receiving the Navy flag from Secretary of the Navy Paul Nitze at an impressive ceremony at Fort Leslie J. McNair in June 1964.

29. Retired Congressman Vinson and President Lyndon Johnson are greeted by Speaker John McCormack and Chairman Mendel Rivers as they enter the Rayburn House Office Building to dedicate the Carl Vinson Room on April 2, 1965. Photo by White House Photographer Cecil W. Stoughton.

30. Reverend Billy Graham, Carl Vinson, President Lyndon Johnson, and House Chaplain Bernard Braskamp in prayer at the dedication of the Carl Vinson Room in the Rayburn House Office Building on April 2, 1965. Photo by White House Photographer Cecil W. Stoughton.

31. Carl Vinson's modest home at River Ridge Plantation, where he lived in retirement. Photo taken in the 1970s.

32. The Vinson-Snead home at 421 Montgomery Street in Milledgeville in the 1970s.

33. Carl Vinson at West Point to receive the prestigious
Sylvanus Thayer Award on September 10, 1966, standing with
Major General D. V. Bennett, United States Military Academy
Superintendent, and General (United States Army Retired)
Cortland Van R. Schuyler, President of the Association of
Graduates, USMA.

34. President Lyndon Johnson and "Lady Bird" Johnson honor
Carl Vinson with a gala birthday party in the White House on his
eighty-fifth birthday in 1968.

35. Carl Vinson and Oneta
Stockstill are pictured at
Warner Robins AFB in
August 1970, attending a
seminar focused on
American servicemen
missing or being held
captive in the Vietnam War.
Mrs. Stockstill was then
Executive Secretary of the
House Armed Services
Committee. Lou Stockstill
was master of ceremonies
for the event.

36. Charles Tillman Snead, III and Karen La-Ru Bodkin at a
pre-wedding shower at the Ponte Vedra Country Club,
Jacksonville Beach, Florida, on April 30, 1972.

37. Elder statesman Carl Vinson chatting with his great-nephew Senator Sam Nunn on the front porch of his farm house in 1973.

38. Lifetime friends Erwin Sibley and Carl Vinson, circa 1973.

39. During a trip to Georgia on November 18, 1973, Vinson's ninetieth birthday, President Richard Nixon announced that a new nuclear aircraft carrier would be named for Carl Vinson. From left to right, President Nixon, Secretary of the Navy John Warner, Carl Vinson, and Secretary of Defense Melvin Laird

40. Carl Vinson and Molly Snead at the christening of the CVN-70 at Newport News, Virginia, on March 15, 1980.

41. Captain Richard L. Martin (on left), the first commanding officer of the U.S.S. *Carl Vinson*; Molly Snead (center); General Sailet, headmaster of Georgia Military College; at the Milledgeville-Baldwin County Airport in Milledgeville in front of the mail-plane from the U.S.S. *Carl Vinson*.

1

A Dream Fulfilled

I saw that the public treasury was being lavishly spent to build battle ship after battle ship to go into the scrap heap to make room for larger battle ships.
Carl Vinson, 1914

After serving in the House of Representatives longer than anyone in history, Carl Vinson, the "Father of the Two-ocean Navy," announced his retirement. On 2 October 1964, near the end of his last term in Congress, the House of Representatives adopted a resolution, which commended "the beloved Dean of the House, for his incomparable record as a legislator, his manifold contributions to the strength of our country, his constant and unimpeachable devotion to the public interest." Knowing his modesty, his friends and longtime colleagues had surprised him with the resolution and numerous statements of effusive praise. Speaker of the House John McCormack of Massachusetts recalled that "his noble, refreshing outlook on life has been an inspiration to all of us." Charles Halleck, a Republican leader from Indiana, was one of several representatives who referred to Vinson affectionately as "Uncle Carl." He stressed Vinson's zeal, dedication, and effectiveness in the defense of our nation. Carl Albert of Oklahoma stated, "Wherever Carl Vinson goes dignity goes with him; wherever he sits there sits wisdom also." Vinson's colleague on the Armed Services Committee, Mendel Rivers of South Carolina, pointed out that "he has led us and the Nation by example." After many others had offered expressions of praise and goodwill, the eighty-year-old Vinson rose, pushed his glasses back from the end of his prominent nose, and thanked the members for their words of praise as well as for their friendship. Visibly moved, he stated that his service literally began with the Springfield rifle and was ending with the Polaris submarine and the intercontinental ballistic missile. In closing his brief speech, the venerated old man remarked, "I have received my reward, and you have made my day in this Congress of the United States a complete fulfillment of what I have sought in life."[1] A few weeks later, before the next Congress assembled, the recipient of those accolades quietly went to Union Station, and without any fanfare boarded a train and returned to Milledgeville, Georgia.

Vinson was born in Milledgeville on 18 November 1883, and although he spent half a century working in Washington, DC, the quiet little town in central Georgia remained his home and refuge throughout his life. There on his 600-acre farm a few miles south of town, amid friends, neighbors, and familiar surroundings, he found peace and contentment.

Milledgeville, the county seat of Baldwin County, is located in the Piedmont on the Oconee River, near the geographical center of the state. In the nineteenth century local entrepreneurs tried to make the town a significant port, but it was agriculture, especially cotton, that flourished on the gently rolling hills and rich river bottoms, that dominated the economy of Baldwin County. Soon after the area was opened to settlers, large agricultural units emerged throughout the "Cotton Belt" or "Black Belt." The planters, who dominated the area economically and socially, usually grew cotton as the money crop but also produced grains, vegetables, livestock, and some even experimented with grapes, other fruit, and pecans. Many planters built graceful and elegant residences in Milledgeville or on their plantations. Quite a few of these beautiful white-columned structures still stand in Baldwin County, attesting to their owners' wealth and standing in society. By definition, a planter owned at least 20 slaves, and the 1860 census showed that Baldwin

---

[1] House, *Tributes in the House of Representatives to Carl Vinson Representative from Georgia October 2, 1964*, 89th Cong., 1st sess., 1965, H. Doc. 310, 1–38.

County had 65 planters. Twelve of them owned 50 or more slaves, and 4 planters owned more than 100 slaves. The planters were exceptional, as most slaveholders owned only one or two families, and the majority of white farmers were hard-working yeomen who owned no slaves. The Civil War destroyed the plantation-slave system as well as much of the county's wealth, but agriculture continued to dominate the Baldwin County economy throughout the ninteenth century.[2]

State government also played a major role in the development of Milledgeville. In fact, the town was laid out and designed to be the state's capital. As settlers flocked into the central part of Georgia after the Revolutionary War, the legislature decided to move the capital from Louisville to a new city named for Governor John Milledge. For sixty-one years, from 1807 to 1868, it served as the capital of Georgia. It also became the site of the state's penitentiary in 1817 and the state hospital for the insane in 1842. Several years before Vinson's birth, the capital had moved eighty miles northward to a thriving railroad center known as Atlanta. The state buildings, however, remained. The Gothic Revival Capitol, a three-story structure with walls four-feet thick, resembled a Gothic castle. Recently restored by the state, it may be the oldest public building of the Gothic architectural style still standing in the country. For several years it served as the Baldwin County Courthouse, but in 1879 it became part of the Middle Georgia Military and Agricultural College (later Georgia Military College), as did the Executive Mansion.[3] Milledgeville gained a second college in 1891, when the Georgia Normal and Industrial College (later Georgia State College for Women and currently Georgia College and State University) opened its doors to eighty-eight students. A part of the University of Georgia, it stressed industrial arts, including typing, bookkeeping, telegraphy, cooking, and dressmaking, as well as teacher education. As part of the agreement to secure the new college, the old Executive Mansion was transferred to the new institution and was partitioned into thirty-five dormitory rooms. For

---

[2] James C. Bonner, *Milledgeville: Georgia's Antebellum Capital* (Athens: University of Georgia Press, 1978) 21–24, 122–26, 155.
[3] Inge Whittle, "Milledgeville: Georgia's Capital, 1807–1868," *Teaching Georgia Government* 24 (Summer 2001): 1–2, 7.

a community of fewer than 1,700 white inhabitants to acquire two flourishing colleges was an exceptional achievement.[4]

Long before Milledgeville existed, five Vinson brothers sailed from Northern Ireland to America. According to family researchers, the Vinsons, originally from France, had settled in Scotland in the 1600s and subsequently had moved to Northern Ireland prior to crossing the Atlantic like thousands of other families in the 1700s. They settled in Maryland.[5] The Reverend John Vinson (1771–1850), a Methodist exhorter, brought the family from Maryland to Middle Georgia. One of the earliest settlers of Hancock County, he married Margaret Callaway there in 1796. One of his seven children, Ebenezer Callaway Vinson (1807–1857), who suffered from a physical ailment (probably tuberculosis), decided to move to Stewart County in Southwest Georgia, where the family had landholdings, hoping that the climate there would be more agreeable to his health. Traveling by horseback, he only got as far as Milledgeville in the adjoining county when his deteriorating health convinced him to go no farther. He had visited the capital city many times, accompanying his older brother, Tully Vinson, who represented Hancock County in the state legislature. He purchased a plantation three miles east of Milledgeville as a temporary abode, but two years later, on 25 December 1857, he died, leaving a widow and ten children.[6] His widow, Martha Dickson Vinson (1813–1894), had descended from two of Georgia's most prominent families: the Dicksons and the Crawfords.

---

[4] Bonner, *Milledgeville*, 240–47.

[5] The Vinson genealogy is based largely on two older publications— Elizabeth Pollard Hood, *Lest We Forget* (Columbia SC: McDonald Printing, n.d.) and Mrs. Anna Maria Green Cook, *History of Baldwin County Georgia* (Anderson SC: Keys-Hearn Printing Co., 1925)—as well as the careful contemporary research of Laura Vinson Northrop, who has graciously shared her Vinson family research with the author. Hereafter cited as Vinson Genealogy Files.

[6] Ebenezer Vinson's house was partially dismantled and moved to a new location, eight miles west of Sparta, Georgia, on state route 16. It was attached to another house and totally restored by its owners, Ben and Christina Lovejoy. Hood, *Lest We Forget*, 162–67.

A woman of extraordinary character, she reared her large family and managed the plantation for nearly fifty years after her husband's death.[7]

The eighth child of Ebenezer and Martha Vinson was Edward Storey Vinson (1850–1938), the father of Carl Vinson. Born in Hancock County, he was five when the family moved to Baldwin County. As the oldest male member of the Vinson family living at home during the Civil War, much responsibility fell on his youthful shoulders. As basic necessities became scarce and could not be replaced locally, Edward and one of their trusted slaves drove a wagon to and from Savannah to buy supplies, especially salt, which was desperately needed for curing meats. The arduous trip, which required several weeks of travel over dangerous roads and flooded streams, was successful. In 1864, when General Sherman's troops approached Milledgeville, Edward, then fourteen, and one of the elderly slaves hid in the swamp to guard the family's valuables, packed in trunks and buried there. Another slave, however, told a Union officer where the valuables had been hidden and led him to the swamps. When the officer saw the boy and the old slave, he said he was not making war on women, children, or the elderly, and that the family's prized possessions were of no use to the Army.[8]

Another family story has young Edward hiding in a gully with the livestock. When the Yankees carried off the mules, Edward emerged from the gully and, with typical Vinson persistence, followed the Yankees for ten miles. After nightfall, he crept in, retrieved one of the mules, and brought it back to the family farm.[9]

Since the Vinson property was conveniently located, some of the invading troops camped on it and their commanding officer stayed in the Vinson home. According to family legend, the officer noticed a fine piano in the parlor and inquired who played it. Edward's older sister, Lucie Kathryn, twenty years old, was an accomplished pianist and, at the officer's request, played a concert. Her performance, as well as the

---

[7] Cook, *History of Baldwin County Georgia*, 457–62.

[8] Hood, *Lest We Forget,* 161–68.

[9] Beverly Smith, "He Makes the Generals Listen," *Saturday Evening Post* 223 (10 March 1951): 137.

gentility of the family, so impressed the officer that he ordered his troops to kill no livestock and destroy no supplies or property of the Vinsons.[10]

Edward Storey Vinson, the only one of the ten children of Ebenezer and Martha Vinson who remained in Milledgeville, married Annie Adela Morris (1855–1937) on 4 February 1875, at the home of her widowed mother, Harriet Singleton Morris. In many ways the history of the Morris family paralleled that of the Vinsons. Starting out in poverty, both families, through hard work and advantageous marriages, had taken advantage of the opportunities America offered. With a few exceptions, both families produced an abundance of sturdy, independent men and women who lived long and productive lives. Like the Vinsons, the Morris family was part of the Scots-Irish migration to America in the 1700s. Settling in the northern area, it gradually drifted southward from Pennsylvania to Virginia and the Carolinas. Shortly after the Revolutionary War, a branch of the family had settled in Jones County, Georgia. Thomas Henry Morris (1829–1862) and his wife Harriet Singleton Morris (1831–1912) moved from Jones County to Baldwin County, where they purchased a large plantation a few miles north of Milledgeville. About 250 acres of the plantation was a vineyard, and twice a year a French wine specialist supervised the culture of the vines and the winemaking. When their first child was old enough for school, they hired a tutor from England, who brought along a fine classical library. Thomas Morris, upon hearing the news of a major Confederate victory, became so excited that he suffered a stroke and died suddenly at age thirty-three, leaving a thirty-year-old widow and five children. Annie was the middle child.[11]

Like Martha Dickson Vinson, Harriet Singleton Morris was a strong and capable widow. She continued to live on the plantation and managed it with great skill for many years. Her plantation in the Pleasant Grove area, located on one of the main roads to Milledgeville, also suffered

---

[10] Hood, *Lest We Forget*, 168; Elizabeth Pollard Hood, interview with the author, Griffin GA, 26 November 2001.

[11] Hood, *Lest We Forget*, 168; Elizabeth Pollard Hood, interview with the author, 26 November 2001; Laura Vinson Northrop, Vinson Genealogy Files, a copy in author's possession.

deprivations in the Civil War. Carl Vinson enjoyed telling a story about his grandmother, Harriet Singleton Morris. It seems that some of General Sherman's forces had camped on the Morris property. As soon as the commanding officer entered the house, a slave girl cried, "Da wine's in da cellah! Da wine's in da cellah!" Her disloyalty to the family brought swift retribution. Shortly after the soldiers left, Harriet Morris took the slave girl to Macon and sold her for two good mules. By showing her deceased husband's Masonic apron to the commanding officer, Harriet possibly saved her plantation. The officer, who happened to be a Mason, ordered that the property be spared from burning and destruction of crops and stores. Unfortunately, some property already had been destroyed, including the fine classical library.[12]

Edward and Annie lived with his widowed mother, Martha Crawford Dickson Vinson, for several years and helped her run the farm. There the first five of their nine children were born: Edward Eugene, who died in childhood; Harriet Thomas (called Hattie); Lelia Crawford; Mabel; and Carl on 18 November 1883. Although the Vinsons generally earned their livelihood from the soil, they recognized the importance of education and could boast of several college graduates and professionals among the extended family. Ebenezer Vinson made provisions in his will for educating his children—the girls as well as the boys. The Morris family, linked by marriage to the Singleton, White, and Walker families, also esteemed education highly. Certainly Annie Morris Vinson did. When Hattie was old enough to attend school, her mother, not wanting her to attend a country school, urged her husband to find a place in town. When he failed to act promptly, she went to Milledgeville and bought a house near the center of town so that Hattie and the other children could attend Georgia Military College, an institution that taught both sexes and all grades beginning with the first. Annie reportedly told her husband that she was staying in town. He could stay on the farm and visit her on weekends or live with her in the house at the corner of North Clark and West Montgomery Streets. He moved to town. Four sons were born in

---

[12] Hood, *Lest We Forget*, 135–36; Emmett Hall, Mary Anne Pollard, and Patricia Pollard Kinnett, interview with the author, Jekyll Island GA, 22 November 2001.

the town house: Edward Augustus, Morris, Fred Louis, and Wilbur Henry. In time, all of the Vinson children would earn college degrees.[13]

Though living in town, Edward continued to farm all his life. He and Annie purchased a farm of their own a few miles south of Milledgeville on the Irwinton Road, and as property became available they added to their landholdings. Like all farmers in that area, he grew cotton as the money crop, but he also grew grain, vegetables, fruit, beef, and pork to supply the needs of the family and the farmhands he employed. In his mature years, he was recognized as one of the most progressive and successful farmers in his section of the country.[14]

He was also fearless and resourceful, as one unfortunate burglar discovered. Tall, slender, and strong, Edward woke up one night and saw a giant burglar, armed with a shotgun, standing by the bed. Undaunted, he tackled the intruder, subdued him, tied him up, and flung him into the farm wagon. After delivering him to the sheriff, he returned home and slept peacefully. Edward worked hard on the farm, and even in his seventies reportedly could work the fields with a 200-pound sack of guano on his back.[15] But Sunday was a day of rest, and he and Annie invariably attended the Methodist Church. Fervent Christians, they rarely missed a Sunday service, and they liked to discuss the sermon on Sunday afternoons as they relaxed on their front porch. For many years Edward was a member of the Board of Stewards of the Methodist Church. In 1909, when the Methodists decided to build a handsome new brick church, the congregation immediately subscribed nearly $20,000. In listing the contributors, the local newspaper recorded that Mr. and Mrs. E. S. Vinson had subscribed $100 and Carl Vinson $75.[16]

---

[13] Hood, *Lest We Forget*, 127–39, 161–68; Laura Vinson Northrop, Vinson Genealogy Files.

[14] Hood, *Lest We Forget*, 168; *Union-Recorder* (Milledgeville GA), 13 October 1938, 1.

[15] Smith, "He Makes the General's Listen," 138.

[16] Ibid.; Elizabeth Pollard Hood, telephone interview with the author, Corpus Christi TX, 16 October 2000; *Union-Recorder*, 23 February 1909, 1. In his later years, Carl Vinson was not an active church member, but he obviously supported the Methodist Church at this stage of his life.

A natural storyteller, Edward enjoyed relating tales about his own experiences, Civil War exploits, and stories he had heard from slaves and black farmhands. It was his custom to call all his children around the fireplace every night and tell them Bible stories. Carl inherited his father's talent, and at a very young age began to plead with his father, "Papa, let me tell. Let me tell." Carl quickly became an accomplished storyteller too. His older sister Lelia recalled that by the time he entered Georgia Military College, he knew many Bible stories by heart. When his first-grade teacher, Miss Carrie Fair, learned about Carl's precocity, she insisted on giving him prominent billing in the chapel programs. The chapel, prophetically, was the legislative assembly hall of the old State Capitol. Years later, as part of his public speaking course, Carl recalled that he had to speak there every Friday afternoon.[17]

Since Edward Vinson had worked hard on the farm all his life, he expected his children to work too. A firm disciplinarian, he gave his sons a choice: either help him on the farm or find jobs in Milledgeville after school and in the summer. Carl chose to work in Milledgeville. For a while he worked at the soda fountain in Culver & Kidd's drugstore, a job that paid little but provided all the ice cream and sodas he wanted. Then he took over the job of delivering the *Atlanta Journal*. "I had all of Milledgeville—about 300 papers," Vinson recalled. He walked a mile to get his heavy bundle of Atlanta papers off the eight o'clock train, and then tramped several more miles delivering them. "The paper cost 10 cents a week. I got 5 cents for delivering it and had to give the *Journal* 5 cents." A friend remarked in 1951, "Nowadays you might say he was a poor boy, but that never occurred to Carl. He was a brash little hustler if I ever saw one."[18]

When he was fifteen Carl worked in two local department stores, P. J. Cline's and Joseph's. He earned $4 a month at Joseph's as a "cash boy." Salesgirls gave a customer's money to Carl, who dashed to the cash desk and returned with the receipt and change. Later he was promoted to "bundle wrapper," earning $15 a month. Judge Erwin

---

[17] Louis R. Stockstill, "'Uncle Carl' Vinson: Backstage Boss of the Pentagon," *Army Navy Air Force Journal* 98 (18 February 1961): 25.

[18] Ibid., 26; Smith, "He Makes the Generals Listen," 138.

Sibley, his friend since boyhood, remembered that Carl, in his free time at the department store, would corner the boys in the cellar and make speeches to them. At this time the Spanish American War was brewing and free silver was a burning domestic issue. Carl, a loyal Democrat, already had political aspirations. In fact, he had informed one of his teachers that he wanted to be a congressman.[19]

In addition to his political aspirations, Carl also displayed leadership qualities at an early age. After school and on weekends, the Vinson home, centrally located and with a big yard, became the gathering place for many of the town's young people. They played croquet, baseball, and other games and enjoyed the food Carl's parents provided. From the farm his father brought home watermelons, cantaloupes, peaches, and apples, and his mother baked cakes and cookies for the children. "Carl was the ringleader," Lelia recalled. "We had to do what he said. He was the boss." Lelia also remembered that "Carl was always popular, but he was never a ladies man. He was so busy studying and working and trying to make money that he never had time for anything else."[20]

Vinson left few records about his boyhood and steadfastly refused to divulge much to interviewers. His typical response was, "I just had a good average boyhood. Nothin' interestin'." Even in his youth he seems to have kept his own counsel. He once fell out of a tree, broke his shoulder, and said nothing about it to his family. When they found out, it was too late to set the bone. The shoulder had a slight droop thereafter.[21]

Following in the footsteps of Hattie, Lelia, and Mabel, Carl attended Middle Georgia Military and Agricultural College, which was divided into a Primary Department and a Collegiate Department. In 1898 nearly two-thirds of the 456 students were in the Primary Department. The curriculum of the Primary Department (grades one through eight) provided the usual emphasis on reading, writing, and arithmetic, but it also stressed spelling, penmanship, and geography. The Collegiate

---

[19] Stockstill, "Backstage Boss," 25; Smith, "He Makes the Generals Listen," 138; Susan Landrum, "Carl Vinson: A Study in Military Preparedness" (master's thesis, Emory University, 1968) 4–5.

[20] Stockstill, "Backstage Boss," 26.

[21] Smith, "He Makes the Generals Listen," 138.

Department, which began after the eighth grade, required 4 years of English, 4 years of mathematics, 1 year of English history, 1 year of world history, 4 years of Latin, 3 years of Greek, 1 year of physiology (biology), 1 year of natural philosophy (physics), 1 year of chemistry, and 1 year of geology. With high academic standards and such an impressive curriculum, it is easy to see why Annie Vinson insisted that her children attend. In addition to this classical curriculum, military training in uniform was required of "every male student in the College classes." Typical of that era, rigid discipline was the order of the day. Classes began at 8:15, and the catalog declared that "Perfect order shall be preserved in the schoolrooms." Although the institution was co-educational, School Law 7 stated, "There shall not be any communication between the sexes in school or out of school, nor will they be allowed to associate at any time except when excused by the president or faculty." After listing a host of offenses, such as drinking, fighting, cheating, swearing, etc., Rule 8 concluded, *"No pupil using tobacco in any form shall be retained in school."*[22]

School lessons came easy to Vinson, but for some reason he did not earn a degree at Middle Georgia Military and Agricultural College. He did receive good academic training, however, and soon decided to further his studies in the field of law. When interviewed late in life, he could not remember what attracted him to the legal profession, but he may well have viewed it as a steppingstone to a political career. Before entering law school, he went to see a local attorney, County Judge Edward R. Hines, and told him he wanted to study law. Hines, who possessed a substantial law library, agreed to let Carl use his books. Sometimes he read at the office, other times he took books home. By 1900, with help from his father, he had saved enough money to enter Mercer University Law School in Macon. The preliminary reading with Judge Hines undoubtedly was a great help during his first months at Mercer. In 1902 he was graduated twenty-ninth in a class of fifty and simultaneously admitted to the Bar. One of his classmates was E. E. Cox of Camilla, also

---

[22] *Middle Georgia Military and Agricultural College Annual Announcement and Register, 1886–1887, 1896–1897, 1898–1899* in Carl Vinson File, Special Collections, Georgia Military College, Milledgeville GA.

destined to be a U.S. Representative from Georgia, and eventually the ranking Democrat on the House Rules Committee. Another classmate remembered Carl as "ambitious and confident of himself" and boasting "that someday in the future he would represent his home district in Congress."[23]

Returning to Milledgeville, the eighteen-year-old Carl became a junior partner with Judge Hines, and a new shingle—Hines and Vinson—went on display. Judge Hines, a brilliant, leisurely gentleman of the old school, wore a plaid shawl over his shoulders and carried a silver snuffbox. The two made a good team. Carl contributed ingenuity and energy, while the judge, with his mellow ways, softened the rough edges of the younger man's brashness. The practice of law in Milledgeville, then a town of about 4,000, was not a booming enterprise. The new partners spent most of their time doing the routine work of preparing deeds and wills and drawing up contracts. Carl later recalled, "We took anything that came along. Just as a country doctor accepts any patient who comes in, country lawyers don't specialize. If they did, they wouldn't have much business."[24]

Ambitious and energetic, Vinson won appointment as Baldwin County court solicitor in 1905. An effective prosecutor, he won 108 of the 128 cases he prosecuted the first year. Reappointed to a second term, he served until 1 April 1909. In assessing his performance, Milledgeville's *Union-Recorder* complimented him for performing his duties "fearlessly" and considered his record "quite creditable."[25] When the city recorder died late in 1907, the Milledgeville City Council named Vinson, already one of the most popular attorneys in town, to fill the unexpired term. Within less than a month, however, he resigned that position, apparently because he had higher ambitions—serving in the Georgia legislature.[26] In local races in Southern small towns, the

---

[23]Stockstill, "Backstage Boss," 26; *Catalogue and Annual Announcement of Mercer University, 1901–1902,* 71–72; Carl F. Hutcheson, "Alumnus Writes of Vinson and Watson," *The Mercerian* 45 (December 1958): 4.

[24] Stockstill, "Backstage Boss," 26; Smith, "He Makes the Generals Listen," 138.

[25] *Union-Recorder*, 30 March 1909, 1.

[26] Ibid., 3 December 1907, 1; 24 December 1907, 1.

candidates' image, personality, and family reputation often are more important than issues. The biggest issue in this campaign was prohibition, and both candidates were strongly in favor of it. But campaigning can also make a difference. In this, Vinson's first campaign for elected office, he displayed a talent for organization, expressed his views clearly both in campaign speeches and in newspaper articles, and spent long hours campaigning. Small-town Southern voters expect the candidate to talk to them, shake their hands, and personally ask for their votes, and no one was more adept at doing this than Vinson. When this spirited four-month campaign concluded, the local newspapers predicted a close vote, but Vinson trounced Stetson Sanford in the Democratic primary by vote of 618 to 346.[27]

When the Georgia General Assembly was in session—50 days each year—Vinson lived at the old Kimball House in Atlanta and drew a salary of $7 a day, barely enough to cover his expenses. The financial rewards were nonexistent, but Vinson flourished in the legislative environment. He received appointment to key committees (Appropriations, General Agriculture, Penitentiary, and Georgia State Sanitarium). Serving on these committees put him in a position to influence legislation that could benefit his constituents, and he quickly earned the reputation as a hard-working, bright young man who could get things done. He wasted no time in introducing bills for increased appropriations to the State Sanitarium and the Georgian Normal and Industrial College, and to establish a city court in Milledgeville. In appreciation for his staunch support, the employees of the State Sanitarium presented him with a handsome gold-headed cane.[28]

When Vinson announced that he would seek reelection, the *Union-Recorder* editorialized that "he was alert and active in the performance of the duties of his office, and no one can deny that he looked carefully after the interests of the state institutions located in this county. He

---

[27]Ibid., 7 January 1908, 1; 24 March 1908, 4; 31 March 1908, 1; 4 April 1908, 1; 21 April 1908, 1, 7.

[28] Ibid., 29 June 1909, 1; 13 July 1909, 1; 11 January 1910, 1; *Milledgeville News*, 11 June 1909, 1; Stockstill, "Backstage Boss," 26; *Georgia, Journal of the House, 1909*, 8–9, 390, 399–414.

secured every appropriation asked for."[29] His talent for securing state appropriations so impressed members of the legislature that they wondered if he had the "power of hypnotism."[30] The *Dublin Courier-Dispatch*, which described Vinson as "the most popular man in the legislature," said, "If he will move to Laurens we will keep him in the legislature for life or send him to congress from the Twelfth district, as he prefers."[31] With such a record of accomplishment, he had little trouble defeating Eli B. Hubbard. The vote in the Democratic primary was 602 to 346.[32]

When the legislature convened in June 1911, Vinson was elected Speaker Pro Tempore, an impressive accomplishment for a twenty-seven-year-old representative beginning his second term. In the absence of the Speaker, Vinson presided over the House, and whenever that opportunity arrived he made the most of it. On one occasion in August 1912, when Speaker John N. Holder was away, the House met on a Saturday. It was late in the legislative session and the members were in a surly mood. The members wanted to go home, but Vinson kept them working and allowed no one to leave. The result was a productive session, with Vinson earning the praise of an Atlanta journalist who noted, "Vinson is an expert parliamentarian and is quick in handing down rulings and opinions."[33]

During this session, Vinson also designed a strategy that he hoped would elevate him into the U.S. Congress. The Sixth Congressional District, of which Baldwin County was a part, had been dominated for years by Bibb County, which held the district's largest city, Macon. Carl doubted that he would ever be able to penetrate very deeply into Bibb's entrenched political structure in a bid for a Sixth District seat. When the Assembly undertook the task of redrawing the congressional districts following the 1910 census, Vinson managed to get appointed to the

---

[29] *Union-Recorder*, 8 March 1910, 1.
[30] Ibid., 12 July 1910, 1; *Milledgeville News*, 15 July 1910, 2, quoting the *Atlanta Constitution*.
[31] Quoted in *Milledgeville News*, 5 August 1910, 3.
[32] *Union-Recorder*, 23 August 1910, 1.
[33] Ibid., 13 August 1912, 1; *Georgia, Journal of the House, 1911*, 149–51.

Reapportionment Committee. There he did some fast-talking and convinced the House to shift Baldwin County to the Tenth Congressional District. Known as the "Bloody Tenth" for the bitter battles that had taken place there, it was dominated by Columbia County and the city of Augusta. Since Baldwin County was at the western end of the district and Augusta was at the eastern extremity, Vinson believed that he could win Baldwin, its neighboring counties, and perhaps three or four others not bordering Columbia. It was a long shot, but it seemed to offer better prospects than a fight with Bibb County.[34]

His strategy was sound as far as it went, but it overlooked one crucial factor. The voters of Baldwin County, perhaps angered by the arbitrary shift to the Tenth District, refused to send Carl back to the General Assembly for a third term. He lost to J. H. Ennis by five votes, 486 to 481. Ennis, considered one of the most popular men in the county, served as captain of the famed Baldwin Blues, the local militia unit. He also came from a distinguished family, operated a large farm, and was engaged in several businesses. In a political career that spanned more than half a century, this was Vinson's only defeat at the hands of the voters.[35] The setback was temporary, however, for when a vacancy occurred in the Baldwin County court, Vinson prevailed upon the governor to appoint him judge. Governor Joseph M. Brown swore Vinson in as judge six weeks after his defeat.[36]

While serving as judge, Vinson kept a careful watch on political developments in the Tenth District so that he could implement his plan of attack. He did not have to wait long. On 14 February 1914, Augustus O. Bacon, Georgia's senior U.S. Senator, died. Representative Thomas W. Hardwick of the Tenth District quickly became a candidate for the vacant Senate seat, whereupon Vinson immediately became a candidate for the House seat made vacant by Hardwick's resignation. Three other

---

[34] Stockstill, "Backstage Boss," 26.

[35] Ibid.; *Union-Recorder*, 5 September 1911, 1; 9 April 1912, 3; 18 August 1927, 1; *Milledgeville News*, 23 August 1912, 1. Ennis had a distinguished political career, serving as mayor of Milledgeville and serving several terms in the Georgia House and Senate.

[36] *Union-Recorder*, 8 October 1912, 1.

candidates entered the race: Joseph Reynolds of Richmond County, A. W. Evans of Washington County, and Judge B. T. Rawlings, also from Washington County. It was soon apparent that his strongest opponent was Joe Reynolds, who had risen from poverty to represent Richmond County in the legislature and for twelve years had served as solicitor general of the Augusta Circuit. Miss Martha Thomas, then a stenographer at Hines and Vinson and later Carl's first secretary in Washington, said, "Most people didn't think he had a chance of being elected. He had three opponents, all wealthy men."[37]

Vinson opened his whirlwind campaign with a speech at Sparta on 23 March and he continued to campaign non-stop throughout the district until the votes were cast on 19 August. Vinson had little money and his staff consisted of three people—Miss Thomas, his campaign manager Dave Howard, and a driver of a Model T Ford. But whatever they lacked in money or sophistication, they made up for in energy and determination. A neighbor recalled that at 4 A.M. a red-haired boy in a Model T would stop in front of Carl's house and honk. "Carl would come out on a run, pulling on his coat. The boy wouldn't bring Carl back until midnight. He would spend twenty straight hours ranging the towns and villages, the piney woods and the creek bottoms, speechifying, talking, shaking hands—and he had to take a fresh chew of tobacco from every farmer who offered one. No paved roads in those days. It was rough going."[38] When the votes were counted, Vinson had achieved an impressive victory, carrying eight of the district's twelve counties. Reynolds had carried Richmond and Columbia counties, and Evans had carried Washington and Lincoln counties. Vinson's popular vote nearly equaled the total of his three opponents combined. Carl's father, who had always said his son "inherited his brains from his mother and his brawn from me," looked back on the long, hard campaign trail and told Carl, "This time it was your brawn that paid off."[39]

---

[37] Stockstill, "Backstage Boss," 26; *Milledgeville News*, 6 March 1914, 1; 20 March 1914, 1; 26 June 1914, 1; 3 July 1914, 3; 17 July 1914, 6.

[38] Smith, "He Makes the Generals Listen," 238.

[39] Stockstill, "Backstage Boss," 26; *Milledgeville News*, 28 August 1914, 1.

Georgia then operated under the county unit system, a unique method of tabulating the votes for candidates in primary elections. The number of county unit votes allocated to each county was twice the number of members of the State House of Representatives from the county. The 8 counties with the largest population were given 6 county unit votes each; the next 30 counties were given 4, and the remaining 121 counties were given 2. The candidate who received the most popular votes in the county was awarded all of the county unit votes in that county. In the Bloody Tenth District, Columbia County had six county unit votes, Washington County had four, and the remainder had two each. By winning eight two-unit-vote counties, Vinson had garnered a total of sixteen of the district's thirty county unit votes. Thus he had sixteen votes (delegates) at the district convention, which nominated him by unanimous vote. This system gave disproportionate power to small rural counties, and as the state became more urbanized after World War II, representation became woefully unbalanced. Yet, the county unit system remained in effect until 1962 when a U.S. district court overturned the county unit system and instituted elections based on popular votes.[40] Georgia also was a one-party state, perhaps the most Democratic state in the country. The Republican Party—the party of the Union Army, Radical Reconstruction, and civil rights—was thoroughly discredited in the South after the Civil War. Democrats regained control of the state and subsequently adopted the poll tax, the grandfather clause, literacy tests, and other devices that circumvented the Fourteenth and Fifteenth Amendments. Such measures systematically disfranchised black voters and thereby eliminated a key Republican constituency. Perhaps even more important in a one-party state, in 1900 the Georgia Democratic Party restricted its primary to white voters. Georgia had not had a Republican governor since Reconstruction, and soon afterwards Republicans gave up any attempt to win the state. Thus, winning the

---

[40] J. Harmon Smith, "History of Georgia's County Unit System," Georgia Department of Archives and History, *Georgia Official and Statistical Register, 1961–1962*, 943–44.

Democratic primary was tantamount to election because usually there was no opposition in the general election in November.[41]

A week after the election, the Tenth District convention at Sparta formally nominated Vinson. In his acceptance speech, Vinson stated that he did not enter the race for "the attainment of a personal ambition" but because he observed gross inequalities in our national laws: "I knew that the back of labor bent under the unequal burdens of governmental duties; I heard the cries of unrewarded labor, and the protests of those the fruit of whose labors were unjustly taken under unequal laws." There was much more of this Populist-style rhetoric, but in view of his later career, his comments about the navy are especially intriguing:

> I saw that the public treasury was being lavishly spent to build battle ship after battle ship to go into the scrap heap to make room for larger battle ships, which in turn went the same way to make room for still larger ones. I saw battle ships, each costing more than the total annual income of the state of Georgia, being used for targets at gun practice. This profligate waste of money was made possible by a false conception of patriotism, encouraged by the chieftain of the steel industry who profited by the nation's cost.[42]

As a result of the immediate House vacancy created by Hardwick's elevation to the Senate, Carl was elected to both the unexpired term in the Sixty-third Congress and to the new term in the Sixty-fourth. His term of service began on 3 November 1914, fifteen days before his thirty-first birthday. Resigning his position as judge, he hired John C. Evans of Warrenton as his executive secretary and Martha Thomas as his private secretary, and set out for Washington. When the third session of the Sixty-third Congress convened on 7 December, Vinson walked onto the House floor and was sworn in as the country's youngest

---

[41] James F. Cook, *The Governors of Georgia, 1754–1995* (Macon GA: Mercer University Press, 1995); Kenneth Coleman, ed., *A History of Georgia* (Athens: University of Georgia Press, 1977).

[42] *Milledgeville News*, 4 September 1914, 1.

congressman. His strategy had worked. He had achieved his ambition of being a congressman from Georgia, and he ahd done it sooner than he possibly could have imagined.[43]

---

[43] Ibid., 6 November 1914, 1; Stockstill, "Backstage Boss," 26.

2

A Narrow Victory

No government which fails to provide for its own preservation against the assaults of every probable foe is entitled to the support of its people.

Carl Vinson, 1916

The city of Washington that Vinson encountered was quite different from the sprawling metropolitan center it became after World War II. The census of 1910 listed the District of Columbia's population as 331,069—up more than 50,000 in ten years, but only half of what it would be thirty years later. The city, designed by Pierre L'Enfant, had wide avenues emanating from Capitol Hill, but many of the famous buildings on Capitol Hill and the Mall that contemporaries associate with Washington had not yet been built when Vinson arrived. The Capitol, the White House, the Washington Monument, and the Library of Congress were there, but the Supreme Court Building, the Lincoln and Jefferson Memorials, the National Gallery of Art, the Archives Building, and a host of government office buildings would not arrive until the 1920s, 1930s, or later. Government, of course, was the city's reason for being, and the federal government then employed 30,000 workers. Although government had grown a bit as a result of Progressive era reforms, it was still small by contemporary standards. Indeed, in 1915 total federal expenditures were only $760,587,000, and the national debt stood at a little more than $1 million, or $11.85 for each of America's 100,000,000 citizens.[1] When Vinson saw Washington for the first time, he must have been impressed not only by the Capitol and other buildings but also by the beauty of the city, with its impressive monuments, magnificent trees, numerous parks, and abundant open space. Pedestrians then walked the streets safely, and things still moved at a slow, leisurely pace, much like Atlanta and the Southern towns with which he was familiar. All things considered, it was a pleasant place to live.[2]

Vinson took a room at the Burlington Hotel at $90 a month and quickly settled into the congressional routine. Moving into the office vacated by Congressman Hardwick, he opened early and stayed late. From his experience in the Georgia legislature, he had learned that constituents are favorably impressed when a representative answered correspondence quickly and accurately. From the beginning, Vinson insisted that letters leaving his office reflect his views clearly and that they be typed flawlessly. Thinking far into the future, he explained to his secretary, Martha Thomas, that if one of his letters is read "forty or fifty years" later, he hoped "no one will have to be ashamed of what it says." His attention to detail in responding to constituents meant that his office staff would stay busy. Miss Thomas, his first secretary who worked for him four years, remarked that she "never caught up with the work." Oneta Stockstill, one of his last secretaries on the Armed Services Committee, said the same thing.[3]

The young congressman's high standards placed heavy burdens on his staff. When Miss Thomas took her first paid vacation from his office, she went to visit friends who lived in the country near Washington. Before leaving she had hired a replacement stenographer so that the office would continue to function efficiently. She had been gone three

---

[1] U.S. Bureau of the Census, *Historical Statistics of the United States, Colonial Times to 1957* (Washington, DC: Government Printing Office, 1960) 8, 12, 711, 718–21.

[2] Judith Waldrop Frank, *Washington By Night* (Washington: Starwood Publishing, Inc., 1992); Myrtle Cheney Murdock, *Your Uncle Sam in Washington* (Washington: Monumental Press, 1948).

[3] Louis R. Stockstill, "'Uncle Carl' Vinson: Backstage Boss of the Pentagon," *Army Navy Air Force Journal* 98 (18 February 1961): 26; Neta Stockstill, interview with the author, 21 June 2001.

days when a cab drove up at her friend's house. The driver told Miss Thomas that Mr. Vinson wanted her and that it was urgent. Assuming that he was sick or that some tragedy had befallen him, she packed quickly, climbed into the cab, and rushed back to the city. When she got to the office she found the congressman looking healthy but unhappy. "What's wrong?" she asked.

Pointing to a stack of unsigned letters, Vinson said, "I've had three stenographers since you left. Look at those letters. There's not a letter there I could send out."

Miss Thomas took off her coat and proceeded to retype the letters. It was the last she ever heard of her vacation.[4]

In debt from the campaign, Vinson expected his finances to improve with his congressional salary of $625 a month. He soon discovered, however, that after he had paid his staff, his office postal expenses, his hotel bill, and bought all his meals, little remained for debt payment and other living expenses. Forty-two years later, when congressional salaries were boosted to $22,500, he joked, "Well, if they are going to pay that kind of money in Congress, I think I'll make a career out of it."[5]

From his Georgia legislative experience, Vinson knew that the real work of Congress was done in committee. As a newcomer entering Congress in the midst of a session, he had to take whatever committee assignments were available. On 19 December 1914, he was elected to the Coinage, Weights, and Measures Expenditures in the Agriculture Department Committee and the Pension Committee.[6] Subsequently, he was named to the District of Columbia Committee. He had little interest in either the Pension Committee or the District of Columbia Committee, but he worked on both committees with his usual diligence and submitted reports for both committees.[7] Since his district was largely

---

[4] Stockstill, "Backstage Boss," 26.

[5] Ibid.

[6] *Congressional Record*, 63rd Cong., 3rd sess., 19 December 1914, 429.

[7] House Pensions Committee, *Report Granting Pensions and Increase of Pensions...*, 63rd Cong., 3rd sess., 21 January 1915, House Report. 1307; Committee on District of Columbia, *Appointment of Recorder of Deeds, District of Columbia,* 64th Cong., 1st sess., 11 February 1916, H. Rept. 170; Committee on District of Columbia, *Inquiry into the Cost of Living in the District of*

agrarian, he was keenly interested in agricultural matters and worked consistently to secure better prices for agricultural products.

Vinson did not let his youth prevent him from seeking public works projects for the Tenth District. In fact, in his first session, he introduced bills to erect public buildings in Sparta, Tennille, and Thomson as well as a bill to extend the time for completion of dams across the Savannah River.[8] Throughout his career, Vinson, like all effective congressmen, would make sure that his district received an ample amount of public works projects. The young freshman legislator also introduced a host of measures designed to enhance his political standing in his district. As a member of the District of Columbia Committee, he submitted two bills dealing with segregation. One bill called for separate streetcars and apartment buildings in the District for Negroes and Whites. The other bill banned racial intermarriage in the District. He also introduced a bill to separate Africans from Whites in civil service employ. He introduced an amendment to the Constitution that would limit the terms of office of judges, and another that would repeal the Fifteenth Amendment in order to prevent former slaves from voting.[9] Taken at face value, these measures mark Vinson as a racist. A product of a racist society, his thinking at this time was representative of his time and place. To his credit, he that knew his proposals would never be enacted and very likely would die in committee. That was his intention. But he also knew that they would impress the people he represented in the rural, racially segregated Tenth District. To them, his proposals would indicate that their congressman was actively championing their interests. Vinson was never a racist like James K. Vardaman or Eugene Talmadge, but at this

---

Columbia, 64th Cong., 1st sess., 9 March 1916, H. Rept. 310; Committee on District of Columbia, *Salaries of Police Officers in the District of Columbia,* 64th Cong., 1st sess., 29 July 1916, H. Rept. 1061.

[8] *Congressional Record,* 63rd Cong., 3rd sess., 16 December 1914, 291, 17 December 1914, 329 .

[9] *Congressional Record,* 63rd Cong., 3rd sess., 23 December 1914, 631; 64th Cong., 1st sess., 6 December 1915, 14, 27, 31; Susan Landrum, "Carl Vinson: A Study in Military Preparedness" (master's thesis, Emory University, 1968) 8–9.

vulnerable stage in his political career he was not above resorting to racial bigotry to enhance his political standing.[10]

On 22 December 1914, only two weeks after he was sworn in, Vinson made his first speech on the floor of the House of Representatives, a clearly reasoned defense of state rights. Vinson, who did not drink alcohol and who had supported state and local prohibition measures, spoke emphatically against national prohibition because it violated the sacred principles of state rights. Although Vinson longed for the day when every state would prohibit the sale and consumption of liquor, he was unwilling to achieve that goal by national prohibition. To Vinson, national prohibition was repugnant to the American theory of government. The Constitution, he argued, gave the states the right to regulate and control their internal affairs. "This Nation is too large to have its affairs entirely directed from Washington." Moreover, "The people of Georgia do not need Congress to regulate their local self-government." Prophetically, he added, "To break down this safeguard and destroy this great principle of State rights is but the entering wedge, and who can tell to where it will lead?"[11]

During his first term Vinson spent much of his time looking out for the needs of his district and individual constituents, but he also expressed his views on three issues of national concern—immigration, farm credits, and national defense. The first two issues were closely related in that both affected the plight of hardworking Americans. On 24 March 1916, Vinson delivered a carefully prepared speech in favor of immigration restrictions. There is strong sentiment throughout the country, he began, that the time had come to amend our immigration laws "to prevent the thousands upon thousands of ignorant, dishonest, vicious, and physical defectives from entering our country." While acknowledging that a large percentage of the recent immigrants had been a great blessing to the country, he was concerned that when the European war ended the better

---

[10] Ralph Reed, "'Fighting the Devil with Fire': Carl Vinson's Victory over Tom Watson in the 1918 Tenth District Democratic Primary," *Georgia Historical Quarterly* 67 (Winter 1983): 454.

[11] *Congressional Record*, 63rd Cong., 3rd sess., 22 December 1914, 580–81.

element would not be permitted to leave, "but the ignorant, vicious, and criminal will pour into this country as never before." To prevent that from happening, the law should be changed immediately, he reasoned. He called for a reduction in the total number of immigrants, and to insure that the immigrants were desirable he advocated a literacy test and a character test. Such ideas were not new, Vinson noted, as Congress previously had passed similar measures only to have them vetoed by Presidents Taft and Wilson. "The people of this country have become aroused on this subject," he declared, and numerous bodies have endorsed the proposed changes. Among those who had endorsed restrictions, he listed several state legislatures, the American Federation of Labor, the Knights of Labor, the Farmers National Congress, and a host of other labor and farm organizations. The corporations, large business interests, and the moneyed institutions oppose the reform, he stated, but American labor must be freed from the competition of cheap foreign labor "that comes to this country through our present lax immigration laws."[12]

A month later Vinson delivered a fifteen-minute speech on the House floor calling for this session of Congress to pass "a rural-credit bill with Government aid, extending to the farmers of the country the same opportunity to borrow money at a low rate of interest and for a long period of time as is now enjoyed by other business." Vinson rarely displayed emotion in his speeches, but the plight of farmers was special. The farmers, he declared, "are entitled to a square deal and fair play, and so help me, God, as long as I am a Member of this body I will fight to see that they obtain it." The speech reflected much study and Vinson provided abundant factual data to support his views. The average American farmer's gross income was only $791 per year, he pointed out, and the farmer received only 35¢ out of every dollar that the consumer spends for the products of his labor. Vinson believed that "the lack of credit and the failure to receive a just compensation for the products of his labor has done more to depopulate the farms of the country than anything else." The farmers constituted one-third of the population, but the banking institutions had extended to them only one-ninth of the credit

---

[12] *Congressional Record*, 64th Cong., 1st sess., 24 March 1916, 4786–89.

of the country. "The banks in this country invest $97.50 in stocks and bonds and other forms of security for every $2.50 invested in farm lands." The situation had become so serious that both parties had addressed the issue of farm credit in their platforms. Arguing that American farming must conform to the best methods of twentieth century progress, he concluded that "The weak link in the chain of agricultural success to-day is the absence of a sound and safe system of agriculture finance."[13]

On 27 May 1916, Vinson addressed for the first time the subject that would become his specialty—military preparedness. After witnessing the devastating war in Europe for nearly two years and studying the defense needs of the country, Vinson completely reversed the position he had taken in his 1914 acceptance speech. He now supported "the largest building program ever undertaken by any government at one time in the history of the world for strengthening a navy." The bill would cost $150,000,000, an increase of $49,000,000 over the previous year's bill. Vinson had become convinced that the security of America demanded such expenditures. In supporting this program he enunciated principles that he adhered to steadfastly throughout his career. First, the most important duty of government is self-preservation. "No government which fails to provide for its own preservation against the assaults of every probable foe is entitled to the support of its people." "No sophistry of logic can justify it in stripping itself of its means of defense and relying for its preservation upon the mercy, the pity, or the love of other nations." Secondly, defense should be non-partisan. "I am a Democrat, a believer in the creed of Jefferson and Jackson, but my country and its safety comes ahead of any party." Thirdly, peace can be achieved only by a strong defense. "I am a hater of war and a devoted lover of peace, but…I am fully convinced and realize that peace to be had must sometimes be battled for. That to be preserved it must be guarded and protected, and that to be protected it must be surrounded by impregnable barriers." After discussing the specifics of the bill, he then went on record as being "unalterably opposed to the issuing of bonds to provide the revenue to meet the provisions set forth in these bills." Instead of

---

[13] Ibid., 13 April 1916, 6078–82.

saddling the people with bonded indebtedness, he favored increasing the rate of the income tax, establishing a federal inheritance tax, and establishing an excise tax on the profits of munitions of war. These taxes, he believed, "would consist in pulling the most feathers with the least squawking."[14]

When Congress adjourned, Vinson returned to Milledgeville, where he opened an office in the Sanford building. He spent the time between sessions traveling throughout the district, meeting people, listening to their concerns, and giving speeches—a pattern he followed throughout his career. His activities received favorable comment in the local press. D. W. Brannen in the *Milledgeville News* gushed that "recent events are making manifest more and more clearly that the Tenth district is being represented in Washington by an astute, able and progressive representative, in the person of Milledgeville's own son, Hon. Carl Vinson."[15] After he had been in office only thirteen months, the *Marietta Courier*, located miles outside his district, urged its readers to keep their eyes on "the gifted statesman from the Tenth." "People outside of Georgia," it asserted, "already are asking about him."[16] The most impressive indication of his popularity came in fall 1916, when he sought reelection. No one challenged him in the Democratic primary, so he won without opposition—an unheard of development in the Bloody Tenth.

Since the beginning of his congressional career, Vinson had been looking for a better committee assignment, and in 1917 vacancies opened up on several desirable committees. He selected Naval Affairs. It was a bit strange for a representative from a landlocked district to be appointed to that committee, but he had already demonstrated a keen interest in military affairs. He clearly saw the need for increased spending for defense, and he expected sea power to grow in importance. He believed the Naval Affairs Committee would provide a needed arena in which to fight for his views. Years later he told journalist Lou Stockstill of a personal motive for serving: "I wanted to serve on a committee where I

---

[14] Ibid., 27 May 1916, 8807–10.
[15] *Union-Recorder*, 16 March 1915, 1; 1 June 1915, 1; 10 August 1915, 1; *Milledgeville News*, 26 January 1917, 1.
[16] Quoted in Stockstill, "Backstage Boss," 26.

could see the results of my labors. When you authorize the construction
of a military base or a big carrier you can see the results." It was a
fortuitous choice. During the next seven years, eight Democratic
members of the Naval Affairs Committee were defeated, died, or
resigned, so that by 1923 Vinson had become the ranking Democrat.[17]

The young Georgian supported President Woodrow Wilson loyally,
even his call for a draft, which seven of Georgia's twelve representatives
opposed.[18] He had no reservation in voting for the declaration of war on
6 April 1917, declaring, "Prussianism must perish from the earth."
Previously he had emphasized the importance of bipartisanship in
national defense, and in wartime it was absolutely essential: "In this hour
of our national trial, party lines are no more; party politics are
obliterated; internal differences forgotten; and to-day we stand as one
people against the common enemy of our country."[19] Vinson admired
President Wilson and backed him throughout the war. World War I was a
war in defense of civilization and a "war to make the world safe for
democracy," but for Vinson and countless others, it also was a personal
war. Two of Carl's brothers, Fred and Wilbur, saw service in France.[20]

Through his efforts in Congress as well as his untiring work
throughout the Tenth District, Vinson had achieved such popular support
that no rival seemed willing to challenge him in the 1918 Democratic
primary. Newspapers printed articles about Vinson going back without
opposition.[21] But at the very last minute, Tom Watson, "The Sage of
Hickory Hill," announced his candidacy. Watson, one of the most
powerful political voices ever to emerge from the red hills of Georgia,
was "hated and vilified by some, idolized and lauded by others."[22] He
had once represented the Tenth District, but that had been many years

---

[17] Ibid., 27; *Congressional Record*, 65th Cong., 1st sess., Special sess., 2
April 1917, 114.

[18] *Union-Recorder*, 1 May 1917, 4.

[19] *Congressional Record*, 65th Cong., 1st sess., Special sess., 5 April 1917,
358.

[20] *Milledgeville News*, 26 October 1917, 1; 7 August 1918, 7.

[21] *Milledgeville News*, 24 July 1918, 1; *Augusta Chronicle*, 4 August 1918,
8.

[22] Reed, "Fighting the Devil with Fire," 451.

ago. Out of office since 1895, he had not sought political office for himself in twenty years, aside from symbolic races for president as the last Populist candidate. Yet, through his writings and speeches, he had remained the spokesmen for Georgia's agrarian interests. So loyal were his thousands of supporters that no one could get elected governor of the state without his backing. Despite his obvious political clout and oratorical skill, a race against Vinson in 1918 seemed daunting if not foolhardy. Vinson was then riding the crest of public support as an effective legislator and a loyal backer of President Wilson and the war effort. Watson, by contrast, had fallen on hard times. In August 1917 the U.S. Postmaster-General had denied the *Jeffersonian,* his weekly newspaper, access to the mail because of his opposition to the war effort. One week later, on 30 August, his only daughter Agnes died. Watson's general health deteriorated as he, reeling in sorrow, began to drink heavily and take narcotics to escape his deep depression. In January he moved to his Florida home to forget his sorrows and to enjoy life on the beach, where the ocean air helped his asthma. On 8 April Watson's only surviving child, John Durham, suddenly died from convulsions in his father's arms. With all his children dead and his printing presses in Thomson rusting, Watson was overwhelmed with grief. Severely depressed, he stayed intoxicated for days at a time. Shortly after Durham's death, a Negro servant found him wandering down the beach babbling old stump speeches from the 1890s.[23]

Watson had supported Vinson in 1914, and some believe that his endorsement was the decisive factor in Vinson's victory.[24] Why at age sixty-two and beset with tragedy he decided to challenge Vinson is baffling to say the least. Vinson's secretary, Martha Thomas, gave one explanation to Lou Stockstill. Shortly after he arrived at the Capital, an influential constituent sent Vinson drafts of a number of bills he wanted

---

[23] Ibid., 454–55; Edward Cashin, "Thomas E. Watson and the Catholic Layman's Association" (Ph. D. diss., Fordham University, 1962) 188–89; *Walter J. Brown, J. J. Brown and Thomas E. Watson: Georgia Politics 1912–1928* (n.p., 1988) 65–68.

[24] Warren D. Evans affidavit, 12 November 1997, Tom Watson Brown Private Papers, Marietta, GA.

introduced. Most members of Congress ordinarily honor such requests. The young Georgian, however, sent the requests back to their author with alacrity, she recalled. When warned that he might be creating a powerful enemy, he replied, "I wear no man's collar." The constituent, Miss Thomas related, was Tom Watson.[25] Some journalists speculated that he was making the race merely as a preparation for running against his longtime rival Hoke Smith for the U.S. Senate seat in 1920.[26] After Watson returned to Georgia in July, his friends and supporters urged him to run, but he resolutely declined. They persisted, however, even promising to finance his campaign. Finally, on the day before the qualifying deadline, Watson allowed his name to be placed on the ballot. In his opening address, Watson acknowledged that one reason for making the race was "to divert his mind and give him employment needed to prevent melancholia." [27]

As the campaign began, Vinson faced a family crisis too. He received disturbing news that his younger brother, Morris, was ailing. Morris, five years younger than Carl, had advanced rapidly in the railroad business. Starting out with the Central of Georgia, he subsequently joined the Southern Pacific in San Francisco, where he became city passenger agent in 1911. When the government took over the railroads with the onset of war, Morris was ordered to Washington for training. In July 1917 he entered the quartermaster's department of the Army and in August was promoted to the rank of captain in the Railroad Division, serving under the Regional Director and stationed in Charleston, South Carolina. He was in Fayetteville, North Carolina when Carl was notified that he was seriously ill. Carl rushed to Fayetteville and was with him when he died on 15 August 1918. Carl had been concerned about his brothers Fred and Wilbur fighting on the Western Front, but it was Morris, who had stayed in America, who perished while Fred and Wilbur—though wounded in the Argonne—came out of the war intact. Only thirty years of age, Morris was one of the early casualties of the

---

[25] Stockstill, "Backstage Boss," 26–27.

[26] *Augusta Chronicle*, 22 August 1918, 1, 2, 5.

[27] *Augusta Chronicle*, 25 August 1918. 1, 2; Reed, "Fighting the Devil with Fire," 455–57.

Spanish influenza epidemic that would take far more lives than all of bullets fired in World War I.[28]

Despite Watson's troubles, Vinson knew that he faced an extremely formidable challenge. On 20 August, he secured an indefinite leave of absence from Congress "on account of important business," apparently the business of getting reelected.[29] After planning his strategy in Washington, he returned to the district prepared for the fight of his life. Watson was to open his campaign on 24 August, but Vinson beat him to the punch by issuing his first campaign statement on 22 August. In a newsletter published on that day in all the newspapers in the Tenth District, Vinson established the issue upon which the campaign would be fought—loyalty versus disloyalty. Declaring that he had been in "complete accord" with President Wilson's administration and the war effort, he asked that the same yardstick be applied to his opponent. When that is done, Vinson declared, the voters of the Tenth District would find "a man whom this government of ours, just entering upon war with a brutal foreign foe, found it expedient and necessary to silence for his well-nigh seditious utterances and un-American writings, by excluding his disloyal incendiary publications from the mails." Tom Watson, Vinson continued, has a "holy hatred" of Woodrow Wilson and holds him "personally responsible for silencing his seditious publications." His goal is to get into Congress so that he can "criticize, embarrass and hamstring our great president and his administration." Regardless of "his fair words and specious promises," Watson "has no more intention of loyally supporting the administration in the prosecution of this war than I have in supporting the Kaiser, or the devil himself." Moreover, the newsletter continued, Watson had not purchased "out of his well-filled coffers a single Liberty Bond, or contributed a dollar to the Red Cross or Y.M.C.A." Summarizing the contrasts, Vinson pledged to campaign on his record in Congress and his career as a loyal Democrat against his opponent's record "as an enemy to democracy and as a pur-blind

---

[28] *Milledgeville News*, 13 January 1911, 1; 14 August 1918, 1; 16 October 1918, 1; Ed and Betty Vinson, interview with the author, Atlanta GA, 7 August 2001.
[29] *Congressional Record*, 65th Cong., 2d sess., 20 August 1918, 9281.

purveyor to every passion and prejudice that would put a penny in his purse."[30]

By taking the initiative, Vinson shrewdly established Watson's past opposition to Wilson's prosecution of the war as the central issue of the campaign. He placed his famous opponent, thirty years his senior, on the defensive for the first time in a generation. It was apparent to everyone that this campaign would be a barn-burner in the finest tradition of the "Bloody Tenth."[31]

Watson promised that he would go after Congressman Carl Vinson's seat "hammer and tongs," and he did so.[32] His opening address at Crawfordville, the home of Confederate Vice President Alexander Stephens, drew a crowd of nearly 2,000 supporters from a dozen counties. Arriving by train from Thomson, Watson showed the effects of his recent illness but seemed healthy enough to conduct a vigorous campaign. Mounting a table in front of the courthouse at 11:00, he brushed back his reddish gray hair and without any preliminaries began to speak. He pointed out that it had been twenty-six years since he had appeared in Taliaferro County on his own behalf. He was in the race because "an almost unanimous voice" from supporters had persuaded him to run for Congress, and "I am now ready to fight until the end of the campaign."[33] The audience roared when he referred to Vinson as "King Karl," a good German name. He denied Vinson's charge that he had obstructed conscription laws or refused to support the Red Cross. He said conscription was "a settled issue," since it had passed Congress and the president had approved it. Regarding the war, he declared that "now that this country was in it he was in favor of continuing it to a successful finish." If sent to Congress, he would not "obstruct President Wilson, but he would do his duty as he saw it." In closing, he claimed to be a

---

[30] *Augusta Chronicle*, 22 August 1918, 1, 2; Reed, "Fighting the Devil with Fire," 458–59; Landrum, "Carl Vinson: A Study in Military Preparedness," 15–17.

[31] Reed, "Fighting the Devil with Fire," 459–60.

[32] *Union-Recorder*, 21 August 1918, 1.

[33] Reed, "Fighting the Devil with Fire," 460.

Democrat; he had stood for Democratic principles in the past and was prepared to support them in the future.

After speaking a little more than an hour, Watson ended his speech abruptly and dismounted the table unsteadily, worn from the exertion.[34] Age and illness had taken away the fire that his followers expected from him, and his voice rarely rose above a conversation level. Although favorably received, the subdued speech failed to generate the rowdy applause, yelling matches, or fistfights that characterized Watson gatherings in the 1890s. But, all things considered, Watson had made an impressive beginning. Even the *Augusta Chronicle,* whose managing editor was Vinson's campaign manager, acknowledged that the Tenth District was in for a horse race, "not by any means a walk-over for either contestant."[35]

During the next three weeks both candidates crisscrossed the district, rallying their supporters and reiterating the themes they had already presented. Vinson, campaigning with his usual energy, announced a speaking schedule for the week beginning 26 August. It called for two speeches a day, each in a different town. On that day he spoke at Louisville at 11:00 and at Wadley at 3:30. The next day it was Bartow at 11:00 and Davisboro at 3:30. Following this schedule, he intended to reach every town and hamlet in the Tenth District.[36]

To win the election, Vinson knew that he had to keep the campaign focused on the issue of loyalty and patriotism. Although he lacked Watson's reputation as an orator, his speeches had clarity, force, and conviction. In each speech, he declared that Watson was anti-war and anti-administration. Maintaining the offensive, he bombarded Watson's record and consistently hammered in the idea that Watson would obstruct the administration because of his hatred toward Wilson. Typical was his tirade at Louisville: "He wants to throw a monkey wrench in the machinery of the government and break it up where possible. He wants to get there to vent his wrath again on President Wilson and ham-string the administration of the greatest president this country has ever known.

---

[34] *Augusta Chronicle*, 25 August 1918, 1–2.

[35] Ibid.; Reed, "Fighting the Devil with Fire," 461.

[36] *Augusta Chronicle*, 21 August 1918, 1, 4; 27 August 1918, 1.

He wants to get here to obstruct the war measures, to prevent the winning of the war, to fight the loyal, patriotic democracy of this country."[37]

J. C. McAuliffe, Vinson's campaign manager, and other strategists carefully reviewed back issues of the *Jeffersonian* looking for especially embarrassing statements by Watson. They found many, which they distributed throughout the Tenth District. Between 27 August and 10 September, they published fifteen large advertisements in the *Augusta Chronicle* and the *Augusta Herald* contrasting the old and the new Watson. The first one—titled "Can a Leopard Change His Spots?"—displayed selections from Watson's campaign speeches beside contradictory phrases from the *Jeffersonian*. That ad asserted, Mr. Watson, "YOUR OWN WORDS ARE GOING TO RISE TO PLAGUE YOU." And they did. Watson had described President Wilson as a "pusillanimous tool of a foreign potentate," a "periodical clown tanked up on verbosity and bellicosity," a "hypocrite," and a "charlatan," who "richly deserves impeachment." Entering the war had been "a wicked, unconstitutional and foolhardy thing"; America was a "moral accomplice in much of its bloodshed, rapine and crimes, because we have fed the war." Each day preceding the primary revealed more of Watson's own words that contradicted his present positions.[38]

Watson, of course, tried to shift the emphasis of the campaign away from the loyalty-disloyalty issue. Before a crowd of 800 at Sparta, he advocated direct loans to farmers, a holdover from his Farmer's Alliance days. He also called for "a government system of loans so that every man who is blacklisted by the state and national banks will know where to go to get money." Continuing the economic theme, he urged the government to stop issuing bonds and issue greenbacks instead. The government should "have confidence in the people and issue money direct." In the same speech, he lambasted the government for taking over the railroads, the telephone and telegraph, and the express companies.[39]

---

[37] Ibid., 27 August 1918, 1.

[38] Ibid., 27 August–10 September 1918; Reed, "Fighting the Devil with Fire," 462–63.

[39] *Augusta Chronicle*, 30 August 1918, 1, 2; Landrum, "Carl Vinson: A Study in Military Preparedness," 19.

Besides Vinson's relentless attacks, Watson's campaign was handicapped by Liberty Bond drives, Red Cross campaigns, and Creel Committee propaganda, which demanded allegiance to Wilson and the war effort. Opponents of Wilson became politically isolated throughout the South. In Mississippi, James K. Vardaman, the only Southern senator to vote against the war resolution in 1917, lost his seat to a strong supporter of Wilson's war measures. On 27 August, Coleman L. Blease, former governor of South Carolina, failed in a comeback attempt similar to Watson's. Senator Thomas W. Hardwick, former Tenth District congressman and Watson protégé, had opposed conscription and other war measures. After President Wilson urged Georgia Democrats to defeat him, his campaign quickly collapsed.[40]

As the primary deadline approached, tension increased. The personal animosity between Watson and Vinson, apparent from the outset, intensified, and their rhetoric grew more strident. The crowds increased in size and emotion, and after the candidates' speeches, loud shouting and fistfights often erupted. Vinson took his campaign to Watson's home of Thomson, and Watson, in turn, spoke for two hours in Milledgeville, within two blocks of Vinson's home. On the last day of the campaign, Watson traveled over 100 miles by car, crisscrossing the district and speaking to thousands. His strenuous campaign ended with an evening address in Augusta before a crowd of 5,000.[41]

On 11 September, 11,000 votes were cast and counted. Vinson won six counties: Baldwin, Columbia, Hancock, Richmond, Taliaferro, and Wilkinson. Watson also won six counties, but Vinson received sixteen county unit votes to Watson's fourteen. A shift of fifty votes in either Taliaferro or Columbia counties would have changed the outcome. Watson immediately claimed fraud and challenged the results in three counties: Taliaferro, Wilkinson, and Columbia. Vinson took the high road, postponing his formal nomination by convention until all of the

---

[40] Reed, "Fighting the Devil with Fire," 463–64; *Augusta Chronicle*, 29 August 1918, 1.

[41] Reed, "Fighting the Devil with Fire," 465–69; *Augusta Chronicle*, 3 September 1918, 1; 5 September 1918, 1; *Union-Recorder,* 4 September 1918, 1; Sam Nunn, interview with the author, Atlanta GA, 4 April 2001.

charges were cleared. Despite unanimous rulings against him in all three disputed counties, Watson refused to concede defeat. When the State Democratic Convention in Macon rejected his appeal on 3 October, the press declared that Watsonism was dead.[42] (Their obituaries were premature, however, as Watson defeated Hoke Smith for the U.S. Senate seat in 1920.[43]) Finally, on 10 October at the Tenth District convention in Milledgeville, Vinson received the official Democratic nomination for Congress by unanimous vote.

Vinson barely had time to savor the accolades he received for defeating Watson when rumors began to circulate that Sam Olive, president of the Georgia State Senate, was considering a race against him. Early in May 1920, Olive made his formal announcement and began his campaign in earnest. Six weeks later, after Congress adjourned, Vinson returned to Milledgeville and expressed confidence that the voters would reelect him.[44] In studying Olive's campaign platform, Vinson discovered a political flaw and made it the central issue of the campaign. Olive advocated national aid for common schools. Knowing how the voters of rural Georgia feared racially integrated schools, Vinson put Olive on the defensive from the beginning. To drive the point home, he had a a *Washington Post* staff member draw a cartoon that depicted a school with Negro and white children entering together. Standing in the foreground was a caricature of "Uncle Sam" saying, "Of course, Olive understands that national aid means federal control and no color line in southern schools."[45] Uncle Sam held a copy of Olive's platform promise "to introduce and press for passage of a bill providing national aid for common schools." At the bottom of the cartoon, Vinson interpreted Olive's idea to mean:

---

[42] Reed, "Fighting the Devil with Fire," 470–77; *Augusta Chronicle*, 12 September–4 October 1918.

[43] While serving in Washington, Watson befriended Vinson, and in 1922, when he was dying, called Vinson to his deathbed. Landrum, "Carl Vinson: A Study in Military Preparedness," 21.

[44] *Union-Recorder*, 4 May 1920, 1; 15 June 1920, 1.

[45] Landrum, "Carl Vinson: A Study in Military Preparedness," 21.

1. that Georgia school laws will be prescribed by the federal government.
2. that our schools will be conducted according to the dictates of autocratic bureaus in Washington.
3. one school for both races and social equality in our schools.
4. centralization of more power in the national government.
5. destruction of home rule and local self-government.[46]

By stressing the dangers of federal aid to schools, Vinson offended his hometown paper. The *Union-Recorder*, a Milledgeville weekly that normally praised him, "advised the people of the Tenth district to beware of trusting with public office the man who would appeal to prejudice instead of reason. He is not a safe leader."[47]

Olive waged a vigorous campaign throughout the district, even speaking twice in Baldwin County. Even though he had a commendable record and was considered a forceful speaker, he could not match Vinson's appeal to the voters of the Tenth District. When the votes were counted on 8 September, Vinson had won a decisive victory. He carried seven counties, including Richmond, Olive's home county, with a total of twenty county unit votes to Olive's five counties with only ten county unit votes. The *Union-Recorder* acknowledged that Vinson had visited every section of every county in the district and had "met the voters face to face and discussed the issues of the campaign." Praising him as "a man of energy and determination" who works hard and has "stood by the administration of President Wilson," it wished him "two years of splendid service to his country."[48] Even more favorable was the *Augusta Chronicle*, which editorialized that Vinson's record was "so excellent that his opponent could make no charges against it."[49]

---

[46] Ibid., 21–22.

[47] *Union-Recorder*, 13 July 1920, 4.

[48] Ibid., 14 September 1920, 1, 4.

[49] Quoted in Landrum, "Carl Vinson: A Study in Military Preparedness," 22.

By defeating Olive and Watson, "the single most formidable political figure in Tenth District history," Vinson established a reputation as an unbeatable campaigner. Indeed, so intimidating was his reputation that no one thereafter dared oppose him in the Tenth District. He was reelected without opposition from 1922 to 1930.[50]

---

[50] Ibid.; Reed, "Fighting the Devil with Fire," 478.

3

The Not-So-Roaring 1920s

We destroyed ships which a prudent nation would have retained; we kept some ships that should have been eliminated.

Carl Vinson, 1923

Serving in Congress can be an all-consuming vocation, demanding all of a congressman's time and energy. For the conscientious representative there is never enough time in the day to accomplish all that needs to be done. Besides participating in debate on the floor of the House, there is committee work, meeting constituents, answering correspondence, discussing issues with colleagues, preparing speeches, studying reports, and attending ceremonies and dedications. Since a congressman faces an election every two years, he needs to spend much time in his district, meeting people, listening to their concerns, and giving speeches. No congressman of this era was more conscientious than Carl Vinson.

Upon arrival in Washington, Vinson learned his way around and quickly developed friendships, some of which would last a lifetime. His closest associates, quite naturally, consisted of the Georgia congressional delegation, including Senators Walter George, Hoke Smith, and then Tom Watson, as well as his colleagues on the Naval Affairs Committee. Vinson also befriended an ambitious young congressman from Texas who had entered the House one year before he did. Sam Rayburn, who also came from a small Southern town, showed remarkable political instincts and dedication to congressional service. The two aspiring young Democrats shared a common outlook on most issues, including an abiding concern for both the well being of the common man and the defense of the country. They fought many a battle side by side and served as colleagues nearly half a century, longer than anyone else in congressional history. Rayburn's mentor was John Nance Garner, an older man who had entered the House in 1903. Colorful and extremely capable, "Cactus Jack," as he was known, rose through the ranks to serve as Speaker of the House and vice president. Garner gave Rayburn and many others advice on how to be a successful congressman. His advice consisted of three inflexible rules: Always take care of the needs of your home district, keep quiet until you know what you're talking about, and become the foremost authority in the House, through work and study, in one particular field of legislation. "You can't know everything well," he continued. "Learn one subject thoroughly and find out as much as you can about the others. Get useful information for the members of this House when you are going to speak. You can't spend your time better. It's finer recreation than fishing. There is nothing more useful or more thrilling than facts. Your colleagues here want information and will listen to a man who has knowledge of his subject. They ought not to have to give ear time to anyone else."[1]

Whether Vinson heard this advice directly from Garner cannot be determined, but he followed it nonetheless. He consistently looked out for his constituents and secured abundant "pork barrel" projects for his district. After his appointment to the Naval Affairs Committee, he applied himself to learning all he could about military affairs. He spent long hours poring over reports and mastering the intricacies of all aspects of the military process. At committee hearings, when military experts testified, he carefully absorbed information about America's obligations and her capacity to meet those obligations. He pondered such matters and became a storehouse of information. His colleagues on the Naval Affairs

---

[1] D. B. Hardeman and Donald C. Bacon, *Rayburn, A Biography* (Austin: Texas Monthly Press, 1987) 70–71; Bascom N. Timmons, *Garner of Texas* (New York: Harper & Brothers Publishers, 1948) 112.

Committee quickly recognized the young Georgian's expertise, and soon afterwards the whole House did.

From the beginning of his political career, Vinson had been so ambitious and so focused on doing the job well that he had little time for social activities. Rather than secure dates, he sometimes escorted family members to social functions he was expected to attend.[2] Newsmen sometimes referred to him as president of the "Congressional Bachelor's Club." Like many bachelors, Vinson had been waiting for the right woman. As far as can be determined, he had shown no serious interest in any woman until he met Mary Greene McGregor. A native of New Philadelphia, Ohio, Mary came from a prominent family. Her father, J. E. Greene, a graduate of Hopedale College and the University of Michigan Law School, had served two terms as a prosecuting attorney; her mother, Anna Shilling Greene, was a graduate of Beaver College and taught school for several years. A widow, Mary had previously been married to Donald McGregor, a well-known representative of the *Paris Herald*, and had lived in Washington for five years. Vinson quickly succumbed to her beauty, charm, and intelligence. Always well groomed, she possessed a natural grace and dignity that Vinson found irresistible.[3] They decided to get married on 6 April 1921, the fourth anniversary of American entry into World War I. Vinson seemed to be such a confirmed bachelor that when he informed a group of congressmen that he was going to get married, they were "blown off their feet."[4]

Carl and Mary were married in a quiet ceremony at the Foundry Methodist Church with the Reverend Herbert F. Randolph officiating. Only a few intimate friends had been invited. They included Representative and Mrs. Edgar R. Kiess of Pennsylvania; Mrs. Willis Howard of Milledgeville; Mrs. and Mrs. Claude Stone, formerly of Crawfordville; and Miss Edna L. Lytle, Vinson's secretary. Immediately

---

[2] Henry Jennings, telephone interview with the author, Gainesville GA, 22 August 2001.

[3] Louis R. Stockstill, "'Uncle Carl' Vinson: Backstage Boss of the Pentagon," *Army Navy Air Force Journal* 98 (18 February 1961): 27; *Macon Telegraph*, April 6, 1921, 1; *Augusta Chronicle*, April 6, 1921, 10.

[4] *Atlanta Constitution*, 5 April 1921, 5.

after the ceremony, Carl and Mary spent a few days honeymooning in
Atlantic City before returning to Washington for the opening of Congress
on 11 April. Vinson was serious by nature, and in practically all of the
hundreds of photographs that exist, he displays a serious countenance.
The one exception is the photo of Carl and Mary leaving the church that
appeared in the *Atlanta Constitution*. In it, a dapper Vinson, dressed in a
stylish suit with vest and hat, is smiling from ear to ear.[5] He had good
reason to be elated, for he had found the woman of his dreams, and she
had become his wife.

By all accounts, the marriage of Carl and Mary was extremely
happy. Devoted to each other, they enjoyed each other's company and
shared life's adventures. They purchased a bungalow at 4 Primrose Street
in Chevy Chase, Maryland, a fashionable suburb on the northwest side of
Washington, and it became their permanent home. It had a big front
porch with four columns and an upstairs with two gables. Carl never had
taken time for a pet, but Mary, a devoted dog-lover, always had a dog,
usually a terrier. Mary also was fond of playing bridge, and they often
had other couples visit to play bridge. Since Carl never drove a car, Mary
served as the family chauffeur. She enjoyed vacationing in Florida,
which they did many times, and she also enjoyed meeting his friends and
family in Georgia. Despite being a transplanted Yankee, Mary was
popular with the old Southern families in Milledgeville, as her
graciousness and charm easily overcame any "defects" they might have
detected in her non-Southern heritage. Carl refused to fly in an airplane
and rarely set foot on a ship, but Mary convinced him to take a
Caribbean cruise. Before boarding the ship, they stopped in Jacksonville,
Florida, to visit his sister Mabel and her family. While walking on the
beach where the St. Johns River enters the Atlantic, Mary slipped and cut
her leg severely on the barnacles on a jetty. But after she received
medical attention, the newlyweds were on their way. This cruise in the
early 1920s was the first time—and one of the very few times—Carl ever
left the country.[6]

---

[5] Ibid., 10 April 1921, K2.
[6] Vinson Scrapbooks, book Mary Vinson, on loan from Tillman Snead to
Georgia College and State University, Milledgeville, GA; Tillman and Karen

Since the vast majority of Vinson's constituents were farmers, he too became a farmer. Five years after his marriage, he purchased a 615-acre farm three miles south of Milledgeville, where he grew abundant crops of cotton, tobacco, and vegetables and raised sheep, cattle, and hogs. Some of the gently rolling hills were well-timbered, and the farm included a large pasture that sloped down to the Oconee River. It was good, rich land, and he later bragged that it was the best farm in Baldwin County. Highway 112 (now the Carl Vinson Highway) bisected the property. On an attractive knoll, where a local road veers off from the highway and marks a boundary to his property, Vinson built his farmhouse. He moved two small frame houses to the site and transformed them into one comfortable house with a hallway down the middle. A big front porch dominated the entrance, and flanking the center hall was the living room, dining room, and kitchen on the right, and his bedroom, bathroom, and guest bedroom on the left. At the rear of the house was a cozy den decorated in red, his favorite color. There was nothing pretentious about the house, for Vinson had simple tastes. He beautified the yard by planting eighty crepe myrtles, two deodars, and several pecan trees and magnolias. As a boy Carl had grown weary of farm chores and preferred living in town, but as a mature adult he developed a great love for his farm, which he called River Ridge Plantation.[7]

In 1925 Carl and Mary purchased a house in Milledgeville near the center of town in the same block as his parents' home. The beautiful two-story white frame house at 421 West Montgomery Street had character. Built in 1832, it had been owned for many years by Judge Iverson L. Harris, a justice of the Georgia Supreme Court. At the time of the Civil War, the family living in the house had a daughter who was engaged to a young man who went into the Confederate Army. On the second floor,

---

Snead, interview with the author, Dale City VA, 8 June 2001; Ed and Betty Vinson, interview with the author, Atlanta GA, 7 August 2001; Elizabeth Pollard Hood, interview with the author, Griffin GA, 26 November 2001.

[7] Tillman and Karen Snead, interview; Joe and Carol McMillan (the current owners of the house), interview with the author, Milledgeville GA, 7 December 2001; Baldwin County, Deed Book 11, 140.

she etched their two names on a windowpane, and her etching is still visible. Carl would have been content living in the farmhouse, but he knew Mary preferred town life. Over the years he refurbished the house with very attractive furniture, including some antiques, to please his wife. In the yard he planted gardenias, his favorite flower.[8]

World War I had a profound impact upon the American psyche. Since Europe had not experienced a major war in a century, many had concluded that all-out war was a thing of the past. Progress was evident everywhere as electricity, petroleum, steel, and chemicals transformed the way people in the Western world lived. The development of the railroad, streetcar, telegraph, and telephone had vastly improved transportation and communication. The worst abuses of the capitalistic system had been eliminated with higher wages, a shorter workday, and the enactment of safety and health regulations. Improvements in sanitation and public health had greatly reduced diseases and epidemics, thereby increasing the lifespan, while widespread public education and public libraries had greatly expanded opportunities for all. With all this progress in technology and political reform, no one expected a four-year war that would kill millions of combatants, cost countless millions of dollars, and topple three ruling dynasties—the Hapsburgs, the Hohenzollerns, and the Romanovs. "The Great War was," writes William E. Leuchtenburg, "a dirty, unheroic war which few men remembered with any emotion save distaste."[9] The destruction of human life and property was so much greater than anyone had expected that the public was thoroughly disillusioned by the war and determined to avoid a repeat. This determination took the form of the twin movements of peace and disarmament, which dominated politics in the 1920s on both sides of the Atlantic. Thoroughly frustrated by the war and the Treaty of

---

[8] Ed and Betty Vinson, interview with the author; Patricia Pollard Kinnett and Mary Ann Pollard, interview with author; Baldwin County, Deed Book 7, 368.

[9] Quoted in Selig Adler, *The Isolationist Impulse* (Westport CT: Greenwood Press, 1957) 3.

Versailles that ended it, America returned to isolationism, unwilling to take on the burdens of world leadership. America not only refused to make any binding commitments to European security, it also refused to join the League of Nations that President Wilson had introduced and worked tirelessly to get the European statesmen to accept. The U.S. Senate rejected the Treaty of Versailles, and a formal treaty of peace with Germany was not signed until 1921. In 1920 the voters thoroughly repudiated Wilsonian internationalism by electing Warren G. Harding as president under the slogan "Return to Normalcy." The Republicans made a clean sweep, capturing control of the House and Senate as well as the presidency—a dominance they would maintain throughout the 1920s.

Despite the opposition of William Jennings Bryan, Henry Ford, Robert LaFollette, Andrew Carnegie, and sixty-three peace organizations operating in 1914, the United States had built an enormous army and navy and transported two million soldiers to Europe, which brought victory to the Allied side.[10] But when victory was assured, that huge military force was quickly dismantled. A clear indication of the change in thinking was evident in the actions of Secretary of the Navy Josephus Daniels. When this North Carolinian first became secretary, he tried "to convert the naval service from a military organization into a vast educational institution specializing in the inculcation of civic values and moral principles not unlike a Boy Scout organization for adults."[11] Yet, he had presided over the unprecedented expansion of the American Navy. In December 1918 he called for a navy second to none and proposed a huge three-year building program. Six months later, he told the House Naval Affairs Committee to disregard his previous suggestion.[12]

From the experience of World War I, American diplomatists made four basic assumptions, which they followed throughout the 1920s. First, they concluded that the Great War was an aberration of European and

---

[10] Armin Rappaport, *The Navy League of the United States* (Detroit: Wayne State University Press, 1962) 45–52.

[11] B. Vincent Davis, *The Admirals Lobby* (Chapel Hill: University of North Carolina Press, 1967) 20.

[12] Rappaport, *The Navy League*, 80.

world history, a departure from the normal course of human events that could not happen again. Second, the diplomatists believed that in the post-Versailles world the nations of Europe could take care of themselves. Third, they believed that Eastern Asia, where teeming masses of Chinese and Japanese lived, could get along with occasional suggestions from the United States. Fourth, they convinced themselves that the real force for peace in the world was moral, not military. The old system of military force and defensive alliances had brought on the Great War, but in the postwar years the moral force of world public opinion would guard the world's peace with an effectiveness that military force could not possibly hope to achieve. The United States, they believed, was a natural leader of the world, the "great moral reserve" of the new postwar era.[13]

Secretary of State Charles Evans Hughes, a former governor of New York, Supreme Court justice, and Republican candidate for president in 1916, convinced President Harding to invite delegates from Great Britain, Japan, France, and Italy to meet in Washington in November of 1921 for the purpose of discussing arms limitations and Far Eastern problems. Invitations were subsequently extended to China, the Netherlands, Belgium, and Portugal to participate in the sessions relating to the Far East. Besides Hughes, the American delegation consisted of Senator Henry Cabot Lodge, chairman of the Foreign Relations Committee; Senator Oscar W. Underwood, ranking Democratic member of the committee; and Elihu Root, former secretary of state. Hughes, keenly aware of the public concern that the United States was replacing Germany as the military pacemaker of the world and the Republican determination to curb government spending and reduce taxes, shocked the delegates by presenting a plan at the opening session that advocated not only limitation of naval armament but the actual scrapping of vessels as well. His plan called for the immediate halt in the construction programs of the three major naval powers and the scrapping of 1,876,043 tons of ships already built or under construction. The British delegates could barely hide their elation, and the Japanese, though stoically calm,

---

[13] Robert Ferrell, *American Diplomacy in the Great Depression* (New Haven: Yale University Press, 1957) 20.

also were pleased. As finally agreed upon, the Five Power Treaty allotted 500,000 tons of capital ships each for Great Britain and the United States, 300,000 tons for Japan, and 167,000 for both France and Italy. Capital ships were defined as vessels displacing more than 10,000 tons and mounting guns larger than eight inches, and aircraft carriers. No agreement was reached on auxiliary craft, which included cruisers, destroyers, and submarines.[14]

In addition to the startling Five Power Treaty, the Washington Conference produced several other treaties, including the Four Power and Nine Power Treaties. The Four Power Treaty attempted to bring a halt to the threat of Japanese expansion in the Far East by non-aggression pledges and provisions for consultation in the event of disputes. The Nine Power Treaty guaranteed the territorial integrity of China and confirmed the principle of the Open Door, a policy the United States had pursued since 1898.[15]

The Washington Conference produced a profound effect upon world opinion. It indicated that great powers could assemble in conference and reach agreements on issues of vital importance. Since World War I had been fought because "the nations were so well prepared for it," naval disarmament seemed to be the path to peace. The Republican Party naturally took credit for the treaty, and in its platform of 1924 called the treaty "the greatest peace document ever drawn." The elated public was oblivious to the fact that the Washington Conference had reached no agreement on auxiliary ships, land armaments, or airplanes. While the public and press rejoiced, a few thoughtful individuals were less sanguine. Elihu Root, expressing the views of many statesmen and experts, viewed the outcome of the treaty as "the complete negation of naval policy." A naval spokesman, expressing an opinion shared by many of his colleagues, concluded that "America resigned to Britain the predominance in Sea Power, and gave up also her power to defend the

---

[14] Raymond G. O'Connor, *Perilous Equilibrium: The United States and the London Naval Conference of 1930* (Lawrence: University of Kansas Press, 1962) 5–7; George T. Davis, *A Navy Second to None* (New York: Harcourt, Brace and Company, 1940) 270–80.

[15] O'Connor, *Perilous Equilibrium*, 7.

Philippines and to accomplish our policies toward China and Russia."
The assessment of Raymond G. O'Connor, a modern scholar, is even
more critical. "Unwilling or unable to resist the clamor for economy and
peace through the reduction or elimination of the weapons of war, the
Secretary of State sacrificed America's freedom of action, lessened her
influence in world affairs, and weakened her ability to promote the
national interest. It was a precarious position for a nation that had
renounced the principle of collective security."[16]

From his earliest years, Vinson had been interested in military
affairs. His imagination had soared from the Civil War stories his father
and his uncle, Henry C. Vinson, related. Henry had enlisted in the
Baldwin Blues and served for nearly four years in the Confederate Army
of Northern Virginia. He was in the thick of the fighting from the
beginning of the war until his capture a few weeks before General Robert
E. Lee surrendered. In describing the battle of Winchester in the fall of
1864, the *Milledgeville Southern* reported that "Sergt. Henry Vinson of
the Baldwin Blues gallantly captured the flag of the 26th Massachusetts
Regiment."[17] After the Civil War, Henry lived in Savannah, Albany, and
McRae before returning to Milledgeville, where he died in 1922. At
family gatherings, Carl heard about Uncle Henry's exciting exploits
many times.[18]

Carl's interest in military affairs increased when he attended
Georgia Military College. When he arrived in Congress in November
1914, World War I already had erupted in Europe, and for the next four
years Congress's chief concern was raising an army and navy. Vinson
had seen how unprepared for war America was and how difficult it was
to raise, equip, train, and transport an army in 1917, when the country
joined the Allied cause. His service on the Naval Affairs Committee
reinforced his belief that the best way to avoid war is to maintain an
adequate defense. Never a military strategist or tactician, he was
perfectly content to leave those matters to the military leaders, but he

---

[16] Ibid., 7–9; Davis, *A Navy Second to None*, 295–301.

[17] *Milledgeville Southern*, 18 October 1864.

[18] Emmett Hall, interview with the author Jekyll Island GA, 22 November
2001 ; Emmett Hall scrapbook.

fervently believed that Congress had the Constitutional duty to "provide for the common defense."[19] Moreover, the Constitution specifically assigned to Congress the duty "to raise and support Armies" and "to provide and maintain a Navy."[20] As a member of Congress, Vinson took those responsibilities very seriously.

Vinson believed that the huge naval expansion plan adopted in 1916 should have been carried out. When completed, it would have given America the largest and best-equipped navy in the world. Rather than build "a navy second to none," the United States accepted parity with the British in capital ships at the Washington Conference. To reach the allotted level of 500,000 tons, America agreed to destroy eleven ships under construction totaling 520,000 tons, plus seventeen other battleships (all but two in active commission) of 267,740 tons, making the total tonnage scrapped by this government 787,740 tons. In a scathing indictment of the Five Power Treaty, Vinson pointed out to the House numerous inequities in the agreement. He noted that the eleven ships America scrapped were from 30 to 45 percent completed and had already cost the taxpayers $350,000,000. By contrast, the ships the British and Japanese scrapped were mostly obsolete vessels or those in the initial stages of construction. The United States, he explained, "actually scrapped 762,940 tons in actual commission and in process of construction, while Japan scrapped in actual commission and in the process of construction 286,182 tons, and Great Britain had no ships in process of construction and only 92,000 tons in actual commission."[21] As for the ships under construction, "the United States agreed to scrap seven battleships and six battle cruisers, against two battleships and two battle cruisers for Japan. The keels of the two battleships agreed to be scrapped by Japan were actually laid after the conference had assembled."[22] To make matters worse, the treaty was based on tonnage alone, with no consideration given to the range of guns or the speed of ships. Thus, "we

---

[19] U.S. Constitution, Preamble.

[20] U.S. Constitution, art. 1, sec. 8.

[21] *Congressional Record*, 67th Cong., 4th sess., 16 February 1923, 3797–98.

[22] Ibid., 3798.

have 3 capital ships of the first line, 11 of the second, and 4 of the third. Great Britain has 15 of the first line, 5 of the second, and none of the third. Japan has 2 of the first line, 8 of the second, and none of the third." Unlike our rivals, Vinson continued, we scrapped "the finest ships that ever sailed the seas" and retained obsolete vessels. In conclusion, he added, "We destroyed ships which a prudent nation would have retained; we kept some ships that should have been eliminated."[23]

Throughout the 1920s, Vinson labored, both in the Naval Affairs Committee and on the floor of the House, to overcome these problems and strengthen America's naval forces wherever possible under the existing restraints. When it appeared that another international conference might be forthcoming to focus on auxiliary ships, he argued that to achieve the aim of prohibiting competitive building among the maritime nations, "it is absolutely imperative and necessary to enter the conference with a strong and powerful Navy." America reached a successful agreement at the Washington Conference, he insisted, "because we had a large naval armament ourselves." He much preferred negotiating from a position of strength, and feared what might happen if we negotiated from weakness. While acknowledging that at the Washington Conference "we got the worst of it, as far as scrapping of ships was concerned," there were positive accomplishments too. "We reduced the naval budget from $815,788,286 in 1921 to $294,991,000 in 1924. We dispelled the hatred and suspicion that was in the minds of other countries and we adopted the policy that our Government was in favor of the reduction of naval armament."[24]

In that same speech on the floor of the House, he articulated principles that should guide American policy-makers. "No government which fails to provide for its own preservation against the assaults of every possible foe is entitled to the support of its people," he asserted. "A primary duty of government is self-preservation, and no sophistry of logic can justify it in stripping itself of its means of defense and relying for its preservation upon the mercy, the pity, or the love of other

---

[23] Ibid.

[24] Ibid., 68th Cong., 1st sess., 28 May 1924, 9751–53.

nations." After setting forth this broad concept, he then dealt with specific issues:

> In making appropriations for the Navy we should be guided and controlled by our ability to successfully defend our insular possessions, to maintain for our commerce the freedom of the seas, to defend the greatest engineering enterprise and commerce carrier of the century, the Panama Canal; to maintain America's open-door policy in the Orient, to enforce our policy of noninterference by monarchial governments in the affairs of Central and South American Republics, to defend our nation's honor and protect and redress American citizens wherever wronged, to maintain the ratio agreed upon at the Washington conference, and by all means to keep the Navy up to the highest point of efficiency.[25]

To Vinson, it was obvious that the navy, in its present condition, was incapable of accomplishing these objectives. Thus, the country should either strengthen the navy or reduce its objectives. Unfortunately, the Republican administrations of Harding, Coolidge, and Hoover did neither during the decade following the Washington Conference. Confident that naval disarmament and international agreements had insured America's defense, they showed scant interest in naval affairs. Under the leadership of Secretary of the Treasury Andrew Mellon, who saw little reason for spending good debt retirement money on "worthless" navy fighting ships, they lowered taxes and balanced budgets. Since such policies were extremely popular, Congress followed the same course of economy.[26] Vinson's role was to remind his colleagues of the inconsistency between goals and means and to convince them to adopt minor improvements in the navy. He repeatedly called for modernizing the fleet in order to maintain parity with the British. This meant converting coal burners to oil burners, protecting the

---

[25] Ibid.

[26] Calvin W. Enders, "The Vinson Navy" (Ph.D. diss., Michigan State University, 1970) 18–21.

decks, and improving the guns. He also reminded Congress of the
manpower needs to keep up with the British as well as the need to build
cruisers, submarines, and other vessels not limited by the Washington
Conference.[27] During this era, the best efforts of the ranking minority
member of the House Naval Affairs Committee did little to motivate a
building program.[28]

While establishing a reputation as the foremost champion of
national defense, Vinson never lost sight of the needs of his constituents
in the Tenth District. In general, farmers faced hard times in the 1920s as
the price of farm produce dropped sharply after World War I. Modern
improvements in agriculture, such as the widespread use of improved
seeds, commercial fertilizers and chemicals, as well as the development
of tractors, and new farm machinery, were largely responsible for the
decline in prices as they greatly increased the output of American farms.
In addition, as soon as European farms went back into production they
eliminated that market for American foodstuffs. The result was
overproduction—a problem that plagued Western farmers throughout
most of the twentieth century. Georgia farmers not only suffered from
lower prices, they also faced the menace of the boll weevil, an insect that
wreaked havoc on cotton production.

Fully aware of the plight of his constituents, Vinson introduced a
host of bills designed to ease their burden. In 1923 he introduced a bill to
eliminate the 25 percent duty on calcium arsenate, another to reduce
railroad rates, and a third to reduce the income tax rate from 4 percent to
2 percent.[29] He devoted much effort to changing the way the government
reported its estimate of cotton production.[30] In 1925 he sought to amend
the law so that farmers could borrow money from the federal land bank
to liquidate any indebtedness.[31] The next year he continued to support the

---

[27] Ibid., *Congressional Record*, 68th Cong., 1st sess., 21 March 1924,
4649–50; 68th Cong., 2d sess., 16 December 1924, 688–90; 68th Cong., 2d
sess., 24 January 1925, 2423–26; 69th Cong., 1st sess., 20 January 1926,
2445–48; 70th Cong., 1st sess., 16 March 1928, 4897–99.

[28] Enders, "The Vinson Navy," 22.

[29] *Union-Recorder*, 5 December 1923, 1.

[30] Ibid., 17 December 1925, 2.

[31] Ibid., 7

previously introduced measures and added a bill to restrict gambling in cotton futures and another requiring the government to disseminate more accurate information on cotton and tobacco crops.[32] In 1927 he introduced a bill "to prohibit the Secretary of Agriculture, or any of the Bureaus of the Department of Agriculture, from issuing or causing to be issued any report, bulletin, or other publication, or give or cause to be given any statement for publication containing any prediction with respect to cotton prices" and another bill requiring the Department of Agriculture to take an actual census of the number of acres planted in cotton each year.[33] In 1928 he authored a bill to "wipe out the manipulation now being carried on by the speculators" on the cotton exchange. He argued that it "will do more to enable the farmers to secure a remunerative price for their cotton than any of the proposed farm relief bills now pending before congress."[34]

Few of these bills became law, and it is doubtful that any of them would have made a major impact on the livelihood of Georgia farmers, but introducing them was a shrewd political move. These measures convinced voters in the Tenth District that their congressman was aware of their plight and was doing all in his power to alleviate their distress. In addition, he continued to address the problems individual constituents brought to him and secure funds for roads and post offices. In May 1919 he introduced bills authorizing post offices in Tennille, Sandersville, Sparta, and Thomson, and no less than twelve bills authorizing the secretary of war to donate a German cannon or fieldpiece to towns in his district.[35] Vinson may have set a congressional record for securing German military pieces as he hardly overlooked a hamlet in the Tenth District. By such actions, he enhanced his political standing to such a degree that no one dared to challenge him from 1922 to 1930. He received high praise from the newspapers throughout his district and often the editors discouraged anyone from challenging him. The *Union-Recorder* and the *Augusta Chronicle* seemed to be in a contest to see

---

[32] Ibid., 18 February 1925, 1; 10 June 1926, 1.

[33] Ibid., 8 December 1927, 1.

[34] Ibid., 9 February 1928, 1.

[35] *Congressional Record*, 66th Cong., 1st sess., 28 May 1919, 378–79.

which one could bestow the most lavish praise on Vinson. His hometown paper editorialized that "Congressman Vinson, during the years he has represented the Tenth District, has studied public questions and has shown an aptitude and determination in championing legislation that was to the best interest of his county. He has always guarded with care and looked after carefully the interest of his constituency. To his willingness and ability he has added an experience which makes his service at this time almost indispensable to the people of the Tenth District."[36] After Vinson had represented the Tenth District twelve years, the *Augusta Chronicle* observed, "Carl Vinson has made thousands of friends throughout the district by his painstaking attention to details, by his prompt handling of large and small matters affecting his constituency, by his consistently being on the job and sticking unswervingly to democratic principles and democratic ideals. He has taken a high stand in Washington and is now ranking democratic member of the powerful naval affairs committee." The lengthy editorial concluded, "Carl Vinson is an able congressman, an outstanding member whose usefulness has greatly increased with the years. And we have an idea that an appreciative electorate will return him without even the suggestion of opposition."[37]

Vinson's career took an upward turn in 1925 when he was named to a prestigious committee to investigate aviation. This committee, known as the Morrow Board, came about in part because of the highly publicized activities of Billy Mitchell, the foremost advocate of airpower. Mitchell, one of the few who came out of World War I with an understanding of how the next war would be fought, launched a public campaign to develop an air force. The rapid demobilization after World War I had "nearly wrecked the nation's armed forces," and "the number of Air Service officers had dropped from 20,000 to a nucleus of little more than 200 regular officers in 1919."[38] These reductions distressed Mitchell, who believed that in future wars, aviation would be far more

---

[36] *Union-Recorder*, 18 February 1926., 1

[37] Quoted in *Union-Recorder*, 17 June 1926, 6.

[38] Alfred F. Hurley, *Billy Mitchell, Crusader for Air Power* (New York: Franklin Watts, Inc., 1964) 41.

important than surface ships. As Director of Military Aeronautics, he declared that American cities were vulnerable to attacks from the air, and he was fond of pointing out that one battleship cost as much as 1,000 planes. His rhetoric produced so many headlines that bombing tests were arranged for June–July 1921. Out-going Secretary of the Navy Josephus Daniels—no friend of Mitchell—allegedly offered to stand bareheaded on the bridge of any ship Mitchell tried to bomb. Fortunately Daniels was not on the ex-German battleship *Ostfriesland* on 22 July when Mitchell's crew dropped six 2,000-pound bombs on it, sending it to the bottom of the sea sixty miles off the Virginia coast. In August he repeated the triumph by sinking the *Alabama.* These bombing tests took place shortly before the Washington Naval Conference, and Mitchell argued that they "greatly facilitated" the decision to limit battleships.[39]

Mitchell's unorthodox tactics and bitter criticism of the Navy and War Departments led to his court-martial in 1925. President Calvin Coolidge, aware that an aviation policy was badly needed and unwilling to let the court martial be the focus of national attention, called on his friend Dwight Morrow, a lawyer and a partner with the J. P. Morgan firm, to lead an aviation inquiry. Together Coolidge and Morrow selected a group of prominent men who would inspire the confidence of the American people, the Congress, and the military. Serving with Morrow were Judge Arthur C. Denison of the Sixth Circuit Court of Appeals; Dr. William F. Durand of Stanford University, president of the American Society of Mechanical Engineers and a member of the National Advisory Committee for Aeronautics; Senator Hiram Bingham of the Military Affairs Committee; Representative James S. Parker, chairman of the House Committee on Interstate and Foreign Commerce; retired General James G. Harbord, president of Radio Corporation of America; retired Admiral Frank E. Fletcher, an early supporter of naval aviation; Howard Coffin, consulting engineer and expert in aeronautics; and Carl Vinson, the ranking Democrat on the Naval Affairs Committee. The *New York Times* reported that Vinson, the only Democrat, had been "chosen so that he may guide his party colleagues when the findings of this board go before Congress for action." Moreover, the *Times* continued, "He ranks

---

[39] Ibid., 58–70.

as a thorough examiner into all questions affecting national defense."
After meeting with the president at the White House, the Morrow Board
held its first public meeting on 21 September, five weeks before the
Mitchell court-martial began.[40]

The Morrow Board completed its hearings by the time the Mitchell
court-martial got under way on 28 October. During those weeks, it
thoroughly examined every aspect of aviation in the United States. It
heard the testimony of ninety-nine witnesses, among them were Orville
Wright, Billy Mitchell, the secretary of war, the secretary of the navy, the
postmaster general, the secretary of commerce, technical advisors, heads
of bureaus and departments, representatives of the National Advisory
Committee for Aeronautics, and leaders of the aircraft industry. Indeed,
the Morrow Board heard from "all the prominent men in civilian flying"
as well as the grievances, hopes, and suggestions of industry. The four
printed volumes reporting the Board's hearings and its conclusions
constitute "an exhaustive, indeed a monumental study of all aviation
problems up to the time of sitting."[41]

In part 1 the Board recommended that the military and civilian
services should remain distinctly separate and that a separate Department
of the Air Force was not advisable at this time. Furthermore, contrary to
Billy Mitchell's rantings, it concluded that the United States was not in
danger of air attack from any potential enemy. After discussing these
broad issues, it analyzed the army, the navy, and the industry in part 2.
Regarding the navy, which was Vinson's bailiwick, it found that there
were 398 service airplanes in naval aviation, plus about 200 airplanes
used for training. In personnel there were 623 officers and 3,330 men
whose major duties were concerned with aviation. Of the officers, 377
were qualified pilots. After discussing numerous strengths and
weaknesses of naval aviation, it made twelve specific recommendations,

---

[40] Ibid., 99–102; Calvin Coolidge to Carl Vinson, 12 September 1925, Lou
and Neta Stockstill Papers, in author's possession; U.S. Senate, Committee on
Military Affairs, *Aircraft in National Defense*, 69th Cong., 1st sess., 10
December 1925, S. Doc. 18, 1; Enders, "The Vinson Navy," 9–10.

[41] Archibald D. Turnbull and Clifford L. Lord, *History of United States
Naval Aviation* (New York: Arno Press, 1972) 249–58; Senate, *Aircraft in
National Defense*, 2–3.

the most important of which was the appointment of an additional assistant secretary of the navy.[42]

The Morrow Board put an end to numerous longstanding dissensions and pointed the way to solving many vexing problems. Congress immediately began to take up the Board's recommendations, and within six months had enacted three laws. The act of 21 May 1926 provided for certain aids to civilian flying and created the post of assistant secretary of commerce for air, the act of 2 July covered many recommendations for the army, and the act of 24 June made several reforms for the navy. The naval bill, which Vinson steered through the Naval Affairs Committee and the House, authorized a five-year program for building 1,000 planes, provided for the purchase of two dirigibles and one metal-clad airship, and authorized the appointment of an assistant secretary of the navy to "assist in furthering naval aeronautics."[43]

Serving on this blue-ribbon committee enhanced Vinson's prestige both in Washington and in his home district. The *Union-Recorder* proudly announced his appointment and printed in full President Coolidge's letter thanking Vinson for his service.[44] That he would be appointed to such a prestigious committee showed the high standing he had achieved in the field of national defense. From the testimony of the expert witnesses, he gained knowledge and insight that would serve him well in the future. He understood how important the airplane would be in repelling an attack on American shores, bombing naval and fixed targets, and in reconnaissance. In determining America's defense needs, he made building new and improved aircraft carriers and airplanes a high priority.[45]

[42] Senate, *Aircraft in National Defense,* 1–35.

[43] Turnbull and Lord, *History of United States Naval Aviation,* 257–58; *Congressional Record,* 69th Cong., 1st sess., 8 April 1926, 7154–59; 9 April 1926, 7227, 7237–38; U.S. House, Naval Affairs Committee, *To Encourage Development of Aviation,* 69th Cong., 1st sess., 7 June 1926, Rep. 1396.

[44] *Union-Recorder,* 24 September 1925, 1; 10 December 1925, 1.

[45] *Congressional Record,* 69th Cong., 2d sess., 4 January 1927, 1092, 1095–97; 28 February 1927, 5084, 5088; *Congressional Record,* 70th Cong., 1st sess., 16 March 1928, 4897–99.

Statesmen from the major naval powers had been dissatisfied with various aspects of the treaties adopted at the Washington Conference and subsequently sought changes. At Geneva in 1927, no agreement could be reached and the effort was a complete failure.[46] In 1928, however, the Kellogg-Briand Pact was adopted by most of the nations of the world. This treaty outlawed war; or more precisely, the signatories "condemn recourse to war for the solution of international controversies, and renounce it as an instrument of national policy in their relations with one another."[47] The treaty made no provision for punishing violators, so aggressor nations violated it with impunity in the 1930s. But at the time of its adoption, many serious statesmen considered it a noteworthy accomplishment toward avoiding war. In discussing the treaty in the Senate, Senator Carter Glass of Virginia had it about right when he remarked that the treaty was "worthless, but perfectly harmless," and thus might as well be ratified.[48] Enthusiastically endorsed by a grand alliance of the Committee on the Cause and Cure of War, the World Peace Foundation, the Carnegie Endowment for International Peace, the American Committee for the Outlawry of War, the Commission on International Justice and Goodwill of the Federal Council of Churches of Christ in America, the World Alliance for International Friendship, plus a host of churches and women's clubs, the Kellogg-Briand Pact was ratified by the Senate by a vote of 85 to 1.[49]

Although the Kellogg-Briand Pact received much attention in the press, a far more important agreement was reached in London in 1930. The American delegation, led by Secretary of State Henry L. Stimson, included two senators, Secretary of the Navy Charles Francis Adams, Ambassador to Mexico Dwight Morrow, and two other ambassadors. This delegation, "as distinguished a group of men as the United States had sent abroad since the Conference of Ghent in 1815," agreed to the first complete treaty of naval limitation, in all categories of vessels, in the

---

[46] Rappaport, *The Navy League*, 109.
[47] Robert H. Ferrell, *Peace in Their Time: The Origins of the Kellogg-Briand Pact* (New Haven: Yale University Press, 1952) 268.
[48] Ibid., 251.
[49] Ibid., 232–52.

history of the modern world.[50] The London Naval Treaty extended the capital ship limit established at Washington until 1936, limited tonnage levels for cruisers, destroyers, and submarines until 1936, and established agreements for the five powers to replace, scrap, and convert war vessels. After months of wrangling, the Senate ratified the treaty on 21 July by vote of 58 to 9. Hailed as the "great outstanding international success of the year 1930," the treaty actually made little change to the agreements already made. Distinguished diplomatic historian Robert Ferrell found in the treaty "a certain moral value, being an affirmation of faith in the limiting of armaments," but "such affirmation was of more than doubtful utility at the beginning of so hectic a decade as the 1930s."[51] In their fervent dedication to peace, the statesmen had created, historian Raymond O'Connor observes, "an unstable and illusory equilibrium of armaments."[52]

When he had finished half a century of lawmaking, Sam Rayburn looked back upon the Republican years between 1919 and 1931 as "the most frustrating, least productive, and unhappiest of his entire career."[53] Vinson was not as pessimistic as his friend and colleague for several reasons. During the 1920s, he had become the undisputed master of the Tenth Congressional District, had gained considerable acclaim for his expertise in national defense, had served on the prestigious Morrow Board, had become ranking Democrat on the Naval Affairs Committee,

---

[50] Ferrell, *American Diplomacy*, 87–88, 102.

[51] Ibid., 102–105; Henry L. Stimson and McGeorge Bundy, *On Active Service in Peace and War* (New York: Harper & Brothers, 1947) 162–74; John Chalmers Vinson, *William E. Borah and the Outlawry of War* (Athens: University of Georgia Press, 1957) 149–75.

[52] O'Connor, *Perilous Equilibrium*, 118.

[53] Hardeman and Bacon, *Rayburn*, 105.

and had married the woman of his dreams. Yet, despite these positive accomplishments, he shared with Rayburn a frustration over the domestic policies of the Harding, Coolidge, and Hoover administrations and a concern over ominous developments in international affairs. Both men longed for the day the Democratic Party would once again regain the White House and control of the House of Representatives.

4

"Mr. Chairman"

I am a Democrat by conviction; by environment; by principles; by heritage; and by application of native common sense.

Carl Vinson, 1960

The collapse of the Stock Market in October 1929 abruptly ended the exuberant prosperity of the 1920s and thrust the nation into the greatest financial crisis in its history. The onset of the Great Depression severely weakened the Republican Party, but the majority party still managed to retain razor-thin majorities in both houses of Congress in the 1930 off-year election. Republican control of Congress was so tenuous, however, that by the time the Seventy-second Congress convened thirteen months later, special elections caused by the deaths of several members had given the Democrats control of the House of Representatives for the first time since 1919. As a result of the financial collapse, Republican domination had come to an end, and the Democrats were on the way to becoming the majority party. As such, they would soon dominate Capitol Hill, and after 1933, the White House as well. When the Democrats organized the House of Representatives, John Nance Garner replaced Nicholas Longworth as Speaker, Henry T. Rainey of Illinois was installed as majority leader, and Carl Vinson was named chairman of the Committee on Naval Affairs. The selection of the forty-eight-year-old Georgian was expected, since he had been the ranking minority member of the committee since 1923. Indeed, under the seniority system, it was a foregone conclusion.[1]

The appointment elevated Vinson to the ranks of the elite in Congress, but outside of his congressional district in Georgia and the halls of Congress he remained obscure. He cut a pale figure beside his flamboyant predecessor, Fred A. Britten (Republican, Illinois), a hard-nosed ex-pugilist noted for his sartorial distinction and penchant for controversy. By contrast, Vinson dressed conservatively in three-piece suits and avoided unnecessary controversy. Basically shy and retiring, he was a man of modest tastes and frugal habits who shunned the spotlight and habitually turned down all invitations, except those to the White House, which he considered command performances. Although a clear and forceful speaker, he was not a spellbinding orator. Neither in committee nor on the floor of the House did he deliver speeches merely to call attention to himself; he left grandstanding to others, like Britten. On the floor of the House he occupied a seat on the seventh row equipped with a spittoon, as he was fond of chewing tobacco and chewing on inexpensive cigars. At six feet, he was a bit taller than average, but his most distinctive feature was his voice—loud with a pronounced Middle Georgia drawl. "Although he was respected for his considerable expertise in naval matters and his conscientious committee work, there was little reason to believe that his appointment represented a watershed in Congressional attitudes or legislative activity involving the Navy," observed Michael West, the most careful student of Vinson's role as chairman of the Naval Affairs Committee.[2]

Appearances can be misleading, as many representatives, admirals, and corporate executives found out when they encountered Vinson's keen analytical mind and extraordinary political skills. One of the

---

[1] Michael A. West, "Laying the Legislative Foundation: The House Naval Affairs Committee and the Construction of the Treaty Navy, 1926–1934" (Ph. D. diss., Ohio State University, 1980) 57–58; Calvin W. Enders, "The Vinson Navy" (Ph.D. diss., Michigan State University, 1970) 25–26.

[2] West, "Laying the Legislative Foundation," 57–8; Louis R. Stockstill, "'Uncle Carl' Vinson: Backstage Boss of the Pentagon," *Army Navy Air Force Journal* 98 (18 February 1961): 24–25; Susan Landrum, "Carl Vinson: A Study in Military Preparedness" (master's thesis, Emory University, 1968) 29–32.

shrewdest men ever to serve in the House, he had quickly learned the intricacies of the legislative process and mastered the arcane rules and traditions that governed that body. In time he became a brilliant tactician, who steered countless bills through congressional mine fields to become laws. Speaker Sam Rayburn later remarked that Vinson "was the best legislative technician in the House."[3] An omnivorous reader, he customarily read three daily newspapers (The *Washington Post*, the *Washington Evening Star*, and the *New York Times*; or in Georgia, the *Atlanta Constitution*, the *Atlanta Journal*, and the *Macon Telegraph*) and devoured classics, histories, biographies, Western novels, murder mysteries, and "just about anything I get my hands on."[4] After spending nine hours on the Hill, he devoted much time at home to studying committee reports and other official documents. Consequently, his mind became a storehouse of knowledge, and on naval matters no one could approach his comprehensive mastery of details.

Vinson understood politics and human nature as well as he did the costs of battleships and submarines. From his early career in local politics, he seemed to have a sixth sense about the potentialities of a political environment and knew intuitively when to press his demands, retreat, or stand firm. Always a realist, he concentrated his attention on what was politically possible and avoided tilting at windmills. In the House, his uncanny sense of timing was used to good advantage and accounted for much of his success in committee and on the floor. Independent by nature, he knew that successful legislation depended upon establishing a winning consensus through persuasion and accommodation, and he was abundantly endowed with this talent. He followed the longstanding congressional tradition of using good manners and flowery language when addressing colleagues, and he almost never lost his temper or resorted to personal attack. In defending his proposals, he appealed to colleagues' better nature and patriotism, especially on

---

[3] West, "Laying the Legislative Foundation," 78; Jerome Doolittle, "The Gentleman From Georgia Goes Home," *Saturday Evening Post* 237 (5 December 1964): 27; Landrum, "Carl Vinson: A Study in Military Preparedness," 36.

[4] Stockstill, "Backstage Boss," 24–25.

defense issues. He had the talent of disagreeing with colleagues without offending them, and he was adept at massaging egos to gain support. Although determined and tenacious in achieving his goals, the cagey Vinson masked these traits with dry wit, a disarming guise, and a pronounced Southern accent that deflated or diverted unwary opponents and earned for him the sobriquet "The Swamp Fox" from his appreciative colleagues.[5]

Even though Vinson was frustrated by Congress's failure to adopt a comprehensive naval construction program, Fortune had smiled upon him during his years on the Naval Affairs Committee. By 1923, eight senior committee Democrats had either died, resigned, or been defeated, enabling him to rise to the position of ranking minority member after only six years of service on the committee. This was an important development because the ranking minority member played a significant role in conducting committee business. From 1919 until his death in 1928, the chairman was Thomas C. Butler of Pennsylvania, a kind and experienced lawyer of Quaker ancestry, who had served in the House since 1897. He worked closely with Vinson to secure bipartisan support on important issues. In return for his cooperation, Butler kept Vinson well informed about major developments and contemplated actions by the House and committee leadership. The two men enjoyed a positive working relationship, and Vinson learned much from the older Republican's leadership, especially the importance of a strong sense of bipartisanship in the committee's handling of naval issues coming before Congress. The position also gave Vinson the opportunity to develop his parliamentary skills, as the ranking minority member normally controlled half the time allotted to the committee for floor debate on measures that it reported to the House. In time he would master those techniques and become "one of the most successful and feared floor managers in the annals of the House of Representatives."[6]

---

[5] West, "Laying the Legislative Foundation," 60–83; Sam Nunn, interview with the author, Atlanta GA, 4 April 2001; Landrum, "Carl Vinson: A Study in Military Preparedness," 36.

[6] West, "Laying the Legislative Foundation," 73–83; *Congressional Record*, 70th Cong., 2d sess., 20 February 1929, 3885–86; *Biographical*

At the time Vinson became chairman of the House Naval Affairs Committee, the most important work of the committee was its power to authorize in principle the size and composition of the United States Navy. While the president and the secretary of state decided how the navy should be used, Congress and its Naval Affairs Committees largely determined the number and types of ships, the number and status of personnel, the extent and location of the shore establishments, and the administration of the Navy Department. Since World War I, the House Naval Affairs Committee had gained ascendancy over its Senate counterpart because its members were more experienced and more knowledgeable. This came about in part because of its status as an exclusive committee. First designated as such in the Sixty-fourth Congress, this meant that its chairman could not serve on any other committee and discouraged the assignment of other members to additional major committees. By focusing attention on naval matters without the distraction of other committees, the House Naval Affairs Committee gained recognition for competency and expertise.[7] The committee consisted of twenty-one members, but "the chairman was the hub around which all else orbited." His power and prerogatives were "awesome," writes Michael West, and he dominated "virtually every aspect of committee activity." The chairman appointed the sub-committees and the staff of the committee;[8] he determined which bills the committee would consider; and, as presiding officer, he controlled debate and the questioning of witnesses. Once a piece of legislation was approved, he decided who would prepare the legislative report and serve as floor manager. As floor manager he enjoyed many procedural prerogatives. Procedurally, "he controlled every phase of a bill's consideration from full committee through enactment." No wonder West writes, "A formal listing of his powers would have warmed the heart of

---

Directory of the American Congress, 1774–1971 (Washington, DC: Government Printing Office, 1971) 683.

[7] Landrum, "Carl Vinson: A Study in Military Preparedness," 29–31; West, "Laying the Legislative Foundation," 84–96.

[8] In 1931, the staff consisted of a clerk, assistant clerk, and a janitor, but after World War II it was greatly enlarged.

any self-respecting despot."[9] Besides the formal powers, the chairman also could influence legislation in countless informal ways through his relationships with the Navy Department, the Speaker of the House, and the press.

A month before his formal installation as chairman, Vinson began working toward the enactment of a comprehensive naval building program in the Seventy-second Congress.[10] On 1 December 1931, he discussed the possible programs for building warships with Secretary of the Navy Charles Francis Adams. The next day he met with out-going chairman Fred Britten and Senators Frederick Hale, Republican of Maine, and Claude Swanson, Democrat of Virginia, chairman and ranking minority member, respectively, of the Senate Naval Affairs Committee. All of these leaders agreed with Vinson that the navy should be built up to the treaty limits and that a comprehensive ship construction program should be introduced in the upcoming session of Congress.

In the previous session Representative Britten had proposed a naval expansion bill which gained the approval of the House Naval Affairs Committee, but he never convinced the leadership to bring it to the floor of the House. When the first session of the Seventy-second Congress opened, he introduced a similar measure, while the Senate Naval Affairs Committee considered a naval construction bill introduced by Senator Hale. Vinson was not impressed with either of these approaches. In his judgment, Hale's bill was too vague on program implementation and Britten's bill would only scratch the surface of the navy's needs. Vinson declared the country needed a "program which will lay down ships, not blueprints."[11] The bill Vinson introduced on 4 January 1932, provided for a ten-year construction program that would build 120 ships at a total cost of $616,000,000. In the first year his program would begin the construction of one aircraft carrier, two light cruisers, nine destroyers, and six submarines. By 1942, it would have added three aircraft carriers, nine light cruisers, eighty-five destroyers, and twenty-three submarines to the American fleet. This program, Vinson argued, would bring the

---

[9]West, "Laying the Legislative Foundation," 109–23.

[10] *New York Times*, 3 December 1931, 12; 5 December 1931, 2.

[11] Ibid., 5 December 1931, 2.

navy up to the size permitted by treaties by replacing old and obsolete vessels. By utilizing shipyards and resources in a systematic long-range plan, the plan would save the taxpayers money and produce an adequate navy.[12]

On 7 January, Vinson wrote an article for the *Washington Herald* in which he explained why America needed the program he had introduced. While other countries had continued to build their navies during the last ten years, the United States had refrained from doing so. As a result, the United States Navy had fallen well below the quotas permitted under the Washington and London treaties, thus jeopardizing national security. Vinson favored a navy "second to none," not to rule the waves, but to preserve the freedom of the seas for peaceful commerce. National defense, he added, "is not a partisan issue."[13] In a speech to the National Republican Club of New York City on 16 January, Vinson discussed the needs of national defense in more detail. After surveying the international scene, he took issue with the pacifists and internationalists who claim that military and naval strength cause war. "Such a statement," he argued, "is about as logical as one which declares that crime can be abolished by destroying our police forces; that disease can be eradicated by abolishing our hospitals and our doctors; that fires can be eliminated by abandoning our fire departments." He then expressed the deeply held convictions that guided his actions:

It is my belief that peace can best be assured and the interests of the United States most securely preserved by this country building up to the limits of the London treaty and by maintaining our naval strength at that level until some further limitation agreement is reached between the great maritime powers. Of all the countries in the world, the United States can the most easily afford to maintain its Navy at the treaty strength. No country requires the safety that a navy alone can give more than does the United States with her vast commerce, frontiers on

---

[12] Ibid., 4 January 1932, 1–2.

[13] *Washington Times-Herald*, 7 January 1932, quoted in Landrum, "Carl Vinson: A Study in Military Preparedness," 45–48.

both the Atlantic and the Pacific, and outlying possessions lying thousands of miles from the North American Continent.

Since no man can foresee the future clearly, it must be evident that a nation that requires a military or naval force requires one adequate to function efficiently in the hour of need. The defense of the country must not be based upon the fluctuations of the stock or commodity market. A country does not need a navy of one strength when she is prosperous and a navy of another size when there is an economic depression. At all times we need a navy that is strong enough to defend our possessions and to support our policies, policies framed by statesmen to assure the safety of our country and development of our commerce. For the protection of our commerce our Navy was first established. With the greatly increased value of that commerce, which totals over $8,000,000,000 annually, and with the keen rivalry for world markets, it is but reasonable that we should provide for its insurance in the form of an adequate Navy, and by adequate I mean one that we can rely upon for victory beyond the shadow of a doubt.[14]

In the committee hearings, which Chairman Vinson carefully orchestrated, both Secretary of the Navy Adams and the chief of naval operations, Admiral William V. Pratt, endorsed his bill. Other naval officials supported it too, as did several influential newspapers. The Republican *New York Herald Tribune* declared: "The whole country, regardless of party lines, should be grateful to Representative Vinson for his straightforward bill providing for the upbuilding of the American Navy."[15] In the *New York Times*, noted military-naval analyst Hanson Baldwin praised the Vinson bill as "a forward-looking measure, commendable both for its economic advantages and its naval benefits."[16] Attempting to take advantage of these positive developments, Vinson

---

[14] *Congressional Record*, 72d Cong., 1st sess., 21 January 1932, 2426–28.

[15] "More Than Half a Billion Asked For Naval Increase," *Literary Digest* 112 (23 January 1932): 8.

[16] *New York Times*, 10 January 1932, E1–2.

requested a meeting with President Herbert Hoover, a consistent opponent of naval expansion, who was then making preparations for the upcoming Geneva Disarmament talks. The meeting took place on 7 January and lasted nearly an hour. The chairman went over his bill item by item with the president, explaining its provisions, clarifying its intent, and hoping to convince Hoover not to oppose the bill. He failed.[17] The House Naval Affairs Committee endorsed the measure by vote of 17 to 2, but the president's opposition thwarted the navy's support and ultimately doomed the measure. Vinson's last recourse was to attempt to enlist the support of the Democratic leadership of the House in an effort to pass the bill in spite of administration opposition. The Democrats, sensing victory in November, preferred caution to controversy. Opposed by the administration and abandoned by the House leadership, Vinson put the best face possible on his defeat. On 25 January, he announced to the House that even though the House Naval Affairs Committee had endorsed a compromise measure to bring the navy up to treaty strength by vote of 18 to 0, because "of the very abnormal economic conditions which now confront us at home and abroad, and the hope that some substantial results may be achieved at Geneva, the committee, in agreement with the chairman, has voted for the time being not to report the bill to the House." At the conclusion of his remarks, the House broke into an enthusiastic round of applause.[18]

As Vinson licked his wounds and analyzed the reasons for his failure, he could take solace in the publicity his program had generated and in the importance of relationships that had been fostered during the procedure. Vinson and the Navy Department developed a close and enduring bond based on mutual respect and trust that would make future collaboration easier and more effective. He had developed a good working relationship not only with Admiral Pratt and Admiral W. A. Moffett, chief of Bureau of Aeronautics, but also with Captain Emory S. Land and other mid-level Navy Department representatives who would

---

[17] West, "Laying the Legislative Foundation," 242–43.

[18] Ibid., 227–49; *Congressional Record*, 72d Cong., 1st sess., 25 January 1932, 2663.

later rise to positions of greater authority.[19] For the present, Vinson realized that no significant naval legislation could be passed as long as Hoover was president and eventually he quit trying. Content to wait for the next administration, he lamented that the Hoover administration had not authorized a single ship.[20]

When Congress adjourned on 16 July, Vinson hurried home to begin a hectic eight-week campaign for reelection, for he faced opposition for the first time since 1920. In 1931 the legislature had been forced to make major changes in the Georgia congressional districts since the state had lost two of its twelve seats. The new law restored Baldwin County to the old Sixth District, where Vinson was pitted against two incumbent congressmen. He convinced one to retire, and the other died before the campaign got underway. A third opponent, Judge R. Earl Camp of Dublin, emerged to challenge Vinson for the Democratic nomination. In an open letter, he promised Vinson, "I am going to give you hell, and when I say hell, I mean nothing but merry hell, and I don't mean maybe. I am going to take the flesh, bone, marrow, hide and hair off of you."[21]

Judge Camp criticized Vinson's stand on prohibition, claimed Mrs. Vinson was on the federal payroll, and charged the congressman with "wasting the substance of the people." Lambasting Vinson's role on the Naval Affairs Committee, he asserted, "Congressman Vinson, in the last few years, has helped to sink to the bottom of the sea over $500,000,000 worth of the finest war vessels ever set afloat by this or any other nation."[22] As always, Vinson took his opposition seriously and campaigned vigorously throughout the Sixth District. The outcome of the 14 September Democratic primary, however, was never in doubt. Vinson carried twelve of the district's sixteen counties as well as the decisive

---

[19] West, "Laying the Legislative Foundation," 267–72.

[20] Landrum, "Carl Vinson: A Study in Military Preparedness," 49.

[21] Congressman Sam Rutherford died on 4 February 1932, and Congressman William Larsen was not a candidate in 1932. Stockstill, "Backstage Boss," 27; *Macon Telegraph & News*, 31 July 1932, 5.

[22] "Vinson's Stand on Prohibition Attacked by Judge Earl Camp," 9 July 1932, Vinson Scrapbooks, book 1919–1939, on loan from Tillman Snead to Georgia College and State University, Milledgeville, GA.

thirty-two county unit votes. Years later, when Vinson was nominated for his eighteenth consecutive term, Judge Camp seconded the nomination with the comment, "I'm glad he defeated me."[23]

Besides his own victory, the 1932 election affected Vinson's career in significant ways. Eugene Talmadge, the flamboyant "Wild Man from Sugar Creek," having served three terms as Georgia's commissioner of agriculture, won a decisive victory as governor. Although never particularly close to Vinson, the red-gallused spokesman for the "wool hat boys" would be the dominant force in Georgia politics from 1933 until his death in 1946. Another victor in the Democratic primary was Richard Russell of Winder, who after a successful term as governor won his first election to the United States Senate, where he would serve with distinction for thirty-eight years until his death in 1971[24]. In contrast to Talmadge, Russell and Vinson became friends and worked together harmoniously, especially on military legislation.

As a loyal Democrat, Vinson consistently supported his party's presidential nominee and, unlike many Southern Democrats, he had campaigned enthusiastically for Al Smith in 1928.[25] An early and ardent supporter of Franklin D. Roosevelt, Vinson predicted in July 1931 that the New York governor "would not only be nominated by the Democrats, but that he would be overwhelmingly elected by the people of the United States."[26] Vinson's relationship with President Hoover, Roosevelt's opponent, was never warm and it became decidedly colder. Indeed, the chairman later confided in an interview with Michael West that Hoover's animosity toward him reached the point where he hesitated to meet with the president alone because "I was afraid he might throw me through a window."[27] Since Vinson disdained Hoover, he did all in

---

[23] Stockstill, "Backstage Boss," 27; Landrum, "Carl Vinson: A Study in Military Preparedness," 27; *Union-Recorder*, 25 August 1932, 1; 1 September 1932, 1; 15 September 1932, 1.

[24] James F. Cook, *The Governors of Georgia, 1754–1995* (Macon GA: Mercer University Press, 1995) 222–34.

[25] *Union-Recorder*, 20 September 1928, 1; 25 October 1928, 1; 1 November 1928, 1.

[26] Ibid., 2 July 1931, 9.

[27] West, "Laying the Legislative Foundation," 187.

his power to ensure Roosevelt's election. When a Roosevelt Club was organized in Baldwin County, he became a member of the executive committee.[28] Vinson had been impressed with Roosevelt's work as assistant secretary of the navy in the Wilson administration and later stated that every member of the Naval Affairs Committee knew that Roosevelt "had a more intelligent grasp of details than any man connected with his department." He was convinced that as President Roosevelt would reverse the pacifism of the Hoover administration and would maintain "the Navy at the highest possible point of efficiency essential to existing and potential requirements." When a reporter queried Vinson about Roosevelt's naval policies, he replied, "Mr. Roosevelt knows more about the Navy, its needs and value if properly organized and managed than any man who has entered the White House since Theodore Roosevelt left it."[29]

Shortly after a sweeping victory, Roosevelt left Hyde Park for a brief vacation at Warm Springs, Georgia, less than a hundred miles from Milledgeville, where he had an extended meeting with Vinson on 29 November. Exactly what the two men said was not recorded, but Roosevelt's ideas must have shocked and greatly disappointed Vinson. When Vinson spoke with reporters after the conference, he unveiled what became known as the "Democratic naval program." As agreed to by the president-elect and Vinson, this program called for a reduction in the navy budget of $100 million, and instead of the $616 million building program Vinson had advocated, it placed an annual ceiling of $30 million in shipbuilding outlays over the next five years. In place of the treaty navy, this program contemplated a "compact, self-contained navy, powerful and effective enough to meet the country's needs." Vinson expressed confidence that substantial savings could be achieved through the more efficient use of navy resources and the closure of obsolete and underutilized naval facilities and air stations. To that end, he announced

---

[28] Enders, "The Vinson Navy," 37.
[29] Louis Seibold, Universal Services, 8 January 1932, http://www.cvn70.navy.mil/vinson/vinson9.htm.

that he would leave for Washington immediately to conduct a committee inquiry into the "problem of naval expenditures and efficiency."[30]

Roosevelt, it should be remembered, had campaigned as a fiscal conservative. He had blamed Hoover for excessive spending and had promised to balance the budget. Campaigning in Sioux City, Iowa, in September, Governor Roosevelt stated: "I accuse the present Administration of being the greatest spending Administration in peace times in all our history. It is an Administration that has piled bureau on bureau, commission on commission, and has failed to anticipate the dire needs and the reduced earning power of the people." In Pittsburgh the next month he declared: "I regard reduction in Federal spending as one of the most important issues of this campaign. In my opinion, it is the most direct and effective contribution that Government can make to business."[31] From this meeting, it appears that Roosevelt was willing to accept second-class naval status in order to balance the federal budget. The navy, after years of stringent economies, could not absorb a $100 million cut and carry out its assigned missions. Why Vinson, the foremost champion of naval expansion, went along with such a program that contradicted his fundamental beliefs is baffling indeed.

With classic understatement, James Hagerty, reporting for the *New York Times*, observed, "There seemed to be reason to believe after the conference that Governor Roosevelt influenced Mr. Vinson more than Mr. Vinson influenced Governor Roosevelt."[32] From the results of the meeting, it is difficult to see how Vinson influenced Roosevelt at all, as all of the concessions went one way. Perhaps out of a sense of party loyalty, coupled with the knowledge that resisting a popular president was futile, Vinson publicly agreed to policies he abhorred. Certainly a factor contributing to Vinson's uncharacteristic behavior was that he

---

[30] *New York Times*, 30 November 1932, 1, 12; West, "Laying the Legislative Foundation," 275–76.

[31] William E. Leuchtenburg, *Franklin D. Roosevelt and the New Deal* (New York: Harper & Row, 1963) 11.

[32] *New York Times*, 30 November 1932, 1.

suffered, as Michael West points out, "a bad overdose of the vaunted Roosevelt charm."[33]

Roosevelt's charm wore off in less than a month. On 28 December 1932, Vinson sent Roosevelt an eight-page single-spaced letter about "the major problems concerning the Navy," which showed clearly that he had repudiated the "Democratic naval program." In embracing that program he had acted against his better judgment, and he wanted his reversal to be a matter of record. Emphasizing his long experience on the Naval Affairs Committee that had enabled him to keep "in close touch with the Navy, with its development, and with its needs," the chairman stated his views and urged the president-elect to reciprocate. In great detail he pointed out how the United States had "led the world in its efforts to reduce and limit armaments," but now lagged far behind our rivals in constructing new ships and replacing old ones. Since 1922, he pointed out, we have provided for but 40 ships compared to the 148 ships for Great Britain, the 164 ships for Japan, the 196 ships for France, and the 144 ships for Italy. The chairman bolstered his arguments with charts showing the number of ships, the types of ships, and the tonnage of the five leading naval powers. Calling attention to the age of the vessels and the construction schedules, he noted that "unless steps are taken immediately to improve our position, in 1936 we will have a total underage tonnage smaller than that of Great Britain, of Japan, and of France." To remedy the situation, Vinson advised the enactment of a well-defined year-by-year schedule that would bring the navy up to Treaty strength. The passage of such a program, he argued, "would provide for the construction of ships in an orderly and systematic manner, which would result in great economies." He advocated a program costing $63 million annually, which he thought should begin immediately, as its postponement would only make for larger expenditures later. He also pointed out that the building program would provide jobs both for naval shipyards and private ones, which were

---

[33] West, "Laying the Legislative Foundation," 278.

closing for lack of work, and maintaining the shipyards was important in case of war.[34]

Although Vinson always argued that defense budgets should be determined by the security needs of the country, he did not hesitate to stress the economic impact of increased shipbuilding to the president-elect who was inheriting a shriveling economy with nearly 25 percent of the work force unemployed:

> The money appropriated for the upbuilding of the Navy goes directly toward the relief of unemployment, and affects not merely the communities in which shipyards are located, but goes far into the interior, where iron ore and copper are mined, where steel is rolled, cast and forged, where steam and electric machinery is manufactured, and where other materials required in smaller quantity are produced, such as aluminum, cotton, cork, hemp, linseed, oil, nickel, paint, pigments, rubber, tin, wood, wool, and zinc. Fully 85% of the total cost of ships goes directly into the pockets of labor, and to give employment to labor.[35]

This letter shows clearly that at this stage Vinson and Roosevelt held divergent views regarding the navy. The president-elect had altered his views substantially since the time he was a "big navy" advocate as assistant secretary of the navy. For him, balancing the federal budget had taken priority over defense needs. During that same period, Vinson had become a staunch and undeviating proponent of naval readiness. A clash between the two Democratic leaders was inevitable.[36] Vinson understood Roosevelt's political dilemma. He knew that as President-elect Roosevelt was being bombarded with requests for spending from all sides—more

---

[34] Carl Vinson to Franklin D. Roosevelt, 28 December 1932, President's Personal File, 9501, Roosevelt Library, Hyde Park NY.

[35] Ibid.

[36] John C. Walter, "Congressman Carl Vinson and Franklin D. Roosevelt: Naval Preparedness and the Coming of World War II, 1932–1940," *Georgia Historical Quarterly* 64 (Fall 1980): 294–96.

requests than he could possibly satisfy. Plus, he had some concern about honoring his campaign pledge. But unlike Hoover, he understood the needs of the navy, and if funds were available, he would support the navy. Thus, despite Roosevelt's public commitment to retrenchment, Vinson believed that he could be swayed to his way of thinking on naval matters. It would take tremendous political pressure backed by public opinion to convince his friend to build the needed ships, and Vinson was determined to generate that pressure. For the next several months, he was a whirlwind of activity, coordinating plans behind the scenes while issuing a steady stream of pronouncements to the media. While presiding over the Naval Affairs Committee's efforts to find ways to economize, he worked closely with congressional and naval leaders to drum up public support for naval expansion. On 2 January, he announced that plans to build up the navy would be halted until the advent of the Roosevelt administration.[37] A week later, the chairman stated, "I am very hopeful there will be a change in naval policy after March 4. We all know Mr. Roosevelt believes in an adequate national defense and with that end in view a new policy is necessary." One of the first acts of the Naval Affairs Committee in the new Seventy-third Congress, he said, "will be the working out of a definite and at the same time economical program, which would be spread out over a series of years so that the drain on the Treasury would not be heavy in any one year." Specifically, this program would involve the replacement of practically the entire destroyer fleet, a large percentage of the submarine fleet, and a considerable tonnage of new aircraft-carrying ships.[38] On 13 February, Vinson stated that his ten-year replacement program was "cheap insurance for a country like ours," and that he felt sure the incoming president "would give serious consideration to the future of the navy."[39]

Rear Admiral William A. Moffett, chief of the Bureau of Aeronautics, powerfully reinforced Vinson's position in a speech at the Annual Dinner of the Naval Academy Graduates of New York on 17 February. His address, which was widely broadcast, began: "Since the

---

[37] *New York Times*, 3 January 1933, 13.
[38] Ibid., 11 January 1933, 1, 7.
[39] Ibid., 14 February 1933, 2.

administration of President Wilson and the signing of the Washington Treaty in 1922, our Navy has progressively declined." The root cause of the navy's plight, the admiral said, was that "Uncle Sam" had been "hoodwinked and bamboozled" by a coalition of wily Europeans and inscrutable Orientals and had "lost everything but his shirt tail when he signed the Washington Treaty." Noting the failure of the United States to match the efforts of Great Britain and Japan, he proclaimed the decadence of the American Navy. By allowing the navy to become decadent, Moffett warned that America was risking not only her honor and glory "but her very existence." The sentiments he expressed were widely shared by his fellow officers, especially after the signing of the London Naval Treaty in 1930.[40]

A week after Moffett delivered his fiery speech, Vinson announced to the House that he intended to introduce at the convening of the Seventy-third Congress a bill providing for the strengthening of our navy and to use his best efforts to have it enacted into law. "The time has not yet come," he added, "when America must depend upon the Navy of some foreign power for its safety and the protection of its interests." In justifying his program to the House of Representatives, Vinson placed the navy's needs in perspective:

> Why, gentlemen, the citizens of this country spend more each year upon perfume alone than is spent for the maintenance, upbuilding, and operation of the Navy. They spend approximately one-third of the sum necessary for the Navy on chewing gum alone. The income derived from the tax upon tobacco would build and maintain our Navy with ease. In other words, gentlemen, the cost of armament in this country does not constitute the crushing burden which the pacifist would have you believe. The Navy costs each person in this country less than one cent per day. Armament and preparedness are not the things that cost so much; it is the result of unpreparedness that is so costly. Again and again history repeats itself.

---

[40] West, "Laying the Legislative Foundation," 7–8; on 3 April, two months after delivering this speech, Moffett died in the crash of the Navy airship *Akron*.

Our national defense in time of peace is allowed to decline and to grow weak, and when war comes, as unhappily it does, billions of dollars are poured out in the vain effort to build up our Navy and to create an Army to meet the emergency that we find upon us. Again and again we must be taught that soldiers cannot be made in a day and that it takes years to create ships.[41]

The change of administrations in March 1933 brought a host of new personalities into key positions, and their policies and ability to work with Congress would become major factors in determining Vinson's success in strengthening the navy. Roosevelt chose seventy-one-year-old Claude Swanson, Democratic senator from Virginia and member of the Senate Naval Affairs Committee since 1914, as secretary of the navy. Concern over Swanson's frail health figured in the appointment of Henry Latrobe Roosevelt as assistant secretary of the navy. Distantly related to the president, he followed in the footsteps of three other Roosevelts who had previously held that position. An energetic ex-Marine lieutenant colonel, he served ably until his untimely death in 1936. Another important personnel change within the Navy Department was the promotion of Emory S. Land to Rear Admiral and his appointment as chief of the Bureau of Construction and Repair. A trained naval architect and aeronautical engineer, Land had extensive experience in the Bureau of Construction and Repair, the Bureau of Aeronautics, and in the Office of Naval Operations. Considered one of the Navy Department's most progressive leaders, he had a history of collaborating with Vinson.

The navy fared less well in the appointment of Lewis Douglas as director of the budget. The thirty-nine-year-old ex-congressman from Arizona played the heavy for Roosevelt by seeking out waste and cutting expenditures. The Democratic landslide increased the Democratic majority in the House of Representatives from nine to 100 and gave the Democrats firm control of the Senate for the first time since 1920. John Nance Garner, the former Speaker of the House, now presided over the Senate as vice president, and seventy-two-year-old Henry Rainey became the new Speaker. The change in party control of the Senate

---

[41] *Congressional Record*, 72d Cong., 2d sess., 22 February 1933, 4720–23.

meant that there would be a Democratic chairman of the Naval Affairs Committee. As ranking minority member, Senator Swanson had been in line for the post, but his departure led to the appointment of Senator Park Trammell of Florida. Trammell was by no means a strong leader, but he could rely on Frederick Hale, Republican from Maine, and David I. Walsh, Democrat from Massachusetts, the ranking minority and majority leaders of the committee, for assistance and advice. In the House Naval Affairs Committee eighteen Democrats and eight Republicans served in the Seventy-third Congress, a dramatic improvement—from Vinson's perspective—over the 12 to 10 ratio in the previous session. Representative Fred Britten remained the ranking minority member, but his influence was waning. The committee also received an infusion of new members—nine Democrats and five Republicans—and Vinson ordinarily restricted freshmen to establishing a quorum and voting. Taken as a whole, Vinson must have been well pleased by these changes.[42]

Months before Roosevelt was inaugurated on 4 March, Vinson had been working quietly with Admiral Land and Admiral Parsons, chief of the Bureau of Yards and Docks, on a new way of securing funds for shipbuilding. Anticipating Roosevelt's emphasis on relief measures in his first hundred days, they devised plans to justify shipbuilding as part of the public works program. Vinson became the navy's point man in the House and Senator Robert Wagner of New York served in that capacity in the Senate. Vinson kept constant pressure on the administration and made sure the public was well aware of the navy's needs. In a *Washington Herald* article on 19 February he noted that "the twelve years of Republican control have been sad years for the Navy." That service had declined, he continued, to the extent that the United States had fewer underaged aircraft carriers, heavy and light cruisers, destroyers and submarines than Japan. Furthermore, he declared: "This is an astounding situation, and one of great importance to our country. Our position as a world power and the strength of our policies are closely related to the strength of our Navy. Without doubt our influence in the

---

[42] West, "Laying the Legislative Foundation," 282–90; Richard Bolling, *Power in the House* (New York: Dutton and Co., 1968) 124–26.

Far East has been greatly lessened with the weakening of our Navy and the decrease in its strength relative to that of Japan."[43]

Major efforts on behalf of the navy were desperately needed because Director of the Budget Louis Douglas, demonstrating "a parsimony worthy of a Scrooge," slashed the navy's appropriations for fiscal 1934 from $330 million to $260 million. The protests of Vinson and the Navy Department eventually restored $10 million, leaving the navy badly underfunded for performing its mission.[44] On 27 March, three weeks into the hundred days, Vinson, alarmed at the trend of affairs, called upon the Navy League to try to influence public sentiment against the economy measures that jeopardized the fleet's well-being. The League president promptly whipped up a statement, got it approved by Admiral Land, and sent it to approximately 3,000 newspaper editors on 1 April. Using chart and text, he sought to demonstrate that naval construction was the ideal instrument for economic recovery by providing both security and employment. He estimated that 260,000 persons from 116 trades, using materials made in 48 states, would be engaged in warship construction. A month later the Navy League issued two more statements that reiterated the arguments of the earlier release. In June two editions of a statistical table were issued in support of naval construction.[45]

While the Navy League was generating public support for shipbuilding as a means of unemployment relief, Vinson was busy on Capitol Hill. After conferring with Speaker Henry Rainey, Majority Leader Joseph Byrns of Tennessee, and other administration supporters in the House, he announced to the press on 31 March that he would present the navy's program to President Roosevelt the following Tuesday. As announced, he met with Roosevelt on 4 April, at which time he explained the navy's proposed building program and its underlying rationale. Vinson had already garnered the support of Secretary Swanson, Speaker Rainey, and organized labor, and after the conference, he told waiting newsmen that the president appeared impressed with the

---

[43] Quoted in Enders, "The Vinson Navy," 46.

[44] Walter, "Congressman Carl Vinson and Franklin D. Roosevelt," 297.

[45] Rappaport, *Navy League,* 157–58.

possibilities of using naval construction to alleviate unemployment. Obviously pleased by the president's attitude, Vinson remarked, "I am entirely satisfied with the conference and hopeful that the plan will be adopted."[46] Despite the president's favorable reaction, he had not made a firm commitment to the project. Consequently, Vinson kept pressure on the president and kept the issue before the public. By the end of April, it seemed apparent that the program advocated by Vinson had received official sanction. After leaving a conference at the White House on 1 May, Secretary of the Navy Swanson told reporters that the president had agreed to include within a public works program $46 million to begin work on thirty warships. On 4 May Vinson wrote the president indicating the language he wanted in the proposed bill. He also detailed the number and types of ships that should be included in the program.[47] Political maneuvering continued, and much uncertainty remained until the administration's National Industrial Recovery Bill was introduced on 17 May. As introduced, the bill gave the president blanket authorization to request such appropriations as he deemed necessary to undertake naval construction allowed within treaty limits.[48] To strengthen the president's resolve, Vinson confidentially advised him in early June that the Japanese naval budget for 1933–1934 had been increased significantly over the previous year.[49] Meanwhile, Vinson, Wagner, and the other naval advocates kept a low profile while Congress considered the measure. It breezed through Congress with minimal opposition, and Roosevelt signed the N.I.R.A. into law on 15 June 1933. The next day the president announced that he had signed an executive order authorizing $238 million for the construction of thirty-two ships.[50] A month later bids were opened and private shipyards were awarded

---

[46] West, "Laying the Legislative Foundation," 314–15; *New York Times*, 5 April 1933, 3.

[47] Walter, "Congressman Carl Vinson and Franklin D. Roosevelt," 297.

[48] West, "Laying the Legislative Foundation," 315–26.

[49] Carl Vinson to Col. Louis McHenry Howe, White House, 3 June 1933, Official File 197, Roosevelt Library.

[50] West, "Laying the Legislative Foundation," 326–30; Walter, "Congressman Carl Vinson and Franklin D. Roosevelt," 297–98.

contracts for twenty-one new ships, including the carriers *Yorktown* and *Arizona*.[51]

The use of N.I.R.A. funding for shipbuilding and aircraft construction, West concludes, was a successful and innovative approach given the political and economic realities of 1933. By increasing naval construction in fiscal 1934 from five to thirty-seven ships, it had a far-reaching effect on the U.S. shipbuilding industrial base. It forced private and government yards to "substantially upgrade their production facilities and drastically expand their work forces." The N.I.R.A. program did not cure the navy's material deficiencies, but it was a major step towards revitalizing its fighting capacity and it provided momentum that would contribute to future successes in shipbuilding.[52]

Although President Roosevelt's support of shipbuilding in 1933 had been reluctant and tentative, to say the least, he nonetheless claimed credit for the authorship of the shipbuilding provisions of the N.I.R.A. In a gleeful aside to Secretary of the Navy Swanson, Roosevelt later observed, "Claude, we got away with murder that time."[53] "While the President's role in this episode should not be denigrated," West asserts, "it would be more accurate to say that he pulled the trigger after Admirals Parsons and Land loaded the weapon, Secretary Swanson cocked the hammer, Senator Wagner placed the primer, and Carl Vinson pointed the barrel."[54]

Vinson deserved as much credit as anyone for the enactment of the naval provisions in the National Industrial Recovery Act. He had worked closely with the Navy Department in formulating the program, kept constant pressure on the president, made sure the issue received constant coverage in the press, and worked behind the scenes to secure for the navy as much funding as possible for shipbuilding and aircraft construction. Undoubtedly pleased with the enactment of the largest shipbuilding program since World War I, he was uncomfortable with the

---

[51] West, "Laying the Legislative Foundation," 331–32.
[52] Ibid., 340–41; Robert H. Levine, *The Politics of American Naval Rearmament, 1930–1938* (New York: Garland Publishing, Inc., 1988) 91–3.
[53] West, "Laying the Legislative Foundation," 341–42.
[54] Ibid., 342.

means employed to get it. Using public works and unemployment relief as a rationale for naval construction was not the way he wanted defense measures enacted. He had resorted to this approach in 1933 as a temporary expedient, when he realized that it was the only way to secure funding for shipbuilding. Always the pragmatist, he did what was necessary, but he did not like it, and he doubted that the N.I.R.A. approach would work again. In future years more traditional means would have to be employed to address the navy's remaining needs, and Vinson looked forward to the challenge.

5

Success At Last

This act is not a mere piece of paper. It means real fighting ships.

Carl Vinson, 1934

For several years Vinson had watched developments in Japan with a wary eye. Unlike the United States, Japan had quickly built her navy up to treaty limits. Moreover, as Vinson had publicly stated many times, the Japanese Navy consisted largely of modern ships of the latest design, whereas the American Navy was antiquated. Aside from capital ships, which were limited by treaty, the Japanese had equaled or surpassed the Americans in several naval categories by 1930 and continued expansion seemed likely.[1] Without the assistance of the British Navy, the United States could not defend the Philippines, China, or other American interests in the Pacific from Japanese aggression.

Even more disturbing to Vinson than Japanese naval expansion was the increasingly militaristic and aggressive nature of the Japanese government. On 18 September 1931, a small section of track on the South Manchuria Railway's main line a few miles north of Mukden was destroyed. Exactly what happened was not clear at the time, but the Japanese Army used the Mukden Incident as a pretext for attacking the Chinese positions in South Manchuria. The Japanese easily subdued the

---

[1] Meredith W. Berg, "The United States and the Breakdown of Naval Limitation, 1934–1939" (Ph.D. diss,, Tulane University, 1966) 21–22.

much larger Chinese forces, and the speed and precision of their attacks seemed to be positive proof of an elaborately preconceived plan. Japan's naked aggression violated the League Covenant, the Nine-Power Pact of 1922, and the Kellogg-Briand Pact of 1928, but neither the Western powers nor the League of Nations was prepared to take strong retaliatory action that would risk war with Japan. As Japan was destroying the last resistance in Manchuria, her troops landed at Shanghai and clashed with Chinese forces. During the fighting, thousands of men, women, and children were bombed or burned to death. The aerial bombardment of civilians produced a wave of revulsion in the United States, and diplomatic pressure from America and Britain convinced the Japanese to withdraw from Shanghai in May 1932. On behalf of the League of Nations, a commission headed by Lord Lytton investigated the crisis in Manchuria. Its lengthy report published in September 1932 condemned Japan's invasion. President Hoover and Secretary of State Henry Stimson refused to recognize Japanese territorial gains, but international condemnation had little effect on the leaders in Tokyo. After crushing resistance in Manchuria, Japan established the puppet state of Manchukuo, and in March 1933 gave formal notice of its intention to withdraw from the League of Nations. Energetic steps by the League and the United States might well have stymied Japanese aggression in 1931 and averted the calamitous chain of events that followed. But the depression-ridden Western powers, fearing war and hoping to preserve trade and investments in the Far East, had no stomach for taking resolute action. Famed diplomatic historian Thomas A. Bailey is correct in his assessment: "The inability of the powers to act in unison proved that the Kellogg-Briand Pact was a parchment pretense, and that the League could be bluffed with impunity. In a very real sense the Open Door collapsed, the League fell apart, collective security perished, and World War II began in 1931 on the wind-swept plains of Manchuria."[2]

---

[2] Thomas A. Bailey, *A Diplomatic History of the American People*, 10th ed. (Englewood Cliffs NJ: Prentice-Hall, Inc., 1980) 694–99; Robert Ferrell, *American Diplomacy in the Great Depression* (New Haven: Yale University Press, 1957) 122–27; James B. Crowley, *Japan's Quest for Autonomy* (Princeton: Princeton University Press, 1966) 82–83, 185–89.

President Roosevelt shared Vinson's concern about the danger of war with Japan. At his first working cabinet meeting on 7 March 1933, the president discussed a possible war with Japan in terms of a short-range defeat and an eventual American victory. America would be obliged to abandon the Philippines, he said, because the fleet could not operate efficiently over long distances. As Postmaster General James A. Farley recalled the discussion, "There was general agreement that we could defeat Japan by starvation, but that it would take from three to five years to do so."[3] The president's chief advisors on Japan were Secretary of State Cordell Hull, chief of the Far Eastern Division of the State Department Stanley K. Hornbeck, and American Ambassador in Tokyo Joseph C. Grew. Hull, a serious, slow-talking Tennesseean, had become a judge at age thirty-one, and then served in the U.S. House and Senate. His self-discipline was notable: after having smoked fifteen cigars a day for thirty-five years, he paused to consider whether or not the habit was necessary and then quit entirely. He applied a stern sense of moral outrage to the Japanese, who were breaking international law. Hull relied for advice on Hornbeck, the son of a minister, who had taught in China for five years and lectured on the Far East at Wisconsin and Harvard before entering the State Department in 1928. Although an isolationist, he retained a basic sympathy for China. At the time of the Manchurian incident, he urged economic sanctions against Japan and staunchly supported the policy of nonrecognition. Grew, a nineteenth-century optimist, hoped that Japan would come to her senses and resume cooperation with the powers. His contacts in Japan were limited largely to prominent people, such as high-ranking diplomats, wealthy businessmen, and the court circle.[4]

Japanese intentions to build up her navy regardless of world opinion became obvious in the spring of 1933 when she increased her naval budget for 1934 by 25 percent.[5] In May, Hornbeck and Hull endorsed

---

[3] Stephen E. Pelz, *Race to Pearl Harbor* (Cambridge: Harvard University Press, 1974) 75.

[4] Ibid., 73–74.

[5] Carl Vinson to Col. Louis McHenry Howe, White House, 3 June 1933, Official File 197, Roosevelt Library, Hyde Park NY.

and transmitted to the president a dispatch from Tokyo in which Ambassador Grew described Japan as a great power in terms of land mass, industry, and national spirit, which "probably has the most complete, well balanced, coordinated and therefore powerful fighting machine in the world today." The Japanese were superior on land and equal on sea to the United States, he reported.[6] The Roosevelt administration responded to these developments cautiously. It reminded the Japanese of their treaty obligations, but tried to avoid any type of crisis with Japan.

The president had received much criticism for allocating funds for a naval building program in 1933, but the continued arguments of Vinson and the Navy Department convinced him that a longterm building program was essential if the navy were to keep pace with Japan.

With Roosevelt's backing, Vinson introduced a bill on 9 January 1934, authorizing the president to build the navy to treaty limits by 1942. The Vinson bill, H. R. 6604, authorized a 15,000 ton aircraft carrier to replace the *Langley*; 99,200 tons aggregate of destroyers and 35,530 tons aggregate of submarines to replace vessels that would become obsolescent by the time the program was completed. Although providing no cost estimate of the program, Vinson stated that it would provide exactly the number of ships authorized by treaties.[7] While Japan had already built to treaty strength, the United States needed to build 1 carrier, 6 cruisers, 65 destroyers, and 30 submarines—a total of 102 vessels to reach that goal.[8] The Vinson bill, which had been prepared by the Navy Department, was similar to bills introduced previously by Senator Trammell and Congressman Britten. One difference between H. R. 6604 and previous measures was the absence of any mention of specific annual increments or mandated deadlines for the completion of the program to insure executive compliance. With Roosevelt in the

---

[6] Pelz, *Race to Pearl Harbor,* 76.

[7] *New York Times*, 10 January 1934, 2.

[8] Calvin W. Enders, "The Vinson Navy" (Ph.D. diss., Michigan State University, 1970) 49.

White House, Vinson was quite willing to grant the president broad discretion in carrying out the replacement program.[9]

After formally referring H. R. 6604 to the Navy Department, Vinson urged Admiral William Standley, chief of naval operations, to endorse the bill. The chief stumbling block, the admiral pointed out, was the Bureau of the Budget and the administration. The president made it clear that he did not oppose the bill as long as it was not identified as an administration measure. Continued pressure from the navy and Vinson forced Budget Director Douglas to capitulate. On 17 January, he advised the secretary of the navy that the navy's draft legislation could be submitted to Congress. Soon afterwards, the Navy Department recommended that H. R. 6604 be enacted, and Vinson announced that the Naval Affairs Committee would begin hearings.[10]

Vinson wanted to expedite the hearings on his bill for three reasons. First, he wanted to capitalize on the public support for naval construction generated by the N.I.R.A. program. Second, he wanted the bill adopted before the peace and disarmament lobbies had time to mobilize their full might on Congress. Finally, he wanted to act before Senator Trammell could hold hearings that might promote an alternative proposal. Consequently, the hearings before the House Naval Affairs Committee lasted only two days, 22–23 January, and only Navy Department witnesses were invited to testify. After hearing the testimony of Acting Secretary of the Navy Henry Roosevelt, Admiral Standley, and other navy professionals, the committee voted unanimously to favorably report H. R. 6604 to the House. Vinson, West notes, had been in firm control throughout and made sure that all the major issues were addressed. The result was "a concise, positive, and useful record that could be effectively employed to garner support within the House or for the cultivation of public opinion."[11]

---

[9] Michael A. West, "Laying the Legislative Foundation: The House Naval Affairs Committee and the Construction of the Treaty Navy, 1926–1934" (Ph. D. diss., Ohio State University, 1980) 352–71.

[10] Ibid., 371–76.

[11] Ibid., 376–86.

Vinson acted expeditiously to get his bill to the floor of the House. On 30 January, he began the debate with a concise explanation of his proposal. "First, the measure establishes the strength of the United States Navy in respect to the categories of ships that are limited by international agreement; second, it authorizes the President to undertake the construction of such ships as are required to maintain the Navy in underage units at the strength prescribed by treaty; third, it authorizes the appropriations necessary for such building." In the final analysis, he continued, "It is simply an authorization for replacement of obsolete ships, plus a definite statement that it is the policy of the United States to maintain the Navy at whatever limits may be established by international agreements." He estimated that building the 102 ships needed to bring the navy up to treaty strength would involve an expenditure of approximately $380,000,000 over a period of 7 or 8 years. The greatest weakness of American sea power, he asserted, had been the lack of a definite policy as to the building and maintenance of the navy. While the United States had for many years affirmed an intention of maintaining a navy of sufficient strength to support and protect national policies, commerce and territories, the fact remains that "we have never had such a Navy, and unless this bill is enacted into law we never will have one."[12]

Mincing no words, he bluntly told his colleagues, "The country and Congress should thoroughly understand that the policies of the Government cannot be maintained and supported with obsolete ships. For the first time in the history of this country we are now trying to provide a logical, orderly plan for the maintenance of the Navy at a level which is sufficient to provide against emergencies. This measure will give no offense and involve no threat to any foreign power and will require the least possible burden on our taxpayers."[13] After tracing the recent history of the leading naval powers since the Washington Treaty, he closed his thirty-minute address with a theme he had used many times: "No government which fails to provide for its own preservation against the assaults of every probable foe is entitled to the support of its people. The primary duty of government is self-preservation, and no

---

[12] *Congressional Record*, 73rd Cong., 2d sess., 30 January 1934, 1597.
[13] Ibid.

logic can justify it in stripping itself of its means of defense, and relying for its preservation upon the mercy, the pity, or the love of other nations."[14]

House debate followed the usual pattern, with proponents arguing that disarmament by example had not worked and that a large navy was needed to defend America and protect commerce around the world. Critics countered by predicting that a large building program would lead to a naval race and probably produce war. They also wanted to know who the United States was going to fight with its big navy since the airplane and submarine had made invasion impossible. Both sides brought Japan into the discussion. Supporters claimed that a larger fleet would restrain Japanese aggression, while opponents insisted that additional building would only exacerbate Japanese suspicions of America. The economic consequences of the program provided another point of contention. While admitting that the program was costly, backers pointed out that a defeat resulting from unpreparedness would be even more expensive. They also emphasized how the measure would be an economic stimulus to the shipbuilding industry and all those industries related to it. Opponents saw the bill as a disastrous diversion of resources away from needed internal improvements and relief, which was certain to cost more than the projected estimates.[15]

After the time for general debate expired, amendments were taken up. At the request of Admiral Standley and Rear Admiral Ernest J. King, chief of the Bureau of Aeronautics, Vinson's committee had approved a motion to amend the bill to include authority to procure aircraft in numbers commensurate with a treaty navy. The House quickly approved the amendment. Representative William Hastings, a Democrat from Oklahoma, offered amendments to limit the total cost of the program, but Vinson convinced his colleagues to vote down his amendments. A more serious threat to the bill came from Representative Chester Charles Thompson, a Democrat from Illinois, who introduced an amendment to require half of the construction to be done in government navy yards. Anticipating such an amendment, Admiral Land had given Vinson the

---

[14] Ibid., 1598.
[15] West, "Laying the Legislative Foundation," 390–94.

following substitute amendment: "That, insofar as practicable, vessels constructed under the authorization of this Act shall be built on the basis of one half in Navy Yards and one half in private ship yards, final decision in each case to be at the discretion of the President."[16] A heated debate ensued and the Thompson amendment was adopted by vote of 143-90.

Representative Charles W. Tobey, a Republican from New Hampshire, then introduced a hastily drawn amendment to limit profits to 10 percent. Apparently the amendment was not based on any objective study of navy contracts, but it sounded right and would allow the House to make a simplistic political statement that would sound good back home. Neither Vinson nor the navy had anticipated this amendment, and they were unprepared to resist it. After Vinson failed to quash it on a technicality, he reluctantly agreed to it, assuming he could deal with it later in conference committee. The House then approved H. R. 6604 by voice vote. In only three weeks, Vinson had steered his bill through the House with only minimal changes. Even with a strong Democratic majority, steering such a controversial measure through the House so quickly was a formidable achievement.

Following the passage of the bill, Vinson took a brief respite from the battles in Congress to visit his ailing parents in Milledgeville. Both were in poor health and his eighty-three year-old-father had been bedridden for three months. On 4 February, they celebrated their fifty-ninth wedding anniversary. Vinson stayed with them a few days and found that his father was "doing about as well as could be expected for a man of his age."[17]

Vinson had moved so swiftly that the opposition forces had not been able to mobilize their forces effectively, but they were determined to stop the bill in the Senate. The most vocal opponent of Vinson's program was the National Council for the Prevention of War led by its executive secretary, Frederick J. Libby, a Congregationalist minister turned Quaker. In a letter to Park Trammell, chairman of the Senate Naval

---

[16] Ibid., 394–402.

[17] Carl Vinson to Charles J. Bloch, 14 February 1934, box 1, folder 3, Charles J. Bloch Papers, Middle Georgia Regional Library, Macon, GA.

Affairs Committee, he charged that the bill was "railroaded" through Vinson's committee and that the hearings were merely "perfunctory," with no opportunity for opponents of the bill to present adequately their side.[18] When Trammell introduced the bill in the Senate, Libby warned him that "the peace organizations are terribly disturbed by this Vinson naval building program."[19]

The Council's associate secretary, former Congresswoman Jeannette Rankin of Montana, declared that an enemy could not land on our shores and therefore the United States did not need these ships for protection. Their only value, she maintained, was to provide contracts for the shipbuilders and the munitions makers. "These war scares come," she said, "every time the shipbuilders want a big building program; and so the real reason that we are having this war scare is so that the shipbuilders can make more profits in peacetime."[20]

The isolationist anti-war sentiment Miss Rankin expressed, already strong in the 1920s, gained additional strength in the early 1930s. Centered in the Midwest, it had attracted countless adherents through popular novels and films, such as Ernest Hemingway's *A Farewell to Arms* and Erich Maria Remarque's *All Quiet On the Western Front,* plus a host of scholarly works that argued that American entry into World War I had been a mistake and that American participation could have been avoided had Wilson strictly adhered to international law. Among the more influential works in the latter category were Walter Millis's *The Road to War*, Edwin M. Borchard and William P. Lage's *Neutrality for the United States*, and Charles C. Tansill's *America Goes to War.* The theory that Wall Street's satanic network had beguiled the country into war was emphasized again during the Great Depression, at a time when Big Business had been found guilty at the bar of public opinion of ruining prosperity. In 1934 two popular books, H. C. Engelbrecht and F. C. Hanighen's *Merchants of Death* and George Seldes's *Iron, Blood and Profits,* accused the munitions-makers of thriving on "bloodshed for profits." *Fortune's* lead article in March 1934, "Arms and Men,"

---

[18] *New York Times*, 29 January 1934, 2.
[19] Enders, "The Vinson Navy," 52.
[20] Ibid.

assumed the existence of a sinister worldwide conspiracy of arms manufacturers operating continuously to prolong war and disturb peace.[21]

Another influential opponent of the Vinson bill was Oswald Garrison Villard, longtime editor of *The Nation,* who told reporters, following a meeting with the president, that he believed that the United States was courting disaster by embarking on a naval race with Great Britain and Japan. He was particularly upset by the House Naval Affairs Committee's haste in pushing through its naval building scheme before the opposition could express its views.[22]

Strong protests against the Vinson naval building program were made at a luncheon of the Women's International League for Peace and Freedom in New York City on 5 February. The speakers included Nevin Sayre, executive secretary of the Fellowship of Reconciliation; Dr. John H. Lathrop, president of the American Unitarian Association; Miss Myra Smith, national secretary of the Y.W.C.A.; Mrs. Estelle Sternberger, executive director of the World Peaceways; and Rabbi Nathan Stern of the West End Synagogue. Sayre asserted that "if the bill was passed," peace organizations must continue to "pile up protests in Washington," and warned that "the world is drifting pretty fast into a new great war."[23] On 10 February, twenty-one of New York City's leading clergymen sent the president a telegram protesting the Vinson bill.[24] On 21 February, Secretary of State Cordell Hull informed Vinson that the White House had received over 200 letters and telegrams a day regarding the navy bill, and more than 99 percent of them were in opposition.[25] A mass meeting on 25 February, sponsored by the Women's International League,

---

[21] Selig Adler, *The Isolationist Impulse* (Westport CT: Greenwood Press, 1957) 256–59; H. C. Engelbrecht and F. C. Hanighen, *Merchants of Death: A Study of the International Armament Industry* (New York: Dodd, Mead, & Co., 1934); George Seldes, *Iron, Blood and Profits: An Exposure of the World-wide Munitions Racket* (New York: Harper & Brothers, 1934); "Arms and Men," *Fortune.* 9 (March 1934): 53–57, 113.

[22] Enders, "The Vinson Navy," 53.

[23] *New York Times,* 6 February 1934, 24.

[24] Ibid., 11 February 1934, 32.

[25] Cordell Hull Statement, 21 February 1934, President's Personal File, 5901, Roosevelt Library.

opposed the "billion-dollar" appropriation for increased naval armament. A thousand people heard Senator Gerald Nye declare that if an honest investigation into the activities of the munitions makers were undertaken, the Vinson naval building bill would never pass. "No nation on earth spends so much money to get ready for war as our country," he argued, "yet we set ourselves as an example for the rest of the world to follow in preserving peace."[26] Harvey O'Connor, the author of the critical *Mellon's Millions*, maintained that Andrew Mellon was thoroughly in sympathy with the Vinson bill inasmuch as he held a monopoly on aluminum. He lamented that "there's a billion dollars for the Vinson Bill, but not one cent for C.W.A. (work relief) funds after May 1." Another such mass meeting was held in mid-March to honor the congressmen who had fought the Vinson bill.[27]

To counter such arguments, Vinson reiterated the reasons for expanded naval construction in numerous congressional speeches and newspaper articles. He declared that the American policy of disarmament-by-example had not been a positive factor in achieving world peace, but had become a menace to peace. Although the United States had contributed to and supported wholeheartedly the limitation of armaments, this system would never work, he pointed out, unless "the various powers should maintain about the same proportion of the maximum strength permitted." All must maintain the ratios agreed upon or an imbalance might permit a stronger naval power to attack a nation which had not continued building. Unfortunately, other countries had progressed much farther toward the goal of full treaty strength than the United States. At the Washington Conference, "as an altruistic contribution to world peace," the United States had taken the unprecedented action of surrendering voluntarily its pending naval supremacy, but no other country had "made a contribution to the cause of disarmament which can even be mentioned in the same breath." During the decade following the Washington Conference, Great Britain had provided for 134 new combatant ships, Japan for 130, France for 166, and Italy for 115. By contrast, the United States made provisions for only

---

[26] Enders, "The Vinson Navy," 78–79.
[27] Ibid., 79.

thirty-four ships, and during the Hoover administration no new ships were authorized. America has allowed its strength in light cruisers, destroyers, and submarines to slip to fifth place and "a very poor fifth at that." If America did not build up its navy, it could not guard its interests or discharge its responsibilities.[28]

Vinson warned that America's destroyer strength was "shockingly and dangerously deficient." Although it had enough destroyers, every one of them would become overage in the next few months, compromising their military usefulness. Between 1922 and 1932, while the Japanese had laid down 43 vessels of this type, the Italians 39, the British 36, and the French 55, the United States had not brought a single destroyer off the ways. A gap existed in the fleet that needed rectification. Recently, under the leadership of President Roosevelt, a start had been made to remedy this bad situation. Thirty-two destroyers were under construction at this time. However, Vinson emphasized, "this program must be recognized as a start only and it is imperative that we continue uniformly."[29]

In defending his program, Vinson frequently called attention to the threat posed by Japanese naval expansion. By the end of 1936, according to Admiral Osumi's figures, Japan's navy would be 68 percent that of the United States, and if only underage tonnage were considered, the Japanese fleet would be 81 percent that of the American fleet. Of the 372 ships in the American Navy on 30 December 1933, only 84 were underage. If the Japanese underage cruisers, destroyers, and submarines were compared to the American underage vessels of these categories, the Japanese would have 103 percent of the American strength. To make matters worse, when the current agreements expired, he pointed out ominously, Japan needed no longer to abide by the treaties, but could build as she wished. As long as the Japanese Navy was built up to the limit in all categories and the American Navy was far short of the limits, the cause of peace was gravely jeopardized, Vinson reasoned.[30]

---

[28] Ibid., 60–62; *Atlanta Constitution*, 28 January 1934, A7.
[29] *Atlanta Constitution*, 28 January 1934, A7.
[30] Enders, "The Vinson Navy," 64–65.

When critics charged that aviation companies had made excessive profits from navy contracts, Vinson responded with alacrity. Upon hearing that one airplane engine manufacturer had made a profit of 36 percent on a navy contract, Vinson declared, "If profits like that are being made, we'll stop it—even if it's necessary for the Government to go into the airplane-making business itself." The House Naval Affairs Committee obtained a special audit of aircraft-makers books from 1927 to 1933, which failed to convince Vinson that the companies had made excessive profits. But the chairman, disturbed by the possibility of excess profits and favoritism in obtaining contracts, made it clear that these were issues that required thorough investigation. While Vinson was the strongest advocate of increased spending for defense, he had no tolerance for waste or corruption in defense contracts. In announcing that his committee would conduct a thorough investigation, he said, "We are not going to stand by and let the Government be at the mercy of any private company; we are not going to be held up. If they're making too much, we'll put a stop to it." If additional legislation is required, "we'll pass it."[31]

Vinson sought a definite naval policy in order to have an orderly building program. Such a plan, he believed, would not only be more economical but also would "contribute to better designs, better workmanship, less disruption of industry," and maintain the national defense at a higher level than would be possible "under old wasteful methods of building a navy by alternate spasms of intense activity and practically complete idleness."[32] Since it would take approximately three years to complete the vessels under construction, Vinson wanted the navy to be ready to lay a new keel to replace each launched vessel.[33] This systematic building program, Vinson added, would enable the navy to correct any defects in design and incorporate technological innovation at minimum cost. To bolster these arguments, Vinson could call on navy

---

[31] *Washington Post*, 2 February 1934, 1, 4; *New York Times*, 1 February 1934, 4.

[32] House, Committee on Naval Affairs, *To Establish the Composition of the United States Navy*, 73rd Cong., 2d sess., 24 January 1934, H. Rep. 338, 2.

[33] *Atlanta Constitution*, 28 January 1934, A7.

spokesmen such as Admiral Standley and Admiral Land. He also received strong support from other members of the House Naval Affairs Committee, especially Representative Britten.

In the Senate, Park Trammell realized that his bill was doomed and agreed to endorse the Vinson bill. On 26 January, he introduced S. 2493 that differed from Vinson's bill by incorporating the navy's amendment to increase the authorized number of useful airplanes to 2,184. By so doing, he was able to abandon his bill and share sponsorship of H. R. 6604, which eventually became known as the Vinson-Trammell Act. Vinson had ramrodded his bill through the House in less than a month, but Trammell needed nearly two months to get it through the Senate. The Senate Naval Affairs Committee heard the same naval arguments the House committee had heard, but it also listened patiently to pacifist and disarmament groups that Vinson had shunned. Once on the floor of the Senate, H. R. 6604 faced the determined opposition of an anti-navy faction led by William H. King of Utah. Senator King had once served on the Naval Affairs Committee, but left in disgust following the passage of the 1916 Naval Appropriations Act. Since then he had carried on a vendetta against the navy, and the passage of time had not moderated his hostility. He was joined by several like-minded senators from the northern plains and upper Midwest states. From 9 February to 6 March, King and his colleagues Lynn Joseph Frazier and Gerald Nye tied up the Senate with delaying tactics to keep Vinson's bill from coming to a vote.[34]

To Vinson and other proponents of the bill, this delay was intolerable. They had the necessary votes for Senate passage, but they could not be sure how long their consensus would hold. Some senators already appeared to be weakening as a result of the intense pressure exerted by pacifist and disarmament groups, and if the debate continued defections were certain to occur. Proponents were relieved when Senate Majority Leader Joseph T. Robinson offered a unanimous consent agreement providing that consideration of H. R. 6604 would be completed on 6 March and limiting debate by any member to ten minutes. His action indicated that the Senate leadership wanted to

---

[34] West, "Laying the Legislative Foundation," 405–16.

expedite consideration of H. R. 6604 and that the delaying tactics of opponents should cease. As a senior administration spokesman, Robinson also made it clear that the White House wanted the measure considered in a timely manner. Robinson's measure quickly gained Senate approval.[35]

Opponents of the bill, however, did not give up without a fight. The debate in the Senate on 5 and 6 March reached new heights of bitterness. Senator Nye, who was just beginning his investigation of munitions makers, charged that the measure was "a bill for the relief of the munitions makers of the United States."[36] Crusty Senator William Borah of Idaho, in one of the most vigorous speeches of his long career, branded the munitions makers as "international criminals," who were spreading propaganda in the Orient about a possible war between the United States and Japan to spur the sale of more armaments. As long as there is profit in making instruments of war, he said, the munitions makers are going to see to it that war fears are kept alive. "Capone and Dillinger," Borah said, "are no more heartless or bloodthirsty than those who make arms and munitions for the disemboweling of human beings."[37] In the Senate Office Building, representatives of the Women's International League for Peace and Freedom called upon Senator Robert Wagner of New York to oppose the bill. Their prepared statement asserted that "armaments do not prevent war" and "it is foolish to suppose that protection is given by great armaments." Their statement urged Wagner: "Do all in your power to save our government from spending vast sums of money, while people are starving and homeless, on building armaments that have been proved dangerous and futile."[38] Despite such impassioned pleas, the Senate passed H. R. 6604 by vote of 65 to 18 with 13 not voting.[39]

---

[35] Ibid., 414–18.

[36] *Congressional Record*, 73rd Cong., 2d sess., 6 March 1934, 3780.

[37] *New York Times*, 6 March 1934, 12; *Atlanta Constitution*, 6 March 1934, 6.

[38] *New York Times*, 6 March 1934, 12.

[39] *Congressional Record,* 73rd Cong., 2d sess., 6 March 1934, 3793–94, 3801, 3813.

Throughout the legislative process, the bill had received bipartisan support. In the final vote in the Senate, 24 Republicans joined 41 Democrats in supporting it, while 10 Democrats, 7 Republicans, and Senator Henrik Shipstead of the Farmer-Labor Party opposed it. The negative votes, concentrated in the Midwest and upper plains states, brought few surprises: Borah and Pope of Idaho; Frazier and Nye of North Dakota; King and Thomas of Utah; Dickinson and Murphy of Iowa; Bulow of South Dakota; Costigan of Colorado; Norris of Nebraska; Capper of Kansas; Clark of Missouri; Thomas of Oklahoma; LaFollette of Wisconsin; and Shipstead of Minnesota. The only unexpected opposition came from Carter Glass of Virginia and Huey Long of Louisiana. Aside from Glass and Long, all of the opponents were from the West.[40]

The differences between the House and Senate bills necessitated a joint conference to resolve them. Four senators—Park Trammell, Millard Tydings, Frederick Hale, and Jesse Metcalf—and five representatives— Carl Vinson, P. H. Drewry, Stephen Gambrill, Fred Britten, and George Darrow—were named to the Conference Committee. Working closely with the Roosevelt administration, the Conference Committee agreed to several minor changes. The Conference Committee gave the president greater flexibility in dividing ship construction and aircraft manufacture between government and private facilities. It reduced the percentage of aircraft and engines to be built in government facilities from 25 to 10 percent, when it was pointed out that the government lacked the facilities to manufacture more than 10 percent of the authorized naval aircraft and engines. As Vinson had expected, the Conference Committee adjusted the Tobey amendment. When the Income Tax Division of the Bureau of Internal Revenue explained how costly auditing all contracts of $10,000 or more would be, the Conference Committee decided to apply the Tobey amendment only to contracts involving $50,000 or more. After incorporating these changes, the Conference Committee filed its report

---

[40] West, "Laying the Legislative Foundation," 422–23.

on 20 March 1934.[41] Both houses quickly approved the report, and the
bill was then engrossed and sent to the president for his signature.

Immediately after the Conference Committee report had been
accepted by both houses, Vinson praised the bill as "the biggest naval
program ever authorized at one time by Congress." The construction
program, he added, "will go a long way toward putting our navy in the
class it belongs." Explaining that the bill provided for 65 destroyers, 32
submarines, 4 cruisers, 1 aircraft carrier, and 1,184 airplanes at a cost of
$580 million, he believed the measure would, either directly or
indirectly, provide employment for thousands. Delighted with his
success, he was confident the president would sign the measure.[42]

Despite Vinson's exulting, pacifist groups were not yet resigned to
defeat. They continued their frantic efforts to convince Roosevelt to veto
the measure. They did not succeed, but they did get the president's
attention and managed to delay his signing the bill a few days. Roosevelt,
who preferred the devious to the straightforward approach, took a
cavalier attitude toward the bill and asserted in a press conference on 23
March that the bill was nothing more than a resolution depending on the
action of future Congresses to appropriate the necessary funds. He tried
to reassure the critics of the bill by stressing America's continued
moderation in the building of naval armament. When he signed the bill
on 27 March, he issued the following statement:

> Because there is some public misapprehension of the facts
> in relation to the Vinson bill, it is only right that its main
> provisions should be made wholly clear.
>   This is not a law for the construction of a single additional
> United States warship.
>   The general purpose of the Bill is solely a statement by the
> Congress that it approves the building of our Navy up to and not
> beyond the strength in various types of ships authorized, first, by

[41] Ibid., 425–31; House, Conference Committee, *Conference Report to
Accompany H. R. 6604*, 73rd Cong., 2d sess., 20 March 1934, H. Rep. 1024.
[42] *Atlanta Constitution*, 23 March 1934, 7.

the Washington Naval Limitation Treaty of 1922 and, secondly, by the London Naval Limitation Treaty of 1930.

As has been done on several previous occasions in our history, the Bill authorizes certain future construction over a period of years. But the Bill appropriates no money for such construction and the word 'authorization' is, therefore, merely a statement of the policy of the present Congress. Whether it will be carried out depends on the action of future Congresses.

It has been and will be the policy of the Administration to favor continued limitation of Naval armaments. It is my personal hope that the Naval Conference to be held in 1935 will extend all existing limitations and agree to further reductions.[43]

The president's statement was "disingenuous" and, as West notes, "wholly consistent with his handling of the naval authorization from its inception."[44] For political reasons he was unwilling to see H. R. 6604 emerge as an administrative proposal and had maintained a respectable distance from it during its consideration by Congress. Yet he was keenly interested in it and made significant contributions to its passage. Once the bill had been introduced, he saw to it that the measure received prompt administration endorsement and prompt scheduling of House floor debate by the Rules Committee and House leadership. When the bill was stalled in the Senate, he instructed Senator Robinson to curtail debate and secure a Senate vote. During the House-Senate conference, the president was closely involved with Vinson and others in fine-tuning the final product. Overt support of H. R. 6604 might well have alienated Democratic and Republican progressives whose support he needed on other measures, so Roosevelt worked behind the scenes and skillfully used surrogates to achieve his goals.[45]

---

[43] *New York Times*, 28 March 1934, 1; Press Release, Statement by the President Upon Signing the Vinson Bill, 27 March 1934, Miscellaneous File, Roosevelt Library.

[44] West, "Laying the Legislative Foundation," 436.

[45] Ibid., 449–51.

Standing behind the president at the signing ceremony were Carl Vinson, Assistant Secretary of the Navy Henry L. Roosevelt, and Representative Fred Britten, each of whom had had a part in the success of the Vinson-Trammell Act. It was significant that the president had invited Britten, the ranking Republican on the House Naval Affairs Committee, but failed to invite any senators. His presence called attention to the key work of the House Naval Affairs Committee. The omission of both Park Trammell, the Democratic chairman of the Senate Naval Affairs Committee, and the ranking Republican member on the committee, emphasized their minor roles. By such action, the president was indicating for all to see that the Vinson-Trammell Act he was signing was in fact the Vinson bill.[46]

Despite the president's remarks, naval supporters knew that once congressional approval had been won, appropriations would follow.[47] After the president signed the bill, Vinson gave this candid appraisal: "This act is not a mere piece of paper. It means real fighting ships. We will provide the money this session to start work on part of the vessels authorized."[48] Vinson's confidence stemmed from the fact that the president had told both him and Henry Roosevelt that new vessels for fiscal 1935 would be financed by the public works allotment in the emergency budget.[49] True to his word, on 29 June, Roosevelt formally allotted $40,661,000 for fiscal 1935 to begin the construction of the first twenty ships and 225 aircraft authorized by the Vinson-Trammell Act. By November, the contracts had been signed and work was underway, with nine vessels going to private yards and eleven to navy yards.[50]

Although the Vinson-Trammell Act provided only authorization, it reversed a fifteen-year policy of naval retrenchment and was the first important act to strengthen the navy between the World Wars.[51] "In

---

[46] Enders, "The Vinson Navy," 82–83.

[47] George T. Davis, *A Navy Second to None* (New York: Harcourt, Brace and Company, 1940) 361–62.

[48] Enders, "The Vinson Navy," 83.

[49] Robert H. Levine, *The Politics of American Naval Rearmament, 1930–1938* (New York: Garland Publishing, Inc., 1988) 240.

[50] West, "Laying the Legislative Foundation," 436–42.

[51] Enders, "The Vinson Navy," 92.

number of ships and expanded aircraft authorized," historian George T. Davis observed that "the Vinson-Trammell Act stands as one of the most significant measures in American naval history."[52] In a 1966 article for a navy publication, Charles F. Elliott declared that "the Vinson-Trammell Act was, in effect, the genesis of the modern U.S. Navy."[53] Michael West, a careful and thorough scholar, declared that the "Vinson-Trammell Act represented an accomplishment of great and lasting significance." He considered the bill "a major turning point in U.S. naval policy and development during the interwar period involving fundamental changes in force structure, fleet manning, and organization. Moreover, it profoundly influenced naval procurement practices, the shipbuilding and aviation industries, and the industrial mobilization base." From the perspective of World War II, West continued, "it would be difficult to overemphasize the contribution of the Vinson-Trammell Act in enhancing the readiness and material condition of the U.S. fleet." The act, "eventually provided authorization for the construction of 8 battleships, 1 aircraft carrier, 4 light cruisers, 5 destroyer-leaders, 46 destroyers, and 28 submarines—the core of the fleet's modern combatant vessels in commission at the outbreak of hostilities."[54] Upon returning to Milledgeville, Vinson declared the session of Congress just closed "the most constructive and important in the history of the nation."[55]

In 1931, when Carl Vinson became chairman of the House Naval Affairs Committee, he suddenly moved from obscurity into the limelight. As the chief congressional spokesman for naval expansion and an intimate friend of President Roosevelt, he emerged over the next three years as one of the most powerful voices in Congress. The successful passage of the Vinson-Trammell Act made Vinson a household name, as his words frequently appeared in the national press and his photo graced numerous publications, including the *New York Times, Literary Digest,*

[52] Davis, *A Navy Second to None,* 161.

[53] Charles F. Elliott, "The Genesis of the Modern U.S. Navy," *U.S. Naval Institute Proceedings* 92 (March 1966): 62.

[54] Ibid., 453, 476–77.

[55] *Union-Recorder,* 28 June 1934, 1.

National Republic, and *Newsweek*.[56] A clear indication of his new celebrity status came when famed artist S. Robles did a caricature of him for The National Gallery, which appeared in the *Washington Post* on 17 May 1934. In the caption under the caricature Robles astutely observed that "Admirals and even his enemies like him while knowing that he is the sharpest, shrewdest politico that ever cultivated a district." Born on a farm fifty years ago, his oratory is "undistinguished, but as effectively strong as any wire ever pulled. A modern Talleyrand. Hobby: Mixing political hemlock."[57]

---

[56] *New York Times*, 10 January 1932, IX, 2; "More Than Half a Billion Asked for Naval Increase," *Literary Digest*112 (23 January 1932): 8; Hancock Adams, "Uncle Sam's New Naval Plan," *National Republic* 19 (March 1932): 5–7; "Navy: House Launches Bill for Construction up to the Limit," *Newsweek* 3 (3 February 1934): 11.

[57] *Washington Post*, 17 May 1934, 6.

6

The Clouds of War

We must buy the defense the nation must have, regardless of cost.

Carl Vinson, 1950

Eugene Talmadge, who served as Georgia's governor from 1933 to 1937 and from 1941 to 1943, ran the state in a near-dictatorial fashion. Popular and flamboyant, he thrived on controversy and kept the state in turmoil throughout his tenure. When the General Assembly refused to adopt his program, he ruled by executive decree; when labor unions tried to gain a foothold in the textile industries, he called out 4,000 national guardsmen and brutally crushed the unions; when he was about to be impeached for misusing state funds, he explained to the people, "Shore [*sic*] I stole, but I stole it for you." To appeal to his rural supporters, the red-gallused governor erected a henhouse and grazed a cow on the Executive Mansion grounds. Although he voted for Roosevelt in 1932, he soon became disillusioned with the New Deal. He once referred to CCC workers as "bums and loafers." By 1935 he had become a bitter critic of Roosevelt and had aspirations of supplanting him in 1936. When his preliminary organizational efforts failed disastrously, he lowered his sights to the United States Senate. In 1936 Richard Russell, then a supporter of the New Deal, defeated him soundly, and two years later Walter George defeated him too. Despite his failure to gain an office in Washington, he maintained popular support in Georgia, winning the governorship again in 1940 and in 1946, the year of his death.[1]

Carl Vinson, who was never close to Talmadge personally, disliked the governor's style and his ultra-conservative policies. He was not considered anti-Talmadge, however, and their contact at Democratic Party functions was civil, if not friendly. Vinson basically tended to his own business and tried to stay out of Talmadge's way. But he, too, was drawn into one of Talmadge's controversies. The governor, rebuffed in his attempt to reorganize the Highway Department, the patronage center of Georgia's government, which spent 53 percent of the state budget, declared martial law, ousted the Highway Board, and appointed a new board consisting of his friends and relatives.[2] The federal government responded by withholding $10 million in road funds until the courts had accepted the legality of the new board. Vinson, who was always eager to secure federal funds for roads, wanted a bridge constructed over the Oconee River in Milledgeville, another bridge over the Ocmulgee River in Macon, and a third bridge across the Oconee River at Ball's Ferry. He also sought several paving projects throughout his district.[3] The pragmatic Vinson, concerned about the thousands of Georgians out of work, thought squabbling over the terms and conditions of the road fund was utterly foolish.[4] When he publicly advocated accepting the $10 million under federal supervision, Talmadge accused him of betraying the state. Vinson countered by strongly implying that Talmadge had refused the money with federal controls only because "he will be unable to play politics with this money."[5] Vinson met with the Georgia congressional delegation both in Atlanta and in Washington in futile efforts to secure the release of the $10 million.[6] The dispute continued

---

[1] William Anderson, *The Wild Man from Sugar Creek* (Baton Rouge: Louisiana State University Press, 1975); James F. Cook, *The Governors of Georgia, 1754–1995* (Macon GA: Mercer University Press, 1995) 228–34.

[2] Anderson, *The Wild Man from Sugar Creek*, 86–95.

[3] *Union-Recorder*, 31 August 1933, 1.

[4] Carl Vinson to Charles J. Bloch, 26 August 1933, box 1, folder 3, Charles J. Bloch Papers, Middle Georgia Regional Library, Macon, GA.

[5] *Union-Recorder*, 31 August 1933, 1.

[6] Ibid., 17 August 1933, 4; 24 August 1933, 1.

throughout 1934, an election year, which saw Talmadge carry 156 of the state's 159 counties in the Democratic primary.

Early in 1935, when the federal government notified the Georgia Highway Board that the funding would start with the construction of a bridge over the Oconee River to be called the Ball's Ferry Bridge, Talmadge exploded. An avid states' righter, he did not want that bridge built and he bluntly refused to accept federal interference in a state matter. He stumped the state blaming the federal government for holding up Georgia's federal road money.[7] Hoping to resolve the dispute, mutual friends arranged for Talmadge to meet with FDR in the White House on 17 July. The meeting was a fiasco, as Thomas McDonald, chief of the Federal Bureau of Roads, insisted that nothing would be spent until the Ball's Ferry Bridge had been built—whether Georgia liked it or not. Before a gathering of newsmen in the lobby of the Mayflower Hotel, Talmadge then loudly berated Roosevelt as a "damned communist."[8] Vinson, visiting his parents in Milledgeville for a few days, refused to comment on the controversy except to say that he would insist on the construction of the Ball's Ferry Bridge.[9] On 15 August, Roosevelt wrote to Georgia's congressmen explaining that the sole question is the adequacy of the state highway organization to provide plans and supervise the expenditure of these millions. Tired of the lengthy controversy, he suggested that the Ball's Ferry Bridge issue could be decided later. With that concession, Talmadge agreed to reorganize the Highway Department and the controversy finally ended.[10] Some years later, when the Ball's Ferry Bridge was constructed, the Highway Board placed a plaque on the bridge honoring Vinson.[11]

Rumors circulated that former Representative Carlton Mobley of Forsyth, Governor Talmadge's secretary, was planning to challenge

---

[7] Anderson, *Wild Man from Sugar Creek*, 131–33.

[8] Ibid., 133–34.

[9] *Union-Recorder*, 1 August 1935, 1.

[10] Anderson, *Wild Man from Sugar Creek*, 134–36; Thomas H. Coode, "Georgia Congressmen and the New Deal, 1933–1938" (Ph. D. diss., University of Georgia, 1966) 148–50.

[11] *Union-Recorder*, 12 January 1939, 1.

Vinson in the 1934 Democratic primary.[12] Mobley decided against the race, and Vinson, as usual, was elected without opposition. Two years later, ex-Congresswoman Jeannette Rankin waged a vigorous campaign against Vinson. The Montana pacifist had moved to Georgia in 1924, purchasing a farm ten miles west of Athens and fifty miles north of Vinson's farm. Working for the National Council for Prevention of War, she had toured his district in 1930 trying to build up peace sentiment. In a luncheon visit with Congressman Vinson in Milledgeville, she explained what she was doing, and he replied, "What you are doing is getting a lot of these people so they will write to you next winter when the Navy bills come up."[13] She continued to organize peace societies on the local level and to oppose Vinson in 1932 and 1934. But in 1936, following the passage of the Vinson-Trammell Act and neutrality legislation, she, along with college students trained in the Emergency Peace Campaign, waged a vigorous ten-week campaign against the reelection of Vinson. Her methodology included thousands of personal contacts, extensive literature distribution, several mass meetings, and parades. Unfortunately for Rankin, the two candidates she had hoped to put up against Vinson declined to run, and a desperate attempt to recruit a third candidate came too late to certify. Vinson won the Democratic primary without opposition and polled 30,603 votes—almost 10,000 more votes than he had received in 1934. Instead of hurting him, the peace campaign, as historian Ted Harris notes, "actually brought out the voters to give him the largest victory to that date."[14] Vinson's popular support was so great that between 1920 and 1946 he had opposition only in 1932, and in that race he easily crushed R. Earl Camp. Yet, despite such success, he never took his reelection for granted. His sensitive political antennae were always on the alert for potential opposition, and his numerous friends kept him well informed of developments in the Sixth District. From Washington he expressed gratitude to his friends, especially Charles Bloch in Macon and Erwin Sibley in Milledgeville for

[12] *Atlanta Constitution*, 4 March 1934, A12.
[13] Ted Carlton Harris, *Jeannette Rankin: Suffragist, First Woman Elected to Congress, and Pacifist* (New York: Arno Press, 1982) 180, 202–205.
[14] Ibid., 249–54.

"keeping down opposition" and keeping him informed of any rumors of opposition.[15] Whenever Congress was not in session, he was back in the Sixth District, tending his farm, chatting with constituents and learning of their particular needs, and giving speeches throughout the district. His close, personal contact with the voters certainly contributed to his remarkable success at the polls.

Another reason for Vinson's continued success at the polls was his careful attention to the needs of constituents. He had gained national attention by his leadership on the Naval Affairs Committee, but since he represented a landlocked agrarian district, he devoted much time to agricultural issues and "pork barrel" projects for his constituents. When he represented the Tenth District, he secured for Augusta one of the largest veteran's hospitals in the South and supported a river and harbor bill that included a survey of the Savannah River. He also introduced a measure calling for the investigation of the New York Cotton Exchange and another to change the Federal Farm Loan Act so that applicants were eligible to obtain money from a local bank for the liquidation of debts. He opposed the tariff bill, the $500,000,000 railroad refunding bill, and the anti-lynching bill.[16] In December 1923 he introduced a soldiers' bonus bill, a bill to reduce railroad rates, and a bill to reduce the income tax.[17] After he had represented the Tenth District four terms, the *Augusta Chronicle* editorialized that he had "ably and energetically" represented the people and had won their "complete confidence."[18] In December 1927 he introduced several bills to benefit the cotton farmers, including a bill to prohibit the secretary of agriculture from issuing any publication containing any prediction with respect to cotton prices, another requiring the Department of Agriculture to take an actual census of the number of acres planted in cotton each year, and a third to take calcium arsenate

---

[15] Carl Vinson to Charles Bloch, 14 February 1934, Charles Bloch Papers, box 1 folder 3, 9 May 1936 and 14 May 1936, box 2, folder 8; Carl Vinson to Erwin Sibley, 26 April 1932, U. Erwin Sibley Papers, 1932–April 1933 folder, Special Collections, Ina Dillard Russell Library, Georgia College and State University, Milledgeville, GA.

[16] *Union-Recorder*, 7 March 1923, 1.

[17] Ibid., 5 December 1923, 1.

[18] Ibid., 24 September 1924, 4, quoting the *Augusta Chronicle*.

from the dutiable list and place it on the free list.[19] After he switched to the Sixth District and achieved distinction as chairman of the Naval Affairs Committee, he continued to do all he could for the farmers and used his considerable influence to secure funding for roads, post offices, and other projects.[20] One of the projects he was particularly interested in was the Ocmulgee National Monument at Macon, which was secured in 1936.[21]

Beginning in the early-1930s and continuing thereafter, rumors circulated that Vinson was in line for some federal appointment. Erwin Sibley heard such a rumor in the spring of 1933, and Vinson acknowledged that someone else had heard that he was going to be named assistant secretary of the navy.[22] Press reports also indicated that Vinson had been urged to run for governor against Talmadge. At the same time another rumor claimed that Secretary of the Navy Claude Swanson was going to resign due to ill health and that Vinson might be named his successor.[23] Vinson's response to such rumors was always the same; namely, that he had no "interest in any position other than the one for which I have been elected."[24] In July 1939 when Secretary Swanson did die, there was a groundswell of support for Vinson to replace him. Members of the House Naval Affairs Committee circulated a petition urging Vinson as his successor, and members of the Georgia congressional delegation launched a similar boom. In a letter of recommendation to President Roosevelt, Representative Robert Ramspeck lauded Vinson as the "best informed" layman on naval matters in the country. Moreover, Ramspeck continued, "He has been a

---

[19] Ibid., 8 December 1927, 1.

[20] Ibid., 29 May 1930, 1, 6; 10 December 1931, 16; 26 May 1932, 1; 28 June 1934, 1; 13 December 1934, 1; 11 February 1937, 5; 11 November 1937, 1.

[21] Carl Vinson to Marvin McIntyre, 23 January 1936; White House Memorandum, 31 January 1936; Marvin McIntyre to Carl Vinson, 4 February 1936, President's Personal File, 5901, Roosevelt Library, Hyde Park NY.

[22] Carl Vinson to Erwin Sibley, May 3, 1933, Erwin Sibley Papers, May–July 1933 folder.

[23] *Union-Recorder*, March 15, 1934, 6.

[24] Carl Vinson to Erwin Sibley, May 3, 1933, Erwin Sibley Papers, May–July 1933 folder.

loyal supporter of you and the Democratic Party. He is able and capable, and I believe would reflect much credit upon you." Vinson, however, had no desire to leave the House for any position. In withdrawing his name from consideration, he stated, "I do not aspire to this honor."[25]

Although the navy was Vinson's primary interest, he also supported Roosevelt's domestic reforms with enthusiasm. Like most Democrats, he followed the president's leadership during the first "Hundred Days" and consistently voted for New Deal reforms thereafter. Despite some concern about concentrating more power in Washington, Vinson believed the AAA, CCC, TVA, REA, Social Security, and a host of New Deal measures regulating business, creating jobs, and providing direct relief were necessary to combat the Depression. Clearly "the most ardent New Dealer in the [Georgia] congressional delegation," he often heaped praise upon President Roosevelt.[26] In accepting the Democratic Party nomination in September 1936, he concluded his address by saying that "one name shall shine upon the pages of history that is darkened with the account of the depression. It will be the name of that great humanitarian, that bold and courageous leader, whose every pulsation of heart beats in harmony and unison with that of the average man. It will be the name of Franklin Delano Roosevelt."[27] Yet, his admiration for the president did not prevent him from pursuing an independent course from time to time. Roosevelt opposed paying veterans a bonus, whereas Vinson had championed their cause for years. While the Vinson-Trammell Act was being enacted, Congress passed a bill providing veterans a bonus and federal workers a pay increase, which Roosevelt vetoed. Vinson was among the 310 members of the House who overrode the president's

---

[25] Vinson Scrapbooks, book 1919–1939, on loan from Tillman Snead to Georgia College and State University, Milledgeville, GA; White House Memorandum, 13 July 1939, President's Personal File, 5901, Roosevelt Library. In subsequent years, Vinson was often rumored to be in line for the position of secretary of the navy. His standard reply was, "I'd rather run the Pentagon from up here."

[26] Coode, "Georgia Congressmen and the New Deal," 72.

[27] *Union-Recorder*, 17 September 1936, 1.

veto.[28] Vinson saw the need for New Deal relief measures, but he forcefully criticized the wasteful practices of some agencies. After observing relief programs in Georgia and talking to constituents, he returned to Washington in November 1934 and declared that federal relief was being administered by a "bunch of school children." Agreeing with Senator Borah, he announced, "There is a huge waste in these enormous expenditures and there should be no hesitancy in starting an investigation."[29] Whether it was military procurement or federal relief, Vinson never forgot that all government expenditures came from the taxpayers, and he expected a dollar's worth of value for every dollar expended.

The peace societies, frustrated by the passage of the Vinson-Trammell Act, did not give up the fight to reduce armaments. Indeed they redoubled their efforts. Operating on the premise that armaments themselves create wars, they attempted to convince the American people that disarmament was the surest road to world peace. Senator Gerald Nye of North Dakota, a tense, determined, humorless man, who had little knowledge of either the munitions industry or the disarmament problem, but equipped with a high school education, some journalistic experience, and nine years of experience in the Senate, chaired a Senate investigative committee that was destined to leave a strong imprint on American politics in the pre-war years. Dominated by isolationists, the Nye Committee intended to prove that the munitions trade, unless curbed by the government, was likely to involve the United States in foreign wars. Shortly after the passage of the Vinson-Trammell Act, it began searching through the files of the major munitions companies for evidence to present at the public hearings, scheduled to begin in September.[30]

During the period 1934 to 1936, the Nye Committee questioned nearly two hundred witnesses, spent more than $130,000, and published

---

[28] *Atlanta Constitution*, 13 March 1934, 1, 9; 15 March 1934, 1; 27 March 1934, 1; 28 March 1934, 1, 9; 29 March 1934, 1; Carl Vinson to Erwin Sibley, 28 April 1932 and 27 May 1932, Erwin Sibley Papers, 1932–April 1933 folder.

[29] *New York Times*, 24 November 1934, 3.

[30] Robert A Divine, *The Illusion of Neutrality* (Chicago: University of Chicago Press, 1962) 62–67; Selig Adler, *The Isolationist Impulse* (Westport CT: Greenwood Press, 1957) 256–57.

thirty-nine volumes of testimony totaling 13,750 pages of fine print.[31] A Nye Committee report, made public in 1935, was some 1,400 pages long. "Only those inured to cruel and unusual punishment read it in its raw form," Selig Adler dryly observed; "the rest absorbed the message after it had been pre-digested and garnished."[32] But it is safe to say that the main ideas of the highly publicized report reached the public in some fashion. In tedious detail it revealed that munitions makers had an international cartel, that their agents had lobbied Congress and international conferences, and that their profits had increased dramatically in World War I. All of this was true, but it did not prove that munitions makers and Wall Street bankers had somehow convinced or coerced President Wilson and Congress to intervene on the side that owed a few of its citizens a great deal of money. The events of 1914–1917 were too complex for any simplistic interpretation, as many competent historians have demonstrated. But in 1935 the country was in a mood to give credence to the Nye theory, as events in Europe and Asia jeopardized peace and scholars, such as Walter Millis, Charles Tansill, and Charles Beard, elaborated on the disillusionment theory.[33]

In *Road to War: America, 1914-1917*, Walter Millis, an editorial writer for the *New York Herald Tribune*, implied that American participation in the war was due to British propaganda, unwise American decisions on neutrality, and the close economic ties between the United States and the Allies. *Road to War* became a Book-of-the-Month Club selection and sold over 20,000 copies.[34] A few years later, Professor Charles Tansill published *America Goes to War*, which for many years was the most comprehensive account of the collapse of neutrality in 1917. Although scholarly and restrained, it implied that a German victory would have been preferable to an Allied triumph at the expense of

---

[31] Wayne S. Cole, *Senator Gerald P. Nye and American Foreign Relations* (Minneapolis: University of Minnesota Press, 1962) 79.

[32] Adler, *The Isolationist Impulse*, 257.

[33] Ibid., 257–59.

[34] Divine, *The Illusion of Neutrality*, 77–78; Walter Millis, *Road to War: America, 1914–1917* (Boston: Houghton Mifflin Company, 1935).

American participation in the war.[35] Professor Charles Beard, perhaps
America's most prominent historian, wrote a series of books and articles
that reinforced the findings of the Nye Committee. He argued that the
United States had entered World War I because it had supplied the Allies
with such vast quantities of money and goods that it had to insure the
military victory of our debtors. Although Beard deplored the triumph of
barbarism abroad, he, like many liberals of the day, placed a higher
priority on the future of domestic reform than on the fate of freedom in
the world.[36]

By the summer of 1935, many Americans had become deeply
concerned by the aggressive actions of Germany, Italy, and Japan and
feared that continued aggression might well produce another world war
that inevitably would involve the United States. As the aggressor nations
threatened the status quo in Europe and the Far East, Americans
desperately looked for a way to insulate themselves from the possibility
of war. Adolf Hitler, who became chancellor of Germany at the same
time Roosevelt was inaugurated as president, had quickly established a
Nazi dictatorship and eliminated all opposition parties. In the fall 1933
Germany withdrew from the Geneva Disarmament Conference and
severed its ties with the League of Nations. After secretly building up his
military in violation of the Treaty of Versailles, Hitler announced on 16
March 1935, that Germany was inaugurating a policy of universal
military conscription designed to raise an army of 500,000 men. Britain
and France protested this violation of the Treaty of Versailles, but Britain
essentially condoned it by signing a treaty with Germany in June
allowing Hitler to build a navy one-third the size of the British Navy.[37]

Benito Mussolini, who had seized power in Italy in 1922, harbored
vague ambitions of reviving the grandeur of ancient Rome. After
establishing a Fascist state, eliminating all opposing parties, and building
up his military, he embarked on a series of foreign conquests. In
December 1934 he sent troops into Ethiopia. After a border clash at

---

35 Adler, *The Isolationist Impulse*, 259; Charles C. Tansill, *America Goes
to War* (Boston: Little, Brown and Company, 1938).

36 Adler, *The Isolationist Impulse*, 259–60.

37 Divine, *The Illusion of Neutrality*, 81–82.

Walwal, he sent in reinforcements, and by summer 1935 it was clear that Mussolini intended to march against Ethiopia. Since Emperor Haile Selassic was going to resist the Italians, there would be war.[38]

Japan, which had conquered Manchuria and withdrawn from the League of Nations, seemed determined to expand her empire in the Pacific. Increasingly controlled by militarists, that island nation continued to build up its army and navy and chafed under the 5-5-3 ratio in effect since 1921. Indeed in December 1934, ten days after the termination of the preliminary negotiations of the London Conference, where British, American, and Japanese delegates failed to negotiate an agreement, Japan gave formal notice of its denunciation of the Washington Treaty to take effect on 1 January 1937.[39] Henceforth there would be no treaty limitation on the size of the Japanese Navy.

Contrary to what some believed, Vinson did not want an arms race, nor did he object to arms limitation. In fact, he repeatedly reiterated his commitment to arms limitation. What he objected to was the British and Japanese building to the limits of the treaty or beyond, while the United States lagged far behind its treaty limit, thereby jeopardizing its security. He sincerely hoped that Japan would not scrap the Washington Treaty, but when it became apparent that she intended to do so, he stated unequivocally that the United States "cannot grant naval equality to Japan at any price." It must maintain superiority over the Japanese Navy by the same ratio, with or without a treaty. Convinced that the Washington Treaty ratio was fair, he declared, "I will insist that the Naval Affairs Committee and Congress make enough money available to build five ships for each three laid down by Japan."[40] Some months later, when reports indicated that Great Britain planned to embark on a new naval building program, President Roosevelt publicly declared his commitment to the 5-5-3 ratio. Traveling to the Pacific to view naval maneuvers, the president told reporters that the United States adhered to the Washington and London treaties and "only in the event that other

---

[38] Ibid., 82–83; Adler, *The Isolationist Impulse*, 261.

[39] Meredith W. Berg, "The United States and the Breakdown of Naval Limitation, 1934–1939" (Ph.D. diss,, Tulane University, 1966) 78–79.

[40] *New York Times*, 28 November 1934, 9.

nations exceed the limits provided by these treaties" would American policy change.[41]

Having secured legislation to bring the American Navy up to treaty strength by 1942, Vinson, working closely with the Navy Department and the Roosevelt administration, sought to remedy three remaining deficiencies in the navy—aircraft, personnel, and auxiliary ships. In August 1934 he told reporters he was drafting a new five-year air expansion program for presentation to the next Congress. "While the navy now has around 1,000 planes, only 400 are suitable for wartime service. We need more of the fighting types," he said. Congress, he pointed out, had already authorized 2,100 planes, but had not yet appropriated the money for construction. As always, he favored a systematic construction schedule in preference to haphazard and sporadic purchasing of planes, which leads to waste.[42]

In explaining to the House H. R. 7672, the Naval Appropriations bill, which called for an appropriation of $460,000,000, the largest peacetime appropriation for the navy, Vinson attempted to allay the fears of pacifists and other critics of increased armaments by emphasizing the peaceful nature of America. He again outlined the sacrifices the United States had made at the Washington Conference and noted that the appropriation was so high only because the navy had been "woefully neglected" for many years. Other nations did not follow the United States' lead to "disarm by example," he pointed out; instead they increased the size of their navies. The United States would be the first to applaud limitation to a lower level, but must maintain a navy of underage ships substantially in the ratio now fixed by international agreement. Every ship authorized by Congress, he emphasized, had been strictly in accordance with the terms of the treaty. "Each and every one of them is a replacement ship. There will be no naval race, unless some country goes beyond the ratio fixed by the Washington and London Treaties, and this country does not propose to go beyond those ratios." Putting the matter in a different perspective, he then asked Congress several questions:

[41] Ibid., 28 September 1935, 1, 3.
[42] Ibid., 14 August 1934, 12.

Are the people of this country willing to send their sons to meet an enemy in ships that are old, slow, and obsolete and inferior in strength in order to save a few dollars? Is the defense of our country to be jeopardized? Are the lives of your sons and grandsons to be offered up as a living sacrifice because you are unwilling to provide the funds for the support of a proper navy in times of peace? The answer to all is emphatically "No."[43]

Vinson explained that when the navy had been brought up to treaty strength in 1942, it would consist of 15 battleships, 6 aircraft carriers, 18 heavy cruisers, 17 light cruisers, 13 heavy destroyers, 84 light destroyers, and 38 submarines, as well as about 1,910 planes. To support a fleet of 191 fighting ships required 122 other ships, such as minecraft, supply ships, hospital ships, oilers, transports, repair ships, ocean tugs, repair ships and tenders, and patrol vessels. To operate such a fleet in peace times necessitated additional personnel, and Vinson estimated that the navy would require 7,941 line officers, of which 1,908 would be aviators, and approximately 110,000 enlisted men. H. R. 5599, a bill defining the strength and distribution of the navy, provided for a gradual increase in navy personnel.[44]

In addition to writing legislation which provided for the construction of new vessels, Vinson also introduced a bill early in 1936 that would provide an extensive modernization of the older vessels in the fleet. This measure supplemented the Vinson-Trammell Act and aided in providing a treaty-strength navy by 1942.[45] Before pushing through legislation to permit the laying down of two additional battleships, the chairman awaited the call of the president. Hoping to avoid a naval race, Roosevelt held back the authorization until other nations began building battleships. Vinson agreed with this approach. After the London Treaty expired on 31 December 1936, and it was apparent that Britain and Japan

---

[43] *Congressional Record*, 74th Cong., 1st sess., 25 April 1935, 6388–91.

[44] Ibid., 27 March 1935, 4550–53.

[45] Calvin W. Enders, "The Vinson Navy" (Ph.D. diss., Michigan State University, 1970) 96–97.

were building battleships, Roosevelt ordered the construction of two new battleships.[46]

While Vinson and Roosevelt were trying to strengthen the navy to face a threatening international scene, isolationists and pacifists were moving in the opposite direction. Isolationists opposed any form of international commitment, and pacifists sought a reduction in armaments as a means of avoiding war. Their strength was growing, as the president discovered when he sought Senate approval of American adherence to the World Court. Roosevelt expected an easy victory in this innocuous measure to honor a campaign promise, but when an avalanche of letters and telegrams, stimulated by the Hearst press and the Detroit radio priest, Father Charles Coughlin, descended on the Senate opposing the Court as a backdoor entrance to the League of Nations, the mood shifted. The final vote on 29 January 1935 fell seven votes short of the required two-thirds majority.[47]

The growing isolationism of the American people in the mid-1930s was accompanied by a surge of pacifism among college students. In spring 1933 the Brown University campus newspaper, reacting against newsreels that glorified military and naval preparedness, conducted a poll of college opinion on war. Of the 20,000 students who participated in 65 colleges, 72 percent voted against serving in the armed services in wartime, with nearly half stating that they would not bear arms even if the United States were invaded.[48] On 13 April 1934, an estimated 25,000 students left their classes to attend anti-war demonstrations where students and faculty members gave impassioned speeches denouncing military service and urging the youth to pledge themselves never "to support the Government of the United States in any war it might conduct."[49] On 12 April 1935, a reported 60,000 students participated in the anti-war strike. In New York City, 10,000 youths paraded on campuses carrying placards that read, "Life Is Short Enough," "Build

---

[46] Ibid., 97; *New York Times*, 29 April 1936, 7.
[47] Divine, *The Illusion of Neutrality*, 83.
[48] Ibid., 84.
[49] *New York Times*, 14 April 1934, 1.

Schools—Not Battleships," and "Abolish the R.O.T.C."[50] "Though representing only a tiny fraction of the nation's youth, the college pacifists," historian Robert Divine points out, "reflected the distaste for war which underlay the dominant isolationism of the American people."[51]

Capitalizing on the fears and uncertainty of the period, isolationists and pacifists joined together to pressure Congress to pass neutrality legislation. The Neutrality Act of 1935 mandated an arms embargo to all belligerents. It also prohibited the carrying of munitions in American ships to belligerents and proclaimed that American citizens traveling on belligerent ships do so at their own risk. Although Roosevelt had misgivings about the bill, he was unwilling to jeopardize important domestic legislation to wage a costly political battle over it. Therefore, hoping the next Congress would adopt a more flexible policy, he signed the bill on 31 August 1935, and declared, "it is entirely satisfactory."[52] On 3 October 1935, Mussolini launched his long-expected invasion of Ethiopia. Most Americans sympathized with Emperor Haile Selassie and the victimized Ethiopians, who were no match for a modern army backed with aircraft, artillery, and tanks, but the Neutrality Act prevented the United States from taking sides. The law prevented the sale of armaments, but it said nothing about raw materials. In many ways, raw materials—especially oil—proved more valuable than arms in the Italian-Ethiopian War. As a result, both the isolationists and the internationalists agreed that broader legislation to include controls on all categories of exports was needed. Congress responded by adopting the Neutrality Act of 1936, which continued the arms embargo and travel restriction of the first act and added the prohibition of loans. Rather than giving the president greater flexibility, as Roosevelt desired, it restricted his options in foreign policy. The old law provided that, if an existing war spread, the president was authorized to extend the arms embargo to the new belligerents; the new one *directed* him to extend the provisions of the law to all nations which entered an existing conflict. This meant

---

[50] Ibid., 13 April 1935, 1, 3.
[51] Divine, *The Illusion of Neutrality*, 84.
[52] Ibid., 85–117.

that if France or England should go to war to defend Ethiopia against the aggressor Mussolini, the president would have to embargo munitions and loans to them.[53]

The Neutrality Act of 1936 passed the House on 17 February by vote of 353 to 27, with 50 not voting. Vinson voted with the majority. Debate in the House was limited to forty minutes, and only one speaker, Vinson's colleague on the Naval Affairs Committee Melvin Maas of Minnesota, opposed the fundamental concept of neutrality legislation. Maas, a veteran of World War I who would later serve with distinction in the South Pacific in World War II, warned that rigid neutrality aided aggressors. He called the bill "cruel," "un-American," and "a dangerous surrender of American ideals to timid political expediency." With uncanny foresight, he prophesied:

> While for a time we may escape involvement in foreign wars, the ultimate outcome will be that a few powerful, militaristic nations, unchecked by anything, will gradually create a situation of world-wide conquest, and the time will come when we alone will be left in the way of their complete world dominance. As surely as we take this attitude of smug indifference now, we ourselves will then become the object of attack and invasion.[54]

When the three-year Spanish civil war broke out in the summer of 1936, it revealed that the neutrality laws did not apply to internal conflict. General Francisco Franco, who led the rebels, received valuable support of arms and men from both Hitler and Mussolini. Hitler, especially, seemed to view Spain as a testing ground for new weapons and bombing techniques. The Fascist press celebrated the fall of Malaga,

---

[53] Ibid., 122–61; Adler, *The Isolationist Impulse*, 262–63; Thomas A. Bailey, *A Diplomatic History of the American People*, 10th ed. (Englewood Cliffs NJ: Prentice-Hall, Inc., 1980) 701.

[54] *Congressional Record*, 74th Cong., 2d sess., 17 February 1936, 2246–53; *Biographical Directory of the American Congress, 1774–1971* (Washington, DC: Government Printing Office, 1971) 1320.

and the Nazis made no attempt to disguise the airplanes that bombed Bilbao. The Loyalist regime received a smaller amount of aid from the Russians as well as the services of a few thousand American volunteers who fought in the Abraham Lincoln brigade and other Loyalist units. At Roosevelt's request, Congress extended the existing neutrality legislation to civil conflict with only one dissenting vote in both houses on 6 January 1937. A few months later Congress enacted "permanent" neutrality legislation. The Neutrality Act of 1937 was, as historian Warren Kimball notes, a "curious compromise." While the law extended the arms embargo and the ban on loans and forbade American citizens to sail on belligerent ships, it also allowed the president to authorize the cash sale of goods to belligerents, providing they were not shipped in American vessels.[55] This controversial "cash and carry" provision showed that Congress, while determined to avoid all risks of war, still hoped to reap some of the profits of foreign trade. Although the "cash and carry" provision received harsh criticism from both internationalists and nationalists alike, the measure passed both houses by huge majorities (376 to 16 in the House, 63 to 6 in the Senate). Vinson voted with the majority. The president, suffering a backlash from his ill-fated proposal to enlarge the Supreme Court, momentarily had minimal influence on Congress. Yielding to expediency, he signed the bill on 1 May, the day the old law expired.[56]

Responding to the unpopularity of American involvement in World War I, the American government, backed by a majority of the American people, had adopted neutrality laws that would keep the country out of a 1914 war. The *New York Herald Tribune* jeered that the Neutrality Law of 1937 should read: "An Act to Preserve the United States from

---

[55] Warren F. Kimball, *The Most Unsordid Act: Lend-Lease, 1939–1941* (Baltimore: Johns Hopkins Press, 1969) 2–3.

[56] Divine, *The Illusion of Neutrality*, 162–99; Adler, *The Isolationist Impulse*, 262–65; Bailey, *A Diplomatic History*, 701–703; William E. Leuchtenburg, *Franklin D. Roosevelt and the New Deal* (New York: Harper & Row, 1963) 217–25; *Congressional Record*, 75th Cong., 1st sess., 18 March 1937, 2410; Louis Fischer, "Keeping America Out of War," *Nation* 144 (27 March 1937): 347–49.

Intervention in the War of 1917–1918."[57] Unfortunately, the neutrality laws did not keep the country out of the next war. Indeed, as Selig Adler notes, "The congressional isolationists, so anxious to keep out of war, actually helped invite a foreign catastrophe of such immense proportions that no nation could have escaped its consequences."[58]

Vinson had not been directly involved in the passage of neutrality legislation. As usual, he supported the president, but aside from backing an occasional farm bill, honoring individual constituent needs, and delivering eulogies for dead or retired colleagues, his speeches on the floor of the House were confined to naval affairs. He also backed the president's controversial attempt to streamline the executive branch of government in 1938. After the measure had been defeated in the House, he informed his best friend Erwin Sibley that there was no cause for "anyone to fear dictatorship," but the opposition sent telegrams to Washington by "the hundreds of thousands" and they had the desired result.[59]

In early February 1935 as the first neutrality law was being debated, Vinson left Congress briefly for a special event in Milledgeville—the sixtieth wedding anniversary of his parents. It was a gala occasion, as Carl, along with his sister Hattie Cannon from Cordele, his sister Mabel Guyton from Dublin, their spouses, several grandchildren, and other family members enjoyed a turkey dinner together. The Vinson house was filled with flowers and messages of congratulations from every section of the country. Carl's brothers Ed in Cordele, Fred in Newport News, Virginia, and Wilbur, a captain in the United States Army stationed in Fort Howard, Maryland, were not able to attend, nor was his sister Leila Pollard in Jacksonville, Florida. The *Union-Recorder* offered the following tribute to the couple that had lived so many years in Milledgeville: "They have lived wisely and well, for they have reached ripe old ages and can look back on years that have been filled with good works which have been a blessing and benediction to all who have come

---

[57] Adler, *The Isolationist Impulse*, 265.

[58] Ibid.

[59] Carl Vinson to Erwin Sibley, 9 April 1938, Erwin Sibley Papers, March–December 1938 folder.

under their influence. They are sustained in their declining days by a faith in a Divine Providence, which has guided and sustained them as they have traveled life's pathway together. "[60]

Edward and Annie Vinson, Milledgeville's "good couple," as the local newspaper described them, celebrated their sixty-first anniversary the following year and remained healthy enough to have an "open house" during a convention of the Georgia Press Association in June 1936. They also celebrated their sixty-second wedding anniversary quietly at home among friends, as none of their children could be with them. But that would be their last one. Seriously ill for several weeks, Annie died on 17 August 1937, at age eighty-two.[61] Her death brought sorrow to the Vinson family and to her many friends in Milledgeville, where she had lived for half a century. The *Union-Recorder* editorialized that "a more generally loved citizen cannot be found."[62] After Annie's death, her daughter Leila lived with Edward, who remained clear-headed and enjoyed visiting friends, neighbors, and the farm until the end. Carl spent much time with him when Congress was not in session and had lengthy visits with him in March and April. Edward's fatal illness lasted only a few days. He died on 10 October 1938, at age eighty-eight, and was buried beside Annie in the Vinson family plot in Memory Hill Cemetery in Milledgeville.[63]

Speaker of the House Joseph Byrns of Tennessee, who had succeeded Henry Rainey of Illinois, died near the end of the 1936 session and William Bankhead of Alabama was selected as his successor. Bankhead became the seventh Speaker Vinson had served under. When he entered the House in 1914, Champ Clark of Missouri presided over the House. During the Republican-dominated 1920s, Frederick Gillett of Massachusetts was Speaker in the Sixty-sixth, Sixty-seventh, and Sixty-eighth Congresses, and Nicholas Longworth of Ohio presided over the

---

[60] *Macon Telegraph and News*, 3 February 1935, 4; *Union-Recorder*, 7 February 1935, 10, and other undated issues in Vinson Scrapbooks, book 1919–1939.

[61] *Union-Recorder*, 25 June 1936, 9; 19 August 1937, 1.

[62] Ibid., 26 August 1937, 4.

[63] Ibid., 24 March 1938, 1; 7 April 1938, 10; 28 April 1938, 1; 13 October 1938, 1.

Sixty-ninth, Seventieth, and Seventy-first Congresses. Married to Theodore Roosevelt's acerbic daughter Alice, Longworth was nearly as witty as his wife. Once a presumptuous congressman passed his hand over Longworth's bald head and remarked, "Feels just like my wife's bottom." Longworth immediately passed his own hand over his own head and said thoughtfully: "By golly, it does, doesn't it?"[64] When the Democrats regained control of the House, John Nance Garner of Texas, a very capable representative, served as Speaker for the Seventy-second Congress. His election as vice president created a vacancy filled by Rainey, a weak Speaker, who died in August 1934. Byrns also failed to manage the House business well, and he died in June 1936. After so much rapid turnover, Bankhead provided some stability, serving until his death in September 1940. Prior to becoming Speaker, Bankhead had been Democratic majority leader of the House. To succeed him, a heated contest emerged between John J. O'Connor of New York and Sam Rayburn of Texas. Vinson, who admired Rayburn and had developed a warm friendship with him, served as one of his campaign managers. He buttonholed members and worked assiduously for Rayburn's election. Vice President Garner publicly backed his protégé, and behind the scenes Roosevelt did too. Rayburn won 184 to 127.[65]

Within months of the passage of the Neutrality Act of 1937, the neutrality policy received a severe test in the Far East. In July 1937 Japanese troops clashed with elements of the Chinese Army at the Marco Polo Bridge near Peking. The fighting continued intermittently. After occupying Peking, the Japanese launched a full-scale attack on Shanghai by air, land, and sea. Although neither side declared war, this fighting proved to be the beginning of the Pacific phase of World War II. Since war had not been declared, Roosevelt did not have to invoke the neutrality law, and much to the dismay of isolationists, refused to do so.

---

[64] Stewart Alsop, *The Center: People and Power in Political Washington* (New York: Harper & Row Publishers, 1968) 80.

[65] Alfred Steinberg, *Sam Rayburn: A Biography* (New York: Hawthorn Books, 1975) 136-38; Booth Mooney, *Roosevelt and Rayburn, A Political Partnership* (Philadelphia: Lippincott, 1971) 79–82; *Members of Congress Since 1789* (Washington: Congressional Quarterly Inc., 1977) 173–74; Bascom Timmons, *Garner of Texas, A Personal History* (New York: Harper, 1948) 204.

Convinced that an arms embargo would harm China, he told the press that invoking neutrality legislation was on "a 24-hour basis." Isolationists in Congress railed at the president until Congress adjourned on 21 August; afterwards the *Christian Century*, the *New Republic*, and various pacifist groups demanded that the president immediately proclaim neutrality and warned that any attempt to choose sides would lead to disaster. Advocates of collective security, on the other hand, endorsed the administration policy. The public, though largely indifferent, tended to uphold the president's decision to avoid invoking legislation that favored Japan. When asked by a Gallup poll in early August which side they favored in the Far Eastern conflict, 55 percent replied neither, 43 percent named China, and only 2 percent listed Japan.[66]

While the fighting raged in China, Roosevelt, engaged in a speaking tour of the West, gave a major address on foreign policy in Chicago on 5 October. In forceful language, he described the breakdown of peace in the world and the spread of an "epidemic of lawlessness" by 10 percent of the population. "When an epidemic of physical disease starts to spread," he observed, "the community approves and joins in a quarantine of the patients in order to protect the health of the community against the spread of the disease." Although mentioning no aggressors by name, everyone understood that he meant Germany, Italy, and Japan. Calling for "positive efforts for peace," he presented no specific proposals either in the speech or in the weeks and months following it. Consequently, as Robert Divine notes, his "intentions remain as mysterious today as they were to contemporary observers in 1937." Nevertheless, the speech, vague as it was, incensed the isolationists. Compared to his last major address on foreign policy, the Quarantine Speech indicated that Roosevelt had abandoned his previously expressed isolationist and pacifist sentiments and had become an internationalist, concerned over rampant aggression and determined to find a means of preventing world war.[67] The president was dismayed by the widespread criticism of the

---

[66] Divine, *The Illusion of Neutrality*, 200–205; Hadley Cantril and Mildred Strunk, eds., *Public Opinion, 1935–1946* (Princeton: Princeton University Press, 1951) 1081.
[67] Divine, *The Illusion of Neutrality*, 211–13.

speech and indignant that many members of his own party refused to support his policy. "It is a terrible thing," he told a close advisor, "to look over your shoulder when you are trying to lead and find no one there."[68]

American relations with Japan deteriorated further in mid-December when the Japanese brutally bombed and sank the American gunboat *Panay* on the Yangtze River, killing three and wounding fifty. The Japanese apologized and eventually paid an indemnity of over $2 million, but the assault severely strained relations with Japan. Although the *New York Times,* the *New York Herald Tribune*, the *Washington Post*, the *Boston Herald*, the *Chicago Tribune*, and other major newspapers condemned the Japanese sinking and defended Roosevelt's policy of keeping naval forces in Chinese waters, a wave of isolationist sentiment swept through Congress demanding the withdrawal of all American nationals and armed forces from China. In the Senate, William E. Borah took the lead in opposing any firm action over the episode. He told a constituent, "I am not prepared to vote to send our boys into the Orient because a boat was sunk which was traveling in a dangerous zone." Leading the fight for an isolationist program in the House was Maury Maverick of Texas, who informed the House that "we should learn that it is about time for us to mind our own business." The public seemed to agree, as a Gallup poll taken in January 1938 revealed that 70 percent favored a complete withdrawal from China.[69]

Since 1935, Representative Louis Ludlow, an Indiana Democrat, had been sponsoring a constitutional amendment that would require a nationwide referendum before Congress could declare war. The measure had been bottled up in the Judiciary Committee, but two days after the *Panay* incident, he secured the necessary 218 votes needed to discharge his resolution from the Judiciary Committee. Church and pacifist groups hailed the referendum idea, but most newspapers severely criticized it. The *New York Times* pointed out that the entire United States fleet could be sunk anywhere overseas, but under the amendment, the government could not retaliate until a nationwide referendum was held. The *New*

---

[68] Manny T. Koginos, *The Panay Incident: Prelude to War* (Lafayette IN: Purdue University Studies, 1967) 19.

[69] Ibid. 34–74.

York Herald Tribune bluntly called it "a lunatic proposal." In a press conference on 17 December Roosevelt denounced the measure as "incompatible to the security of the nation" and went to extraordinary lengths to block its passage. Speaker Bankhead left the chair to read a warning from Roosevelt that the amendment "would cripple any President in his conduct of foreign relations and...would encourage other nations to believe that they could violate American rights with impunity." Supporters of the referendum plan, who seemed oblivious to the effect this amendment would have on the future conduct of foreign policy, fought back vigorously. New York Republican Hamilton Fish, a decorated combat veteran of World War I who represented Roosevelt's own Hyde Park district in the House, insisted that "we could do nothing better or greater for world peace than to give the American people the right to vote to stay out of war." Mrs. Caroline O'Day, a Georgia-born Democratic representative from New York, who had studied art in Paris, Munich, and Holland, lauded the Ludlow plan as "the essence of popular government." Fortunately for the country, the House rejected Ludlow's motion by a vote of 209 to 188. Carl Vinson voted with the majority, but 111 Democrats had disregarded the president and voted to strip Congress of the power to declare war. The bloc of 188 votes that supported Ludlow, William E. Leuchtenburg points out, "are a measure both of the President's tenuous control of foreign policy and, as late as 1938, of the hardrock strength of isolationist sentiment in America."[70] As war clouds were gathering in Europe and Asia, the American people were beginning

---

[70]Ibid., 80–97; Divine, *The Illusion of Neutrality*, 219–21; Leuchtenburg, *Franklin D. Roosevelt and the New Deal*, 229–30; Selig Adler, *The Uncertain Giant, 1921–1941:American Foreign Policy Between the Wars* (New York:Macmillan, 1965) 200–201; *New York Times*, 11 January 1938, 1, 18; *Biographical Directory of the American Congress*, 943, 1485 .

to understand that this nation could not remain aloof from world events. A Gallup poll in January 1938 found that only 16 percent believed that the United States could stay out of another world war, but it would take nearly four more years of aggression, including the Japanese attack on Pearl Harbor, to finally convince the isolationists in Congress.[71]

---

[71] Cantril and Strunk, *Public Opinion*, 966.

7

Father of the Two-Ocean Navy

Now, Admiral, no hemming and hawing. Let's get to the bottom of this thing.

Carl Vinson, 1939

During the years before the attack on Pearl Harbor, Carl Vinson became a regular visitor to the White House as he worked closely with President Roosevelt in formulating policies for the navy. One of the more important meetings took place on 5 January 1938. The troubling international situation had prompted Roosevelt to summon Vinson; Admiral William Leahy, chief of naval operations; Charles Edison, assistant secretary of the navy; Representative Edward Taylor of Colorado, chairman of the House Appropriations Committee; and Representative William Umstead of North Carolina, chairman of the naval subcommittee of the Appropriations Committee, to the White House for a conference. By this time, Hitler, with a rapidly improving army, navy, and air force, already had marched into the demilitarized Rhineland, was preparing to incorporate Austria into the Third Reich, and was making demands on Czechoslovakia. He had joined with Mussolini to form the Rome-Berlin Axis in 1936, and both provided aid to General Franco in the Spanish Civil War. Hitler also formed a pact with Japan, which Mussolini joined in 1937, to create the anti-democratic, anti-communistic Rome-Berlin-Tokyo Axis. The immediate causes for the conference, however, came from the Far East, where the Japanese attack on the *Panay* was followed within days by an article in an Italian newspaper which indicated that Japan had a total of 294,640 tons of new naval vessels under construction. This total meant that Japan had far exceeded the five to three ratio established at the Washington Conference, a ratio American naval experts considered crucial. Even more important, the article indicated that the new Japanese naval program included three super-battleships of 45,000 tons each and mounting 16-inch guns. By contrast, the United States had observed the 35,000 ton limit of the London Treaty of 1936 in building its newest battleships, the *North Carolina* and the *Washington*. To maintain American naval strength in comparison with other nations, the leaders at the White House conference agreed that the 1938–1939 program would have to be expanded to include two additional battleships and two light cruisers. They began to make plans to increase the total tonnage of the Navy by 20 percent above the limit established by the Vinson-Trammell Act of 1934.[1]

A well-orchestrated campaign for new armaments began a week later when Admiral Leahy, on behalf of the Navy Department, formally recommended to Roosevelt that Congress be asked for authorization to build war vessels in excess of the limits of the existing Vinson-Trammell Act. In his annual message to Congress, the president stressed the need for keeping "adequately strong in self-defense." Upon the advice of Majority Leader Sam Rayburn and others, the president delayed announcing the new plan until after the regular Naval Appropriation bill had been adopted. On 21 January 1938, the House passed the 1938–1939 naval budget of $553 million in order to continue the completion of vessels currently under construction. In steering the bill through the House over the strenuous objections of Representative Fish of New York, Vinson called for "a Navy second to none." Refusing to be drawn into the controversy over battleships versus aircraft, he insisted that it was "absolutely essential" for this nation to have both airplanes and battleships. "Aviation," he said, "is the eye of the Navy; battleships are the backbone of the Navy." While Vinson longed for the day when

---

[1] Manny T. Koginos, *The Panay Incident: Prelude to War* (Lafayette IN: Purdue University Studies) 103–104; *New York Times*, 6 January 1938, 11.

agreements can be reached limiting armaments, he pointed out that "we are forced to lay down the same kind of ships that other nations do."[2]

A few days later, the specific details of the program were worked out at a two-hour White House conference attended by Roosevelt, Vinson, Taylor, Umstead, Chairman Andrew J. May of the House Military Affairs Committee, and Chairman J. B. Snyder of the House Army Appropriations sub-committee.[3] On 28 January, the president recommended to Congress a long-range construction program for the navy and several improvements for the army, at an estimated cost of $800,000,000. This new program called for a 20 percent increase in naval authorizations for new building and replacements, the laying down this year of two additional battleships and two more cruisers, and the appropriation of $15,000,000 for new types of small ships. When completed, the United States Navy would have more combat ships than any navy currently had, but fewer than Britain would have in 1942. On the same day, Vinson, in total agreement with the president's plan, introduced in the House a bill to implement his program. In addition to the ships the president requested, the Vinson bill also authorized the president "to acquire or construct additional naval airplanes" to bring the number of useful naval aircraft to 3,000.[4]

Vinson promptly opened hearings on H. R. 9218 in the Naval Affairs Committee on 31 January. The first and most important witness to testify was Admiral Leahy. Having chaired the committee for several years, Vinson had developed a reputation as a forceful and eccentric chairman. Critics called him a dictator. But all agreed that he got things done in a unique manner. Since he frowned on closed meetings, reporters often attended Naval Affairs Committee meetings, which one writer

---

[2] Koginos, *The Panay Incident*, 104–105; *Congressional Record*, 75th Cong., 3rd sess., 19 January 1938, 917; Memorandum for the President, 15 January 1938, President's Personal File, 5901, Roosevelt Library, Hyde Park NY; *New York Times*, 14 January 1938, 2; 22 January 1938, 1, 4.

[3] New York Times, 23 January 1938, 1, 29; Calvin W. Enders, "The Vinson Navy" (Ph.D. diss., Michigan State University, 1970) 101–102; *Washington Post*, 26 January 1938, 1, 7.

[4] *Washington Post*, 29 January 1938, 1, 5; *New York Times*, 29 January 1938, 1, 4, 5.

described as "one of Capitol Hill's best shows." Since Capitol Hill is overrun with "professional" witnesses who spend their days trying to tell Congress how to run the country, the ability to control testimony is an essential asset for a congressional chairman. When testimony before the Naval Affairs Committee proved unproductive or repetitious, Vinson emptied the witness chair in a hurry. A lady who was in and out of the Capitol as often as famed doorkeeper "Fishbait" Miller persuaded Vinson to give her ten minutes to talk to the committee about the draft act. When her turn came, she unfolded an impressive sheaf of notes and began a rapid-fire recitation. Five minutes elapsed and Vinson banged his gavel. "Your time has run out," he said. The lady was indignant. "I was supposed to talk ten minutes," she protested. The chairman peered down at the witness from his lofty seat. "You talk so fast," he said, "You put an awful heap in the five minutes." When a naval engineer told the committee there was no reason why a well-built hangar at Miami should collapse under a hurricane wind, Vinson put on his horn-rimmed spectacles, peered over them, and pointed to the witness. "That's just the kind of an architect they have been looking for down there," he said. The chairman had no patience for equivocation or unnecessary delay from any witnesses, including the highest-ranking officers in the navy. After lengthy questioning, he said to Rear Admiral Arthur B. Cook, chief of Naval Aeronautics: "Now, Admiral, no hemming and hawing. Let's get to the bottom of this thing." On one occasion, the committee decided the navy needed a new pay system to replace the existing complicated arrangement. Admiral Leahy was summoned. Vinson asked him to work out a new system, taking care to keep it simple. "Keep it all on the back of an envelope so the average layman can understand it," Vinson cautioned. The chairman, who was fond of chewing tobacco and gnawing on cigars, kept a spittoon nearby. At the beginning of testimony, the spittoon was close to his chair. But as testimony began to drag, he would move it farther away. When it reached a certain distance, the committee members knew that his patience had been exhausted.[5]

---

[5] Ben Grant, "Wit of Vinson Has Made Him Popular in Capital," *Macon Telegraph*, 20 February 1939, 1, 7; Louis R. Stockstill, "'Uncle Carl' Vinson: Backstage Boss of the Pentagon," *Army Navy Air Force Journal* 98 (18

When important witnesses appeared before the Naval Affairs Committee, the chairman ordinarily began the questioning. After he finished, ranking members held forth, while junior members were expected to say very little. Lyndon Johnson later stated that as a young representative from Texas he served on the committee for four years before Vinson allowed him to ask a question.[6] He probably exaggerated, but not by much. In 1937, when Johnson and Warren Magnuson of Seattle, both in their first term in the House, peppered witnesses with questions at their first committee hearing, the chairman gaveled the hearing into recess and called the two young representatives into the back room. In his small, bare private office behind the hearing room, Vinson "let us have it," Magnuson recalled. "You two are nice young fellows, and I'm sure you have the interest of the Navy at heart," he said. "But we have a rule in this committee. We call it seniority. Each of you is entitled to ask only one question this whole year, and two next year." Coping with the Vinson rules, Johnson and Magnuson soon learned how to "play up" to the chairman. "Lyndon and I always called Carl Vinson Admiral," Magnuson said. "We could get around him easily after the first few years—Lyndon more easily than I because he used me as a straightman and he had the southern syrup."[7]

After H. R. 9218 was read and Admiral Leahy had read a lengthy prepared statement, Vinson proceeded to question the chief of naval operations in lawyerly fashion, eliciting the information he wanted in the record and setting the tone for the entire hearing. He first asked about the fixed policy of the navy, to which Leahy replied: "The approved naval policy is to maintain the Navy in sufficient strength to support national policies and commerce and to guard the continental and overseas

---

February 1961): 24; Lou and Neta Stockstill, interview with the author, Indialantic FL, 21 June 2001.

[6] Lyndon Johnson, "Remarks at the Dedication of the Carl Vinson Hearing Room in the Rayburn House Office Building, 2 April 1965," Public Papers, folder 1965 I, Lyndon Baines Johnson Library, Austin TX.

[7] Robert A. Caro, The Path to Power (New York: Alfred A. Knopf, 1982) 537; Robert Dallek, Lone Star Rising: Lyndon Johnson and His Times, 1908–1960 (New York: Oxford University Press, 1991) 165; Alfred Steinberg, Sam Johnson's Boy (New York: Macmillan, 1968) 137–39.

possessions of the United States." After elaborating on that policy, Vinson then shifted to the term "adequate navy." To defuse the arguments of critics, the chairman stated: "The object and purpose of this legislation, then, is not to construct a Navy for the purpose of attacking foreign shores, but is solely for the purpose of affording adequate defense." Leahy agreed. The chairman then delved into the inadequacies of the Navy:

The Chairman: "As the ranking naval officer giving your military opinion, you state that this addition to the Navy is not sufficient for aggression against a first-class naval power."

Admiral Leahy: "That is correct."

The Chairman: "The statement was made on the floor in the debates that this might be an effort toward policing the world. Is the addition called for sufficient for any such undertaking?"

Admiral Leahy: "It is not sufficient for any such undertaking…. The proposed Navy is barely adequate to provide defense against attack on our shores and our island possessions, and beyond that it should not go."

The Chairman: "It would not under any conditions be sufficient to protect us on both oceans and the Panama Canal at the same time."

Admiral Leahy: "It would not be sufficient for that."

The Chairman: "Then as a matter of fact, this addition places us in the position that we have only a Navy that can afford protection to one coast at a time."

Admiral Leahy: "That is correct."

After other members questioned Admiral Leahy, Vinson had more questions for him on Wednesday, his third day before the committee.

The Chairman: "On Friday of last week the statement was made on the floor of the House that this program seemed to be justified only on the theory that we intended to join with the British and French navies to police the world. What have you to say about such statements as that?"

Admiral Leahy: "That statement is incorrect. This program is justified by the need to provide naval strength in the same proportion or approximately the same proportion that was provided in the Washington and London treaties by the 5-5-3 ratio."

After discussing the president's message and the history of naval armaments, Vinson emphasized the American increase was caused by the increase in other navies.

The Chairman: "When other nations are building battleships, submarines, destroyers, and airplanes, it is incumbent upon us to construct the same kind to give to the people an adequate defense."

Admiral Leahy: "It is necessary, and that is the purpose of this proposed authorization bill."

The Chairman: "Do you think that the increase provided for in this bill would tend to better promote peace or will it have the opposite effect—that of inviting war?"

Admiral Leahy: "I think it will definitely tend to promote peace."

After Admiral Leahy had testified for a week, some of the news reports of his testimony bothered Vinson, so he had Leahy respond to those issues to clarify his position and avoid any misunderstanding. The admiral addressed them succinctly:

The Navy does not have in mind any particular possible enemy, but does consider all foreign navies in its studies of the sea defense needed by the United States.

The Navy has no thought of obtaining assistance from any other nation.

It has no thought of giving assistance in the solution of the problems of any other nation.

It has no foreign commitments.

There are no understandings regarding assistance to be given or received.

There has been no talk of giving or receiving assistance.

The Navy expects to solve naval defense problems that may confront the United States in the Navy's traditional way, without alliance.

It expects to stand on its own feet in providing protection to the United States, and it expects to succeed.[8]

After Admiral Leahy concluded his testimony, the Naval Affairs Committee heard the testimony of several critics of the bill, including Jeannette Rankin, Charles Beard, Representative Hamilton Fish, Representative Caroline O'Day, Frederick Libby, executive secretary of the National Council for Prevention of War, and others. Vinson took a special interest in Libby's testimony as the following animated exchange reveals:

The Chairman: "Do you make contributions to political campaigns?"

Mr. Libby: "No, sir; we do not have any money to support that."

The Chairman: "Do you make contributions to individual campaigns?"

Mr. Libby: "No; never have."

The Chairman: "Do you go around and seek to get opposition to various Members of Congress?"

Mr. Libby: "We do not."

The Chairman: "Answer my question."

Mr. Libby: "I will answer your question in a sentence. We do not carry on campaigns against Congressmen as such. We carry on campaigns for the promotion of our policies through Congressmen that are sympathetic with those policies."

The Chairman: "In other words, you carry on campaigns against individual Members of Congress who do not share your beliefs?"

Mr. Libby: "We might."

The Chairman: "Answer the question."

Mr. Libby: "Yes. We have not done it much."

The Chairman: "How often have you done it?"

---

[8] House, Committee on Naval Affairs, *To Establish the Composition of the U.S. Navy, To Authorize the Construction of Certain Naval Vessels, and for Other Purposes*, 75th Cong., 3rd sess., 31 January and 1–4, 7–11, 14–19, 21, 23–26, 28 February 1938, Hearings No. 620, 1937–2053.

Mr. Libby: "Miss Rankin was down in your district once."

The Chairman: "That is right. They did it in my district against me. Miss Rankin carried on a campaign in my district because I do not share your beliefs."

Mr. Libby: "I would not put it so crudely."

The Chairman: "How crudely should it be expressed?"

Mr. Libby: "I would say that radical disagreement is necessary."[9]

Vinson sought unanimous support from his committee before sending a bill to the House, and usually, by the strength of his arguments, the testimony of witnesses, and the incorporation of minor adjustments in the bill, he succeeded. In this instance, however, twenty members supported the bill, but three opposed it. Ralph Brewster of Maine, W. Sterling Cole of New York, and Ralph Church of Illinois filed a minority report.

In presenting the bill for House consideration on 14 March, Vinson delivered one of his best speeches, a thirty-minute address that reiterated many of the points discussed in the committee. Defending the need for 46 new warships, 22 auxiliaries, and 950 airplanes, which H. R. 9218 would authorize, he said it would furnish the minimum national defense to preserve the republic. A strong navy, he argued, should prevent war, or should that fail, wage war effectively in order to bring hostilities to a close as soon as possible. The building program, he maintained, was "solely for the purpose of affording adequate defense for the continental United States and its insular possessions." He emphasized to his colleagues that the bill represented no militaristic campaign or aggressive movement; on the contrary, it was "to make America impregnable from any direction." The bill was an "insurance policy for peace for the American people." Even though it would involve the expenditure of more than a billion dollars, it would still be "cheap insurance." Nothing

---

[9] Ibid., 2175.

would "contribute more to guarantee to the people security and peace than a defense as provided for in this bill."[10]

As expected, there was much opposition to the bill. Representative Maury Maverick, a fiery, liberal Democrat from Texas, and Representative Ralph Church, an Illinois Republican, led the opposition on the floor of the House. But Vinson, liberally quoting President Roosevelt and Secretary of State Cordell Hull and aided by Majority Leader Sam Rayburn, prevailed. The majority of the House seemed to agree with Vinson's conclusion about the navy—"It is far better to have it and not need it than to need it and not have it"—as they approved H. R. 9218 by vote of 294 to 100. The Senate approved it with practically no changes, and Roosevelt signed the Naval Expansion Act into law on 17 May 1938.[11] In adopting the Second Vinson Bill, the largest peacetime naval appropriation to date, the United States was the last of the great powers to initiate a major new naval building program since Great Britain, Japan, Germany, and Italy had already begun to increase their navies beyond the prescribed limits established by the naval conferences.[12]

Included in the 1938 Naval Expansion Act was a provision authorizing the secretary of the navy to appoint a board of officers to investigate the need—for the purposes of national defense—for additional naval bases on United States territory. The report of this board, headed by Rear Admiral Arthur Hepburn, recommended new bases and improvements on existing facilities at nine Pacific, one Atlantic, and two Gulf locations. The Hepburn Report was transmitted to Congress in December 1938 and was embodied by Vinson and the Naval Affairs Committee in H. R. 4276, which was debated in the House on 21 February 1939. The measure, known as the Naval Air and Submarine Base Bill, authorized an expenditure of $53,800,000 on construction of

[10] *Congressional Record*, 75th Cong., 3rd sess., 14 March 1938, 3322–24; Enders, "The Vinson Navy," 107–109; Susan Landrum, "Carl Vinson: A Study in Military Preparedness" (master's thesis, Emory University, 1968) 53–54.

[11] *Congressional Record*, 75th Cong., 3rd sess. 3322–34, 3391–94, 3767, 7124; *Biographical Directory of the American Congress, 1774–1971* (Washington, DC: Government Printing Office, 1971) 736, 1352.

[12] Koginos, *The Panay Incident*, 123.

more defense facilities on the mainland and island possessions. The only item in the bill that aroused any controversy was the proposal to improve the harbor facilities at Guam by the expenditure of $5,000,000 over the next three years. Because of Guam's proximity to Japanese holdings, congressional opposition focused its campaign on that island. Tall, broad-shouldered Hamilton Fish of New York, an All-American football player at Harvard, the grandson of President Grant's able secretary of state, and the ranking minority member of the House Foreign Affairs Committee, assailed the proposal as a "dagger at the throat of Japan, an arrow aimed at this country's heart." Warning against war hysteria, he stated that he knew of no more dangerous proposal that could come before the House than the plan to prepare Guam for an air base. Representative Church, second ranking minority member of Vinson's committee, insisted that fortification would provoke counter moves by Japan. Pleading for a policy that would keep the United States out of Far-Eastern politics, he warned that this project "may be the first step that may involve us in the power politics of Asia." Such arguments carried the day, as twenty-five Southern Democrats joined the Republicans in defeating the Guam item by vote of 205 to 168. Vinson took his rare defeat with good grace. He felt the Guam defeat was more than compensated for by the convincing manner in which the House later approved his amended bill. Only four out of 372 Congressmen participating recorded themselves against final passage.[13]

In following the advice of the Hepburn Board, Congress eventually appropriated $65,000,000 for the establishment and development of naval aviation facilities at Kaneohe Bay; Midway Island; Wake Island; Johnston Island; Palmyra Island; Kodiak, Alaska; Sitka, Alaska; San

---

[13] *Congressional Record*, 76th Cong., 1st sess., 1710–22, 1744–82, 1832–44; House, Committee on Naval Affairs, *Report on Need of Additional Naval Bases*, 76th Cong., 1st sess., 3 January 1939, Document No. 65 (the Hepburn Report); Landrum, "Carl Vinson: A Study in Naval Preparedness," 57–59, Enders, "The Vinson Navy," 114; Wayne S. Cole, *Roosevelt and the Isolationists, 1932–45* (Lincoln: University of Nebraska Press, 1983) 333; Gladstone Williams, "Guam Base Vote First Vinson Loss," Vinson Scrapbooks, book 1919–1939, on loan from Tillman Snead to Georgia College and State University, Milledgeville, GA.

Juan, Puerto Rico; Pensacola, Florida; Hampton Roads Naval Operating
Base, Norfolk, Virginia; Quonset Point, Rhode Island; Tongue Point,
Oregon; and Pearl Harbor, Hawaii; but nothing for Guam.[14]

In introducing H. R. 4278 on the House floor, Vinson went far
beyond the tenor of the bill to outline a national policy of strong
rearmament. In clear, forceful terms, he ranged the United States on the
side of Great Britain and France in what he regarded as the ultimate
showdown against the world's dictatorships. Some of his colleagues
considered the speech a masterpiece. His approach, as Calvin Enders
points out, "was considerably ahead of that which the Roosevelt
Administration could take at this particular time and certainly far beyond
that which the American people were willing to engage in as of early
1939."[15] In the key portion of the address Vinson declared:

We must be prepared to stand alone. National defense
is of utmost importance to America and to the Western
Hemisphere.

Let no one think that with the world being overrun by the
dictator powers—Germany and Italy in Europe and Japan in the
Far East—that it is not of the utmost importance that we be
forever vigilant in looking to our defenses.

It is not only necessary that we look to our own defenses but
it is to our advantage to allow our airplane manufacturers to
furnish planes to those other two great democracies—France and
England—in order that they may not be destroyed by the dictator
powers.

Every right-thinking American approves the
administration's decision in this case, for if England and France
are unprepared they will surely be destroyed and the last stand of
the democracies will be in this hemisphere, with the United
States carrying the load.

---

[14] George T. Davis, *A Navy Second to None* (New York: Harcourt, Brace
and Company, 1940) 381.

[15] Enders, "The Vinson Navy," 115.

America now finds it necessary to answer the dictators in their own language. The world might just as well know that America is not going to submit to being destroyed with other unprepared democracies.

There are even those who believe that the ills of this mad world could be cured by conferences and covenants between the democracies and the dictatorships.

There is not a man within the sound of my voice who would not welcome such a conference if it meant a return to world sanity, a resurgence to the good old-fashioned principles of national honor, national ethics, and national respect of obligations—if one iota of good could come out of it.

Every meeting so far with the dictators has meant unequivocal surrender. Peace on the terms of the dictators is a Carthaginian peace.[16]

While his remarks flirted openly with the possibility of United States involvement in war, Vinson received a standing ovation when he concluded: "We do not seek war with anyone. We do not intend to get entangled in any alien quarrels. As a democratic people we are a peaceful people. We respect the rights of other nations; we expect other nations to respect our rights. We do not covet one foot of soil of any other nation. The purpose of this program is to insure that no covetous nation shall secure a foot of ours."[17]

The conflicts in Europe and Asia, growing in intensity and frequency, seemed to be heading inevitably to a bloody climax. War in Europe had been averted at the last minute by the now-maligned Munich Conference of October 1938, which rendered Czechoslovakia defenseless by awarding Hitler the Sudetenland with more than three million citizens in return for his promise of peace. That was the height of appeasement, and the next spring, when he took the remainder of Czechoslovakia, many concluded that he could not be appeased. The

[16] *Congressional Record*, 76th Cong., 1st sess., 21 February 1939, 1711–12.
[17] Ibid., 1712.

British and French responded by promising to defend Poland, which appeared to be Hitler's next target. A growing number of Americans became convinced that America's military defenses and industries must be brought to wartime efficiency. In a world ruled by naked force, delay could be fatal, as Vinson had pointed out many times. Polls consistently showed that the American people favored increased commitments to defense. When asked on 22 November 1938, "Do you think the United States should increase the size of its navy?" 86 percent said "yes." When asked the same question ten months later, the positive responses had increased to 88 percent. When asked on 23 September 1938, "Would you be willing to pay more taxes for a large army?" 53 percent replied affirmatively. On 10 October 1939, the same question received a favorable response of 64 percent. When the same question was asked about the navy, the favorable responses increased from 57 percent to 67 percent. A poll on 9 April 1939, asked, "If England and France go to war against Germany, do you think this country should declare war on Germany?" Only 5 percent answered "yes" and 95 percent answered "no." Yet, despite America's overwhelming aversion to declaring war, several polls in 1939 showed that a strong majority of the respondents believed that a war in Europe between the major countries would draw the United States into it.[18]

Despite the opposition of isolationists, several defense measures were adopted in the summer of 1939. Vinson steered through the House the Battleship Overhaul Act of 25 July 1939, which authorized major alterations for the modernization of the battleships *Tennessee, California, Colorado, Maryland,* and *West Virginia,* and the Coast Guard Defense Act of 2 June 1939, which authorized a coast guard base and air station on the coast of Alaska. President Roosevelt appointed Admiral Leahy as Governor of Puerto Rico, confirming plans to transform that island into a powerful Caribbean air base. The secretary of the navy announced that the creation of a special "mosquito fleet," consisting of torpedo boats and submarine chasers, was underway. Large sums were spent in increasing navy-yard building facilities, and the president ordered a comprehensive

---

[18] Hadley Cantril and Mildred Strunk, eds., *Public Opinion, 1935–1946* (Princeton: Princeton University Press, 1951) 939–41, 966–67.

survey of all government plants and facilities available for war activity.[19] Following the Nazi-Soviet Pact of 23 August 1939, and the outbreak of World War II a week later, President Roosevelt in a fireside chat to the American people on 3 September declared, "This nation will remain a neutral nation, but I cannot ask that every American remain neutral in thought as well.... Even a neutral cannot be asked to close his mind or his conscience."[20] While keeping America out of the war, the president fully intended to aid Britain and France. To that end, he called for a revision of neutrality legislation. He told a joint session of Congress on 21 September that he wanted to return to a neutrality based on the fundamentals of international law. Regarding the Neutrality Acts of 1935 and 1937, he said, "I regret that Congress passed that Act. I regret equally that I signed that Act." The president went on to argue that by returning to "real and traditional neutrality," the United States would stop aiding aggressors, enhance its trade, and preserve its peace. The president's firm leadership succeeded, and on 4 November he signed the Neutrality Act of 1939, which placed all trade with belligerent countries, munitions or not, on a cash-and-carry basis. The new law was presented as a peace measure, but Roosevelt clearly intended to use it in an unneutral way to benefit Britain and France.[21]

On the same day Roosevelt signed the Neutrality Act of 1939, Vinson, with the backing of the president, the Navy Department, and a majority of his committee, announced plans for the third great authorization program of the Roosevelt era. This Third Vinson Bill called for an expenditure of $1,300,000,000 during the next four years on 3 aircraft carriers, 8 cruisers, 52 destroyers, 32 submarines, and 22 auxiliaries. An additional measure authorized longterm government loans at low rates of interest to shipbuilding companies. It discarded the former practice of building half of the ships of the navy in government yards and empowered the Navy Department to award contracts without competitive

---

[19]Davis, *A Navy Second to None*, 381–82.

[20] David Reynolds, *From Munich to Pearl Harbor* (Chicago: Ivan R. Dee, 2001) 63.

[21] Ibid., 63–67.

bidding. All signs pointed to an attempt to accelerate the speed of naval construction.[22]

Following the end of the special session that dealt with neutrality legislation, Roosevelt was vacationing at Warm Springs when he suggested that national defense expenditures be placed on a "pay-as-you-go" basis as an alternative to heavy federal borrowing. Apparently the president, concerned about raising the statutory debt limit of $45 billion, was unleashing a trial balloon for the purpose of discussion. The entire Georgia congressional delegation except Senator Walter George, whom Roosevelt had tried to purge in the 1938 election, called on the chief executive at the Little White House and agreed with him. As the spokesman for the delegation, Vinson declared: "I have been thinking about this question for some time and have even discussed it with a number of members of the House. It seems to me that this generation ought to bear the burden of the cost of protection. By a proper adjustment of the income tax in the lower brackets, and of the inheritance and gift taxes, sufficient money could be raised to support an adequate defense."[23] Vinson's statement reflected his loyalty to the president and his innate fiscal conservatism. Although the idea might have merit in peacetime, it was unrealistic when the nation went to war.

Hearings for H. R. 8026, the Vinson Naval Expansion Act, began in January 1940. Admiral Harold R. Stark, the recently-appointed chief of naval operations, was the chief witness before the Naval Affairs Committee. A calm, reserved man with white hair, blue eyes, and pink cheeks, he was respected for his honesty, fairness, and careful planning. Never confusing what was desirable with what was possible, he trusted in methodical planning and precise thinking. In expressing strong support for the bill, he raised a troubling question: "What if the dictators won?" That possibility, he said, made it imperative that Congress pass the $1,300,000,000 Vinson Naval Expansion Act, "for if the United States should wake up some day to face a hostile world of alien ideologies, it

[22] Davis, *A Navy Second to None*, 383.
[23] *New York Times*, 26 November 1939, 1, 41.

would be too late for precautions."[24] As first proposed, the bill would have authorized a 400,000 ton, or 25 percent, increase in the combat ship strength of the navy. While Vinson's committee discussed the bill, it became obvious that Congress had developed a critical eye toward preparedness bills. The House had lopped off $7 million from a $264 million Emergency Defense Bill that the president had sought to implement the Neutrality Act. In the Senate, a Republican drive to bear down on every item of defense appropriations gathered force, waiting for bills to come over from the House side. Even more ominous was the evidence of a revolt in the Democratic Party. Speaking for a strong Midwestern farm bloc, Senator Alva B. Adams of Colorado called for a diversion of the $460 million in new taxes from defense to farm benefits. Senator Scott Lucas of Illinois claimed that "it might be possible to cut several hundred million dollars from defense appropriations and use it for farm parity payments." David I. Walsh of Massachusetts, chairman of the Senate Naval Affairs Committee, also took a stand against the Vinson bill. Walsh, a notorious homosexual who sought companions in the lower rungs of the Naval Academy staff, drank a great deal, and hobnobbed with isolationists, contended that until the navy built its present "paper fleet," there was no point in authorizing another.[25]

Vinson explained to Senator Walsh that "all battleships, carriers and submarines authorized by the act of 1938 have been provided for," and the baffled chairman was "at a loss to understand how any one conversant with naval matters can confuse the situation."[26] Nevertheless,

---

[24] "Vast U.S. Navy Program Is Put Under Congressional Microscope," *Newsweek* 15 (22 January 1940): 11–12; Patrick Abbazia, *Mr. Roosevelt's Navy* (Annapolis: Naval Institute Press, 1975) 66–67.

[25] Ibid.; *New York Times*, 11 January 1940, 1, 14; 12 January 1940, 1–2; Steinberg, *Sam Johnson's Boy*, 138.

[26] The disagreement between the two headstrong leaders was so great that for two months each chairman permitted naval bills from the other house to pile up without action by his respective committee. Finally, at the suggestion of the legislative counsel, Rear Admiral George Russell, Vinson made a generous gesture to Walsh and buried the hatchet. Robert Greenhalgh Albion, "The Naval Affairs Committee, 1816–1947," *Proceedings of the United States Naval Institute* 78 (1952): 1236.

sensing that the 25 percent expansion goal would not pass over the growing opposition, the Georgia Swamp Fox simply cut the proposal to a 10 percent increase. Always the realist, Vinson was willing to accept a temporary setback to achieve his long-range goals. "If world conditions are like they are today," he pointed out, "the committee can go along and authorize the other 15 percent next year or the year following." He admitted that the 10 percent increase would provide for the laying down during fiscal 1941 and 1942 of all the vessels that the navy yards and private ship-building industry could handle. Since no more could be laid down, his strategy compromised on the surface, but in reality conceded nothing.[27]

On 12 March, Vinson opened debate on H. R. 8026 on the floor of the House. He pointed out that the bill, passed unanimously by the Naval Affairs Committee, authorized a two-year building program with an 11 percent increase in the combatant strength of the navy at a total cost of $654,902,270. This limited expansion, much less than the Navy Department had requested, would not maintain parity with Great Britain or a 5-3 ratio with Japan. Nor would it be adequate to meet all possible needs, in the Atlantic and the Pacific, should they arise simultaneously in both oceans. The proposed increase, he asserted, was "the minimum that should be considered." Had world conditions remained as they were when the 1938 Expansion Act was passed, there would be no need for the 1940 act, and the existing authorization would have been sufficient, he readily admitted. But "the international situation has altered substantially," he continued, and we now face the possibility of "a general European war" and "a threat of world conflagration." Since 1932, "Japan has invaded China and possessed herself of a good portion of that country. Italy has taken Ethiopia and Albania; Germany has now the territory formerly occupied by Austria, Czechoslovakia, and part of Poland; Russia has seized the rest of Poland, has to all intents and purposes taken over Lithuania, Latvia, and Estonia, and is now busily engaged in attacking Finland." In summary, "We are living in an age of conquest, [and] today the language of Europe is force. Therefore, it is the

[27] *New York Times*, 14 January 1940, 34; Enders, "The Vinson Navy," 119; *Washington Post*, 30 January 1940, 5.

duty of the United States to be ready to speak the same kind of language."[28]

Republican critics attempted to show that Admiral Stark's fears of a coalition of dictators were unwarranted, that the law of obsolescence would render much of the hastily built tonnage useless in a short time, or that future events might prove such authorization and expenditure useless. Such ideas produced the following dialog:

Mr. White of Idaho. Has the gentleman given any thought to the proposition that the great forces of the world at war now will be so exhausted at the conclusion of hostilities that they will be in no position to attack us after this war is settled and that the warships we are building now will be obsolete in 20 years and therefore the great expenditures we are making now are useless expenditures in adding to the Navy to any great degree. Has the gentleman given any thought to that proposition?

Mr. Vinson of Georgia. No; because that is so farfetched I never let my mind run along those lines. [Laughter.] I only try to give my thought to something that is founded upon facts that history teaches, and history shows that nearly every nation that emerges from war oftentimes is stronger after the war is over than when war commences. Take our own Government. The United States Government was comparatively stronger, from a military standpoint, at the surrender at Appomattox than it has been at any time in the history of the world. The British Government was stronger from a military standpoint at the end of the World War than when it started, and the French Government also was stronger from a military standpoint. There is nothing to the argument that nations will impoverish themselves because they are engaged in war over a period of years if they emerge victorious. [Applause.]

---

[28] *Congressional Record*, 76th Cong., 3rd sess., 12 March 1940, 2731–33.

Mr. White of Idaho. Does the gentleman not know that a battleship is obsolete in 22 years, according to the rules of the Navy?

Mr. Vinson of Georgia. Oh, no; it is not obsolete. It still has fighting ability, but it has not as much fighting ability as the more modern up-to-date ship. It is not obsolete any more than a Ford automobile of 1935 is obsolete and antiquated because you happen to have a 1940 model.[29]

After less than five hours of debate, the House passed the Vinson Naval Expansion Act by vote of 305 to 37. Only two amendments were offered during the debate, and they were shouted down after Vinson argued that the provisions to be amended were essential. The Senate passed the bill intact and it became law on 14 June 1940, the day after Paris fell to the Germans. The law authorized the construction of 21 combatant vessels, 22 auxiliaries, and 1,011 airplanes.[30]

On 19 May 1940, the day newspaper headlines reported the German capture of Antwerp, Vinson announced plans to draft legislation to speed naval construction. Three days later, he and Walsh placed before Congress a huge naval aviation expansion program that would increase the number of planes from 3,000 to 10,000 while providing 16,000 navy pilots and 20 air bases, both on the continent and on insular possessions. Vinson's committee quickly approved the bill, and the House approved it on 28 May by vote of 402 to 1. Representative Vito Marcantonio of New York, a socialist who had left the Republican Party and joined the American Laborite Party, was the only opponent. On the same day, the House passed another Vinson-sponsored bill, which would permit the navy to negotiate contracts instead of submitting them to public bidding, allow the navy to advance up to 30 percent of contract price to contractors, make payments for plant expansion, and reemploy retired skilled craftsmen. The bill further relaxed labor restrictions in order to

---

[29] Ibid., 2735–36.

[30] Ibid., 2752, 9126; Landrum, "Carl Vinson: A Study in Military Preparedness," 66; Enders, "The Vinson Navy," 120–23; *Washington Post*, 13 March 1940, 6.

permit shipbuilding employees to work up to forty-eight hours a week, with time-and-a-half pay for time over forty hours. In urging passage of the bill, Vinson declared, "We are building, but we are not building fast enough, and we are not building as fast as we can." The House, agreeing with Vinson, passed the bill by vote of 401 to 1, with only Representative Marcantonio in opposition.[31]

Marcantonio, representing an ethnically diverse population in East Harlem, was often called the most radical member ever to serve in Congress, but the Georgia Swamp Fox figured out a way to capitalize on his extremism. On one occasion when Vinson was managing the floor debate on a defense bill, allotting time on his side of the aisle to members who wished to speak for or against the measure, Congressman Marcantonio asked if he could have five minutes to speak in opposition to the bill. Turning to Russ Blandford, one of his committee counsels, who was sitting with him to handle the paperwork, the chairman said, "Russ, put Mr. Marcantonio down for five minutes." Marcantonio thanked him and walked away. When he was out of earshot, Blandford, in disbelief, said, "Mr. Chairman, do you realize what you've done. You just gave that man five minutes to speak in opposition, and he's a Communist." Vinson, bemused and with a twinkle in his eye, turned to Blandford and said, "Well, now, Russ, don't you know if we give Mr. Marcantonio five minutes to speak in opposition to the bill, we'll pick up five or six votes."[32]

Although the 1940 measures were significant steps in preparing the United States for any crisis, Vinson was convinced that more could be done. He was especially concerned about developments in Japan. According to naval intelligence, Japan had eight aircraft carriers in

---

[31] Landrum, "Carl Vinson: A Study in Military Preparedness," 66–67; *Congressional Record*, 76th Cong., 3rd sess., 28 May 1940, 7019–26, 7045; Enders, "The Vinson Navy," 124; Jack Purcell, "House Votes Naval and Air Expansion," Vinson Scrapbooks, book 1940–42; *Washington Post*, 19 May 1940, 1, 2; 22 May 1940, 1, 4; *Biographical Directory of the American Congress*, 1336.

[32] Donald C. Bacon, *et al.*, eds., *Encyclopedia of the United States Congress*, 4 vols. (New York: Simon and Schuster, 1995) 3:1352–53; Louis Stockstill to the author, 19 March 2003, Stockstill Papers.

service and was building six more. Persistent rumors also held that Japan was building a fleet of superdreadnoughts, but American naval authorities were not sure because Japan had effectively hidden its construction activities from the outside world since 1936. Despite the progress that had been made, Vinson knew that the American Navy was still woefully inadequate to meet challenges in both the Atlantic and the Pacific. It would be years before the ships Congress had authorized were actually afloat, and he wondered if America had enough time to construct them.[33]

In contrast to the earlier years when Vinson had to struggle to get modest naval expansion plans approved, Congress now adopted major programs involving huge expenditures with great rapidity. As soon as one bill was approved, another, it seemed, was being introduced. On 17 June, three days after Roosevelt had signed the Vinson Naval Expansion Act, another bill, authorizing a 23 percent increase in the size of the navy at an estimated cost of $1,200,000,000 was introduced in the House and Senate with the president's backing. Vinson, however, doubted that the new authorization was adequate, so he went to the White House to discuss yet another major authorization bill with the president. Although the two strong-willed supporters of the navy had had occasional disagreements—such as the president insisting on a smaller authorization, or the president removing a provision in the Second Vinson Bill that would have raised the proportion of commissioned line officers to enlisted men from four and a half to one, to six to one, much to the displeasure of the chairman—they had worked cooperatively for seven years in strengthening the navy. The president had approved Vinson's plans in general and had endorsed all of his rearmament measures to that time, but he was unwilling to act on another bill at this time. As usual, Roosevelt was juggling many concerns. He was about to make important changes in his cabinet; namely, appointing Republican interventionists Henry L. Stimson as secretary of war and Frank Knox as secretary of the navy—changes that were certain to enrage isolationists.

---

[33] Enders, "The Vinson Navy," 123–25; *Congressional Record*, 76th Cong. 3rd sess., 12 March 1940, 2750; *Washington Post,* 14 April 1940, 2; *New York Times*, 2 June 1940, 1, 34.

Moreover, the nominating conventions were soon to meet, and Roosevelt, pondering a third term and concerned that the Republicans had made significant gains in previous elections, decided he had enough problems without adding another. Vinson disagreed. He believed the time was right to push for a two-ocean navy. Later, it might be harder to pass such a measure, he reasoned. Above all, he felt the sooner the navy received approval for an expanded program, the sooner it could begin the expansion of shipbuilding facilities to absorb the extra load he believed was coming.[34]

After leaving the White House, Vinson, disregarding the president's objections, dropped the new authorization bill in the House hopper, and had someone drop a twin copy in the Senate hopper bearing Senator Walsh's name. When President Roosevelt learned that the bill had been introduced, he had Vinson on the telephone, demanding to know why he had introduced the bill after being advised to wait. Vinson answered simply, "There is no time to wait." The chairman understood the president's political dilemmas, but he believed that Roosevelt was being excessively cautious. The sudden collapse of the French military and the subsequent surrender of the French government on 22 June 1940, profoundly shocked Americans, and Vinson was unwilling to accept any more presidential temporizing because he believed that the Congress and the American people now shared his views on naval preparedness. That same afternoon Admiral Stark asked for 399,000 tons of new construction at an executive session of the Naval Affairs Committee. That night, under Vinson pressure, the figure suddenly jumped to 1,250,000 tons—a two-ocean navy. The committee went beyond Stark's recommendations by adding 75,000 tons for additional aircraft carriers, $25,000,000 for building a "mosquito fleet," $150,000,000 for additional shipbuilding facilities, $20,000,000 for expanding the armorplate factory, and $50,000,000 for new gun factories. By 6:00 p.m. the next night, the

---

[34] Cole, *Roosevelt and the Isolationists*, 294, 363–68; John C. Walter, "Congressman Carl Vinson and Franklin D. Roosevelt: Naval Preparedness and the Coming of World War II, 1932–1940," *Georgia Historical Quarterly* 64 (Fall 1980): 301–302; Landrum, "Carl Vinson: A Study in Military Preparedness," 68; *Washington Post*, 18 June 1940, 1, 2.

Naval Affairs Committee, after hearing only three witnesses, gave unanimous approval to the bill. Vinson then moved to secure a speedy passage by the House.[35]

On 22 June, only five days after Vinson's talk with Roosevelt, the measure, H. R. 10100, calling for a 70 percent increase in the size of the navy, came before the House. With minimum discussion, the House passed the bill by a voice vote. In introducing the measure, Vinson reminded the House, "The axis now has at its disposal the shipyards and munitions factories of Germany, Italy, Poland, Denmark, Norway, Holland, Belgium, France, and possibly Spain." In addition, the axis may get British shipyards, and Japan has its own shipyards. Warning of the consequences of a complete Axis victory in Europe, he called for arming "as rapidly as possible" and increasing naval armaments "to the maximum degree possible." Our aim must always be, he declared, "to have complete freedom of action in either ocean while retaining forces in the other ocean for effective defense of our vital security." The $4 billion measure provided for 385,000 tons of battleships, 200,000 tons of aircraft carriers, 420,000 tons of cruisers, 250,000 tons of destroyers, and 70,000 tons of submarines. The Senate passed the bill on 11 July after a one-hour debate "without a single audible no," and the president signed it into law a week later. This program combined with others already authorized would provide a fleet of well over 600 vessels.[36]

With war raging in Europe and the Far East, funding automatically followed authorization. On 1 July, the president signed H. R. 9822, which was designed to speed up contract-letting and shipbuilding. Two hours after the bill became law, the navy let contracts for forty-five ships—the largest single contract-letting operation for warships in history. Soon every shipyard capable of building warships was operating at peak capacity; clearly more shipyards would be needed as the load was

[35] Landrum, "Carl Vinson: A Study in Military Preparedness," 68–69; Stockstill, "Backstage Boss," 28; *Washington Post*, 19 June 1940, 1, 2; Walter, "Congressman Carl Vinson and Franklin D. Roosevelt," 303–304.

[36] Landrum, "Carl Vinson: A Study in Military Preparedness," 69–70; *Congressional Record*, 76th Cong., 3rd sess., 22 June 1940, 9064–65, 9078; 22 July 1940, 9570; Enders, "The Vinson Navy," 125–27; *New York Times,* 23 June 1940, 1, 14.

expected to double. The *New York Times* noted that "the greatest naval expansion in our history has started, and it is already benefiting by the costly lessons learned in the unprecedented expansion of the past seven years." The "costly lessons" which often required radical changes in specific ships were over and the Vinson Building Schedule was providing a new fleet.[37]

The Two-Ocean Navy Law, which came almost a year and a half before Pearl Harbor, enabled the United States to make the necessary preparations for its tremendous wartime expansion. It dwarfed all previous naval construction authorizations, but, as Vinson pointed out repeatedly, changes in the world situation necessitated drastic action. President Roosevelt, whose political antennae were always sensitive to public opinion, did not believe that Congress and the American people were ready for such enormous naval expansion. Vinson believed otherwise and was proved correct. Passage of the bill revealed Vinson as not only a statesman with vision but also as a politician of rare tactical skill.[38] It also demonstrated that Vinson, though usually deferential to the president, had the courage to challenge "the chief" when the security of America was at stake. Technically the Two-Ocean Law bore the names Vinson and Walsh, chairman of the Senate Naval Affairs Committee. Some years later, Senator Walsh said he wanted the record to show that the movement for the two-ocean navy began in Congress, was approved by Congress, and was "largely due to the foresight, ability and judgment of the Chairman of the House Naval Affairs Committee."[39]

---

[37] *New York Times*, 2 July 1940, 1; 21 July 1940, 11, 13; *Atlanta Constitution*, 2 July 1940, 1, 11; Enders, "The Vinson Navy," 129–30.

[38] Albion, "The Naval Affairs Committees, 1816–1947," 1235.

[39] Stockstill, "Backstage Boss," 28.

8

Preparing for War

We can't afford to let England lose.
Carl Vinson, 1939

During the crucial period from the summer of 1940 through 1941, as events inexorably drew the United States into the maelstrom, Carl Vinson followed three guiding principles. First, he believed that America's first line of defense was Europe. Thus, like President Roosevelt, he favored providing aid to Britain, the only country in Europe still resisting the Fascist onslaught. By August 1940, Hitler had conquered Belgium, the Netherlands, Luxembourg, Denmark, Norway, and France. He had incorporated Austria into the Third Reich in 1938 and was allied with Mussolini's Italy, which had aided in the attack on France. He had stabilized his Eastern Front by coming to terms with the Soviet Union, his former enemy. After the signing of the surprising Nazi-Soviet Pact, Hitler took the western half of Poland, and Stalin took the eastern half. Stalin then attacked Finland and incorporated Estonia, Latvia, and Lithuania into the Soviet Union. Since Sweden, Switzerland, Ireland, and Spain had proclaimed neutrality, only Britain stood in the way of Hitler becoming master of Europe. In August Hitler began the massive bombing of British air bases and declared a total blockade of Britain; in September "The Blitz" began, as he subjected London to severe and protracted bombing. Britain's only hope for survival was aid from America, and her new Prime Minister, Winston Churchill, quickly requested it. Vinson had called for an American alliance with Britain even before Roosevelt was willing to express his views publicly, and he consistently backed the president's efforts to bolster British resistance. He was willing to provide Britain with planes, guns, and artillery from America's limited stockpile, for he shuddered to imagine a Europe under the total domination of Hitler. As he stated in an article early in 1941, "We can't afford to let England lose."[1]

A second principle Vinson followed at this time (and throughout his career) was that the Constitution gave to Congress the duty and responsibility of raising an army and navy. Adherence to this principle produced an emotional conflict with the president in May 1940. After two years of work, Congress had passed a personnel bill designed to rid the higher ranks of deadwood and to retain in the service eight of the navy's ablest flyers, slated for retirement largely because they were not Annapolis graduates. The "brass hats" vehemently opposed the bill, and when defeated in Congress, they turned to the president, who agreed to veto the measure. Realizing he had a selling job to do, Roosevelt summoned Chairman Vinson and Chairman David Walsh to the White House and told them he was going to veto the bill. Senator Walsh, no friend of the brass hats, protested, as the president expected. But he was dismayed when Vinson, the navy's strongest supporter in Congress, replied, "You can't do that, Mr. President. That isn't right." The president tried to soothe the angry chairman by arguing that everything proposed in the bill would be done anyway. Ten or eleven admirals would be retired and the eight crack pilots would be retained on active duty, he insisted. "Don't get excited, Carl," intoned the president. "Everything will be all right without this bill." Roosevelt, however, had not grasped the reason for Vinson's anger. "The question isn't whether you will do these things without this bill, Mr. President," shot back Vinson. "The question goes much deeper than that. It is whether Congress or the brass hats shall do the legislating for the Navy. It has always been my understanding that it was Congress, elected by the people, which had this power. But apparently I was wrong, and it's the brass hats who decide Navy policies." Irked by Vinson's blast, the

---

[1] "Building a Navy Second to None," *United States News* 9 (14 February 1941): 13.

president protested that he was not trying to flout the will of Congress and maintained that there was a "better way" to handle the matters covered in the bill. Unmoved by his arguments, Vinson retorted, "I disagree with you. It was the judgment of Congress that these things be done.... Now all our time and efforts are wasted simply because you choose to be guided by the Admirals instead of by Congress."[2]

Shortly after this confrontation, Vinson added a provision to H. R. 10100 that "no vessel, ship or boat now in the U.S. Navy or being built thereof shall be disposed of by sale, charter, or otherwise scrapped without the consent of Congress." Remembering the Washington Disarmament Treaty negotiated by the president and approved by the Senate, he was planning ahead, trying to make sure that House members would have a say in any disarmament treaty negotiated when things returned to normal.[3] Unfortunately, this provision had immediate repercussions—it complicated matters for Roosevelt when he tried to honor Churchill's request for fifty American destroyers. Once again the president summoned the chairmen of the two Naval Affairs Committees, but this time it was for an extended cruise on the presidential yacht *Potomac*. Cruising down the Chesapeake Bay, they inspected the Norfolk Navy Yard, a fleet training station, fortifications at Old Point Comfort, Langley Airfield, and the Newport News shipbuilding facilities. As they traveled, Roosevelt explained how desperately Britain needed America's help and especially how important destroyers were in resisting Hitler. Knowing how difficult it would be to get Congressional approval to provide destroyers to Britain, he solicited their support as he sought to accomplish that goal by other means. Walsh, who had isolationist tendencies, rejected the president's overtures and publicly castigated the "Destroyer Deal." Vinson, by contrast, supported the president.[4]

---

[2] Drew Pearson and Robert S. Allen, "Vinson Angrily Charges Brass Hats Rule As Roosevelt Threatens Navy Bill Veto," Vinson Scrapbooks, book 1940–1942 Tillman Sneed/Georgia College and State University, Milledgville GA; *Congressional Record*, 76th Cong., 3rd sess. 3 May 1940, 5501–502.

[3] *Washington Post*, 19 June 1940, 12.

[4] *Macon Telegraph*, 27 July 1940, 1; Wayne S. Cole, *Roosevelt and the Isolationists, 1932–45* (Lincoln: University of Nebraska Press, 1983) 374.

Vinson later gave two versions of how President Roosevelt secured his support. In her master's thesis, "Carl Vinson: A Study in Military Preparedness," Susan Landrum related the following version based on an interview with Vinson in 1968:

> Vinson was invited, as he had been many times before, to ride down the Potomac River with the President on Roosevelt's yacht. When they approached what appeared to be a good spot on the river to fish, Vinson and the President rowed away from the yacht and fished alone from a small dinghy. It was a relaxing afternoon and conversation centered around fishing techniques rather than increased complexity and seriousness of world events. Only when the afternoon was ending and the yacht was on the way back to Washington did the President tell Vinson of his decision to send Britain the ships she sorely needed. Vinson agreed with the President and replied that he would not oppose such an effort.[5]

A few years later Vinson, sitting on his front porch, gave a slightly different account to his great-nephew Sam Nunn. As Senator Nunn recalled, Roosevelt telephoned "Uncle Carl" and said, "I'm going to take the presidential yacht down to Norfolk on Saturday morning. It will leave early and come back late that night and I would love for you to come with me." Vinson readily accepted. They left at daybreak, had breakfast and lunch aboard, and cruised down to Norfolk. They reached a place where many naval vessels were located and circled them three or four times, and all the while Roosevelt said not a word about a destroyer deal. They headed back to Washington and when they were almost within sight of the dock, the president said, "Carl, you authored that legislation prohibiting any transfer of vessels without Congressional notification. It is very important because England is likely to be knocked out of the war if we do not help them. We've got to get them some vessels and we've got toget them to England soon. If I notify Congress, as your legislation

---

[5] Susan Landrum, "Carl Vinson: A Study in Military Preparedness" (master's thesis, Emory University, 1968) 77.

requires, it would stir up tremendous problems for me. It would test our neutrality laws and so forth." After an intensive, ten-minute pitch, the president said, "I would like to tell you and let you assume the responsibility for the Congress. And I would like for you to keep it secret." Uncle Carl replied, "Mr. President, that would be straining the outside parameters of the law. I will have to think about it." Roosevelt said, "Okay, Carl, call me on Monday." After thinking about it, Vinson called him on Monday and said, "Mr. President, you have notified Congress. You have complied with the law." Soon afterwards, the destroyers were on their way to England. Although no tape or written record of the conversation was made, Nunn stated, "I remember that story very well."[6]

Whether or not Vinson assumed the responsibility of speaking for Congress became irrelevant after the attorney general gave his opinion that the chief of naval operations could certify that the destroyers were "not essential to the defense of the United States if in his judgment the exchange of such destroyers for strategic naval and air bases will strengthen rather than impair the total defense of the United States." After receiving the opinion of chief of Naval Operations Harold Stark that "an exchange of fifty overage destroyers for suitable naval and air bases on ninety-nine year leases in Newfoundland, Bermuda, the Bahamas, Jamaica, St. Lucia, Trinidad, Antigua, and in British Guiana, will strengthen rather than impair the total defense of the United States," Roosevelt concluded an executive agreement. Backed by the ruling of the attorney general as well as the opinions of four leading lawyers, including Dean Acheson, that he did not need the authority of Congress, a jubilant President Roosevelt made public the "Destroyer Deal" on 3 September 1940. Although Roosevelt feared the Destroyer Deal might jeopardize his reelection, most Americans applauded the agreement that helped both nations.[7]

---

[6] Sam Nunn, interview with the author, Atlanta, GA, 4 April 2001.

[7] Robert Dallek, *Franklin D. Roosevelt and American Foreign Policy, 1932–1945* (New York: Oxford University Press, 1979) 244–48; Patrick Abbazia, *Mr. Roosevelt's Navy: The Private War of the U.S. Atlantic Fleet,*

A third principle guiding Vinson was that every effort should be made to strengthen American defenses as quickly as possible. Central to America's defense, of course, was the completion of the two-ocean navy. Consequently, he had no patience with any business or labor union that hindered the defense effort. Nor did he tolerate inefficiency in the Navy Department. These were longstanding concerns for Vinson, but the threat of war magnified their importance. The issue of civilian versus military authority and the relation of the chief of naval operations to the bureaus had been recurring sources of controversy. In 1933 a special board, chaired by Assistant Secretary Henry L. Roosevelt, had studied the problem and found that considerable confusion existed in administrative relations generally. When no changes were made as a result of the board's report, Vinson introduced a navy reorganization bill providing for a sweeping overhaul of the Navy Department. His bill, introduced in December 1933, called for a new Office of Naval Material co-equal in authority with a greatly strengthened Office of Operations. The General Board, however, objected to Vinson's proposal, and it was never reported out of the Naval Affairs Committee.[8]

In 1939 Vinson again submitted a reorganization bill which was based in part on his 1933 proposals. His plan was to abolish the bureau system and create in its place four major divisions: the Office of the Secretary, the Office of Naval Operations, the Office of the United States Marine Corps, and the Office of Naval Material. Unanimous opposition from the commander in chief of the fleet and the chiefs of the various bureaus doomed the Vinson plan. Naval leaders, it seemed, preferred the status quo. In testifying before Vinson's committee, Rear Admiral Chester Nimitz, chief of the Bureau of Navigation, said, "The present organization of the Navy Department has been developed through a long process of evolution. During this evolution practically all the difficulties which have existed at one time or another have been overcome and today the organization functions efficiently, economically and without friction.

1939–1942(Annapolis: Naval Institute Press, 1975) 92–95; Cole, *Roosevelt and the Isolationists*, 370–73.

[8] Robert H. Connery, *The Navy and the Industrial Mobilization in World War II* (Princeton: Princeton University Press, 1951) 23.

It is a historical fact that the bureau system successfully fought the Mexican War, the Civil War, the Spanish War, and the World War."[9]

In a letter to Vinson on 3 January 1940, Secretary of the Navy Charles Edison stated that the Vinson plan was sound but asked him to delay action on it until he could present proposals of his own. Edison later explained that he was overwhelmed with routine paper work, most of it dealing with shore problems. One day's mail, when stacked on the floor, rose four inches above his desk, he complained. To remedy the problem, he proposed the creation of a new Office of Shore Activities. When Captain C. W. Fisher testified that an Office of Shore Activities would relieve Secretary Edison "of a considerable amount of detailed routine matter," Vinson interrupted to inquire, "If it is not going to be a bureau, but is going to be an office, why should it not be headed by an Under Secretary, a civilian? If it is going to be merely for the purpose of taking burdens off the Secretary's shoulders and to settle minor squabbles between the various bureaus, why should it not be headed by a civilian who is classified as an Under Secretary?"[10] Once again, navy leaders opposed any change. Numerous naval officers, including Admiral Stark, chief of naval operations; Admiral Furlong, chief of the Bureau of Ordinance; and Admiral Sexton, chief of the General Board, testified that they preferred no change in the existing administrative organization to the Edison plan.[11]

Following the hearings, a bill was introduced on 13 March 1940, merging the Bureau of Construction and Repair and the Bureau of Engineering into the Bureau of Ships. It also authorized the president to appoint an under secretary who was to be responsible for coordinating the industrial activities of the navy and for any additional duties the secretary of the navy might prescribe. S. 4026 passed both houses and became law when the president signed it on 20 June 1940.[12] As finally adopted, the bill was not exactly what Vinson had proposed, but he was

---

[9] Ibid., 23–24.

[10] Ibid., 26; *New York Times*, 13 March 1940, L11.

[11] Connery, *The Navy and the Industrial Mobilization*, 28.

[12] *Congressional Record*, 76th Cong., 3rd sess., June 1940, 7630–32, 7764, 8026, 8081–83, 8773.

satisfied that it had strengthened the secretary's office and had improved the administrative structure of the navy. Vinson also was pleased when the president named James Forrestal, a short, pugnacious, thin-lipped investment banker, as the first under secretary. A native of Dutchess County, New York, Forrestal had attended Princeton, served in the navy in World War I, and had become president of Dillon, Read and Company, one of the more important Wall Street financial houses. Since June 1940 he had been one of Roosevelt's administrative assistants. Secretary of the Navy Frank Knox assigned him so many duties that Forrestal, in essence, became the wartime chief for material. Throughout the war years, Vinson worked closely with him and developed a high regard for his abilities. When Knox died on 28 April 1944, Vinson urged the president to name Forrestal as his replacement, which he did.[13]

As the vast rearmament program expanded, it became apparent to Vinson that greater efficiency in production was needed. Congress had appropriated enormous sums of money, and Vinson believed that both navy yards and private industry should make progress "commensurate with the appropriations of Congress." He was especially concerned that work on the new aircraft carrier *Wasp* was one year behind schedule. President Roosevelt shared his concerns, and following a meeting at the White House, Vinson and his committee spent two weeks in May 1940 studying the problem. The recommendations of the House Naval Affairs Committee were incorporated in H. R. 9822, even though the president had misgivings about allowing workers to work forty-eight hours a week. Although the new guidelines improved the situation, serious bottlenecks in industrial production remained.[14]

---

[13] Connery, *The Navy and the Industrial Mobilization*, 28–29, 56–57; William D. Leahy, *I Was There* (New York:McGraw-Hill Book Company, 1950) 237; Lewis Compton memos, 2 April and 13 April 1940, E. M. W. memos, 2 April and 12 June 1940, Vinson to Roosevelt, 5 April 1940, Daniel Callaghan to Roosevelt, 8 June 1940, President's Personal File, 5901, Roosevelt Library, Hyde Park NY.

[14] *Atlanta Constitution*, 14 May 1940, 10; "Vinson to Launch Probe of Shipbuilding Program," n. d. in Vinson Scrapbooks, book 1940–42; Lewis Compton memo, 27 May 1940, President's Personal File, 5901, Roosevelt Library.

On 15 September 1940 work in the House stopped suddenly when word arrived that Speaker of the House William Bankhead had died. Weakened by years of heart trouble and stomach ailments, he died of a stomach hemorrhage. The next day, with Bankhead's flower-draped coffin resting in the well of the House, lanky John McCormack of Massachusetts nominated gritty Sam Rayburn of Texas as Bankhead's successor. When the Republican leader Joe Martin of Massachusetts offered no candidate, Rayburn was elected by acclamation. Like John Nance Garner, the last Texan to serve as Speaker, Rayburn was known for keeping his word and keeping his mouth shut.[15] Before going home for the elections, the House had one final chore: selecting a new majority leader. Several members aspired to the job, but at the Democratic caucus Rayburn threw his support to McCormack, who was elected. Although he had served in the House only twelve years and had chaired no major committee, McCormack possessed qualities Rayburn admired: loyalty, a desire to assume responsibility, and a willingness to work long hours. Moreover, the "Fighting Irishman's" quick mind, acid tongue, and zest for a good fight superbly equipped him to advance his party in legislative combat. In time, this Texas-Massachusetts combination would become one of the most effective leadership teams in House history. Vinson was extremely pleased by these developments. Having served with Rayburn throughout his congressional career, Vinson considered him a close friend and the best man for the job. Like Rayburn, he respected McCormack, a fellow New Dealer, and developed an effective working relationship with him.[16]

Vinson also was pleased by the results of the 1940 election. The Democrats retained control of both houses by wide margins, and Roosevelt, with a new vice president, Henry Wallace, trounced Wendell Willkie to secure an unprecedented third term. A noted expert in agriculture, Wallace combined science with mysticism, and he was fascinated with the occult. At times he lived on a diet of cottonseed meal.

---

[15] Richard Bolling, *Power in the House* (New York: Dutton and Co., 1968) 150.
[16] D. B. Hardeman and Donald C. Bacon, *Rayburn, A Biography* (Austin: Texas Monthly Press, 1987) 242–46.

It was Wallace who persuaded Henry Morgenthau, the un-mystic secretary of the treasury, to put a picture of the Great Pyramid on the new dollar bills of 1935. One professional politician remarked, "Henry's the sort that keeps you guessing as to whether he's going to deliver a sermon or wet the bed." Many politicians considered him a "nut," but Roosevelt saw him as a humanitarian and a worthy upholder of the banner of liberalism, and Vinson supported him too.[17] As usual, Vinson, the dean of the Georgia delegation, had no opposition in the Democratic primary, but his election was noteworthy in other respects. He broke two precedents when he was sworn in for his fifteenth consecutive term as a United States representative—he had served longer than any previous member from Georgia, and he had served as chairman of the House Naval Affairs Committee longer than anyone in history. In January 1941 only six members of the House outranked him, even though he was a vigorous and comparatively youthful fifty-seven.[18]

When the Seventy-seventh Congress convened on 3 January a dual inquiry of army and navy defense preparations was undertaken. The House Military Affairs Committee headed by Representative Andrew J. May of Kentucky began a probe of the army's program, while Vinson's Naval Affairs Committee examined the progress of Naval Air Corps expansion, shipbuilding, construction of shore establishments, production of armor plate and heavy guns, and the timetable for completing the program. "The Committee is determined to find where the trouble lies," Vinson declared, "and then seek summary action to put an end to it." After conferring for two hours with Rear Admiral Samuel M. Robinson, chief of the Bureau of Naval Engineering, he said his committee planned to work at top speed for several months, meeting daily, "morning, afternoon and evening, if necessary." The Naval Affairs Committee planned to summon the navy's high command, shipbuilders, airplane manufacturers, and heads of navy shipyards in order to get a complete picture of the whole program. "We want to know how they are

---

[17] Philip Goodhart, *Fifty Ships that Saved the World* (Garden City NY: Doubleday & Company, 1965) 120.

[18] Gladstone Williams, "Vinson Breaks 2 Precedents As Lawmaker," Vinson Scrapbooks, book 1940–1942.

getting along," Vinson declared, and "what is needed, if anything, to speed the program." Emphasizing the seriousness of the task, he added, "The responsibility that devolves upon us all is without parallel. Our country's will to help nations fighting for democracy has increased that responsibility. We must not only expand our defense program, but accelerate production to a point which will permit us to give much needed aid."[19]

Through their investigations, both committees hoped to get an exact picture of loopholes in the rearmament drive so that they could provide the new Congress a working basis for the supplementary multi-billion dollar defense program to be proposed in the first session. In stating the need for the investigations, Vinson revealed that two new battleships were to be commissioned—the *North Carolina* on 15 July and the *Washington* on 30 September. These two new battleships, the first to be completed for the navy since the early 1920s, would give the fleet a total of seventeen capital ships in service. He also revealed that not one single keel had been laid for any of the ships that Congress had authorized in the two naval expansion acts of 1940, but the materials were being assembled for many of them.[20]

After grilling Rear Admiral John H. Towers, chief of the Bureau of Aeronautics (and a fellow Georgian), for a week, Vinson was convinced that industry had to curtail more commercial production in order to obtain full armament output. Declaring that no opportunity to unsnarl any arms procurement tangle would be overlooked, Vinson asserted: "You can't keep making pots and pans as fast as you ordinarily would and turn out all the aluminum needed in the defense program at the maximum rate…. With the shortage of skilled labor, the manpower necessary to rush the arms program at the greatest speed cannot be made

---

[19] Milton Magruder, "New House to Seek Probe of Rearmament Progress," *Washington Times-Herald*, 3 January 1941, Vinson Scrapbooks, book 1940–1942; *Washington Post*, 5 January 1941, 4.

[20] Ibid.; "Vinson Plans Probe of Navy Construction," n. d., "Defense Before Trade, Chairman Vinson Insists," n. d., Vinson Scrapbooks, book 1940–1942.

available if non-defense industries keep production at a normal or increased rate."[21]

The testimony of the heads of leading airplane-manufacturing companies soon convinced Vinson that more of the work needed to be assigned to subcontractors. When Burdette Wright, a vice president of the Curtiss-Wright Corporation, testified that his company was subcontracting only ten percent of its work, Vinson was shocked. He responded, "It is necessary to call in subcontractors so that you would not get all the business yourselves.... We have got to get these planes as quickly as possible, and every industry that can contribute should be given an opportunity to do so so you can speed up your production."[22] He told Glenn Martin, president of the Glenn L. Martin Company, "In these critical times, every subcontractor in America, that is capable of contributing, should be called into the picture."[23]

After the Naval Affairs Committee had heard two weeks of testimony, Vinson explained to the House that five factors were delaying the defense program. While debating a bill to alter naval vessels, he asserted that the government's control of the flow of essential supplies to the British and to American Army expansion was a major handicap to speeding up defense efforts. Vinson explained the effect of government priorities to the House:

> The shipbuilding program, like everything else in the United States, has felt and is feeling the effect of the vast program of the British Government and the expansion of our Army, especially the aircraft industry. All of these compete for machine tools, aluminum products, armament, and so forth. To cope with this situation, a system of priorities has been worked out which enables us to go ahead with the maximum expedition

---

[21] House, Committee on Naval Affairs, *Investigation Into Status of Naval Defense Program*, 77th Cong., 1st sess., 7–14 January 1941, Hearing No. 17, 1941, 247–368; "Defense Before Trade, Chairman Vinson Insists," Vinson Scrapbooks, book 1940–1942.

[22] House, *Investigation Into Status of Naval Defense Program*, Hearing No. 17, 389.

[23] Ibid., 432.

on all light vessels, such as destroyers, submarines, light cruisers, and auxiliary craft, but it has a tendency to slow down such vessels as battleships, large cruisers, heavy cruisers, and airplane carriers.[24]

Vinson identified four other difficulties impeding naval construction. Machine tools were hard to obtain, and there was a lack of trained personnel, but he believed these two problems would be alleviated in less than a year. Obtaining propelling machinery such as diesel engines was the third problem, and the shortage of armor, which restricted the building of large battleships, was the fourth problem he cited. Despite the efforts being made, he believed it would take two years before the full armor capacity could be reached.[25] While acknowledging the existing problems, Vinson kept things in perspective. In placing contracts for ships and additional facilities for the construction of 650 ships and the acquisition of 140 ships within a short period of time, the country had made "a remarkable showing," he pointed out. Overall, he believed the progress had been "satisfactory, especially when it is considered that this is the largest building program that has ever been undertaken by any country at any one time."[26]

Vinson also believed that the aircraft industry had made satisfactory progress thus far. In a March 1941 article in *National Aeronautics* he stated, "By and large the aircraft industry has kept pace with the schedules set by the Navy." As of 1 January 1941 the navy had a total of 2,590 planes on hand, plus 6,290 on order. He expected delivery of 4,000 planes during 1941. The aircraft industry was spreading production as widely as possible by utilizing the automobile industry and by farming out the work on parts and accessories among many smaller producers. "Sometimes as many as 200 or 300 sub-contractors," he noted, "are employed on a single prime contract for bombers or engines." While

---

[24] *Congressional Record*, 77th Cong., 1st sess., 21 January 1941, 205.
[25] Ibid.
[26] Ibid., 205–206.

admitting there had been delays, he found the causes were "mainly beyond the control of the manufacturers."[27]

A resolution adopted by the House of Representatives on 2 April 1941 directed the Committee on Military Affairs and the Committee on Naval Affairs to conduct thorough studies and investigations of the progress of the national-defense program, "with a view to determining whether such program is being carried forward efficiently, expeditiously, and economically." The resolution invested both committees with all of the authority of special investigating committees. To carry out those assigned duties, Vinson's committee appointed Edmund M. Toland, a District of Columbia attorney, as its general counsel, and quickly assembled a staff of attorneys, accountants, investigators, stenographers, and clerks. This investigative staff, after studying all aspects of the naval defense program, delivered a preliminary report on 20 January 1942 and a supplemental report on 22 July 1942.[28]

Long before those reports were completed, however, Vinson took action against organized labor, which he considered the biggest impediment to completing the two-ocean navy. "There are laws against sabotage of machines," he declared, "but the greatest sabotage is the strikes in the defense plants."[29] He had reached that conclusion because of the numerous labor disputes that had curtailed production the navy needed. On the last day of 1940 the United Automobile Workers of the Congress of Industrial Organizations went on strike at an International Harvester truck plant at Fort Wayne, putting 3,200 workers on the picket lines and delaying the manufacture of parts for navy vehicles.[30] On 22 January the United Automobile Workers walked out of the Allis Chalmers plant in Milwaukee, the largest industrial plant in Wisconsin, which was producing turbines, generators, shafts, pumps, and gun mounts for the navy. The strike halted work on defense orders totaling

---

[27] Carl Vinson, "The Aircraft Program Passes in Review," *National Aeronautics* 19 (March 1941): 7–8.

[28] House, Committee on Naval Affairs, *Investigation of the Naval Defense Program*, 77th Cong., 2d sess., 20 January 1942, H. Rept. 1634; 22 July 1942, H. Rept. 2371.

[29] "Building a Navy Second to None," 13.

[30] *Washington Post*, 1 January 1941, 1.

$26,000,000. On the same day, the Pittsburgh Building Trades Council of the American Federation of Labor called a strike of union construction workers engaged in building a $1,000,000 addition to the Mesta Machine Company's plant to house gun forging machinery for making navy ordnance.[31] Four days later the press reported that the ten-day strike of 1,400 men at the International Harvester Company's East Moline, Illinois, plant had been settled, but a new strike was impending at the Atlas Drop Forge Company at East Lansing, Michigan, which was producing plane propellers as well as parts for tanks and machine guns.[32]

Vinson had seen enough. As a loyal New Dealer, he had supported organized labor in the past and recognized the need for unions to balance the power of management, but he could no longer sit back and do nothing as strikes delayed defense production. Consequently, he introduced legislation to forestall strikes in defense plants by setting up a system of compulsory mediation and arbitration covering all naval work. His measure, modeled on the Railroad Mediation Act, would set up a board empowered to step in and take charge whenever labor disputes threatened to interfere with the naval defense program. The bill also would bar "closed shop" agreements in plants handling naval work. All labor disputes on navy contracts, which management and labor could not resolve, would have to be submitted to the three-man Naval Defense Labor Board created by the bill. The board would first try to settle the dispute during a thirty-day compulsory mediation period and then by arbitration if necessary. Either side could refuse the terms proposed by the board of arbitration, and a strike could be called after a three-months "cooling off" period.[33]

Syndicated columnist David Lawrence noted that when something stood in the way of progress for the United States Navy, Vinson would not "let any stone remain unturned to attain his objective." Timid political folks, he pointed out, stayed away from the ticklish labor problem, but someone had to tackle it "or else see the national defense

---

[31] Ibid., 23 January 1941, 1, 6, 7.

[32] Ibid., 27 January 1941, 1.

[33] Ibid., 28 January 1941, 1; 30 January 1941, 2; Landrum, "Carl Vinson: A Study in Military Preparedness," 90–91.

program slowly broken down and aid to Britain retarded." The Vinson bill, Lawrence asserted, was a severe measure that went to the very heart of the problem. Given the friendly attitude of the Roosevelt administration toward labor, legitimate labor organizations seeking legitimate objectives would have nothing to fear, he pointed out. But the "left" or communist wing in American labor circles would have plenty to fear, "and that's why the Vinson proposal...becomes a real fight between hidden influences that wish to break down defense operations and the almost unanimous desire of the American people to get their defense machine built in the shortest possible time."[34]

Throughout early 1941 Vinson continued to demand that labor issues must not halt defense production and must be stopped by law if necessary. He told the House Judiciary Committee on 13 March that strikes in defense industries already had cost enough man-hours of labor to manufacture 325 bombers. He based his estimate on reports from 127 companies involved in strikes. The loss during 1940 and through February 1941 was a total of 7,817,360 man-hours of labor, or 10.5 years of labor.[35] Replying to administration statements that no legislation was needed at that time because fewer national defense strikes had occurred in 1940 than in 1917, Vinson told the Judiciary Committee why this comparison was irrelevant:

> During that prior defense emergency there took place the greatest number of strikes this country has ever experienced; and to say now, with the Nation facing an emergency unprecedented in its history, with our very existence as a free government dependent upon uninterrupted production of arms and munitions for defense, that we must wait until the number of strikes exceeds that of such prior period—that we must wait until it may be too late—is just simply nonsense.[36]

---

[34] David Lawrence, "Vinson Bill Gets to Heart of Problem," *Washington Evening Star*, 30 January 1941, Vinson Scrapbooks, book 1940–1942.

[35] Carl Vinson, "Legislation to Curb Strikes in Defense Industry," *Congressional Digest* 20 (April 1941): 110.

[36] Ibid., 112.

Pointing out the seriousness of the issue, he insisted, "Our country cannot defend itself against enemies from without if it is faced with industrial warfare or even the threat of industrial warfare at home." He reminded the Judiciary Committee that the president, in his 6 January address to Congress, had stated: "We must all prepare to make the sacrifices that the emergency, as serious as war itself, demands. Whatever stands in the way of speed and efficiency in defense preparations must give way to the national need." Others were making great sacrifices for the Nation, but "defense labor," Vinson noted, "has not been, and is not being, asked to make sacrifices with respect to wages, hours, or overtime compensation."[37]

When President Roosevelt announced on 2 April 1941, that he was disposed to give the existing conciliation machinery a fair trial before seeking to cope with strikes in the defense industry by other means, Vinson realized that his bill would not become law anytime soon. The president's statement came hours after Vinson had introduced a bill that would permit the government to take over industrial plants if there was "existing or threatened" failure of production on defense orders. In justifying the bill, Vinson pointed to an existing law that gave the president power to take over and operate manufacturing plants that refused to give the United States preference in the execution of orders, refused to manufacture the material ordered, or refused to furnish them at reasonable prices. The owners of the Allis Chalmers plant had not refused to do any of these things, but because of the strike of their employees they were powerless to cooperate with the government. Vinson reasoned: "Obviously, interference with the national defense is just as serious if occasioned by employees as it would be if it were occasioned by employers, and it follows that existing law is deficient in providing no authority whereby the cause of the interference can be removed, regardless of its source."[38]

---

[37] Ibid., 111–12.
[38] "President Opposes New Strike Curbs," *New York Times*, 2 April 1941, 1, 14.

On April 15 Vinson began hearings on his strike legislation, H. R. 4139. Yielding the chair to Representative Patrick Drewry, a quiet, conservative Democrat from the eastern Tidewater gentility area of Virginia, Vinson explained the specifics of his bill to the committee, after which Secretary of the Navy Frank Knox testified. Knox was favorably disposed toward the proposed legislation, and at the risk of being classed a "scaremonger," he stated, "We are now in the midst of the decisive period of this present World War."[39] Vinson inserted into the record a letter from Knox listing all of the strikes that had taken place in defense industries since September 1939—a total of seventy-one work stoppages.[40] With minimum discussion, the Naval Affairs Committee gave unanimous approval to the bill.[41]

Vinson's bill aroused controversy throughout the country and incurred the wrath of organized labor. Philip Murray, president of the C.I.O., telephoned the chairman of the Rules Committee that the bill should be sent back to the Naval Affairs Committee for further hearings and extended consideration. He said, "This bill drastically and seriously curtails existing rights of labor and will in my judgment provide a basis for more widespread discontent among working men and women, thereby causing grave repercussions throughout our national defense program."[42] George Meany, secretary-treasurer of the A.F. of L., told the Rules Committee the A.F. of L. "is absolutely and unalterably opposed to this bill," and William Green, president of the A.F. of L., sent an open letter to all members of Congress vigorously opposing the legislation. Representative Warren Magnuson, perhaps capitalizing on an opportunity to embarrass the "dictatorial" Vinson, contended the bill would deprive labor of fundamental rights. He saw no reason for anti-

---

[39] House, Committee on Naval Affairs, *Hearings on H. R. 4139, To Further Expedite the National Defense Program*, 77th Cong., 1st sess., 15 April 1941, Hearing Nos. 67, 805.

[40] Ibid., 16 April 1941, 837–44.

[41] Ibid., 18 April 1941, 922.

[42] Landrum, "Carl Vinson: A Study in Military Preparedness," 95–96.

strike legislation at this time and added "Congress is the one that needs a cooling off period."[43]

In the face of such concerted opposition, President Roosevelt was not about to jeopardize his standing with organized labor, a key component in his successful political coalition. Without presidential support, Democratic congressional leaders were not inclined to act on Vinson's bill. Why place their leader in an awkward political position, or why spend time and energy drafting legislation that was certain to be vetoed, they reasoned. Consequently, Vinson's bill languished in the Rules Committee for seven months until the president belatedly encouraged Congress to consider strike legislation.[44]

Vinson was clearly disappointed that his labor bill was not enacted, but he could take solace from the passage of many other bills. The Naval Affairs Committee traditionally was one of the busiest committees in Congress, and Vinson was justly proud of the amount of legislation it produced. So that others could see the fruit of his labors, he had a complete listing of all the naval legislation enacted by the Seventy-sixth Congress, third session, inserted in the *Congressional Record*. The impressive list included twenty-nine laws, albeit some of which dealt with trivial matters, such as accepting real estate from the city of Miami. But the list also included major laws for the construction of ships, planes, and shore facilities.[45] He also inserted in the *Congressional Record* a memorandum prepared by the Bureau of Ships showing the contracts and allocations made for the construction of naval vessels on 9 September 1940. The list shows nineteen shipyards building 201 naval vessels at a total cost of $3,788,745,672.[46]

Major naval legislation continued to be adopted in 1941, with minimum debate and nearly unanimous votes. On 29 January 1941 the president signed a bill providing antiaircraft defenses of combatant

---

[43] Ibid., 96; Hedley Donovan, "House Rules Committee Defers Action on Vinson Compulsory Mediation Bill," *Washington Post*, 24 April 1941, 7.

[44] Landrum, "Carl Vinson: A Study in Military Preparedness," 97–98.

[45] *Congressional Record*, 76th Cong., 3rd sess., Appendix, 14 September 1940, 5721–22.

[46] Ibid., 13 September 1940, 5700.

vessels at a cost of $300,000,000.[47] The next day he signed a bill removing certain limitations on appropriations for the pay of midshipmen.[48] On 31 January he signed a bill authorizing $909,000,000 for additional shipbuilding and ordnance manufacturing facilities. It had passed the House with only two opposing votes—the votes of Vito Marcantonio of the American Labor Party and Republican William Lambertson, a sixty-year-old farmer from Kansas, who had served in the House since 1929.[49] Vinson received special pleasure on 23 March when Roosevelt signed a bill authorizing $58,000,000 for construction at existing naval shore establishments as well as at the eight air bases acquired in the Destroyer Deal. Included in the law was an authorization of $4,700,000 for the development of Guam and Samoa.[50] On two previous occasions the House had voted to strike from naval bills proposals to fortify Guam—the only defeats Vinson had suffered on naval bills he had presented since Roosevelt had been president. With Japan casting covetous eyes on Indo-China, Malaya, and possibly the Philippines, the House now saw the wisdom of fortifying Guam, thus erasing the one blight on Vinson's perfect record of securing adoption of naval bills.[51]

Over the years, Vinson had received much praise on the floor of the House from colleagues, especially members of the Naval Affairs Committee who were most familiar with his accomplishments, such as the following tribute by Representative W. Sterling Cole, a Republican from New York:

I take this opportunity simply to call to your attention the fact that the responsibility for the condition of our Navy today rests, if it rests at all upon the shoulders of one man, upon the gentleman from Georgia himself. [Applause.] For 10 years he

---

[47] Ibid., 77th Cong., 1st sess., 21 January 1941, 204–10; 29 January 1941, 445.

[48] Ibid., 22 January 1941, 228–29, 30 January 1941, 445.

[49] Ibid., 22 January 1941, 230–43, 31 January 1941, 1122.

[50] Ibid., 19 February 1941, 1175–1201, 23 March 1941, 3079.

[51] *Macon Telegraph*, 25 February 1941, 4.

has advocated a bigger, a stronger, and a better Navy. Some of
us have at times disagreed with him in some phases of the
program. Now we are happy that he was successful in his
efforts.[52]

It is doubtful that any tribute, however, gave him as much
satisfaction as the speech of Representative Hamilton Fish of New York
on 25 February 1941. His longtime foe described Vinson as a man "who
knows more about the Navy than anybody in the Navy Department itself,
who is the Navy's best friend, and who is largely responsible for our
having the biggest navy in the world today." Yet, despite the fact that the
United States now has "the finest navy in the world," Fish continued,
"there are millions of people, led astray by deliberate falsehoods and
misleading propaganda," who believe that "our Navy amounts to
nothing, and that we would be helpless without the British Navy to
defend us." Rejecting this "sinister, vicious, and false propaganda," the
isolationist Republican added:

I would say to the distinguished gentleman who is the father
and sponsor of our great Navy—and I cannot give him too much
credit, he deserves it, and I hope the American people realize
that he more than any other one man is responsible for giving us
this Navy—that it is our first line of defense, not the English
Navy. It is the Navy built by the gentleman from Georgia, Mr.
Vinson. [Applause.] This Navy will always be our first line of
defense. We cannot rely on the navy of any other nation.[53]

Events had diminished isolationist strength in Congress, as Fish's
dramatic turnaround demonstrated. Consequently, Roosevelt was able to
secure passage of the Lend Lease Act, one of the most momentous laws
ever passed by Congress. It passed both houses by wide margins early in
1941, and immediately after the president signed it on 11 March, a
shipment of weapons was on its way to Britain and Greece. Roosevelt

---

[52] *Congressional Record*, 77th Cong., 1st sess., 21 January 1941, 210.
[53] Ibid., 25 February 1941, 1389.

declared the vote on Lend Lease marked "the end of compromise with tyranny and the forces of oppression," while Churchill described the bill as the "new Magna Charta" and later ranked its passage as one of the climaxes in the war.[54] An unofficial declaration of war on the Axis, the Lend Lease Act was, as historian Thomas A. Bailey pointed out, "a belated acceptance of the fact that the dictators had already unofficially declared war on all the democracies, including the United States."[55] An alarmed Senator Arthur Capper, a Republican from Kansas, feared that the president might "sell, lend, lease, or give away our entire Army and Navy, except the men."[56] Isolationist Senator Burton Wheeler of Montana branded lend-lease "the New Deal's triple 'A' foreign policy—it will plow under every fourth American boy."[57] Though weakened, the isolationists had not given up the fight, and their power was demonstrated when Roosevelt sought to extend selective service. The original act, passed on 16 September 1940, had called for the training for one year of 1,200,000 troops and 800,000 reserves. Roosevelt, fearing isolationist opposition, was reluctant to bring up the matter in Congress, but General George Marshall declared that failure to pass the extension would result in "disintegration of the Army."[58] It turns out that the president's fears were justified. The Senate passed the extension bill 45 to 30, but in the House it passed by a majority of one vote, 203 to 202.

---

[54] Samuel I. Rosenman, ed., *The Public Papers and Addresses of Franklin D. Roosevelt*, 13 vols., (New York: Random House, Macmillan, Harper, 1938–1950) 10:63. For a good study of the passage of the Lend-Lease Act, see Warren F. Kimball, *The Most Unsordid Act: Lend-Lease, 1939–1941* (Baltimore: Johns Hopkins Press, 1969).

[55] Thomas A. Bailey, *A Diplomatic History of the American People*, 10th ed. (Englewood Cliffs NJ: Prentice-Hall, Inc., 1980) 723.

[56] Arthur Capper, "Let Us Keep Out of Foreign Wars," *Vital Speeches of the Day* 7 (1941): 295.

[57] Wayne S. Cole, *America First: The Battle Against Intervention, 1940–1941* (New York: Octagon Books, 1971) 46.

[58] Robert E. Sherwood, *Roosevelt and Hopkins: An Intimate History* (New York: Harper & Brothers, 1948) 367.

Since early in 1941 America had been engaged in an undeclared naval war with Germany in the North Atlantic. American naval patrols had aided the British by radioing the position of German submarines to nearby British warships and airplanes. American troops occupied Iceland in July and American ships began convoying Lend Lease goods to Iceland, where British patrols then escorted the ships to the United Kingdom. Inevitably armed incidents occurred. In September the American destroyer *Greer* battled a German U-boat near Iceland. After two American-owned merchant ships had been sunk, Roosevelt declared that America would strike first at all Axis raiders operating within the American defensive areas. Although the isolationists loudly protested the president's shoot-on-sight orders, his decisions had Vinson's endorsement and seemed to have the support of the majority of the American people. On 9 October Roosevelt asked Congress to repeal the "crippling provisions" of the Neutrality Act—the provision that prevented arming merchant ships, and the provision that forbade American ships from entering belligerent ports and sailing through combat zones. In mid-October the U.S. destroyer *Kearny* battled a German submarine near Iceland and suffered the loss of eleven lives. In late October the American destroyer *Reuben James*, on convoy duty near Iceland, was torpedoed and sunk with the loss of over one hundred officers and men. It was the first and only American warship sunk by Germany before war was declared. Shortly afterwards, Congress complied with the president's request, despite the shrill cries of the isolationist minority. Henceforth, American merchant vessels could go anywhere and carry any kind of cargo, including munitions.[59]

Eight days after the revision of the Neutrality Act, Admiral Isoroku Yamamoto, commanding a mighty Japanese fleet, set out from the Kurile Islands for a surprise attack on Pearl Harbor. On 7 December 1941, as the carrier-based planes of the Japanese fleet destroyed much of the U.S. Pacific fleet and over 250 aircraft, they also destroyed isolationism in America. The tragic defeat at Pearl Harbor ended partisan bickering overnight and galvanized the American people into action as one nation.

---

[59] Bailey, *A Diplomatic History of the American People*, 730–31; Cole, *Roosevelt and the Isolationists*, 442–53.

"The only thing now to do," declared isolationist Senator Wheeler, "is to lick hell out of them."[60]

Vinson was in his Chevy Chase, Maryland, home when he heard the first radio reports of the Japanese attack at Pearl Harbor. Though disheartened by the magnitude of the losses, he was relieved that at last the United States was a belligerent, an eventuality he had expected for some time. He immediately telephoned the Navy Department. Upon receiving confirmation of the report, he declared with typical brusqueness, "I'm coming down." When he arrived, Admirals Stark and Towers related more of the events to him. Vinson stayed at the department for the remainder of the day conferring with top officials as further reports of the damage arrived.[61]

The next day, Vinson listened intently as a solemn President Roosevelt delivered a twelve-minute address to a joint session of Congress that perfectly captured the mood of the American people: "Yesterday, December 7, 1941—a day which will live in infamy—the United States of America was suddenly and deliberately attacked by naval and air forces of the Empire of Japan.... I ask that Congress declare that, since the unprovoked and dastardly attack by Japan on Sunday, December 7, a state of war has existed between the United States and the Japanese Empire."[62]

After the presidential address, the Joint Session was dissolved and the two houses met separately. Without a word of debate the Senate voted for war, 82 to 0. The House took a bit longer, but voted for war 388 to 1. Jeannette Rankin, the Montana pacifist and Vinson foe, who had voted against American entry into World War I, was back in Congress after an absence of twenty-two years. She cast the only negative vote. Three days later the House and Senate declared war on Germany and Italy, this time with Congresswoman Rankin voting "present."[63]

---

[60] Bailey, *A Diplomatic History of the American People*, 740.

[61] Landrum, "Carl Vinson: A Study in Military Preparedness," 82–83.

[62] *Congressional Record*, 77th Cong., 1st sess., December 8, 1941, 9504–505.

[63] Hardeman and Bacon, *Rayburn*, 275–77.

The damage inflicted at Pearl Harbor was heavy but not irreparable. Fortunately for America, the carriers were at sea when the attack occurred and the Japanese failed to destroy the huge oil depot. The United States was able to recover from the tragedy quickly, in large part because of Vinson's leadership, as Susan Landrum pointed out: "From the Vinson-Trammell Act in 1934 to the events of December 1941, Chairman Vinson had authored and guided through the House measure after measure authorizing an adequate defensive navy and adequate facilities for expansion of the Navy. While the United States was caught by surprise at Pearl Harbor, the military and industrial forces and facilities needed to recover from the tragedy and prepare for war had actually been set into motion three years before in the giant authorization acts of 1938, and then expanded even further by the acts of 1940."[64]

Some years later, when key naval leaders analyzed this crucial era, they acknowledged Vinson's contributions to America's ultimate victory. Fleet Admiral Chester W. Nimitz declared: "I do not know where this country would have been after December 7, 1941, if it had not had the ships and the know-how to build more ships fast, for which one Vinson bill after another was responsible."[65] In his book *I Was There*, Admiral William D. Leahy offered the following praise of Vinson for his work in the critical decade of 1935–1945: "In my opinion, the Georgia Representative had, in the past decade, contributed more to the national defense than any other single person in the country except the President himself."[66]

---

[64] Landrum, "Carl Vinson: A Study in Military Preparedness," 80.

[65] Louis R. Stockstill, "'Uncle Carl' Vinson: Backstage Boss of the Pentagon," *Army Navy Air Force Journal* 98 (18 February 1961): 28.

[66] Leahy, *I Was There*, 22.

9

The War Years

If you attend to things properly you will get good results.
Carl Vinson, 1953

Three years before the outbreak of war in Europe, the Vinson family expanded. Carl and Mary Vinson had no children, but Carl's new aide, Charles Tillman Snead, Jr., became their surrogate son. A native of Baldwin County, Snead grew up on a farm that reputedly produced more corn per acre than any farm in the county. Vinson knew the Snead family well and saw potential in young Tillman. To encourage his development, Vinson got Tillman the job of superintending the building of Ocmulgee National Park soon after he completed his high school work at Georgia Military College in Milledgeville. In 1936 Vinson brought him to Washington to work in his office. It proved to be a mutually advantageous relationship, and Tillman remained on Vinson's staff as his administrative assistant until both men retired at the end of 1964. Throughout that period of nearly thirty years, Snead lived in the Vinson home. Since Vinson did not drive a car, Tillman drove him to and from work and wherever else he wanted to go. Both Mary and Carl were so fond of "Till," as they called him, that he was considered a member of the family.[1]

---

[1] Tillman and Karen Snead, interview with the author, Dale City, VA, 8 June 2001.

A few years after Carl and Mary married, Mary began to experience physical problems. At first the rheumatoid arthritis was only a minor annoyance, but it grew progressively worse. The cold winter climate of Washington increased her discomfort, so Mary found relief by spending some of the winter months in Miami, Florida. On several occasions, Tillman drove Mary, along with her maid and Paddy, her beloved wire-haired terrier, to Coconut Grove near Miami. He stayed with her until their return to Washington and took her to the racetrack practically every night they were in Florida, for Mary had a passion for horse races. Carl, of course, remained in Washington as long as Congress was in session, and when it adjourned he went to his Milledgeville farm, where she joined him.[2]

The devastating disease, for which no cure existed, ravaged Mary's body, and by the outbreak of World War II she had become an invalid, unable to get out of a chair without assistance. Carl, who could be so intimidating when grilling a witness before his committee, was the gentlest of husbands. Despite the demands of his job, he made a point of leaving his office promptly by 4:45 so that he could spend the evenings with his beloved wife. He read to her and kept her informed of the day's events. In the evenings and on weekends Till would carry her to the car and drive her around the Washington area.[3] Although incapacitated, she could still use the telephone, and during World War II she contributed to the war effort by telephoning for bond sales.[4]

Since Vinson left his office early, he managed to put in nine-hour days by arriving early. He routinely went to bed at 9:00, arose at 5:10, left the house with Till by 6:00, and was in the Capitol by 7:00. Much to the dismay of certain late-rising admirals and generals, he liked to discuss matters with them in the privacy of his office at 7:00 a. m. Disciplined in his eating as well as everything else, Vinson began the day

---

[2] Ibid.; Tillman Snead to Mr. and Mrs. C. T. Snead, Sr. and Betty Snead, 31 October 1939, Snead Family Papers, Dale City, VA; *Union-Recorder*, 29 June 1939, 7.

[3] Tillman and Karen Snead, interview with the author.

[4] Ed and Betty Vinson, interview with the author, Atlanta, GA, 7 August 2001.

with a breakfast of two pieces of wheat toast with fig preserves and two cups of coffee. On rare occasions, he would indulge in another cup of coffee after dinner. He liked food prepared in the Southern style: rich and greasy. He ate almost everything and was fond of meats, vegetables, salads, and especially desserts. His favorite desserts were homemade apple and peach pies, but he limited himself to one big piece. He used real butter, not margarine, drank whole milk, ate greasy, fried foods and rich desserts, and smoked cheap cigars and chewed tobacco all his life—all the things modern nutritionists and health specialists advise against doing—but he never got sick, never gained weight, and lived to the ripe old age of ninety-seven![5]

The Vinsons had few visitors, but one who came regularly was Lyndon Johnson. Vinson was fond of the tall young Texan with the long nose and big ears and correctly assumed that his drive and ambition would take him far in the Democratic Party and in national politics. For his part, Johnson understood how Congress operated. He knew who wielded power, and power was what he longed to possess. President Roosevelt had boosted his career and fellow Texan Sam Rayburn served as his mentor, but their support was not enough to satisfy Johnson. He also made every effort to cultivate House leaders including Bankhead, McCormack, Fred Vinson of Kentucky (no relation), and especially Carl Vinson. Johnson quickly adapted to Vinson's idiosyncrasies on the Naval Affairs Committee and developed a warm relationship with the chairman. Since Vinson had become reclusive because of his wife's illness, Johnson made a point of stopping by the Vinson home week after week to tell him ribald stories and the latest congressional gossip.[6]

World War II seemed to affect every family in America in some way, and the Vinsons were no exception. Tillman Snead was drafted into the army and served in an infantry unit in France and Germany. He fought in the Battle of the Bulge and received a Bronze Star with oak leaf cluster. While he was away, Mary Vinson worried about him and

---

[5] Tillman and Karen Snead, interview with the author.

[6] Robert Dallek, *Lone Star Rising: Lyndon Johnson and His Times, 1908–1960* (New York: Oxford University Press, 1991) 162–65; Robert A. Caro, *Master of the Senate* (New York: Alfred A. Knopf, 2002) 158–59.

corresponded regularly with him.[7] Carl's youngest brother, Wilbur Henry, who had made a career of the army, also was in the infantry. He served throughout the war and retired afterwards with the rank of colonel. In addition, Carl had a host of nephews, cousins, and friends in military service. Ed Vinson, the son of his brother Edward from Cordele, had the opportunity to visit his Uncle Carl frequently in Washington during the year before America entered the war. A graduate of Georgia Tech, Ed was working with General Mills in Minneapolis when he received a year's leave to accept an appointment to the National Institute of Public Affairs in Washington, DC. The forty-five interns in the program usually worked with either cabinet or sub-cabinet offices, and did graduate work at American University. Ed shared the highpoints and experiences of this program with his uncle. When he completed the program in June of 1941, he was convinced the United States would soon be at war.

Shortly before Ed left Washington, his attractive fiancée, Betty Alderman, came to visit him for a weekend. A recent Phi Beta Kappa graduate of Agnes Scott College, Betty was articulate and outspoken. When Vinson indicated that he wanted to meet Betty, Ed tried to prepare her for the visit. He explained that Uncle Carl's life was devoted to putting people on the witness stand. "As soon as you enter his office he will start asking you questions," Ed warned, "and he will not give you much time to answer, so you had better be ready for him." Vinson did exactly as Ed had predicted, but Betty was prepared for him. She not only answered his questions, she queried him about topics of interest to her. She brashly expressed the opinion that fortifying Guam was the wrong strategy. She then directed the conversation to the controversial county unit system, which she abhorred and Vinson accepted. Ed, somewhat dismayed at his fiancée's frankness, wondered whether she had offended his uncle. His fears were groundless, however, as Vinson admired spunk and independent thought. A few days later, when Ed saw

---

[7] While Till was in the Army, his sister, Betty Snead, worked in Congressman Vinson's office and lived in the Vinson home until Till returned home. Tillman and Karen Snead, interview with the author; Snead Family Papers.

Uncle Carl again, Vinson remarked: "Ed, I appreciate your bringing Betty over. It was an interesting discussion. And Ed, you marry that girl. She's got sense!" A few years later, long before the county unit system was outlawed, Ed and Betty visited Vinson at his farm and he brought up the subject of the county unit system. "Well Betty," he said slowly in his Middle Georgia drawl, "you were right and I was wrong."[8]

In January 1942 Ed was commissioned an ensign in the navy and was assigned to the Headquarters of the Sixth Naval District in Charleston, South Carolina. He lived at the Middleton Family House on the Battery at Charleston with two other ensigns—Bert Struby from Macon and John F. Kennedy from Boston—and Lieutenant Commander Erwin Sibley from Milledgeville. Struby later edited the *Macon Telegraph,* and Sibley, a bachelor lawyer from Milledgeville, was Carl Vinson's very close friend. He owned a farm near Vinson's and acted as the congressman's chauffeur whenever he was in Milledgeville. The three Georgians could hardly have imagined that the friendly young Bostonian rooming with them one day would be the president of the United States. Ed subsequently saw duty in Britain and in Normandy with the U.S. Ports and Bases France, and in the Atlantic. After the war, when Jack Kennedy was elected to Congress, he wrote Uncle Carl that a bright young man from Boston who had just been elected to the House should be enrolled in the "Carl Vinson College of Congressional Knowledge."[9]

Vinson was never one to look back and rue "what might have been." On the contrary, he took defeats in stride and continually looked forward to new challenges.[10] Thus, in the wake of the tragedy at Pearl Harbor, when Representative John Dingell, a Democrat from Michigan, announced that he would demand court-martial proceedings against five ranking military and naval officers, Vinson denounced the move as "a cheap effort to get newspaper publicity." Continuing, Vinson added: "This is no time to rock the boat. I strongly resent the effort of people who come up here without a scintilla of evidence to indict these men

---

[8] Ed and Betty Vinson, interview with the author.
[9] Ibid; Ed Vinson to the author, 22 April 2003.
[10] Sam Nunn, interview with the author, Atlanta GA, 4 April 2001.

who are offering their lives to their country's service. Congress cannot fight this war and the House of Representatives cannot fight it. We must leave it to the military and the Navy. They must have the privilege, without criticism, of deciding when to make public information for the benefit of the American people."[11]

A week later, Vinson, meeting with David Walsh and Frank Knox, assured his colleagues that "we'll get to the bottom of it."[12] When the Roberts Report on Pearl Harbor came out a month later, Dingell, Hamilton Fish, and others remained dissatisfied, but Vinson took the position that neither an investigation nor court-martial action was feasible at this time. He said that if high ranking officers were detached from duty to testify or serve on boards of inquiry at this time, the armed services in war zones would be impaired.[13]

Working closely with the administration and the Navy Department, Vinson and Walsh, a week after Pearl Harbor, introduced identical bills to increase the size of the navy by 30 percent. Unlike previous bills, this one gave the navy complete flexibility in the types of ships to be built. "The Navy knows what kind of ships it needs to win this war," said Vinson. "If it wants to build all submarines or ships of all types, it can. It will have complete discretion."[14] When Representative Jeb Johnson, a Democrat from Oklahoma, tried to discredit the utility of battleships, which he described as "floating palaces," and to belittle the admirals in charge of naval construction, Vinson, refused to be drawn into a debate between airplanes and battleships. He responded, "We have to have everything in order to win the war." The chairman continued, "You must have battleships, cruisers, submarines, airplanes, and all, to make a forcible attacking unit. You cannot argue against battleships any more than you can argue today that we should abandon the infantry because the aircraft can knock them out."[15] With minimum debate, H.R. 6223 soon became law, as did a host of other measures. H. R. 6392, a measure

[11] *New York Times*, 10 December 1941, 7.

[12] *Washington Post*, 16 December 1941, 2.

[13] *New York Times*, 27 January 1942, 4.

[14] *Washington Post*, 13 December 1941, 2.

[15] *Congressional Record*, 77th Cong., 1st sess., 16 December 1941, 9854.

authorizing the construction of 1,799 auxiliary vessels, was introduced, debated, and passed by a voice vote of the House in precisely ten minutes.[16]

In previous years Vinson had been forced to expend much time and energy to convince skeptical colleagues to approve modest defense measures. Defense measures of all types, even those of unprecedented size, breezed through the House with practically no debate, for all the members agreed that maximum production was needed to win the war. On 28 June 1942 Vinson brought up for debate H. R. 7184: "the largest single authorization bill for the construction of combatant ships that has ever been considered by the Naval Affairs Committee and reported to the House." It authorized an increase in the combatant tonnage of aircraft carriers by 500,000 tons, of cruisers by 500,000 tons, and destroyers and destroyer escort vessels by 900,000 tons, plus the construction of 800 small vessels suitable for use as patrol vessels, mine sweepers, and torpedo boats. In the brief discussion that ensued, Vinson pointed out that of the nearly 4,000,000 tons of combatant vessels that had been authorized for construction, all but 93,629 tons was either in service or under construction. Passage of H. R. 7184, he predicted, would "utilize the country's shipbuilding capacity to the fullest extent." He also predicted that when this program is completed, the United States Navy "will be larger than that of the combined navies of the world." After approximately an hour of discussion, this enormous authorization passed the House 319 to 0. Instead of probing questions or criticism, Representative James Mott of Oregon, the ranking minority member of the Naval Affairs Committee who had served under Vinson for many years, used most of his time to heap praise upon the chairman. In sincere tones he told his colleagues:

> When you listened to the chairman of the Naval Affairs Committee a few minutes ago, you listened to the man who, in my opinion, is the outstanding authority in the United States on

---

[16] Ibid., 77th Cong., 2d sess., 21 January 1942, 514–15; Susan Landrum, "Carl Vinson: A Study in Military Preparedness" (master's thesis, Emory University, 1968) 84.

naval policy. You will note that I said policy—not strategy or tactics, for that is the field of the professional naval expert. This program of building the greatest navy in the world began years ago in the Naval Affairs Committee, just as soon as the expiration of the arms limitation treaty would let us begin. From that time until the present the naval policy of the United States has been made by the Naval Affairs Committee of the House under the leadership of the gentleman from Georgia (Mr. Vinson). He has been years ahead of the country and of the Navy itself in many of the most important features of our great Naval Establishment which have proven most effective and most useful in this war.[17]

With the passage of H. R. 7184 creating a 5-ocean navy, Vinson had sponsored and passed a total of 48 important war measures, authorizing total appropriations of $16,000,000,000, since the session began in January. If the first session of the Seventy-seventh Congress is included, the total number of bills he piloted through the House increased to ninety-nine. Commenting on those statistics, Gladstone Williams of the *Atlanta Constitution* asserted that Vinson "has achieved a record for legislative enactments which has been seldom, if ever, equaled in the history of congress." Vinson's standing in the House is so great, Williams observed, that he could now bring in a bill to fortify the moon and the House probably would approve it.[18] Vinson's naval bills continued to breeze through the House, so that by the end of World War II, despite heavy casualties, the United States had 6 more battleships, 21 more aircraft carriers, 70 more escort carriers, and 127 more submarines than it possessed in 1941.[19] Altogether the navy spent approximately 100 billion dollars in World War II. During the five-year period between 1

---

[17]*Congressional Record,* 77th Cong., 2d sess., 18 June 1942, 5374–83; *Washington Post*, 4 June 1942, 1, 4.

[18] Gladstone Williams, "Washington Parade," *Atlanta Constitution*, 1 July 1942, 8.

[19] C. L. Sulzberger, *World War II* (New York: McGraw-Hill Book Company, 1970) 115–16.

July 1940 and 30 June 1945 additions to the fleet totaled 10 battleships, 18 large aircraft carriers, 9 small aircraft carriers, 110 escort carriers, 2 large cruisers, 10 heavy cruisers, 33 light cruisers, 358 destroyers, 504 destroyer escorts, 211 submarines, and 82,028 landing craft of various types. "Never before in history had any nation spent such sums on construction and maintenance of a navy," observed historian Patrick Abbazia, and Vinson played a key role in steering all of the authorizations through the House.[20]

In an article published shortly after the war ended, economist Eliot Janeway, a prolific author who had served as editor in chief of *Time* since 1932, observed:

> For many years Vinson and his Capitol colleagues have lived together under a nonaggresssion pact. They know that he doesn't care who makes the nation's laws, so long as he can build its Navy, and they have given him a blank check to operate as a one-man Committee of the Whole in naval matters. In return, Congress is assured, from long experience, that the Vinson Navy measures which it votes for will never boomerang. The pact has been justified. In no other field does Congress wield more power, or do individual members suffer less embarrassment.

"During the war years," Janeway continued, "the judgment and foresight of this small-town Southern politician were pretty well vindicated."[21]

Admiral Isoroku Yamamoto, the commander in chief of Japan's Combined Fleet, having studied at Harvard and worked at the Japanese embassy in Washington in the 1920s, had an accurate grasp of America's economic and military capacity. In planning the attack on Pearl Harbor, he told the Japanese premier, "I shall run wild for the first six months,

---

[20] Patrick Abbazia, *Mr. Roosevelt's Navy: The Private War of the U.S. Atlantic Fleet, 1939–1942* (Annapolis: Naval Institute Press, 1975) 3.

[21] Eliot Janeway, "The Man Who Owns the Navy," *Saturday Evening Post* 218 (15 December 1945): 17, 102.

but I have utterly no confidence for the second or third years."[22] His predictions were uncannily accurate. For six months Japanese naval forces were unstoppable as they wreaked havoc upon the American Pacific Fleet at Pearl Harbor and proceeded to capture the Philippines, Guam, Wake, and much of the western Pacific. Nearing Australia, their offensive finally was stopped at the Coral Sea, where the airplanes of the competing carriers fought to a bloody stalemate. A month later at Midway, almost exactly six months after Pearl Harbor, the Japanese suffered a crushing defeat, losing 4 carriers, 250 planes, and 2,200 officers and men. Although outnumbered in ships 162 to 76, Admiral Chester Nimitz had won what proved to be the turning point in the Pacific, the battle that spelled the ultimate doom of Japan.[23] Upon hearing the report of the impressive victory at Midway, Vinson commented it was "just what we expected as soon as we came in contact with the Japanese." It confirms, he said, "that the fighting Americans will whip the Japs at sea just as they will later on land."[24]

The importance of air power and the vulnerability of battleships had been demonstrated clearly in the early stages of the Pacific war when Japanese planes spotted Britain's greatest battleships, the *Repulse* and the *Prince of Wales*, without air escort fifty miles from Singapore, and sunk them in a matter of minutes. Any doubt about the need for carriers was removed by the battles at Coral Sea and Midway. Vinson had long valued the importance of the air arm of the navy and had used his influence to increase production of carriers and airplanes. His five-ocean navy bill made no provision for construction of battleships, and he reported that work had been temporarily deferred "on four or five battleships in order to concentrate on carriers." Moreover, the six new 60,000-ton super-dreadnoughts scheduled to be built were left in the blueprint stage. While the navy had not abandoned the battleship, events,

---

[22] Allen Weinstein and Frank Otto Gatell, *Freedom and Crisis*, 3rd ed., 2 vols. (New York: Random House, 1981) 2:787.

[23] B. H. Lidell Hart, *History of the Second World War* (New York: G. P. Putnam's Sons, 1970) 343–53; Samuel Eliot Morison, *The Two-Ocean War* (Boston: Little, Brown and Company, 1963) 137–63.

[24] *Washington Post*, 6 June 1942, 2.

he said, had proved conclusively that the aircraft carrier "is the backbone of the fleet."[25]

The five-ocean navy had superseded the two-ocean navy, and before the war was over the United States had a seven-ocean navy. In summer 1943, James F. Byrnes, the war mobilization director, noted that new launchings this year will give the navy double its pre-Pearl Harbor tonnage. Secretary of the Navy Frank Knox paid an unusual tribute to the man most responsible for the shipbuilding program now bearing handsome fruit. Carl Vinson, he declared, deserves credit as the father of the seven-ocean navy the United States is now rushing to completion. It was Vinson's foresight, perseverance and influence that enabled the navy to be already embarked on its program for getting ready for war at the time of Pearl Harbor. But for this, the secretary pointed out, our preparation would have been delayed for several years. "I have found in Chairman Vinson one of the most constructive and able associates in the task of building a great new fleet to meet the present emergency," he stated.[26]

As America suffered a series of humiliating defeats in the Pacific during the first six months of the war, the situation in the Atlantic was equally grim. In building up the navy, the emphasis had been on constructing destroyers and larger ships to fight the impending two-ocean war. Small craft were neglected (as were antisubmarine aircraft) in the belief that they could be improvised and rapidly produced in small shipbuilding yards. Consequently, when the United States entered the war, it had practically no defense against German submarines in the Atlantic. The Eastern Sea Frontier, which extended from the Canadian border to Jacksonville, Florida, had no naval planes capable of searching far out to sea. Admiral Karl Doenitz, commander of the German U-boat fleet, took full advantage of America's weakness to devastate the East

---

[25] *Atlanta Constitution*, 17 June 1942, 1; Gladstone Williams, "Washington Parade," *Atlanta Constitution*, 20 June 1942, 4.

[26] Gladstone Williams, "Washington Parade," 6; Paul R. Leach, "Hail Vinson as Father of U.S. 7-Ocean Navy," Vinson Scrapbooks, book 1945–1948, on loan from Tillman Snead to Georgia College and State University, Milledgeville, GA.

Coast shipping lanes. In a little more than 2 weeks in January 1942, his U-boats sank 13 vessels, measuring 95,000 gross tons. During the first 4 months of 1942, the Germans sank 87 ships totaling 515,000 tons in coastal waters. Merchantmen made perfect targets silhouetted by the lights of coastal cities, but Americans, fearing the loss of the tourist trade, refused to darken their cities at night. It was not until 18 April that the Eastern Sea Frontier ordered waterfront lights and sky signs cut off. With no more than twelve U-boats at any one time, Doenitz, placing his vessels at strategic spots from New York to the Caribbean, sank an appalling number of transports month after month. After six months of combat, the United States had managed to destroy only eight German U-boats—about as many as Germany was producing every ten days. "The massacre enjoyed by the U-boats along our Atlantic Coast in 1942," historian Samuel Eliot Morison observed, "was as much a national disaster as if saboteurs had destroyed half a dozen of our biggest war plants."[27] Military historian Edwin P. Hoyt, author of more than a dozen books on World War II, contends that "twenty more U-boats, even ten, made available to Admiral Doenitz for his effort against America in the months from January through July 1942, might have turned the tide."[28]

On 12 March 1942, President Roosevelt signed an executive order making Admiral Ernest J. King the chief of Naval Operations. Since he was already commander in chief of the fleet, King, by holding both positions, had complete military control of the navy. "Never before had an American naval officer exercised the authority and responsibility delegated to King by the President of the United States, and never again could one do so," notes King's biographer.[29] A graduate of the Naval Academy in 1901, the tall, rigid sixty-three-year-old King had shown exceptional ability in almost every branch of the navy. A hard man with little sense of humor, he was more respected than liked; his eagerness to get things done quickly, coupled with an abrupt and rude manner,

---

[27] Morison, *The Two-Ocean War*, 102–22.

[28] Edwin P. Hoyt, *U-Boats Offshore* (New York: Stein and Day Publishers, 1978) viii.

[29] Thomas B. Buell, *Master of Sea Power, A Biography of Fleet Admiral Ernest J. King* (Boston: Little, Brown and Company, 1980) 179.

infuriated many who had to deal with him. Churchill and Stimson hated him. Admirals William H. Standley and Adolphus Andrews had acrimonious relationships with him. Secretary Knox, who brought King to Washington in December 1941, felt threatened by him and tried to dilute his authority. Forrestal respected King and bore him no animosity, but King, on his part, developed an intense dislike of Forrestal. Fortunately, Vinson worked well in private with the acerbic admiral.[30]

Concerned over the staggering losses in the Atlantic, Vinson corresponded regularly with Admiral King, hoping to find a solution to the problem. In response to one of his letters, King bluntly informed Chairman Vinson, "The facts of the matter are that we have not yet got the 'tools' that are necessary to protect shipping in the Eastern Sea Frontier (Florida to Maine)—or anywhere else. Production is months upon months behind schedule." The admiral added, "We have been—and are—taking over, manning and equipping every vessel of every kind that has any worthwhile characteristics for operations off shore and along shore. Included in these is a growing number of small craft which have no real military value but are being used solely as 'rescue vessels' whose primary mission is the rescue of survivors."[31] At Vinson's request, King's chief of staff, Vice Admiral Russell Wilson, appeared before the Naval Affairs Committee on 3 June 1942, to discuss antisubmarine warfare. Following his testimony, Vinson released to the press a lengthy statement on the antisubmarine campaign. Attempting to reassure the public, he asserted that "the anti-submarine warfare organization has now passed through its period of growing pains, is well established and is functioning efficiently." The navy, he continued, was now making substantial progress in the four essentials of organization, material, personnel, and training. In dealing with submarines, the U.S. faces a tough and clever enemy who is building more submarines, he stated, "but he cannot build them in the proportion we are increasing our means of

---

[30] Ibid., 100–101, 237, 450–51; Morison, *The Two-Ocean War*, 35; Arnold A. Ragow, *James Forrestal: A Study of Personality, Politics, and Policy* (New York: The Macmillan Company, 1963) 101–105.

[31] Ernest King to Carl Vinson, 19 March 1942, Ernest King Papers, Manuscript Division, Box 16, Library of Congress, Washington, DC

combating them. The naval committee has full confidence that we shall defeat the submarine."[32] Vinson reiterated some of the same points in an article published in *Collier's* on 31 October. He admitted "we were caught woefully short," but assured the public that "from now on, we can reasonably expect improvement in the situation, until all ships will be as comparatively safe as those in convoys."[33] As American radar, blimps, and planes came increasingly into play, the defenders gradually gained supremacy over the attackers and the U-boat menace was greatly reduced, as Vinson predicted.

Throughout his congressional career, Vinson had always put in long hours, but his workload expanded during the war years. In addition to shepherding unprecedented authorization measures through the House, he also figured prominently in two major issues resulting directly from the enormous industrial expansion for defense. The first was the extensive investigation of the naval defense program, which sought to eliminate waste and excessive profits for business. The other issue was strikes by labor unions in defense industry and the effort to secure legislative restrictions on the strikes. Vinson had already expended much effort on both issues before Pearl Harbor, and his work continued throughout the war.

A week before the Japanese attack on Pearl Harbor, President Roosevelt finally decided that something needed to be done about union strikes disrupting defense programs. In debate on the floor of the House, Vinson declared that union leaders had lost control of a small minority of union "troublemakers" and insisted the government must step in. "The hour has come for this Government to reassert its sovereignty," he shouted.[34] The House, more resolute than the Senate in curbing labor abuses, had three labor bills to consider, all imposing more drastic restrictions on unions than any bill presented in the Senate. A bill by Howard Smith, a conservative Democrat from southwest Virginia, would ban mass picketing and jurisdictional or organizational strikes, freeze the

---

[32] *Washington Post*, 8 June 1942, 4.

[33] Carl Vinson, "The Battle of the Atlantic," *Collier's* 110 (31 October 1942): 18–20.

[34] *Washington Post*, 2 December 1941, 8.

closed and open shops at their present status, require a majority vote of the workers before a strike is called, outlaw boycott and sympathy strikes, assure workers protection from pickets, and require unions to register and report financial operations to the National Labor Relations Board. The second bill, introduced by Robert Ramspeck of Georgia, the ranking Democrat on the Labor Committee, would provide for voluntary conciliation, mediation, and arbitration of defense disputes. It would empower a defense mediation board to enforce a sixty-day cooling off period before strikes and would authorize the government to seize and operate struck plants. The Vinson bill was the third one under consideration. It called for a thirty-day cooling off period and compulsory mediation. It also authorized the government to seize and operate plants in which production had been halted by labor conflicts.[35]

On 3 December, 129 Democrats joined with 123 House Republicans to pass the Smith bill by vote of 252 to 136 over the protests of administration leaders. Vinson voted with the majority. The House apparently had grown weary of the frequent strikes and the unwillingness of powerful union leaders like John L. Lewis to support any of the more moderate proposals.[36] At the same time the House passed the Smith bill, the Congress of Industrial Organizations, with unbelievably poor timing, called a strike at the Pusey & Jones Shipbuilding Corporation in Wilmington, Delaware, halting production of $22,600,000 in cargo ships.[37] The Senate, preferring to enact its own version of strike legislation, refused to act upon the Smith bill. When the House refused to take action on the Senate bill, strike legislation in the first session of the Seventy-Seventh Congress came to a halt.[38]

In the second session of the Seventy-Seventh Congress, Representative Smith introduced H. R. 6790, which provided for limitations on profits and the suspension for the duration of the war of both the closed shop and the forty-hour week. The Naval Affairs

---

[35] *Washington Times-Herald*, 2 December 1941, Vinson Scrapbooks, book 1940–1942.

[36] *Washington Post*, 4 December 1941, 1, 4.

[37] Ibid., 8.

[38] Landrum, "Carl Vinson: A Study in Military Preparedness," 98–99.

Committee opened hearings on the bill on 19 March, and Smith was the first to testify. He was followed over the course of the next month by Under Secretary of War Robert Patterson, Under Secretary of the Navy James Forrestal, Assistant Secretary of the Navy Ralph Bard, Vice Admiral Samuel Robinson of the Office of Procurement and Material, Chairman of the War Production Board Donald Nelson, Secretary of Labor Frances Perkins, Chairman of the United States Maritime Commission Rear Admiral Emory Land, Secretary of the Navy Frank Knox, and a host of labor leaders, members of Congress, and small businessmen. As usual, Chairman Vinson dominated the hearings with probing questions and incisive comments. When Forrestal objected to the bill, Vinson pointedly retorted, "If our plan is wrong, throw it out of the window and bring in another and better plan."[39] Vinson's strongest barbs were directed at Bard and Nelson. When Bard stated that paying double time on Sunday had the effect of slowing up work on other days of the week, Vinson exploded:

> Now, let us get right down to the bottom of it. I am not in a critical frame of mind, because we are all on the same basis. Let us see what the Navy Department has done to correct that. Just tell us frankly. You recognize that condition. You say it has a tendency to slow up production. You are charged in the Navy Department to produce. That is your responsibility....
>
> The President set out a program and he said this was our program: 45,000 tanks in 1942, 8,000,000 tons of ships, 60,000 airplanes, 25,000 antiaircraft guns.
>
> Now, as I figure it, there are about 286 more days left in this year. We have got to produce at this rate 25,000 antiaircraft guns. That is one every half-hour.
>
> We have got to produce 45,000 tanks. That is one every 12 minutes.

[39] House, Committee on Naval Affairs, *Hearings on H. R. 6790, To Permit the Performance of Essential Labor on Naval Contracts....*, 77th Cong., 2d sess., 20 March 1942, Nos. 205, 2517.

We have got to produce 60,000 airplanes, which means 1 every 8 minutes.

Now that is your job, and that is the job of the War Department, and yet you tell the committee that by paying double time on Sundays you have been cognizant of the fact that it slowed up your production. Now, I want you to tell us what you have done in your capacity as Under Secretary to help remedy that condition.[40]

Donald Nelson had been chairman of the War Production Board only sixty days when he came before the committee. He objected to the proposed bill and seemed unwilling to say anything negative about labor. After much probing, Vinson finally got him to admit that strikes were "having some effect" on production. Nelson favored the elimination of double time pay for Saturdays, Sundays, and holidays, but he believed the unions would make these concessions voluntarily. Vinson pointed out that "up to this good hour" he had not yet convinced them to "get away from business as usual." He then asked Nelson how much longer "we should drift with the tide." Nelson assured him that the concessions would be accomplished within thirty days or he would be back before the committee asking for legislation.[41]

After hearing extensive testimony, Vinson offered a substitute bill on 17 April. The revised bill broadened the scope of the original bill from naval contractors to all war contractors and raised allowable profits from 6 percent to 8 percent. Both the original bill and the Vinson substitute eliminated "premium pay for overtime, Saturdays, Sundays, or holidays or night work." Under the substitute, time-and-a-half pay was accepted for work in excess of forty-eight hours per week. Several members of the committee expressed serious reservations about the bill and the substitute. Following his usual practice, Vinson had printed thirty copies of the substitute for the members' consideration, but some members insisted that he print many more copies for public consumption. Seventy-five-year-old Joseph Shannon of Missouri

---

[40] Ibid., 2536–37.
[41] Ibid., 2578–83.

complained, "130,000,000 inhabitants of this country, and only 30 copies printed." The debate showed clearly that Vinson wanted the committee to adopt the bill expeditiously and then publicize and refine it, whereas several members wanted more public input and lengthy debate before voting on the bill. Responding to the criticism, Vinson agreed to have 200 copies printed. After several days of acrimonious debate and parliamentary maneuvering, Democratic Representative Michael Bates of Pennsylvania moved to table H. R. 6790 and the substitute. Vinson, Maas, and Mott tried to convince the committee to approve the bill and then change it later in executive session, but to no avail. In an unusual rebuff to the chairman, the Naval Affairs Committee tabled the bill by vote of 13 to 12, ending two months of careful study by the committee.[42]

The Georgia Swamp Fox, who rarely lost control of his committee, had momentarily lost sight of the political concerns of the committee members. Holding one of the safest seats in Congress and representing a district with few union members, Vinson did not worry about offending organized labor or facing opposition. To him, the issue was crystal clear. As long as American soldiers and seamen were risking their lives in defense of their country, every patriotic American—including union members—should be willing to sacrifice for the duration of the war. Some of his colleagues, however, were not so fortunate. Facing serious opposition every two years, they were unwilling to alienate large blocs of voters. Moreover, they could point to President Roosevelt's statement, delivered less than a week before the vote, that no labor legislation was necessary at this time. The committee would have been happy to impose profit limits on industry, but without the president's backing, the majority was not willing to challenge organized labor. In an interview years later, Vinson recalled the reason his bill failed. "It didn't go down well with some of those big city politicians up North," he remarked.[43] More than a year elapsed before Congress finally passed the War Labor Disputes Act, which provided for a cooling-off period before strikes

---

[42] Ibid., 17 April 1942, No. 209, 3044–3117; *New York Times*, 1 May 1942, 14.

[43] Landrum, "Carl Vinson: A Study in Military Preparedness," 99.

could be called, but it did not contain the strict provisions offered in both the Smith and Vinson bills.[44]

Although Vinson had little success in curbing the power of unions, he fared much better in investigating the naval defense program. The special investigating committee led by Washington attorney Edmund Toland began its work on 13 April 1941, and submitted a Preliminary Report on 20 January 1942. The investigating committee did field investigations at naval bases, naval and private shipyards, and airplane factories, and submitted questionnaires to all contractors doing business with the Navy Department. Covering the period 1 January 1940, through 1 November 1941, the preliminary report admittedly was tentative and incomplete, but it revealed interesting statistics nonetheless. Out of 5,198 navy contractors of all types, responses were received from 1,228, reporting on a total of 19,086 navy contracts. The value of the contracts covered was $3,889,168,760, on which profits of $287,859,448 were reported, an average of 7.99 percent of the cost of the contracts. The report also revealed that more than 60 percent of the amount of all the contracts had gone to 15 companies, which made an average profit of 8.21 percent on the cost of the contracts.[45]

On the whole the report presented a favorable view of the Navy Department and the defense industry, but it found enough abuses to justify several recommendations. The 27 percent profit by the Cleveland Diesel Engine Division of General Motors Corporation amounting to more than $2,000,000 and the excessive profits realized by the Bath Iron Works and other companies convinced the committee to recommend the adoption of a profit limitation on defense contracts. When instances of such abuse were uncovered, the committee insisted on renegotiating the contracts, a policy that saved the government millions of dollars. The report indicated that renegotiated contracts with General Motors already had saved $4.5 million and renegotiated aviation contracts had saved $12 million. Finding that "a great deal of waste" was due to the "lack of

---

[44] Ibid.
[45] House, Committee on Naval Affairs, *Investigation of the Naval Defense Program*, 77th Cong., 2d sess., 20 January 1942, H. Rept. 1634, 2–4.

uniformity in cost-accounting," the report also called for the adoption of "a strict and standardized system."[46]

Perhaps the most surprising part of the report was its direct criticism of labor. By tabulating union assets, it presented an astounding picture of concentrated wealth. From 31 October 1939, to 31 March 1941, the gross assets of 117 unions representing over 6 million members increased from $71,915,665 to $82,594,959, and some of the biggest and wealthiest unions had not reported to the committee. In response to the tremendous financial gains made by labor organizations, the committee recommended that "suitable legislation be enacted requiring all labor unions (along with other special interest groups) to register with a suitable governmental body and to furnish pertinent information concerning their officers, members, and financial condition at periodic intervals." Since the strike tactics of labor organizations had been responsible for much of the delay in defense contracts, the committee also urged Congress to enact "fair and suitable legislation designed to prevent interference with the progress and speed of the defense program by strikes and work stoppages."[47] Seven Democrats on the twenty-seven-member Naval Affairs Committee filed a minority protest to the union portion of the report, and Representative Joseph Shannon asked that the entire labor section "be physically stricken from the report."[48] In view of the determined opposition of the minority to any criticism of organized labor, it was not surprising that Vinson encountered formidable opposition a few months later when he sought to enact legislation curbing unions' power.

During the spring and summer of 1942, the Naval Affairs Committee held lengthy hearings in which it heard the testimony of chief executives, auditors, and attorneys from a host of businesses, both large and small, doing business with the navy. Toland's investigating committee provided the full Naval Affairs Committee ample

---

[46] Ibid., 22, 24, 27.

[47] Ibid., 22, 26, 106–107; "The Congress," *Time* 39 (26 January 1942): 14.

[48] *Investigation of the Naval Defense Program*, H. Rept. 1634, 29; "Probe's View of Arms Profits Raises Cry for Drastic Curbs," *Newsweek* 19 (2 February 1942): 38.

documentation of company financial records before the business leaders were subpoenaed. As usual, Vinson chaired the meetings and dominated the questioning of witnesses. The probing questions of Vinson and other committee members coupled with the public exposure of company records quickly produced impressive results. On 24 April, the Sperry Corporation "voluntarily" renegotiated its contracts with the War and Navy Departments at a savings of $100,000,000. A week later the Bendix Aviation Corporation reduced its prices on navy and army contracts to the extent of $73,354,000. When the former president of Bendix acknowledged that reduction, Vinson remarked, "Over in Jerusalem they have a famous wall known as the Wailing Wall. That witness table is now going to be known as the 'mourners' bench."[49]

The testimony revealed numerous instances of inflated salaries and excessive bonuses, which the executives could not justify. Any unnecessary expense for the navy angered Vinson, but the role of "war brokers," agents who specialized in getting navy contracts for businessmen unfamiliar with the navy, especially irked him. Among the dozen brokers who testified before the committee were William Scrimgeour and Horace Ward. Scrimgeour, whose family firm charged fees ranging from 2.5 percent to 10 percent, made $613,798 in 1941. He denied that he had any pull with the navy, but admitted that he knew "plenty of people down there." When balding, hawk-nosed Ward, who had charged his twenty clients $431,463 in 18 months, experienced a change of heart and told the committee it was wrong for such commissions to be paid on navy business, Vinson inquired, "When did your conscience begin to hurt you?"[50]

Further testimony revealed that A. P. Shirley, onetime army major, formed a "sales engineering" firm with two former navy civilian employees, which engineered war contracts for forty-six munitions makers, yielding them handsome profits in 1941 and 1942. Convinced that the three men had an "inside track" at the Navy Department, an angry Vinson declared, "You three men, sitting here in Washington, are

---

[49] House, Committee on Naval Affairs, *Investigation of the Naval Defense Program*, 77th Cong., 2d sess., 7 vols., (Washington, DC, 1942) 2:239.

[50] "The Congress," *Time* 40 (27 July 1942): 14.

getting $1,150 each a day, every day for the first six months of this year, including Sunday, while boys are dying at Bataan and Corregidor and on the *Lexington*. I am going to see if I can break up this practice of contingent fees. There's no justification for it."[51]

True to his word, Vinson sponsored a bill that sought to outlaw the payment of contingent fees in connection with government procurement. Supported by the War and Navy Departments, it easily passed the House but died in the Senate Naval Affairs Committee.[52] Consequently, despite the adverse publicity generated by the hearings, sales agents continued to flourish in Washington and throughout the country. "The war has given them a heyday," remarked the general counsel for the Naval Affairs Committee, "and they are making the most of it."[53] In 1943 the Naval Affairs Committee held more hearings, which provided additional documentation of the exorbitant profits made by "sales agents." Finally, H. R. 1900, a watered-down version of Vinson's bill, passed both houses of Congress and received the president's signature on 14 July 1943.[54]

Although infuriated by the practices of the "war brokers," Vinson could be forgiving when they testified honestly and admitted their guilt, as demonstrated in the following interchange with Jay A. Mount, a "war broker" operating out of Washington, DC.

The Chairman: "Your conscience worried you."

Mr. Mount: "I think you might say that in essence; yes, sir, in all fairness."

The Chairman: "I think that is very commendable. You felt it was all right to jump from $3,000 to around $75,000, but when it got up to

---

[51] Ibid., "Huge Profits of War-Work Agents Cited, Vinson Scrapbooks, book 1945–1948; *Investigation of the Naval Defense Program*, 15–16 July 1942, 7:1089–1126.

[52] House, Committee on Naval Affairs, *Prohibiting the Payment of Contingent Fees for Services*, 77th Cong., 2d sess., 20 July 1942, Report No. 2356, 1–5; *Congressional Record*, 77th Cong., 2d sess., 20 July 1942, 6409–26.

[53] House, Committee on Naval Affairs, *Investigation of the Progress of the War Effort*, 78th Cong., 1st sess., 25 March–7 April 1943, Hearings pursuant to H. Res. 30 (Washington, DC, 1943), 1–2.

[54] *Congressional Record*, 78th Cong., 1st sess., 3624–29, 7354, 7551.

$95,000 it began to hurt you a little.... Therefore, you had to get rid of two good customers, two good clients, and you just threw them overboard because you began to worry about the enormous amount that you were making. Isn't that correct?"

At first Mount tried to justify his actions, but after more probing questions he soon realized the hopelessness of his situation.

> The Chairman: "You felt, in the condition the country is in, that you were making too much."
> Mr. Mount: "I make no denial; that is absolutely correct."

Mount's frankness and admission of guilt made a favorable impression on Vinson.

> The Chairman: "When anybody's conscience begins to worry him and he begins to adjust his conduct to fit his conscience, that is a very commendable thing, and then when he contributes anything to the efficiency of the Government service, that is worthwhile too. Thank you very much, Mr. Mount. You and your wife are excused."[55]

When the supplemental report of the Investigation of the Naval Defense Program was released on 22 July 1942, it emphasized the success of the renegotiation process. Already, during a short period of time, renegotiation had saved the taxpayers $533,958,887, plus $170,000,000 in indirect savings, for a total of $703,958,887. Moreover, as Vinson pointed out, pending negotiation would increase that total substantially, and many millions of dollars would be saved in future contracts. After surveying 25,000 Navy Department contracts, the committee believed that 95 percent of war contractors were doing an honest and effective job and receiving reasonable profits, while only 5

---

[55]*Investigation of the Progress of the War Effort,* Hearings pursuant to H. Res. 30, 197–217.

percent were taking advantage of the war situation and receiving
excessive profits.[56]

That Vinson, the navy's strongest advocate in Congress, would
chair the committee assigned the task of investigating the navy was akin
to making the fox the guardian of the hen house. But the results showed
that he was as adept at rooting out waste as he was in building up the
navy. In 1941 the Senate created the Truman Committee to investigate
the national defense program, but its functions were largely confined to
army contracts. The apparent discrimination between the two services
reflected a belief in Congress that the specialized Naval Affairs
Committee, under Vinson's leadership, could investigate excess profits
on naval contracts more effectively. Although the Truman Committee
generated more headlines, Vinson proved to be as alert a watchdog as
Senator Harry Truman. He later confided, "We forced the return of more
excess profits than the Truman Committee."[57] Eliot Janeway pointed out
that Vinson was extremely proud of the fact that not once did the Truman
Committee "catch his Navy doing anything wrong." Vinson's own staff
of sleuths "always managed to find the trouble first."[58]

During the latter stages of the war, Vinson received an unusual
tribute. Rarely in the history of the House of Representatives had a
portrait of a sitting member been unveiled, but an exception was made
for Vinson. The members of his committee had commissioned Lawrence
A. Powers, a well-known portrait painter and reserve officer in the navy,
to do the life-size portrait of Vinson, who had then served on the committee twenty-seven years and chaired it thirteen years. Appropriately, it
was hung in the meeting room of the House Naval Affairs Committee.
Joining the committee in honoring Vinson in the unveiling ceremony
were several dignitaries, including Senator Walter George of Georgia,
Assistant Secretary of the Navy Ralph Bard, White House Chief of Staff
Admiral William Leahy, and Admiral Ernest King. President Roosevelt,

---

[56] *Investigation of the Naval Defense Program, Supplemental Report*, H.
Rept. 2371, 26–32.

[57] Calvin W. Enders, "The Vinson Navy," (Ph.D. diss., Michigan State
University, 1970) 141–42.

[58] Janeway, "The Man Who Owns the Navy," 102.

Secretary of the Navy Knox, and Speaker of the House Rayburn, who were unable to attend, sent congratulatory messages. In accepting the portrait for the committee, Vinson's longtime colleague Patrick Drewry called attention to the chairman's "good-natured persistence with his committee," and "his steady and studious and well-informed presentation in the House of the action of his committee."[59]

Emphasizing the nonpartisan nature of Vinson's committee, senior minority member Melvin Maas told the gathering that he had worked in harmony with Vinson and insisted that the House Naval Affairs Committee "is a team with Carl as captain."[60] In praising his longtime colleague, Representative W. Sterling Cole of New York pointed out that Vinson, who began his service in the other world war, "has contributed more to the development and expansion of the American Navy over the past quarter century than any other individual in the Nation during that period of time."[61]

Perhaps the most insightful of all the tributes, however, came from an unexpected source. Admiral King, a man not noted as a gifted speaker or writer, offered the following heartfelt tribute on behalf of himself and "every other Navy and Marine Corps officer who knows the chairman, or who has appeared before his committee." He said:

> For nearly 30 years the distinguished chairman of this committee has influenced naval policy by his sound judgment, by his perspective, and by his foresight. He has come to know the naval service better than any other Member of Congress, and for that matter, better than a great many people who are in the naval services themselves.
>
> As a legislator in naval matters, he has established a record that is not likely to be equaled. Besides all this, he has a way with him.

---

[59] *Atlanta Constitution*, 21 January 1944, 6; Proceedings on the Occasion of the Unveiling of the Portrait of Hon. Carl Vinson, Chairman, Naval Affairs Committee, House of Representatives, Thursday, 20 January 1944, 1261–67, Vinson Scrapbooks, book 1945–1948.

[60] Proceedings on the Occasion of the Unveiling of the Portrait of Vinson, 1268.

[61] Ibid., 1262.

We have learned that we can approach him with our problems and that they will be given due consideration. In keeping with his understanding of naval officers and their strong points, and their faults, Mr. Vinson seems to have a sixth sense which tells him when to support the proposal made to him and when to give us a sound spanking and send us back to the Navy Department. I strongly suspect that this sixth sense is common sense.

Any individual who knows his job can command the respect of his fellow men. When that individual does his job in such a way as to gain not only their respect but their unquestioned loyalty, it is proof of duty well done and of unfaltering devotion to that duty.

In the case of the gentleman in whose honor we meet today, the high regard in which he is held by his colleagues and all who know him is shared in no uncertain manner by the Navy and the Marine Corps. He believes in us and we believe in him. He has earned for himself the confidence and the esteem of the entire membership of the naval services, and I am happy to have the opportunity to say so publicly.

His portrait in this committee room will be a permanent testimonial to his greatness. It will serve as a constant reminder to us all that courtesy, patience, hard work and, above all, a clear perspective, are invaluable in discharging our responsibilities.

May we have the benefit of his wise counsel for many years to come. [62]

By this time, Vinson had already received numerous honors and accolades, and in the course of his long and distinguished career would receive many more. But none touched him as deeply as this simple one-hour ceremony on 20 January 1944, offered voluntarily by friends, colleagues, and those who knew him best.

---

[62] Ibid., 1266.

10

Postwar Conflicts

Concentration of power in a few inevitably brings
about the elimination of personal liberty.

Carl Vinson, 1956

Long before the end of World War II, Vinson began to direct his thoughts to the needs of the postwar navy. While he continued to shepherd huge naval bills through the House in 1944 and 1945 in order to achieve the victory, he pondered what America's defense needs would be after Germany and Japan had been defeated. He knew the country would demand a significant reduction in military expenditures, and he too favored cutting costs. But his great fear was that the American Navy, the largest fleet the world had ever seen, would be summarily dismantled when peace was achieved. The legacy of the Washington Conference haunted him, and he was determined that the folly committed after World War I would not happen after World War II.

Early in 1944 Vinson was appointed to the Select Committee on Post-war Military Policy, a prestigious committee that would exert considerable influence on American military affairs in the postwar years. Chaired by Representative Clifton Woodrum of Virginia and generally known as the Woodrum Committee, it held its first hearings in late April and May, before the launching of the Normandy invasion. The first witnesses called by the Woodrum Committee were representatives of the War Department. All of them, including Secretary of War Stimson, spoke of the desirability of a single military department and recommended that Congress approve the "principle" of unification immediately. Vinson, who believed that the army and navy had distinct missions and that the services should be coordinated rather than united, well understood why the War Department's drive for unification was undertaken while the war was still going on. "Now is the psychological time to do it before it cools off," he observed. Although favoring unification "in principle," Vinson failed to see how creating a separate air force, as the army suggested, would achieve unification. To block the army's plan for unification, Vinson faced a Herculean task, as all of the twenty-three members of the Woodrum Committee except for him and one or two others from the Naval Affairs Committee seemed to support it. Secretary of War Stimson, who believed that unification should be "the primary objective of the postwar period," wanted quick congressional endorsement of the principle of unification so that the issue would not get bogged down in controversy. Vinson, however, thwarted the plan of Stimson and the War Department. His probing questions at the hearings revealed the lack of logic behind the scheme and thrust the issue into the very controversy Stimson feared. The movement for unification received another blow when Navy Secretary Frank Knox, a strong supporter of unification, died suddenly on 28 April 1944, upsetting the War Department's plans. Since his successor, James Forrestal, was skeptical of unification, Stimson soon terminated the hearings.[1]

From the Woodrum Committee hearings the navy had learned that their old prewar ally, the army high command, had abandoned its former opposition to unification and was now engaged in a serious political campaign to get it enacted into law. The navy also learned that the army air force was determined to become an autonomous third branch of the military service, at least equal in stature to the army and the navy. The

---

[1] *Congressional Record*, 78th Cong., 2d sess., 29 March 1944, 3250; Vincent Davis, *Postwar Defense Policy and the U.S. Navy, 1943–1946* (Chapel Hill: University of North Carolina Press, 1966) 58–63; Walter Millis, *Arms and the State* (New York: The Twentieth Century Fund, 1958) 146; Demetrios Caraley, *The Politics of Military Unification* (New York: Columbia University Press, 1966) 25–34.

creation of a separate air force raised serious questions about the future of the navy's aviation component. In response to these perceived threats, the navy developed an agency to devise political strategy for use in the bureaucratic struggle and to prepare those officers who would be sent to the struggle's front line.[2] Three months after the Woodrum Committee hearings ended, Forrestal wrote to Vinson, "The question of a single Department of Defense, I do not think for a moment we can take this lightly, and I have so told Admiral King.... Publicity is as much a part of war today as logistics or training and we must so recognize it. I am happy to say that Admiral King shares these views."[3] Working closely with Secretary Forrestal, Admiral King, and others, Vinson played a major role in the navy's political efforts which culminated in the National Security Act of 1947.

On 12 April 1945, three weeks before the surrender of Germany, the president who had led the nation for twelve years, from the depths of the Great Depression through the Second World War, died suddenly at the Little White House in Warm Springs, Georgia. Like all Americans, Vinson was deeply saddened by the loss of his friend, but not terribly shocked by the news. "I was with the president recently," he told his nephew Ed Vinson, who had spent the night with him en route home from overseas on medical leave: "Roosevelt was very drawn and much thinner and his hearing was much affected."[4] Vinson was named to the official committee of the House to attend the funeral services at the White House.[5] With the death of Roosevelt an era had ended. For many years, Vinson had been a regular visitor to the White House and had worked harmoniously with the president in creating the victorious fleet. It would be many years before Vinson again developed a warm and effective relationship with the occupant of the White House.

---

[2] Davis, *Postwar Defense Policy and the U.S. Navy*, 63–65.

[3] Walter Millis, ed., *The Forrestal Diaries* (New York: The Viking Press, 1951) 9.

[4] Ed and Betty Vinson, interview with the author, Atlanta GA, 7 August 2001.

[5] *Congressional Record*, 79th Cong., 1st sess., 14 April 1945, 3356.

Roosevelt had carefully avoided any commitment whatever on the War Department proposal to create an autonomous air force within a unification scheme. His successor, Harry Truman, however, already had expressed unequivocal support for such a reform, and his newly appointed secretary of state shared his views. Moreover, Truman's military experience was largely confined to the army. An old army captain, he had the highest respect for Stimson and General George Marshall, the army chief of staff, but he lacked similar ties to, or affection for, the navy. Prior to his election as vice president, he had served as a member of the "quote Upper House," as Vinson derisively referred to the Senate, and he was an outspoken partisan who would choose his side and fight for it.[6]

Resolved to beat the president and the army on the issue of unification, the Georgia Swamp Fox carefully planned his strategy. First, he explained to Chairman Andrew May of the House Military Affairs Committee that under the merger, Vinson, by right of seniority, would become head of the combined military and naval committees, leaving May without a position. The following day, May came out against unification. On 19 June Vinson's committee met with the Senate Committee on Naval Affairs in a joint session to hear the Navy Department's overall postwar plans. As orchestrated by Forrestal and Vinson, Forrestal and Admiral King did most of the testifying. In his testimony, Forrestal argued that the navy should be made "flexible," so that its size and composition could be varied in accordance with the "blood pressure of the international community." He then listed the following six criteria so that each congressman could "measure the adequacy of his nation's navy in the light of world conditions then prevailing." He said:

(1) For support of the U.S. commitment to any international peacekeeping force.

(2) For insuring naval superiority over any navy, or combination of navies, 'in the western part of the North or South Atlantic Oceans or anywhere in the Pacific.'

---

[6] Davis, *Postwar Defense Policy and the U.S. Navy*, 118

(3) For police and occupation duties in captured areas.

(4) For local defense and sea frontier forces.

(5) For training naval forces and the continuing development of naval warfare.

(6) For maintaining auxiliary ships and landing craft adequate to support operations by ground forces.[7]

Since the navy presentations made a favorable impression on the two committees, Vinson, Forrestal, and Senator Walsh arranged to have an oral presentation to President Truman a few days later. Vinson next sought from Congress a general preliminary endorsement of the navy's program before the coming storm of controversy diminished the chances of success. The navy's plans were not yet complete enough for a statute, so Vinson decided to introduce a "House concurrent resolution," a form of legislative action not carrying the force of law but that would exert considerable pressure within the government by expressing "the sense of Congress." On 11 September, he introduced House Concurrent Resolution 80, titled "Composition of the Postwar Navy" and Senator Walsh introduced a similar measure in the Senate. The Vinson-Walsh plan called for a peacetime navy of 1,079 combat ships, a reduction of only 229 vessels from its current strength. The biggest change in capital ships was the recommended reduction in the number of battleships from twenty-four to eighteen. The plan called for retaining the three 42,000 ton aircraft carriers as well as twenty-four 27,000 ton aircraft carriers, a reduction of only three from the fleet. Aside from their proposals on carriers and battleships, the chairmen recommended the maintenance of 3 large cruisers, 31 heavy cruisers, 48 light cruisers, 367 destroyers, 296 escort destroyers, and 200 submarines. About one-third of the force would be "kept fully manned and ready for any emergency." Another third would be organized into reserve fleets and partly manned. The final third, in decommissioned status, would be kept available for recommissioning "if and when needed."[8]

---

[7] Ibid., 157–58.

[8] Ibid., 166–82; *New York Times*, 10 September 1945, 1, 3.

On 19 September 1945, only seventeen days after the Japanese formally surrendered on the deck of the giant battleship *Missouri* in Tokyo Bay, Vinson's Naval Affairs Committee opened hearings on his resolution. The hearings ran through 28 September and were dominated by the strong testimony of Secretary Forrestal, Admiral King, and Admiral Frederick Horne. The new focus of the hearings, historian Vincent Davis points out, *"was on naval aviation, carrier task forces, and a postwar Navy to be built around these forces. The new emphasis was on the variety of tasks that these forces could perform, including strategic bombing. The new sense of direction was toward the development of an atomic bombing capability for carrier task forces."*[9] The Naval Affairs Committee approved House Concurrent Resolution 80, and early in November the House also approved it by vote of 347 to 0.[10] The resolution that passed the House unanimously was not even considered in the Senate by request of the president. Truman's quest for a smaller and less expensive navy ran headlong into Vinson's plans and would produce serious clashes between the two headstrong Democrats over the next five years.

As soon as the war ended, the public demanded that the troops be returned home immediately. The public also insisted on lower taxes, economy in government, and a lessening of all forms of federal intervention in private affairs—issues that strengthened the Republicans. Truman, a practical politician, adjusted his policies to the new realities. Although he opposed instantaneous demobilization, he was as powerless as the military to resist an aroused public demanding that "the boys be brought home." By the middle of November 1945 well over half of the eligible men overseas had been returned home. The navy had used battleships, carriers, cruisers—almost any vessels they could find—as troop transports. More than 3 million men had been returned, and the navy had furnished 55 percent of the ships that had done the job, but the political pressure did not abate. Almost every day, statements critical of

---

[9] Davis, *Postwar Defense Policy and the U.S. Navy*, 195. Emphasis by Davis.
[10] *Atlanta Journal*, 4 November 1945, 9–A; *Congressional Record*, 79 Cong., 1st sess., 29 October 1945, 10151–65.

the navy's performance in returning troops or in discharging personnel were inserted in the *Congressional Record*.[11] The wholesale reduction in personnel, however, took a toll on military preparedness. On 16 November Admiral King told the House Military Affairs Committee that the navy was no longer sufficiently strong to fight a major battle. Two months later, Admiral Chester Nimitz, the new chief of naval operations, told the Associated Press Managing Editors Convention in Miami: "At the present moment, less than five months after the defeat of Japan, your Navy has not the strength in ships and personnel to carry on a major military action."[12]

In March 1946 Vinson's committee held a special set of hearings to learn how demobilization had affected the navy. Admiral Nimitz testified that on 20 February the Bureau of the Budget informed the Navy Department that the president had reduced the navy's appropriation for fiscal 1947 from the requested $6,325,000,000 to $3,960,000,000. After a navy protest, the amount was raised to $4,224,000,000. Nimitz went on to point out that in the Budget Bureau's determination of both the first and second figure the Navy Department had not been consulted, nor had it been told what the president desired for the navy to cut or to emphasize. The department was simply issued the dollar amounts and "told to figure it out for yourselves." Vinson got right to the essence of the matter during the following exchange with the admiral:

> The Chairman: "From what you say I gather that you feel the budget cut will jeopardize the security of the nation."
>
> Admiral Nimitz: "That's right."
>
> The Chairman: "Would you go so far as to say it jeopardizes our position in world affairs and the defense of the homeland?"
>
> Admiral Nimitz: "I think it does."
>
> The Chairman: "There are two ways of scrapping a navy—one by straightaway scrapping, the other by strangulation

---

[11] Davis, *Postwar Defense Policy and the U.S. Navy*, 212–15.
[12] Ibid., 216.

resulting from insufficient appropriations. It appears that the Budget Bureau has chosen the latter."[13]

This pattern set by the Budget Bureau was to prevail until the Korean War.[14]

While battling to preserve the navy's budget, Vinson continued to oppose the unification of the military services. A Jeffersonian Democrat, he instinctively distrusted anything as big as a combined army and navy, and he plotted ways to prevent the merger. In September 1945, as reports spread that President Truman might send a special message to Congress recommending a merger, Vinson along with Andrew May, chairman of the House Military Affairs Committee, publicly stated that the House would not even consider such a measure for some time. "There won't be any merger," Vinson declared. "There is no chance of taking up the Army and Navy merger now," he added. "I hope it's off forever. The two services should remain separate and distinct."[15]

In October the Senate Military Affairs Committee opened hearings on the several unification plans. The committee had already heard strong support for unification from Robert Patterson, Stimson's replacement as secretary of war, General Douglas MacArthur, General George Marshall, and General H. H. Arnold, Commanding General of the Army Air Forces, when Forrestal presented a contrasting view on 22 October. He outlined a comprehensive report prepared by Ferdinand Eberstadt, his longtime friend and adviser, which called for three distinct services, headed not by a single department but by a National Security Council that would link the State Department to the three military arms. The Eberstadt plan reflected the principle of coordination rather than unification. Both Forrestal and Vinson believed that it satisfied all the major requirements of an adequate national security establishment.[16]

---

[13] *New York Times*, 20 March 1946, 3.

[14] Davis, *Postwar Defense Policy and the U.S. Navy*, 216–17.

[15] *New York Times*, 28 September 1945, 2.

[16] Millis, *Arms and the State*, 151–52; Arnold A. Ragow, *James Forrestal: A Study of Personality, Politics, and Policy* (New York: The Macmillan Company, 1963) 217–19.

The next step in Vinson's carefully laid strategy came in December when he and May jointly introduced bills to create an independent air force with a civilian secretary of cabinet rank. The measures also would create an Air Force Academy to function like Annapolis and West Point and would continue the war-created Joint Chiefs of Staff of the proposed three defense arms. This action shocked the army, which had been campaigning for months for a combined Department of National Defense. The two chairmen described their bills as "our answer to the merger proposals." In a formal statement they said, "We believe unification is not the answer to the problem of national defense." They added that they did not contemplate action "in any way affecting the air arm of the Navy, since naval aviation presents an entirely different problem of national defense."[17]

Although the Vinson-May bills ultimately failed, they stirred up dissension within the War Department and weakened the army's pro-merger campaign, as Vinson intended. In the Senate, where army support was strongest, Vinson decided to play for time. After the bill was reported out of the Senate Military Affairs Committee, he persuaded Chairman Walsh to hold extensive pro-navy hearings. In the meantime, Vinson quietly circulated through House offices explaining to individual members why the merger was ill-advised. Rarely speaking publicly against it himself, he persuaded important figures in labor, business, and the educational world to campaign against unification.[18]

Vinson, along with Forrestal, Walsh, and Vice Admiral Louis Denfeld, chief of naval personnel, met with the president on 21 November 1945, at which time Truman expressed his opposition to the House concurrent resolution setting the size of the navy. Both Walsh and Vinson took the opportunity to urge the president not to undertake or introduce a bill for unification of the services because it would not pass. Truman ignored their advice and the advice of others who cautioned him about waging an unnecessary fight he might lose. He submitted his unification message on 20 December. It called for a single, overall chief

---

[17] *New York Times*, 11 December 1945, 6.
[18] "The Admiral," *Newsweek* 27 (3 June 1946): 30.

of staff and a single, centralized Department of Defense—an arrangement Vinson and Forrestal heartily opposed.[19]

A bitter and protracted controversy ensued for the next eighteen months. Truman, whose position on unification had been clear from the beginning of his presidency, had patiently listened to the navy's objections for months, but his patience gradually wore thin. In a news conference on 11 April 1946, an unsmiling president denounced lobbying by navy admirals and others against the army-navy merger proposal and warned the Navy Department to fall into line behind the commander in chief or face a possible shake-up. Shaking his head for emphasis, the president vehemently stated that the navy was wrong in not supporting him on unification. The navy was never justified in making a fight against the merger after he had stated the administration policy on the matter, he said. Since this was the third presidential rebuke of the navy in months, observers speculated that Secretary Forrestal, an opponent of all-out unification, might be forced to resign.[20]

Forrestal was not forced to resign. He continued to meet with President Truman, Secretary of War Robert Patterson, and others trying to work out a satisfactory compromise. On 13 May the president called Forrestal, Patterson, and the principal naval and military advisers to the White House. He asked them to resolve their differences and make a report to him by 31 May.

Vinson, having built up considerable support for his position, played his trump card on 19 May. Together with Senator Walsh, he listed eight "major defects" in the army-backed bill approved by the Senate Military Affairs Committee. The joint Vinson-Walsh letter to Secretary Forrestal stated that Congress would not support any compromise in the navy's stand. Specifically their letter said Congress would not approve:

(a) A single Department of Common Defense with a single Secretary at its head.

(b) The placing of a single military officer in supreme command of all the armed forces.

---

[19] Millis, *The Forrestal Diaries*, 115–20.
[20] *New York Times*, 12 April 1946, 1, 13.

(c) Divesting the Marine Corps of its important function of maintaining a Fleet Marine Force to support fleet operations.

(d) Transferring the vital function of naval aviation to the Army Air Corps or to a separate Air Corps.

(e) Removing from the Secretary of War and the Secretary of the Navy the responsibility for initiating the budget of their respective departments and supporting these budgets before the Congress.[21]

Well aware that the administration still hoped that Congress would enact a bill acceptable to both services before the summer adjournment, the joint-letter also stated that the chairmen intended to hold hearings on the administration unification bill. This meant that regardless of any compromise reached under White House pressure, the unification issue would have a long wait before coming to a vote in the House. Vinson wryly remarked: "The sands of time are running out for the advocates of unification."[22]

Forrestal and Patterson reached agreement on most issues when they reported to the president on 31 May. The army accepted most of the navy's plan for a higher organization—a National Security Council, a National Security Resources Board, a Central Intelligence Agency. The army accepted three autonomous departments—army, navy, and air force—each to be headed by its own secretary. The navy recognized that there would have to be an overall secretary of defense, even though no department was created for him. Two main obstacles remained. The army wanted the secretary of defense to be the "boss" of the whole establishment; the navy insisted that he should be a "coordinator" only. Finally, the navy believed that its aviation branch and its Marine Corps were insufficiently protected. President Truman released their report along with his own judgment on 15 June. When Congress adjourned early in August the unification bill had not even reached the floor.[23]

---

[21] Ibid., 20 May 1946, 1, 8.

[22] Ibid.; "The Admiral," *Newsweek*, 30.

[23] Millis, *Arms and the State*, 169–73.

Vinson was especially eager to get back to Milledgeville because for the first time since 1932 he had opposition in the Democratic primary. Why Harvey Roughton, a gaunt, thin-faced local preacher and farmer from Washington County, decided to challenge Vinson at this time is unclear. Although he had practically no chance of unseating Vinson, he had seriously considered running in 1940 and 1942, but local politicos, including former U.S. Senator Thomas Hardwick, had talked him out of it. Having been bitten by the "political bee," however, Roughton could not be dissuaded in 1946.[24] All of the local leaders throughout the Sixt District, no matter how ambitious they might have been, had seen the futility of running against Vinson. Consequently, no candidate with a chance of winning had dared challenge him since Sam Olive in 1920. In 1946 Vinson's political standing was at an all-time high, as the war had greatly enhanced his power and prestige in Washington. Moreover, the war had enabled him to bring home more than the usual amount of "pork." He secured a fuse plant for Macon, a naval hospital for Dublin, and many other projects throughout the district, including a huge military airport, a $15,000,000 military repair and supply depot, a WAVE school, and a military sack factory. Due to him, heavy cruisers were named Macon and Augusta, and an escort ship was named Milledgeville. Despite his busy schedule in Washington, he continued to look after individual constituent needs with great efficiency and maintained close political contacts throughout the district. In each election cycle he encouraged his supporters to do all they could to eliminate opposition, as his correspondence with Charles Bloch in Macon clearly shows.[25]

---

[24] Thomas Hardwick to Carl Vinson, 20 June 1942; Carl Vinson to Thomas Hardwick, 22 June 1942, Thomas W. Hardwick Papers, Series 1, Subseries B, Box 2, Richard B. Russell Library for Political Research and Studies, University of Georgia Libraries, Athens, GA.

[25] *Macon Telegraph*, 24 October 1940, 1; *Dublin Courier Herald*, 7 June 1942, Vinson Scrapbooks, book 1945–1948, on loan from Tillman Snead to Georgia College and State University, Milledgeville, GA; Carl Vinson to Charles J. Bloch, 7 July, 9 September 1942, Charles Bloch Papers, box 5, folder 25, Middle Georgia Regional Library, Macon, GA; Vance Packard, "Uncle Carl," *American Magazine* 149 (April 1950): 122.

Even though his opponent was politically unknown, Vinson took his candidacy seriously. He urged Erwin Sibley to "get as many people to register as you possibly can," as "we can't afford to leave anything undone." Vinson planned to conduct an "active and aggressive" campaign, beginning with a short talk to the Rural Letter Carriers of the Sixth District on 30 May, followed by a visit with the Sixth District Postmasters. The next day he planned to attend the ceremony for the opening of the Research Center at the Dublin hospital. On 3 June he was scheduled to deliver the commencement address at Mercer University and receive an honorary doctorate. From then until the end of the congressional break on 17 June, he planned to campaign all over the district.[26]

His opponent raised such a ruckus lambasting Vinson all over the district that Uncle Carl called upon one of his aides in Washington to come down and help him prepare a "major radio address." Together they spent two days wrestling with the address. It had been so long since Vinson had opposition that he had forgotten how to make a campaign speech. Finally, the address was finished and typed. Vinson looked at it, and then threw it away. He decided he would be "dignifying" his opponent's campaign by paying any attention to him.[27]

The Georgia Swamp Fox thought of a better way to handle this opponent who had criticized him so harshly. One Sunday morning Vinson had Tillman Snead drive him out to Reverend Roughton's home in Sandersville. They arrived about 7:30 in the morning. Vinson went to the door and knocked. Roughton came to the door still half-asleep and wearing his nightshirt. He said, "Well, Carl Vinson. What are you doing here? You don't need to try to talk me into voting for you. You know I can't stand you." Vinson calmly replied, "Preacher, I didn't come here to try to convince you to vote for me. I came here to ask you to pray for me." Stunned by the humble request, Roughton's mouth fell open. After

---

[26] Carl Vinson to Erwin Sibley, May 10, 1946, Erwin Sibley Papers, April–June 1946 folder, Special Collections, Ina Dillard Russell Library, Georgia College and State University, Milledgeville, GA; Spright Dowell to Carl Vinson, June 11, 1946, Vinson Scrapbooks, book 1945–1948.

[27] Packard, "Uncle Carl," 122.

that exchange, he never said one negative thing about Vinson in the rest of the campaign.[28]

The outcome of the primary was never in doubt. Vinson received nearly three-fourths of the 60,000 votes cast, carried all of the counties, and won the county unit vote 42 to 0. For the next decade no one else would be foolish enough to challenge him.[29]

Wild inflation, numerous costly strikes, Truman's advocacy of controversial welfare and civil rights legislation, Russian belligerence and an emerging cold war, plus the resignation of Interior Secretary Harold Ickes and Truman's firing of Secretary of Commerce Henry Wallace—all weakened the Democratic Party's chances in the 1946 congressional races. Few were surprised when the Republicans—using the popular slogan "Had enough?"—won an overwhelming victory. The Republicans won firm control of both houses for the first time since 1928. The Democrats' chief liability was Truman himself. He had convinced millions of voters that he was incapable of leading or governing.[30] Truman was held in such low regard that secretaries remarked, "You just sort of forget about Harry until he makes another mistake."[31] Republican control of the House made Joseph Martin of Massachusetts the Speaker for the Eightieth Congress. It also meant that Representative Walter G. Andrews of New York would chair the new House Armed Services Committee, a merger of the Naval Affairs Committee and the Military Affairs Committee that became effective with the opening of the Eightieth Congress. Having dominated naval affairs as chairman of the Naval Affairs Committee for sixteen years, Vinson now became the minority leader of the Armed Services Committee. With the change in responsibility, Vinson made it clear that he would devote his future efforts not only to the problems of the navy

---

[28] Tillman and Karen Snead, interview with the author, Dale City, VA, 8 June 2001.

[29] Georgia, Department of Archives and History, *Georgia Official and Statistical Register, 1945–1950*, 488.

[30] Arthur S. Link, *American Epoch* (New York: Alfred A. Knopf, 1967) 675.

[31] Eric Goldman, *The Crucial Decade—And After: America, 1945–1960* (New York: Vintage Books, 1960) 44.

and Marine Corps, but those of the army and air force as well.[32] For Vinson, the best thing about the new Congress was that his salary had increased from \$10,000 to \$12,500.[33]

Six months after the new Armed Services Committee was created, the National Security Act became law. The reorganization embodied in this act, Walter Millis points out, "was essentially...that proposed by Eberstadt in 1945." Thus, it was a victory for Forrestal, Vinson, and the navy. The law was the capstone of the new government structure derived from the experiences of World War II. It established a weak secretary of defense and deprived the services of none of their traditional prerequisites. It did not provide for a single military chief of staff. An executive order accompanying the legislation specifically guaranteed that naval aviation forces and the Marine Corps would remain a part of the navy.[34]

As Mary Vinson's rheumatoid arthritis got progressively worse, she was forced to spend much time at Bethesda Naval Hospital. There she developed a warm relationship with her nurse, Amalia Margaret "Molly" Steman. Molly had grown up on a farm in Minnesota in a close-knit, hard-working, German, Roman Catholic family of fourteen children. When her father died of a massive heart attack at age fifty, leaving four boys and ten girls, the family sold the farm and moved to town. Despite the death of the father, almost all of the children became professionals, and most of the girls became registered nurses. The family had little money, but the children received educations by helping each other. As soon as the oldest girl finished nursing school and got a job, she provided financial assistance for the next one to attend nursing school. Every one of the girls repaid the money provided by her older sister. After Molly finished nursing school in North Dakota, she received a commission in the navy. Her first job with the navy was on the psychiatric ward at

---

[32] Louis R. Stockstill, "'Uncle Carl' Vinson: Backstage Boss of the Pentagon," *Army Navy Air Force Journal* 98 (18 February 1961): 28.

[33] "Shaping New-Style Congress: Opposition to Major Changes," *U.S. News & World Report*. 21 (18 October 1946): 27–28.

[34] Davis, *Postwar Defense Policy and the U.S. Navy*, 234; Millis, *Arms and the State*, 177–85.

Parris Island, South Carolina, where she treated marines returning from the Pacific theater. After six months of treating shell-shocked and deranged seventeen- and eighteen-year-olds whose lives had been shattered by the war, she had reached the limit of her endurance. She secured a transfer to Bethesda Naval Hospital, where she became one of the head nurses on the VIP ward. Molly and Mary became friends immediately. One day Mrs. Vinson said to her, "Molly, I have a young man you might be interested in." She was referring to Tillman Snead, who was single and, in Mary's view, ideally suited for Molly. He was then past thirty, and she was six years younger. Despite Mary's entreaties, Molly showed no interest in meeting Till and kept putting her off. Mary persisted. Several days after Mary had left the hospital, Molly finally met Till. They started dating and soon fell in love, as Mary had predicted. Molly and Till were married on 6 June 1947, Till's thirty-third birthday, in the chapel at the Bethesda Naval Hospital. Vinson served as best man. Molly, then a lieutenant commander, resigned her commission, moved in with Till and the Vinsons, and nursed Mary thereafter. The Vinsons and Sneads lived together as one family in the bungalow at 4 Primrose Street in Chevy Chase for more than seventeen years, until Vinson retired from Congress in 1965.[35]

In 1948 Vinson, as usual, supported the Democratic nominee, but with the party shattered by the defection of the Henry Wallace and Strom Thurmond factions, most politicians, pundits, and citizens gave Harry Truman only the most remote chance of winning the election over New York Governor Thomas E. Dewey. Truman campaigned longer and harder than Dewey, traveling more than 30,000 miles and giving 351 speeches. He lambasted the "do-nothing Republican 80th Congress" in some of the roughest English spoken by a presidential campaigner since frontier days. And his aggressive campaigning worked. All the polls said Dewey would win, but Truman made fools of the experts and won "the most spectacular upset in American political history." The Democrats also regained control of Congress by majorities of ninety-three in the House and twelve in the Senate. On 3 January 1949, Sam Rayburn

---

[35] Tillman and Karen Snead, interview with the author.

resumed his position as Speaker of the House, and Carl Vinson became chairman of the Armed Services Committee.[36]

Despite his loss of power and prestige in the Eightieth Congress, Vinson had worked cooperatively with the Republican leadership and had received warm praise from Chairman Andrews in his annual reports.[37] Upon assuming the chairmanship, however, he made several changes in the operation of the committee. He abolished all regular subcommittees, divided the committee into three equal parts, and reserved to himself the power to assign bills to one of the three groups. This action enhanced his power and enabled him to decide who would introduce an important bill, which, as Susan Landrum notes, "was the lever he used to keep the thirty-seven members of the committee in line."[38] Vinson would need all the power he could muster in confronting troublesome issues in the year ahead. During the year 1949, the Berlin Blockade finally ended, the Russians successfully tested an atomic bomb, China fell to the communists, the North Atlantic Treaty Organization was signed, and the trial of Alger Hiss, a high-ranking New Dealer and participant at the Yalta Conference who was accused of spying for the communists in the 1930s, captured headlines for weeks. Hiss was convicted of perjury early in 1950, and ten days after his conviction, Truman announced that work had begun on the hydrogen bomb. Vinson was not directly involved in any of these events, but they all contributed to a growing sense of anxiety and fear that Senator Joseph McCarthy would capitalize on in his outrageous three-year "witch hunt" for communists in government.[39] By intensifying emotions, they also complicated many controversial issues that Vinson and his committee faced.

In its quest to control spending and inflation, the Truman administration continued to place a much lower priority on

---

[36] Goldman, *The Crucial Decade—And After*, 81–90; Link, *American Epoch*, 676–80.

[37] *Congressional Record Appendix*, 80th Cong., 2d sess., 19 June 1948, A4482–87.

[38] Susan Landrum, "Carl Vinson: A Study in Military Preparedness" (master's thesis, Emory University, 1968)110.

[39] Goldman, *The Crucial Decade—And After*, 91–145.

defense—especially air power—than Vinson did. When the Truman administration sought to reduce the air force from fifty-nine to forty-eight combat groups in 1948, Vinson insisted that an air force of seventy groups was needed. If we do not provide additional funds for the air force, "we will be gambling with our national existence," he informed the House, because "in my judgment the sinister forces at loose in the world today are far more dangerous to the very existence of our country than were the forces of Nazi Germany."[40] Navy leaders were dismayed that their former advocate had sided with the air force on building a huge strategic air force. When some of the navy's battleship officers doggedly held on to the battleship after World War II, Vinson finally told them to "get a beautiful picture" of one of the battleships, "bring it up and we will hang it on the wall...the day of the battleship is over."[41] Vinson's actions displeased Secretary of Defense Forrestal, who summoned him for a conference. Vinson took Texas Democrats Lyndon Johnson and Paul Kilday of the Armed Services Committee with him to see Forrestal. The defense secretary, who had worked very closely with Vinson in the past, explained that the proposed cut to forty-eight groups was aimed toward a balanced national defense in which the army, navy, and air force would all have approximately equal status. Vinson was not persuaded. Neither was the Congress. Opposed by Truman and Forrestal, Vinson was not able to secure all of the funds he desired. But after negotiating a behind-the-scenes deal with Appropriations Chairman John Taber and Air Force Secretary Stuart Symington, he managed to obtain an additional $822,000,000 for plane procurement. On 15 April 1948, after weeks of debate, the House voted 343 to 3 to expand the Air Force to 70 groups, and a few weeks later the Senate agreed by vote of 74 to 2.[42]

Despite the overwhelming sentiment of Congress, Truman did not spend the money appropriated for aircraft construction—an action that astounded Vinson. Thus the battle continued the next year. Vinson, chairing the Armed Services Committee, was more determined than ever

---

[40] *Congressional Record*, 80th Cong., 2d sess., April 14, 1948, 4453.

[41] Stockstill, "Backstage Boss," 28.

[42] Landrum, "Carl Vinson: A Study in Military Preparedness," 123–24.

to defeat the president. On March 16 the House approved the initial step of a plan to compel the construction of a 70 group air force. A week later it authorized his program by vote of 385 to 3.[43] In a speech to the House on 30 March 1949, Vinson clearly analyzed the military budget. Initially, he pointed out, the military had requested $30 billion. Knowing that total was unreasonable, they pared it down to $23.5 billion. When the president established a ceiling of $15 billion, they cut some more. But the rock bottom minimum for maintaining a reasonable defensive posture, the military concluded, was $17.5 billion. The president and his Bureau of the Budget insisted on the $15 billion ceiling, and the military budget that finally reached Congress came to a total of $14,765,000,000. After outlining the budget process, Vinson added, "I conceive there to be nothing holy or untouchable about that final budget figure." He then explained how the proposed cuts would affect each branch of the service, after which he offered 8 specific recommendations calling for $1,599,600,000 in additional funding. In concluding his speech, he said, "As between the Bureau of the Budget and the Joint Chiefs of Staff, I will place my confidence in the latter, in regard to what our national defense needs are."[44]

Vinson operated on the principle that "If we do too much in the way of arming, we will just lose dollars. But if we do too little, we may lose American lives, we may lose vital engagements with the enemy, we may bring on global war through our indecision and weakness." Declaring the Truman military budget "unhealthful and shortsighted," he got from Congress $851,000,000, a little more than half of the addition he had sought. It was enough to save some carrier strength for the fleet and four squadrons of Marine Corps air.[45]

On 28 March 1949 Forrestal, exhausted, ill, and at odds with the Truman administration, resigned as secretary of defense. The next day, he appeared before the Armed Services Committee, where Vinson and

---

[43] *New York Times*, March 17, 1949, 1, 4; *Washington Post*, March 23, 1949, 1, 5.

[44] *Congressional Record*, 81st Cong., 1st sess., 30 March 1949, 3540–44.

[45] Beverly Smith, "He Makes the Generals Listen," *Saturday Evening Post* 223 (10 March 1951): 134.

other members lauded his exceptional career and presented him an engraved plaque.[46] A week later, Forrestal, deeply depressed, was hospitalized at Bethesda Naval Hospital. By the end of April he had responded well to the treatment and seemed to be on the road to recovery. By the middle of May his physicians thought he might be discharged in another month or so. They miscalculated badly. Early on the morning of 22 May he committed suicide, hanging himself by jumping through an unguarded window on the sixteenth floor of the hospital.[47] In a eulogy the next day Vinson reviewed his friend's outstanding career, pointing out that he was humble, patient, objective, and "assiduous beyond the point of endurance." In closing he said, "I shall never know a greater American or a finer friend."[48]

Forrestal had had serious misgivings about Truman's economies in defense. His successor, Louis Johnson, a large, blunt-spoken West Virginia lawyer who had raised millions for Truman's election, had no such doubts. Inevitably, he and Vinson would clash over budgetary matters and several other issues as well. The initial conflict between the secretary and the chairman was over who would boss the defense establishment.

Shortly after Johnson was installed as secretary of defense, he announced that he was going to unify the armed forces and run the whole show, even if he had to crack heads together. The Senate quickly adopted the Tydings bill, a series of amendments to the National Security Act of 1947 that substantially increased the power of the defense secretary. Johnson considered the legislation essential in order to weld the bickering military forces into a single team and achieve significant economies. In addition to Johnson, the Tydings bill had the strong support of President Truman, most army and air force officials, and former President Herbert Hoover and his Government Reorganization Commission. It did not, however, have the support of Vinson. He believed the bill concentrated too much authority in one man's hands,

---

[46] *Congressional Record Appendix*, 81st Cong., 1st sess., A1878–80.

[47] Millis, *Forrestal Diaries*, 554–55; Ragow, *James Forrestal*, 18–19, 305–19.

[48] *Congressional Record*, 81st Cong., 1st sess., 23 May 1949, 6641–42.

and would make the defense secretary a potential "man on horseback." He had the support of the majority of his committee and many navy and marine corps leaders. To Vinson, the issue was whether the national defense would be provided by orders in the Pentagon or by Congress, representing the American people.[49]

The National Security Act of 1947 was a compromise measure; the Tydings bill was a move to put the army's original plan into operation. Sponsors of the bill stated that the experience of the past twenty months of its operation proved the concept of a single defense force was sound. Air Force Secretary Stuart Symington said:

> Some two years ago the apostles of half measures had their way. They raised fears of military dictators. They said civilian control would be undermined if we have anything stronger than a coordinator who would seek to persuade the services to agree.
>
> They insisted on continuing a Joint Chiefs of Staff system which could be immobilized by the dissent of any one member.... We have tried out this half-measure organization, and there is unanimous agreement that it is inadequate.[50]

The Tydings bill offered three amendments to the National Security Act. First, it would establish a Department of Defense and reduce the army, navy, and air force to military departments within an overall executive department. Secretaries of the military departments would lose their positions on the National Security Council and would be shorn of policy-making power. Second, the power of the defense secretary would be greatly increased. He would have specific power over the armed forces, would be empowered to reorganize his new department, would be given additional staff, and would be given control over the Munitions Board and the Research and Development Board. Third, a new post of chairman of the Joint Chiefs of Staff would be created. This official

---

[49]Packard, "Uncle Carl," 122; Landrum, "Carl Vinson: A Study in Military Preparedness," 112–13.

[50] John G. Norris, "Defense Titans Face a Showdown," *Washington Post*, 19 June 1949, 6–B.

would become the chief adviser to the president and the defense secretary and would outrank all other members of the Joint Chiefs of Staff.[51]

The Senate passed the Tydings bill on 26 May without a recorded vote. Despite mounting opposition, Vinson avoided scheduling hearings on similar House legislation for a month. Finally, he announced that hearings would begin on 28 June 1949. He also declared that he would support the administration's unification bill if the right of top defense officials to "come to Congress" were specifically guaranteed in the measure. Since Vinson had substantially moderated his previous opposition to the bill, Johnson quickly endorsed Vinson's idea. Vinson explained that a careful reading of the bill convinced him that the present law gives Johnson "ample authority to accomplish what you want to do." Since "you are going to run the department," the whole fight over the bill is "largely academic."[52]

Vinson and Johnson were on friendly terms when the hearings began, but by the first week of July the amity had vanished. On 6 July Vinson offered a compromise plan, which, he stated, would give the secretary of defense "all the power he needs to improve unification and save money" while "making sure we never have a military dictatorship in this country." His long series of amendments retained the main features of the Tydings bill but added major limitations. First, no single chief of staff could be created over the armed forces and no armed forces general staff could be established. Second, the defense secretary would be required to consult with the Senate and House Armed Services Committees before exercising his powers to transfer or consolidate any statutory functions of the three military departments. Third, the civilian and military heads of the army, navy, and air force would be authorized to appear before Congress on any matter after notifying the defense secretary. Fourth, the president's authority to make transfers and consolidations in military services under the recently passed general Government Reorganization Act would be repealed. "This is all the

---

[51] Ibid.

[52] John G. Norris, "Vinson Alters Stand on Unification Bill," *Washington Post*, 29 June 1949, 3.

reorganization they will need in the defense establishment," Vinson declared.[53]

Johnson disagreed vehemently. Regarding one of the proposed amendments, he complained to Vinson that it "would make you the secretary of defense" and "would utterly tie my hands."[54] At one point the impatient Johnson hammered his fist on the table and said, "I think, Mr. Vinson, that this has boiled down to a question of whether you are going to run this country's armed forces or whether I am." Vinson looked steadily at Johnson and replied grimly, "The Congress won't be by-passed, and we will be conversant with what goes on."[55]

Following Vinson's direction, the House Armed Services Committee rejected the Senate bill on 12 July. Subsequently, President Truman called Vinson to the White House and bluntly informed him that he would further unify the armed forces by executive action, unless the Armed Services Committee reversed its action. Convinced that the president had the authority to carry out his threat, the committee then unanimously approved a portion of the bill.[56] It decided to postpone further action on unification until an investigation of the B-36 bomber procurement program was completed. Serious charges had been leveled at the secretary of defense, and the committee did not think it should report out a bill designed to increase the power of the secretary of defense and then immediately investigate him on the B-36 charges. The House acted on the portion of unification the Vinson Committee had approved. The subsequent Senate-House conference committee included Vinson and six of his Armed Services Committee colleagues who shared his views on unification. When the conference committee made its report to the House on 2 August, the conference agreement was essentially the Vinson plan. The House agreed to the conference report by vote of 356 to 7 and President Truman signed the amendments into law on 10

---

[53] John G. Norris, "Vinson Offers Compromise on Unification Plan," *Washington Post*, 6 July 1949, 1, 12.

[54] "Irony in Johnson's Crack at Vinson," *Atlanta Journal*, 7 July 1949, 18.

[55] Vance Packard, "Uncle Carl," *American Magazine* 149 (April 1950): 123.

[56] *Washington Post*, 14 July 1949, 1, 3; 15 July 1949, 1, 16.

August.[57] Vinson had been the key figure in the adoption of the unification amendments, as Dewey Short of Missouri, the ranking Republican on the Armed Services Committee, told the House on 2 August. It was Carl Vinson, he declared, who wrote the bill, contrived reservations on the vast powers granted by this legislation, and had the "capacity, energy, and sagacity to put forth the views of the House conferees and to carry them successfully against the views of the Senate."[58]

While Vinson grappled with issues of national and international importance, he also maintained a keen interest in the condition of his Milledgeville farm. His close friend and neighbor Erwin Sibley regularly kept him informed of local political developments as well as the condition of River Ridge Plantation. On 4 June Vinson queried him about his crops. "Is the cotton half a leg high?" "How does the watermelon patch look in the orchard and has anything else been planted in it?" "How high is the corn?" Sibley assured him that his cotton was "almost knee high," his corn was "generally in good color," and that soybeans had been planted in his oats field and should be coming up soon.[59] A month later, Sibley informed him, "Your cotton is fruiting up as fast as I have ever seen." He added that he had a "good stand" of velvet beans, but his corn and watermelons were "not as good as you have had." Since the farm had received much rain, Vinson, concerned about the boll weevil infestation, was eager to get home. He expected the military unification issue to keep Congress in session until the middle of August. That issue was resolved earlier than he expected, but the B-36 crisis kept him in Washington longer than usual.[60]

---

[57] Ibid., 21 July 1949, 1, 8; 28 July 1949, 1, 4; Landrum, "Carl Vinson: A Study in Military Preparedness," 118–23; *Congressional Record*, 81st Cong., 1st sess., 2 August 1949, 10592–10610; 10 August 1949, 12256.

[58] *Congressional Record*, 81st Cong., 1st sess., 2 August 1949, 10602.

[59] Carl Vinson to Erwin Sibley, June 4, 1949; Erwin Sibley to Carl Vinson, 6 June 1949, Erwin Sibley Papers, June 1949 folder.

[60] Carl Vinson to Erwin Sibley, 23 June 1949; 5 August 1949; 8 August 1949; Erwin Sibley to Carl Vinson, 12 July 1949, Erwin Sibley Papers, June, July and August 1949 folders.

During the spring of 1949 rumors circulated that skullduggery had been involved in the procurement of the B-36, the air force's newest and heaviest bomber. The chief publicist for the rumors was a member of Vinson's Committee, Representative James Van Zandt, a Republican from Pennsylvania. A staunch supporter of the navy, he had access to an anonymous nine-page letter that claimed that the B-36 was sold on publicity and not on performance, that dealings between Consolidated Vultee Aircraft Corporation and American Motors in production of the plane were irregular, and that production of other planes was cut back because of people in the National Military Establishment who wished to favor Consolidated Vultee. Vinson tried to stay out of the controversy, but rather than allow Van Zandt to chair a special investigative committee, he accepted the challenge. On 26 May he announced that the Armed Services Committee would undertake a "thorough and searching investigation" into air force procurement of B-36 bombers.[61] The committee "will find out what lies behind these rumors and innuendoes," and "this will be no whitewash investigation," Vinson assured reporters.[62]

As promised, Vinson's committee hired a staff, investigated the charges, and held daily hearings from 9 through 12 August and 22 through 25 August. During the ten-day break, Vinson went to his farm to assist with the cotton picking and ginning while a subcommittee conducted hearings in California. When Vinson asked Van Zandt to substantiate his charges, the only evidence he could cite were gossip columns in the *Washington Times-Herald* and the *Philadelphia Inquirer* and the anonymous letter. The investigation subsequently revealed that the author of the anonymous letter was Cedric Worth, a forty-nine-year-old special assistant to the under secretary of the navy. He admitted frankly that he had written and circulated the document. In three grueling sessions before the committee, he also admitted that there was no

---

[61] *Atlanta Journal*, 26 May 1949, 22; "Why Air Force Wants B–36," *U.S. News & World Report* 26 (17 June 1949): 18–19; "Carl Vinson, Friend of the Navy and of Air Force Expansion," *U.S. News & World Report* 26 (17 June 1949): 34–37.

[62] *Atlanta Journal*, 31 May 1949, 1.

evidence of corruption in the B-36 procurement program and that neither Louis Johnson nor Stuart Symington had been guilty of impropriety in buying the bomber. After Worth had repented for every item on the statement, Vinson called for a vote. By unanimous vote (including the vote of Van Zandt), the committee agreed that there was not "one iota, not one scintilla of evidence…that would support charges or insinuations [of] collusion, fraud, corruption, influence or favoritism."[63]

The navy suspended Worth and the Armed Services Committee adjourned, but the crisis was far from over. Both the Navy Department and Vinson believed Worth had not worked alone but had received help from a few navy officers who had sought to impede the passage of amendments to the National Security Act, which would have been favorable to the air force.[64] The Worth episode was part of the on-going friction between the navy and the air force as they battled for a larger share of a greatly reduced defense budget. The air force seemed to be gaining the upper hand, as increasingly the public, the Congress, and even Vinson perceived the air force as the chief deterrent to the Soviet Union. Unwilling to allow the air force to monopolize strategic bombing, the navy wanted to build a super carrier of 65,000 tons capable of launching bombers carrying nuclear weapons. When the air force purchased more B-36s and Secretary Johnson cancelled the super carrier in April 1949, navy leaders were aghast. Secretary of the Navy John L. Sullivan resigned in protest. Although Vinson was a strong proponent of naval aviation, he supported the cancellation because of the budget limitations. "I think Mr. Johnson did the right thing," he said. The navy's frustration was understandable. It had lost public support as well as its prized carrier, and it feared the Marine Corps might be abolished and all naval aviation transferred elsewhere. Its role in defense was unclear, its budgets had been cut severely, and neither the president nor the secretary of defense seemed the least bit sympathetic to its cause. Making a bad

---

[63] "Meet the Author," *Time* 54 (5 September 1949) 14; Carl Vinson to Erwin Sibley, 8 August 1949, Erwin Sibley Papers, August 1949 folder; House, Committee on Armed Services, *Investigation of the B-36 Bomber Program*, 81st Cong., 2d sess., 12 January 1950, Report No. 1470.

[64] Landrum, "Carl Vinson: A Study in Military Preparedness," 132.

situation even worse, Vinson, the navy's staunchest defender for many years, had championed the expansion of the air force so strongly that he was now being called "Air Marshal Vinson." All of these factors contributed to what has been called the "revolt of the admirals," which included shameless efforts by the navy to discredit the B-36, of which the Worth episode was one.[65]

Between 6 October and 21October 1949, the House Armed Services Committee held twelve days of "some of the most rambunctious hearings ever held on Capitol Hill" on the subject of "Unification and Strategy." During the first seven days, almost the entire high command of the navy appeared to present the navy's case. On the eighth day two senior officers of the Marine Corps testified. Stuart Symington held forth on the ninth day. He was followed by Air Force Chief of Staff Hoyt S. Vandenberg and General Omar Bradley, the recently appointed chairman of the Joint Chiefs of Staff. Army Chief of Staff General J. Lawton Collins, General Dwight D. Eisenhower, chief of Army Field Forces General Mark Clark, and a civilian management consultant testified on the eleventh day. On the final day, Secretary of State George Marshall, Secretary of Defense Louis Johnson, and former President Herbert Hoover testified.[66] Out of this testimony came an excellent fifty-six-page report written largely by Bryce Harlow, a staff member of the House Armed Services Committee. Its thirty-three specific recommendations made significant contributions to the subsequent defense organization.[67] Regarding the development of weapons for defense, the report stressed

---

[65] Paul Y. Hammond, "Super Carriers and B-36 Bombers: Appropriations, Strategy and Politics," *American Civil-Military Decisions*, ed. Harold Stein (Tuscaloosa: University of Alabama Press, 1963) 467–500; "Air Marshal Vinson," *Newsweek* 33 (28 March 1949): 18–19; *Washington Post*, 24 April 1949, 3; Robert H. Ferrell, *Harry S. Truman, A Life* (Columbia: University of Missouri Press,1994) 338–43; W. F. Halsey interview, "Why the Navy Wants Big Aircraft Carriers," *U.S. News & World Report* 26 (20 May 1949): 24–28.

[66] Hammond, "Super Carriers and B-36 Bombers," 514–37; Ferrell, *Harry S. Truman*, 340.

[67] Stockstill, "Backstage Boss," 28; House, Committee on Armed Services, *Unification and Strategy*, 81st Cong., 2d sess., 1 March 1950, House Document No. 600.

what Vinson had maintained for years: "The Nation must rely upon the judgment of its professional leaders, in their respective fields."[68] According to Paul Hammond, the most thorough student of the subject, the hearings accomplished the following:

> Its primary accomplishment was a demonstration to both the Navy and Air Force that Congress could not be fooled by either, to the Secretary of Defense that Congress could at least embarrass him in his administration of the Department as a sanction against objectionable policies or procedures, to the committee that it must stand above any single service viewpoint, to the Administration that the defense economy program had political costs as well as gains, and to the public that the nation faced the prospects of nuclear counter-deterrence with divided councils.[69]

Vinson had chaired the hearings in his usual manner, eliciting from the participants testimony he wanted in the record and inserting his own observations from time to time. He pointedly told admirals that the low morale of the navy was a legitimate reaction to a severe cutting of all naval forces. He repeated his previously-stated view that Congress "intended to let Navy aviation wither on the vine" because leaders in the Pentagon and the secretary of defense were "out of sympathy with naval air power."[70] But his strongest criticism, expressed several times during the hearings, was directed at Louis Johnson's habit of arbitrarily cutting military budgets below what Congress had approved. "The basic question is whether or not Congress has a voice in this matter or whether it is to be entirely set by the Secretary of Defense," Vinson declared. "After months of careful study," he continued, Congress approves an appropriation and "then Mr. Johnson, without the slightest information as to what effect it is going to have, sets lower figures and tells these

---

[68] Hammond, "Super Carriers and B-36 Bombers," 538–51.
[69] Ibid., 554.
[70] Ibid., 515–20.

departments to disprove them. The country must know what is going on in the Pentagon. It is time Congress knows what is going on."[71]

As the momentous year drew to a close, Vinson knew the armed services were not adequately prepared to meet the Soviet challenge and carry out all of their expanded worldwide responsibilities. He also knew that to bring about any significant improvement would entail bitter clashes with Secretary Johnson and the Truman administration. The loss of his friends Roosevelt and Forrestal, it seemed to him, had left leadership voids that their successors had not been able to fill. Yet, he could derive some satisfaction from what he had accomplished during the year. He had established firm control over the Armed Services Committee, had blocked the worst features of unification and established a coordinated structure with three distinct services, and had secured from Congress additional funds for research and development and aircraft construction. His committee had conducted several lengthy hearings, produced important reports, and significantly impacted legislation affecting the nation's defenses. His heated clashes with Secretary Johnson over budgeting and air power had received so much attention that his photo had graced the covers of both *U.S. News and World Report* and *Newsweek*.[72]

Throughout the year, he had worked at his usual hectic pace, dealing with one controversial issue after another. The amount of energy he expended would have taxed the resources of a young healthy legislator, and in 1949 Vinson was neither young nor in robust health. Already passed the normal retirement age, he began to experience serious physical ailments for the first time in his life. Heretofore he had enjoyed remarkably good health and extraordinary stamina, but in April a kidney stone forced him to spend several nights in Bethesda Naval Hospital.[73] When the Unification and Strategy Hearings ended, Vinson said his

---

[71] Ibid., 520, 527.

[72] *U.S. News & World Report* 26 (17 June 1949); *Newsweek* 33 (28 March 1949).

[73] *Atlanta Journal*, 2 April 1949, 1; Ernest J. King to Carl Vinson, 19 April 1949; Carl Vinson to Ernest J. King, 26 April 1949, Ernest King Papers, box 18, Manuscript Division, Library of Congress, Washington DC.

committee would "go on a little vacation" and then get back to work on 3 January 1950.[74] He himself had very little time for a vacation. Late in November, shortly after his sixty-sixth birthday, he was back in the same hospital again, for eighteen days. His surgery was successful, and when he returned to his office on 14 December, he wrote Erwin Sibley that he was "feeling fine" and that the operation "had added at least ten years to my life." While he was hospitalized, Molly Snead also had surgery. He explained to Sibley that he wanted to come home after Christmas, if Molly had recovered from her surgery. If she were not able to carry on, he would come to Georgia early in January "so we can get things ready for next year's crop."[75]

---

[74] *New York Times*, 22 October 1949, 5.

[75] Carl Vinson to Erwin Sibley, 14 December 1949, Erwin Sibley Papers, December 1949 folder.

11

Getting the Ox Out of the Ditch

*I disagree with the President quite often and I don't hesitate
to say so.*

Carl Vinson, 1950

Vinson had reached his limit. Louis Johnson's policies had gone too far
for him to remain silent. As the House debated H. R. 7786, the General
Appropriation Bill for 1951, Vinson saw an opportunity to condemn
Johnson. His speech on 4 April 1950, was a scathing attack on the
secretary of defense, but he began it gently, heaping praise on his
adversary. Secretary Johnson and his associates, the Swamp Fox
asserted, "deserve the commendation of the entire Nation for having
carried out so successfully the drive…to squeeze the fat out of public
expenditures." Johnson had spent $1.5 billion less than the president had
requested and $2 billion less than Congress had authorized for defense.
About one-third of that total, Vinson declared, was a direct saving to the
taxpayer without injury to the national defense. In releasing 163,000
civilian employees and closing a number of service installations, Johnson
deserved full credit, Vinson said.

The chairman then shifted gears to examine how Johnson's
economy program had affected the military. He found that the economy
measures had reduced the fighting capabilities of the armed forces by
$1.5 billion. The result, Vinson stated emphatically, was "Mr. Johnson's
economy scalpel has not only carved away some service fat but has
cut—deeply in some areas—into sinew and muscle of the armed

services." The secretary is to be commended for cutting the fat, but in the process he also has "impaired the fighting effectiveness of the armed forces." In specific detail, Vinson showed how Johnson's cuts had greatly weakened the army, air force, navy, and marines. He was dismayed by a new thought being germinated in Washington, namely, "that by reducing the armed forces we are, by some magical process, growing in strength and becoming militarily more effective." Vinson refused to believe it.

He was troubled not only by the reductions but also by the concept that the executive department shall decide the size of the armed forces. As Vinson interpreted the Constitution, the Congress provides the forces; the president commands them, as commander in chief. "If we ever get this principle of our Government distorted," he warned, "our whole fabric of government will be in jeopardy." To Vinson, the issue was clear-cut. "It is whether the Congress will say what kind of defense the nation will have, or whether the creature of the Congress, the Secretary of Defense, Mr. Louis Johnson, will tell us what kind of defense he will let the Congress have."

Vinson operated on the premise that "we must buy the defense the nation must have, regardless of cost." He believed that "enemy capabilities, not dollars, determine our defense needs." In studying the individual services, he found the greatest deficiency in air defense. Naval air strength, he said, was lower than it was at the time of Pearl Harbor. A realist, he did not ask for what he deemed appropriate, but he did insist on an additional appropriation of $200,000,000 for the air force and $383,289,221 for naval aviation.[1]

This speech, delivered eleven weeks before the outbreak of the Korean War, was new only in the direct criticism of Louis Johnson; it reflected the principles Vinson had followed throughout the postwar years. He knew America could never return to isolationism and must be concerned with events throughout the world, and he was convinced that a strong national defense was the best way to ensure peace. Lasting peace and security depended upon the success of nations in settling differences at the conference table, and at the conference table "the voice of peace

---

[1] *Congressional Record*, 81st Cong., 2d sess., 4 April 1950, 4680–85.

must be supported by strength."[2] The Soviet Union was the chief threat to the democratic world at this time, and Vinson estimated that the Russians had a 7-to-1 advantage in tanks, a 2-to-1 advantage in first-line aircraft, and a 4-to-1 advantage in submarines. While he sought a substantial reduction in some of these Russian advantages, he did not want to "over-arm." He favored a basic, hardcore preparedness rather than arming to the teeth, which would touch off a gigantic arms race, severely strain the economy, and leave the United States open to the charge of being conquest-minded. He counseled the government to spend defense dollars on men and weapons rather than on posts, camps, navy yards, or airfields.[3]

In an interview with Vance Packard, Vinson explained that a large part of the defense expenditures should go for three general purposes. "First, our dollars should give us weapons and bases to deliver swift, crushing retaliatory blows to the very heart of Russia if we are attacked." Translated into weapons, this meant that heavy bombers, guided missiles, widely dispersed launching bases, and atomic weapons must receive high priority in defense planning. "Second, the money spent should enable us to absorb without critical damage any initial blows Russia can deliver if we ever are attacked." To achieve this goal he wanted America to maintain superbly trained shock troops stationed at home and in strategic areas of Europe and the Far East. He also insisted that America's cities and industrial centers should be adequately protected from enemy aircraft and sabotage and that more resources be directed to aircraft carriers, guided missiles, and a radar screen around the continent. "Finally, our defense dollars should lay a groundwork that will permit us to mobilize swiftly our great national resources and manpower." This meant stockpiling scarce raw materials, keeping hundreds of thousands of war veterans in a state of trained reserve, and spending billions of dollars to develop the best weapons American technology can produce.[4]

---

[2] Susan Landrum, "Carl Vinson: A Study in Military Preparedness" (master's thesis, Emory University, 1968) 105.

[3] Vance Packard, "Uncle Carl," *American Magazine* 149 (April 1950): 121.

[4] Ibid., 121–22.

In response to Vinson's forceful attack on 4 April, Secretary Johnson ordered the Joint Chiefs of Staff to reexamine the administration's military budget to determine whether more funds should be requested for aircraft procurement. General Dwight Eisenhower, the Allied Supreme Commander in World War II, reinforced Vinson's position when he testified before the Senate Appropriations Committee. When Johnson, abandoning his economy program, recommended a $350,000,000 increase in the military budget—$300,000,000 for aircraft procurement and $50,000,000 for antisubmarine vessels—Vinson immediately announced his endorsement.[5] Syndicated columnist Stuart Alsop observed that following Vinson's "remarkable" speech, Johnson was beginning to see how much damage he had inflicted on the military. Alsop predicted that Johnson's economy program would be "quietly abandoned" and that additional increases would be forthcoming.[6]

Vinson had previously thought that the draft was no longer needed, but in the spring of 1950 he reversed his position and steered a bill through the House extending the registration and classification features of selective service until 24 June 1952. Without this measure, which the House approved 216 to 11, the whole selective service structure would have expired on 30 June 1950, five days after the Korean War began. Vinson explained that his committee had concluded that peace would not be realized in 1950 because of a number of recent events. He specifically mentioned the following events:

(1) The unprovoked Soviet attack on an unarmed United States Navy airplane over the Baltic.
(2) Continued Soviet pressure on United States occupation forces in Berlin.
(3) Russian control of the armed forces of Poland.
(4) Soviet demands for United States withdrawal from Trieste.
(5) Communist threats to overrun the Malayan Peninsula.

---

[5] *New York Times*, 5 April 1950, 1, 6; 27 April 1950, 1, 24.
[6] *Washington Post*, 1 May 1950, 9.

When critical Republicans asked why his committee recommended a measure to bolster the country's armed strength despite President Truman's recent declaration that the world situation looked better than it had since 1946, the chairman replied, "I disagree with the President quite often and I don't hesitate to say so."[7]

When the communist forces of North Korea launched a massive invasion across the thirty-eighth parallel into South Korea on 25 June 1950, President Truman responded with alacrity. He ordered General Douglas MacArthur, then stationed in Japan, to use air and naval forces to support the Republic of Korea. He dispatched the Seventh Fleet to the Formosa Strait and approved recommendations to strengthen American forces in the Philippines and to increase aid to the French in Indo-China. With the Russian delegate boycotting the Security Council, he secured a resolution calling on all members of the United Nations to give assistance to South Korea. After meeting with military and congressional leaders including Vinson, the president issued a statement on 27 June explaining the action he had taken.[8]

As the news media brought the grim story of American soldiers retreating and dying in a country thousands of miles away, Vinson addressed the Sixth Congressional District's Democratic Convention in Macon, which had nominated him for a nineteenth consecutive term in Congress. He commended the president for his "prompt action to meet unlawful force with force" in Korea. While favoring a balanced budget, he stated that the country could not blind itself to minimum national defense requirements. These minimum requirements included use of required force wherever necessary to stop communism; economic and military assistance to those nations allied with the United States against communism; an acceptable defense force to fight a nation that respected only military force; and maintenance of a high level of publicity of American standards, ideals, and democratic principles of government for the nations in the world which were being threatened and lured by communism. He ended his speech on a deeply serious note: "Our

---

. [7] *New York Times*, 25 May 1950, 1, 2.

[8] Harry S. Truman, *Memoirs*, 2 vols. (Garden City NY: Doubleday & Company, 1955–1956) 2:337–39.

responsibilities are grave; the outcome of our acts is weighty in portent for freedom on this earth."[9]

A month after the war began, Truman and Louis Johnson asked Congress to appropriate $10.5 billion to meet the challenge of communist aggression. Two months earlier, Vinson had to struggle to secure an additional $300 million from the administration for aircraft construction. Now the Administration sought $3.3 billion for aircraft.[10] How easy it would have been for Vinson to say to his critics, "I told you so." But it was not in his nature to do so. As was the case after Pearl Harbor, he refused to condemn others; instead, he looked ahead to the needs of the country. There was no need for him to "toot his own horn," for others were doing it, sometimes to excess. No one praised him more extravagantly than Representative Mendel Rivers of South Carolina, who had served on Vinson's committees for ten years. He told the House that Vinson was "the greatest chairman that any committee has ever had in the history of the Nation" and "has exhibited more vision than all the Presidents and all the members of the executive branch on matters of defense, since time began."[11] When Democrats and Republicans sought to blame each other for the nation's inadequate defense, Vinson ended the argument with this declaration: "Our great need right now is to get the ox out of the ditch—not spend a whole lot of time and effort trying to find out who pushed him into the ditch. Let's not spend our time looking backwards while Americans are being killed in Korea and our defenses urgently need strengthening. It is time to get action. Let us get on the road and get up speed. This is no time to take a detour to hunt for scapegoats."[12] Vinson steered the $10.5 billion measure and a host of other military bills through the House as Congress passed the necessary measures for the Korean War.

---

[9] Landrum, "Carl Vinson: A Study in Military Preparedness," 138–39; *Macon Telegraph*, 7 July 1950, 16.

[10] *New York Times*, 25 July 1950, 11.

[11] *Congressional Record*, 81st Cong., 2d sess., 25 July 1950, 10995.

[12] Ibid., 10985.

When the war began, Secretary Johnson's economies were widely condemned.[13] Demands for his resignation grew, but President Truman stubbornly backed him. A Drew Pearson column on 25 July reported that Vinson had met with Secretary Johnson on the morning Truman sent his rearmament program to Congress. Johnson, who had cut billions from the armament estimates of the Joint Chiefs of Staff, quietly said to Vinson: "I need your help, Congressman. You were right." The forgiving chairman replied: "We'll let bygones be bygones, Mr. Secretary. The important thing is that we all work together to get the kind of defense we need to win a war."[14] When Johnson explained the plans for an enlarged army, navy, and air force, "they were virtually identical to the demands Vinson has been making like a modern Jeremiah ever since the end of World War II."[15]

The Vinson-Johnson rapprochement lasted only a month. By 25 August the demands for Johnson's resignation had risen to a chorus. At that point Johnson, replying to a critic, quoted from Vinson's speech of 4 April. Amazingly he quoted the polite praise from Vinson's introduction; he did not mention the scathing criticism that made up the body of the speech. Upon hearing of Johnson's quotation, one of Vinson's friends remarked, "That's the last straw for Uncle Carl. Johnson's days are numbered."[16] Eighteen days later Johnson resigned. Truman accepted his resignation and appointed General George Marshall as his replacement.[17]

The appointment of the sixty-nine-year-old General of the Army and former secretary of state provoked heated debate in Congress. In order for him to serve, it was necessary for Congress to waive the law that prohibited a military man from holding the position of secretary of defense. In debating the waiver, some critics objected to any military man in that position, others focused on Marshall's role as secretary of state, and others emphasized his age and health. The most extreme critic

---

[13] *Washington Post*, 23 July 1950, B5.

[14] Drew Pearson, "Korea Proved Vinson Right," *Washington Post.*, 25 July 1950, B13.

[15] Ibid.

[16] Beverly Smith, "He Makes the Generals Listen," *Saturday Evening Post* 223 (10 March 1951): 136.

[17] *New York Times*, 13 September 1950, 1, 10.

was Republican Senator William Jenner of Indiana, who called Marshall "a front man for traitors" and "a living lie." Vinson, however, was not swayed by any of the critics. He commended the president for choosing Marshall for this powerful position at this critical time. "I am wholly convinced," he assured the House, "that the remarkable and outstanding military ability of General Marshall...will have a splendid effect on our defense program." In his thirty-minute speech endorsing Marshall, Vinson took the opportunity to revisit the unification issue. He pointed out that "the person charged with the administration of this entire organization, stupendous in size and of immeasurable importance to our Nation, is bound to be embroiled in endless difficulty of one sort or another." He cannot escape "unceasing and bitter criticism." The two previous secretaries of defense were able to shoulder the burdens no longer than a year and a half. In trying to unify the armed services, Vinson explained to the House, "We may have overreached our mark. We may have concentrated too much power. We may have imposed too much responsibility upon one man."[18]

Representative Dewey Short of Missouri, Vinson's longtime colleague on the Armed Services Committee and a professor of ethics by training, opposed the appointment of any military man to the position and expressed concern about Marshall's age and health. In the course of his remarks, he said: "We all know, the one man for this job is Carl Vinson. If he was (sic) appointed there wouldn't be a single voice against him. He knows more about defense than all the admirals and the generals in the Pentagon." Following that statement, the members of the House expressed their agreement by giving Vinson a standing ovation that lasted nearly a minute.[19]

The North Koreans very nearly succeeded in driving the South Koreans completely off the peninsula before General MacArthur finally managed to stabilize a front. Then, after reinforcements arrived, he

---

[18] *Congressional Record*, 81st Cong., 2d sess., 15 September 1950, 14953–72; *New York Times*, 16 September 1950, 1, 4.

[19] *Macon Telegraph*, 19 September 1950, 4; *Biographical Directory of the American Congress, 1774–1971* (Washington, DC: Government Printing Office, 1971)1673.

launched a daring amphibious assault at Inchon on the west coast of South Korea near the capital of Seoul. With the invaders overextended and caught between two advancing armies, MacArthur quickly liberated South Korea. Having accomplished the initial objective, he proceeded northward across the thirty-eighth parallel. To observers at home, it appeared that the United Nations operation was going so smoothly that it would soon capture all of North Korea and be able to send the troops home for Christmas.[20]

While Vinson was busy directing huge military bills through his committee and the House, he faced a personal tragedy. His beloved wife, who suffered from rheumatoid arthritis and pernicious anemia and had been bedridden for years, took a turn for the worse. She was taken to Bethesda Naval Hospital, but failed to respond to treatment. Vinson was with her when she died. She was sixty-three years old. On Sunday, 19 November 1950, 700 people crowded into the First Methodist Church at Milledgeville for the brief, simple funeral she had requested. A host of top-ranking military and political leaders attended. President Truman sent a large basket of irises and gladioli. A floral arrangement in the shape of a navy anchor and composed of gardenias and orchids was sent by civilian employees, officers, and enlisted men at the Naval Ordinance Plant in Macon. The casket was blanketed with an arrangement of deep red roses. The Reverend George O. King conducted the service, and Helen Long, a friend of the Vinson family, sang two solos. Burial was in historic Memory Hill Cemetery, where other members of the Vinson family had been interred for years.[21]

"Mr. Vinson is a wonderful congressman, but he was an even finer husband. His devotion to Mrs. Vinson was an example you seldom see

---

[20] In a far-ranging interview with Vinson published on 27 October 1950, the editors of *U.S. News & World Report* assumed the Korean War was over. "Why Bigger Draft Is Coming: An Interview with Carl Vinson," *U.S. News & World Report* 29 (27 October 1950): 40–46.

[21] *Washington Post*, 17 November 1950; *Atlanta Journal*, 16 November 1950 and 17 November 1950, Vinson Scrapbooks, book Mary Vinson, on loan from Tillman Snead to Georgia College and State University, Milledgeville, GA; *Union-Recorder*, 16 November 1950, 1; 23 November 1950, 1.

and she loved him for it."[22] Thus did a close friend of the Vinson family express in words the feeling in the hearts of the hundreds who paid respects to the wife of the state's leading congressman. For many years, Vinson kept fresh flowers on Mary's grave. He never remarried, and family members agree that he never showed the slightest interest in another woman.[23]

Comforting to Vinson in his bereavement was the birth of a son to Tillman and Molly Snead. Charles Tillman Snead, III arrived on 27 November, eleven days after Mary's death. Although technically unrelated, Tillman became Vinson's "grandson" and the pride and joy of his latter years.[24]

On 24 November 1950, General MacArthur launched a "final" offensive, designed to crush all remaining resistance in North Korea and leave North and South Korea united under United Nations supervision. "The war," MacArthur told reporters, "very definitely is coming to an end shortly."[25] The old general had miscalculated badly. Suddenly on 26 November, thirty-three Chinese divisions crossed the Yalu River, smashing the United Nations' forces and driving them in headlong retreat. The communist advance continued until all of North Korea and a small portion of South Korea was under communist control. MacArthur, as well as his superiors in Washington, had completely ignored the Chinese warnings and suffered humiliating defeats as a result.

On 1 December Truman met with a group of congressional leaders including Vinson to apprise them of the situation in Korea. The president explained that more appropriations would be needed to meet the "critical international situation," and he emphasized the importance of preventing

---

[22] Bert Struby, "Funeral Rites Held For Mrs. Vinson," *Macon Telegraph*, 20 November 1950, 1.

[23] Tillman and Karen Snead, interview with the author, Dale City, VA, 8 June 2001; Ed and Betty Vinson, interview with the author, Atlanta, GA, 7 August 2001; Elizabeth Pollard Hood, interview with the author, Griffin, GA, 26 November 2001.

[24] Tillman and Karen Snead, interview with the author; Lou and Neta Stockstill, interview with the author, Indiatlantic, FL, 21 June 2001.

[25] Eric Goldman, *The Crucial Decade—And After: America, 1945–1960* (New York: Vintage Books, 1960) 178.

the affair in Korea from becoming a major Asiatic war.[26] At another White House meeting a few days later, Secretary of Defense Marshall described the military situation, and Truman told the group he planned to issue a proclamation of national emergency. Vinson advised him to issue the proclamation immediately and follow it at once with the imposition of allocation systems and price controls on all commodities vital to the national defense.[27]

In Korea the war continued with neither side able to achieve a decisive victory. MacArthur, unwilling to accept a stalemate, sought to expand the war in order to win a total victory. Chafing under the limitations imposed on him by Truman and the Joint Chiefs of Staff, he sought public support for his more aggressive policies. On 11 April 1951, following the advice of the Joint Chiefs of Staff, Truman fired General of the Army MacArthur, Commanding General of the U.S. Army Forces, Far East, U.S. commander in chief Far East Command, Supreme Commander for the Allied Powers in Japan, and commander in chief, United Nations Command. A roar of outrage greeted Truman's decision. Seventy-eight thousand telegrams or letters, running twenty-to-one against dismissal, assaulted the White House. A Gallup poll showed 69 percent for MacArthur and only 29 percent backing the president.[28] Republicans insisted that General MacArthur be invited to address a joint session of Congress. On 19 April the charismatic general delivered his memorable address, which ended with the statement "Old soldiers never die; they just fade away."[29]

Although Vinson had escorted MacArthur into the House Chamber, he emphatically backed President Truman. His position was set forth in a letter to a constituent, which was published in the *Atlanta Journal*. Vinson regretted that MacArthur had stayed fourteen years in the Pacific without returning to the United States, for he felt it was only human that a person staying so long in one area would consider that area more important than other regions of the world. Vinson continued:

---

[26] Truman, *Memoirs*, 2:388–91.

[27] Ibid., 2:421–27.

[28] Goldman, *The Crucial Decade—And After*, 202–203.

[29] *Congressional Record*, 82d Cong., 1st sess., 19 April 1951, 4123–25.

An American war with China…as advocated by the General, would not only sink us in the quicksand of the Far East without any ready means of extraction, but it would lay all of Western Europe open to Russian power, since the Russians would know that our hands were completely filled with our undertaking in the Far East…. It is for this reason that the President and the Joint Chiefs of Staff have been doing their level best to localize the war in Korea….

General MacArthur's disagreement with this strategy…was a direct and deliberate attempt to modify the known program of the Commander-in-Chief…through channels which are not properly open to military commanders.

So from the viewpoint of preserving our constitutional processes of government, from the viewpoint of maintaining the strongest possible combination of free powers in the world against the communist threat, and from the standpoint of achieving and maintaining a lasting peace, I think President Truman not only was correct and courageous in forcing the removal of General MacArthur, but in fact, he had no other course of action open to him in the interest of the American people.[30]

The beleaguered Truman was so delighted by Vinson's quick and forceful support that he sent him a personal letter of thanks. "I can't tell you how very much I appreciate your wholehearted support," wrote the president. "I, of course, had counted on the fact that you would understand that the policy at stake is civilian control of the military."[31]

As the president well knew, Vinson's word carried weight in Washington. Others were becoming aware of Vinson's clout and his unique personality through biographical sketches in popular publications. His power and eccentricities had often been mentioned in news

---

[30] Wright Bryan, "Vinson Says Firing Was Wise Strategy," *Atlanta Journal*, 18 April 1951, 1, 2.

[31] Landrum, "Carl Vinson: A Study in Military Preparedness," 142.

magazines, such as *Time, Newsweek*, and *U.S. News & World Report*, but in 1950–1951, three longer biographical sketches reached a wider audience. Vance Packard in *American Magazine*, William S. White in the *New York Times Magazine*, and Beverly Smith in the *Saturday Evening Post* depicted Vinson in a similar way—intelligent, powerful, cagey, and colorful. Vinson had become one of the more interesting characters in Congress, and their works cited numerous examples of his uniqueness. Previously known as the "Admiral," after military unification he was more often referred to as the "Old Operator" or "Uncle Carl." Both terms had merit. White observed in Vinson "a curious, politically perfect, intermingling of the art of attack and the science of withdrawal and compromise." His skill in getting legislation adopted had become legendary and his appearance—balding with glasses perched on the end his prominent nose, loose-fitting clothes on a stooped six-foot frame with a growing paunch, an ever-present cheap cigar in his hand or mouth, and a kindly and unassuming expression—made him everybody's "uncle." White declared that Vinson had "the outward casualness of any rural Southerner on his front porch" and was "so homespun, in a Georgia way, as almost to suggest a case of art improving upon nature."[32] Although Vinson was a man of great national stature, Packard noted that he "still looks, talks, and acts very much like a county sheriff from the Cracker State who settles world problems while sitting around the barrel at a crossroads store."[33] Vinson, "the unlikeliest of war lords," Smith pointed out, "is the image of an easygoing small-town justice of the peace, a disarming picture of bucolic relaxation, until you note—almost with a sense of shock—the sharpness of the blue eyes which peer over the specs. These are the eyes beneath which, these many years, proud admirals and generals have quailed and fidgeted."[34] Even General of the Army George C. Marshall acknowledged that "he could make me feel like a newly minted corporal. When appearing before his

---

[32] William S. White, "Carl Vinson Has Been Unified, Too," *New York Times Magazine*, 10 September 1950, 12.

[33] Packard, "Uncle Carl," 31.

[34] Smith, "He Makes the Generals Listen," 20–21.

committee, I would sometimes have to look at my shoulder board to be certain that I was a five-star general."[35]

Vinson could sling fine language and purple oratory, but he preferred the pure idiom of Georgia's red-clay hill country, seasoned with "Cracker" wit. When generals spoke of "logistics," he said, "You mean carrying things from here to there." He usually referred to weapons, whether submarines, planes, tanks, or atom bombs, as "hardware." As he dryly observed, "The conditions in the world today require a great deal of hardware."[36] Long-windedness bored him. "Never mind the hemmin' and hawin', Admiral," he said, "Just give us the facts." Always wanting the facts first and conclusions later, he often remarked, "Now General, don't take off your shoes till you get to the creek."[37] To a general he drawled sharply, "Put the cards on the table. Let's talk out loud."[38] Certain words he simply could not (or would not) pronounce correctly. He said "Indigo-China" when he was presumably referring to Indo-China. The phrase "*cessation* plus 60 days" gave him so much trouble he often said "*secession* plus 60 days." House clerks had to be assured that the old Georgian really had no thought of insurrection in mind.[39] He never pronounced correctly the last name of his longtime nemesis Representative Vito Marcantonio or the names of many other House colleagues.[40] When L. G. Clemente, a young member of the Armed Services Committee from Queens, New York City, became exasperated with the chairman, he protested, "I feel like I am playing left field in a cemetery." The other members waited fearfully for Clemente to be stricken by a thunderbolt, but Uncle Carl merely asked mildly, "Does Mr. O'Clemenick, in the outfield, have a question?" In time Vinson came to respect Clemente's vehemence and willingness to work. He sometimes asked, "Any questions from the outfield, Mr. McKlenty?" and even invited Clemente into his office for further discussion. "In his office Mr.

---

[35] *Carl Vinson: A Great Georgian* (Athens: University of Georgia, Georgia Center for Continuing Education, 1972).

[36] Smith, "He Makes the Generals Listen," 137.

[37] Ibid., 21.

[38] Packard, "Uncle Carl," 30.

[39] Ibid., 31.

[40] Sam Nunn, interview with the author, Atlanta, GA, 4 April 2001.

Vinson is as nice as he can be," Clemente told Beverly Smith. "He listens to what you say, and if you've got the facts on your side, he changes his mind. Why, the other day, he even called me by my right name."[41] No respecter of authority, Vinson's haziness about names enabled him to deflate those impressed with their own importance. If some salt-encrusted hero known to most of the world became unduly pompous when testifying before his committee, Vinson peered at him innocently over his specs and asked: "Admuhl, what did you say your name was?"[42]

If more drastic measures were needed to deal with those impressed with their own importance, the chairman willingly used them. When the general counsel for the Defense Department managed to offend practically every member of the Armed Services Committee with his arrogance, the chairman solved the problem immediately. He picked up a telephone and told the secretary of defense, "We can't work with this man. Don't send him back over here any more."[43] At the first meeting with his successor, Vinson told the new general counsel, "Now, I don't want to say anything derogatory about your predecessor, but I just want to say that no matter what kind of job you do, it will be a better job than your predecessor did."[44]

His well-known support of the military did not shield admirals from his wrath if they came before his committee unprepared. In 1947 an admiral was testifying on a minor bill providing for the disposal of some old navy surplus ships, when Vinson, then the ranking Democrat on the committee, read the key sections of the bill out loud and asked the admiral if it wouldn't permit the navy to dispose of the entire fleet. The admiral assured him that the navy had no such intention, but Vinson pressed him. Could he show the committee one word in the bill that would prevent the navy from doing just that? The admiral hemmed and

---

[41] Smith, "He Makes the Generals Listen," 137.

[42] Ibid.; Frank Eleazer, "He controls 55¢ of your tax dollar," *Nation's Business.* 43 (December 1955): 68.

[43] Lou and Neta Stockstill, interview with the author.

[44] Louis R. Stockstill, "'Uncle Carl' Vinson: Backstage Boss of the Pentagon," *Army Navy Air Force Journal* 98 (18 February 1961): 22.

hawed, and finally agreed that theoretically Vinson was right. Vinson
then drew from the admiral an acknowledgment that he had read the bill
for the first time on his way from the Pentagon to the committee hearing
room. The bill was tabled without a murmur. Then Vinson turned to the
admiral: "Now Admiral, don't you ever come back up here again
unprepared."[45]

All observers agreed that "Cahl," as Southerners called the
chairman, presided over the most non-political and productive committee
in Congress. He was the absolute boss of the House Committee on the
Armed Services, a body so big that it sat upon three staggered tiers in its
hearing rooms in the old House Office Building, with Vinson front and
center "rather like an ancient monarch surrounded by ministers whose
proximity to the throne depends upon the years that lie upon their heads."
Senior Republicans sat to his left, senior Democrats to his right, and
junior members so far away that their voices were rarely heard by the
chairman.[46] Despite treating his committeemen with high-handed
indignities, he had the respect and admiration of practically all of them.
Through patient discussion and compromise, he usually secured a
unanimous vote in the committee. The only uprising against the
chairman occurred during the unification hearings in 1949. Freshman
John R. Walsh, a young man from Indiana, stormed out of the hearings
charging that Mr. Vinson was running the hearings by "dictatorial
methods." He refused to go back. Since Vinson picked the members who
served on his committee, this was one time his judgment failed. The
committee members recognized that Vinson was a dictator, but they
insisted that he was a *benevolent* dictator. They acceded to his wishes
because, as Dewey Short explained, "there is no chairman in Congress
who is as well informed on the bill he is sponsoring and all its
implications—as Mr. Vinson."[47]

As the chairman of a prestigious committee, Vinson had the
opportunity to take free "inspection trips" and world-girding junkets, but

---

[45] Rowland Evans, Jr., "The Sixth Sense of Carl Vinson," *Reporter* 26 (12
April 1962): 25.

[46] White, "Carl Vinson Has Been Unified, Too," 12.

[47] Packard, "Uncle Carl," 120.

he never went on one. Instead, he sent committee members on such jaunts, while he traveled only to his Milledgeville farm. When Major General Clovis Byers, testifying before Vinson's committee, incautiously remarked, "As you know, Mr. Chairman, from your travels in Europe—" Vinson cut in firmly: "No, suh, I have never been out of this country. I stay right here."[48] As a matter of policy, Vinson never attended military maneuvers and had not set foot on a warship since boarding a submarine in 1917. When the submarine went down 125 feet, Vinson said, "That's enough." He avoided ships thereafter.[49] He was afraid of flying, and when air force officials lured him into a plane ride after World War II, it was considered a historic event. Before agreeing to fly to Georgia for the Easter holiday, he insisted that the very highest brass accompany him in the air force plane. Among his fellow passengers were Secretary of the Air Force Symington, Chief of Staff Hoyt Vandenberg, and Lieutenant General E. R. Quesada, of air force headquarters. When a reporter asked Vinson why he loaded down the plane with so many dignitaries, he replied, "I figured it all out, and took them along for two reasons: First, I figured that with all those big Air Force people aboard, the pilot would be *very* careful when we got up in the sky. And, second, I wanted to make sure that if the plane did come down unexpectedly, it wouldn't be any page-two funeral."[50]

Somehow Vinson exerted awesome power without raising his voice, using abusive language, or coming any closer to profanity than "Consarn it!" His manner was usually one of easygoing courtesy. But when he spotted trouble at the Pentagon, he did not hesitate to pick up the telephone and call the man responsible. He did not waste time with such formalities as "Hello" or "How are you?" Usually he barked: "All right. Vinson of Georgia. Here's the thing let's do. I'll he'p you." ("I'll he'p you" was a favorite expression of his.) If the problem persisted, the officer or official would be summoned to Uncle Carl's lair. The visitor may have entered at a stroll, but often emerged at a trot, and results followed. Exactly what the chairman said in such meetings is unknown.

---

[48] Smith, "He Makes the Generals Listen," 21.
[49] *Atlanta Constitution,* 13 April 1962, 31.
[50] Packard, "Uncle Carl," 121.

When asked directly how he got his results, Vinson replied amiably, "All I do is fuss with them."[51]

Vinson had always made a point of looking after the needs of his constituents, and his ability to cut through bureaucratic red tape on their behalf was unparalleled. After helping a grateful Milledgeville constituent, he explained how he did it: "Sometimes you have to touch up those folks in Washington. You have to touch 'em up." In 1950 the Milledgeville Police Department decided it needed two-way radio equipment for its police cars. When the city council turned down Chief Eugene "Gene" Ellis's request for $2,000, the police department sponsored a rodeo that raised $2,000. The police still needed an additional $500 to purchase the equipment, and finally, after three meetings, the city council provided it. Chief Ellis then purchased the two-way radios and applied for a license and a construction permit from the Federal Communications Commission. Weeks went by and Chief Ellis heard nothing from the F.C.C. Fifty years after the event occurred, he remembered vividly that he could not even get a response from the F.C.C. It so happened that when Vinson came to Milledgeville by bus, Chief Ellis often met him at the bus station and drove him to his farm. The next time Uncle Carl came by bus he asked Ellis how things were going. "Not worth a damn," he replied, explaining how he had purchased the two-way radios but could not get a license from the F.C.C. Vinson told Ellis that he was returning to Capitol Hill on Monday and instructed him to send a telegram to him at his office on Monday. Uncle Carl said, "I'll see what I can do." As instructed, Ellis sent Vinson the telegram at nine o'clock. At three o'clock that afternoon Ellis received a telegram from the F.C.C. It read: "Construction permit granted, license on the way."[52]

A practical man, Vinson did not like to be annoyed by opposition in the Democratic primary and was adept at discouraging challengers. Once he heard that a Mr. Lewis might engage him for the nomination. Promptly he telephoned Georgia's junior Senator, Richard B. Russell.

---

[51] Smith, "He Makes the Generals Listen," 136.

[52] *Union-Recorder*, 9 November 1950, 1; Eugene Ellis, interview with Emmett Hall and the author, Milledgeville GA, 7 December 2001.

"Dick, I don't want you to let that cousin of yours run against me," he shouted emphatically. Russell protested that to his knowledge he had no cousin with such designs. "Well," Vinson complained, "anyhow he married one of your cousins. Get him out of there, Dick." Russell, hurriedly promising to do what he could, did some research and discovered that Mr. Lewis had married a very distant connection to the Russell family. The crisis for Vinson was averted; he was unopposed.[53]

Vinson's highly developed sense of self-preservation could also be seen in his relationship to Georgia's political leaders. When the time for congressional redistricting came around every ten years, he invariably had been on the side of the man who was going to be governor of Georgia when the districts were redrawn. Consequently, as other districts were reshuffled, his district remained intact, the way he wanted it.[54] Concern for his district may explain why, in the summer of 1950, Vinson took time from his busy schedule to campaign for Herman Talmadge, the son of Gene Talmadge. Vinson said he was endorsing Talmadge because he was "deeply impressed with the record he has made." Talmadge, the incumbent governor, defeated M. E. Thompson, and Vinson's district remained unchanged.[55]

Vinson, who received numerous honors and awards, received an honorary doctor of laws degree from the University of South Carolina on 4 June 1951. It was granted "for his foresight and wisdom in national defense and for his judgment and determination in providing adequately for the armed forces, even in defiance of public opinion." The citation described him as a "wise leader of public opinion, faithful servant of the public welfare [and] strong-willed and skillful guardian of the nation's safety."[56]

Since the end of World War II, President Truman had asked for legislation on universal military training, but Congress did not consider the draft and universal military training until the Korean War. After the

---

[53] White, "Carl Vinson Has Been Unified, Too," 13.
[54] Ibid.
[55] "Vinson to Do All He Can For Talmadge," *Atlanta Journal*, 1 June 1950, 17.
[56] Citation of Carl Vinson, Vinson Scrapbooks, book 1949–1951.

Senate passed the bill, Vinson became Truman's point man in the House, where debate on the bill began on 3 April 1951. House members seemed willing to accept the extension of the draft, but expressed strong objections to the universal training section. In a one-hour speech introducing the bill, Vinson warned the House: "We can choose, as set out in this bill, military preparedness—immediate preparedness and sustained, lasting preparedness. Or we choose to continue that bloodstained, costly, and perilous course of entrusting our freedoms and our national security to the fickle hope that our enemies will in the future, as they have in the past, give us time to prepare."[57] Vinson believed the United States must meet the Korean emergency and at the same time establish a long-range preparedness and training program. He further warned: "This present system of raising large armies for short periods of time, followed by complete and total demobilization, results in waste and extravagance and will lead to economic chaos. And to continue this policy in the face of conditions of modern war will surely invite disaster."[58]

On 13 April, by vote of 372 to 44, the House passed a compromise measure. It amended the draft laws by extending the draft three years and lowering the draft age to 18.5 years, but it did not include universal military training. Only by accepting the compromise did Vinson and universal military training supporters avoid a total defeat in the House.[59] The next year, when the issue was brought up again, the House remained bitterly divided. Vinson led the proponents while Leslie Arends, a ranking Republican on the Armed Services Committee, led the opposition. Critics argued that universal military training was undemocratic, uneconomical, and "a transgression on individual liberties," while Vinson maintained that it provided three benefits. First, the trained reserve forces it would provide would cost less to provide and maintain than a huge standing force. Second, the program would apply equally to all young men. Third, those men who had already served once

[57] *Congressional Record*, 82d Cong., 1st sess., 3 April 1951, 3205.

[58] Ibid.

[59] Landrum, "Carl Vinson: A Study in Military Preparedness," 144; "New Draft: Winners and Losers," *U.S. News & World Report* 30 (8 June 1951): 26.

or twice on the front lines of battle would not do so again. To refute the undemocratic argument, Vinson asked: "Do you think Dick Russell, Harry Byrd, Lyndon Johnson, Estes Kefauver, John Stennis, Russell Long, Styles Bridges, Leverett Saltonstall, Wayne Morse, William Knowland, John McCormack, Sam Rayburn, and many others would approve a program that was not in the best interest of the American people?"[60]

Realizing that the bill in its present form could not pass, Vinson resorted to some last-minute compromises to salvage the bill. His efforts failed. The motion of Dewey Short to table the bill carried by vote of 236 to 162. The defeat on universal military training was one of the few major legislative defeats Vinson suffered in his lengthy congressional career. Susan Landrum correctly attributed the defeat to Vinson's compromise retreat at the last moment, to actual convictions of some members against universal military training, and to the unwillingness of many members to support such a controversial issue in an election year.[61]

Vinson had purchased a house in Milledgeville largely to please his wife. He much preferred living in the country, and after her death he sought to lease the house to a good tenant who would take care of it. As he had invested $1,600 on a new back porch, $1,000 on a fence around the property, $400 on blinds, and $400 on an iron fence, he decided that $125 a month was the minimum he could accept. When Erwin Sibley informed him that the commandant of Georgia Military College would lease the house at that price, a delighted Vinson told him to close the deal. "The truth of the matter is," Vinson added, "that I never did want to move back in town, but I was going to have to do so to take care of the property, as I was unwilling to let the old house go down."[62]

Unlike many Southern leaders of this era, Vinson consistently supported the national Democratic Party ticket, and the election of 1952 was no exception. He rarely attended national conventions, but he went

---

[60] Landrum, "Carl Vinson: A Study in Military Preparedness," 144–46.

[61] Ibid., 148; "The Congress," *Time* 59 (17 March 1952): 18–19.

[62] Carl Vinson to Erwin Sibley, 2 February 1952, Erwin Sibley Papers, January–February 1952 folder, Special Collections, Ina Dillard Russell Library, Georgia College and State University, Milledgeville, GA.

to the Democratic National Convention in Chicago to support the presidential bid of fellow Georgian Richard Russell. When Senator Russell failed to win the nomination, the party chose Adlai Stevenson of Illinois as its standard-bearer. Vinson considered him the party's "second best choice" after Russell.[63] In a press release he declared "there is not an iota of lukewarmness in me" and "I am one hundred percent plus for the STEVENSON-SPARKMAN Democratic Ticket."[64] Unfortunately for Vinson, not many others shared his enthusiasm for the ticket, and the Democrats suffered a resounding defeat. Dwight Eisenhower proved to be the most appealing American political figure in the 1950s and, with Richard Nixon as his running-mate, won by a landslide. The Republicans also captured control of the House by a margin of 221 to 213, making Representative Joe Martin of Massachusetts the Speaker, and Representative Dewey Short of Missouri the new chairman of the Armed Services Committee. Vinson, relegated to ranking minority member of the committee, found out quickly how the change in leadership affected his clout. When a constituent sought a job in Washington, Vinson ruefully informed Erwin Sibley, "There is nothing I can do for him. All jobs—from that of elevator operators up—are under Republican patronage. They are laying off all the Democrats and putting in Republican patronage, so there is no chance of my taking care of him in any position as long as the Republicans are in control."[65]

Eisenhower pursued a moderate course and sought support from Democrats. As one of the ranking Democrats, Vinson was invited to the White House many times. After a luncheon there on 13 February 1953, he was certain the new president wanted to work with Congress. However, in a private letter to Erwin Sibley, he expressed concern that Eisenhower "is going to hesitate in taking the leadership necessary for a president to take, for fear he might get in a fuss with Congress."[66] When

---

[63] *Union-Recorder*, 31 July 1952, 1.

[64] Ibid., 11 September 1952, 11.

[65] Carl Vinson to Erwin Sibley, 12 January 1953, Erwin Sibley Papers, January 1953 folder.

[66] Carl Vinson to Erwin Sibley, 16 February 1953, Erwin Sibley Papers, February–March 1953 folder.

Vinson emphatically endorsed an administration measure to give the chairman of the Joint Chiefs of Staff more management responsibilities, he received warm personal letters of thanks from President Eisenhower.[67]

In the campaign, Eisenhower had pledged to "go to Korea." He fulfilled that promise and the undeclared war came to an end in July 1953, with the boundary separating North Korea from South Korea practically where it was when the war began. In thirty-seven months of combat, America had lost 25,000 dead, suffered 115,000 casualties, and spent $22 billion.[68] Ten months later, as the Geneva Conference was trying to resolve the situation in Indo-China, Vinson wrote Erwin Sibley, "I am fully convinced that there will be no intervention on the part of this Government."[69] After a briefing at the White House on foreign affairs, national defense, and related matters in December 1954, he wrote the same correspondent: "We are further from war now than any time in recent years. I firmly believe we are on the road toward lasting peace."[70]

For many years Vinson had believed that the air force needed a separate academy, similar to West Point and Annapolis. With the Korean War publicizing the need for additional air force training, he introduced legislation to establish a $20,000,000 Air Force Academy. To drum up public support for the measure, he published an article, "For a 'West Point' of the Air," in the *New York Times Magazine* in June 1952.[71] This time the timing was right. On 21 January 1954 the House approved the measure by vote of 331 to 36. Six weeks later the Senate approved it, and on 1 April 1954, President Eisenhower signed it into law.[72] Creating the Air Force Academy was Vinson's most important legislative accomplishment during Eisenhower's first term.

---

[67] Dwight Eisenhower to Carl Vinson, 22 June and 29 June 1953, Vinson Scrapbooks, book August 1951–December 1954.

[68] Goldman, *The Crucial Decade—And After*, 246–47.

[69] Carl Vinson to Erwin Sibley, 8 May 1954, Erwin Sibley Papers, 6–25 May 1954 folder.

[70] Ibid., 14 December 1954, November–December 1954 folder.

[71] "Vinson Bill Asks Air Academy to Cost 20 Million," *Atlanta Journal*, Vinson Scrapbooks, book 1949–51; Carl Vinson, "For a 'West Point' of the Air," *New York Times Magazine*, 22 June 1952, 13, 35.

[72] *Congressional Record*, 83rd Cong., 2d sess., 597, 2796, 4793.

Eisenhower's personal popularity failed to keep his party in power, and in the 1954 off-year election, the Democrats regained control of the House by a margin of 232 to 203. Although Vinson had delivered a rip-roaring partisan address at the Sixth District Democratic Convention in Macon and had campaigned as a loyal Democrat, bipartisanship and mutual respect characterized this era of Congressional history.[73] On 5 January 1955 Speaker Joe Martin praised his successor, Sam Rayburn, as "a man of great parliamentary skill and experience,…a man of character, a man of integrity, a man of fairness, and, above all, one who believes in the great traditions of Congress." Rayburn, in turn, praised his predecessor, calling attention to their personal friendship that had existed for years. "He and I both believe in the same things when it comes to honesty and truthfulness," said Rayburn. "There are no degrees in truthfulness. There are no degrees in honesty. You are 100 percent or you are not. I have found Joe Martin a hundred percent upon both." After calling attention to the dangers that faced the Republic, Rayburn again emphasized the importance of bipartisanship. "We are all in this thing together whether we be Republicans, Democrats, or what not." Pledging bipartisanship, he said, "We are going to look upon the President's recommendations with kindliness because he is the leader of our country. He is the President of the United States and should be honored and respected as that." Vinson administered the oath of office to Rayburn, who was then completing his forty-second year in Congress, and resumed his customary position as chairman of the House Committee on Armed Services.[74]

---

[73] *Union-Recorder*, 23 September 1954, 11.
[74] *Congressional Record*, 84th Cong., 1st sess., 5 January 1955, 8–10.

12

The Eisenhower Years

The Supreme Court may say what the law is; they may not say what the law should be. Only the Congress may write our Federal laws.

Carl Vinson, 1956

The Eighty-fourth Congress opened on 5 January 1955, with Sam Rayburn and John McCormack in their familiar places as Speaker and majority leader in the House, and with Vinson protégé Lyndon Johnson the majority leader in the Senate. Despite Johnson's flair for publicity, "Rayburn was the senior partner of the Texas leadership team in the Congress," observed Richard Bolling, and "it was not until 1960 that Johnson, though dominant in the Senate, became a full partner in the Democratic leadership." Rayburn, resisting any change in the way the Democratic Party operated in Congress, continued the seniority system for choosing committee chairmen because he doubted that any better system existed.[1] Consequently, Southerners held disproportionate power in the Democratically-controlled Congress. With Rayburn holding the

---

[1] During the 1950s and 1960s the seniority system came under widespread attack, as critics demanded that younger, ostensibly abler members be allowed to chair committees. Vinson, of course, owed his position as chairman of the Naval Affairs Committee and then the Armed Services Committee to the seniority system. By the end of his career, some maintained that Vinson was "the best argument ever devised for the seniority system." "Fifty-Year Man," *Newsweek* 64 (28 December 1964): 20.

balance of power, the Eighty-fourth and subsequent Congresses backed Eisenhower on foreign policy and generally supported his conservative domestic agenda too.

Richard Bolling, a reform-minded congressman from Missouri, called the Eisenhower-Rayburn years the "dismal years," but Vinson had a much higher regard for the period.[2] In fact, he approved of much of the Republican military program and foreign policy. When Secretary of Defense Charles E. Wilson explained the administration's military programs for 1956 to the House Armed Services Committee, Vinson could barely restrain his enthusiasm. "I've been here a long time," the chairman replied, "and I have heard many resumes on world situations, and defense needs, but I believe your statement is the most comprehensive and the most forthright one I have ever heard. Your reasoning is sound and your candor is highly commendable." Vinson was pleased that Wilson had set a floor on the size of the armed forces at 2,850,000 men at an annual cost of approximately $34 billion, and he was especially pleased that the secretary sought stability for the armed services instead of the wasteful "feast or famine" of the past. Vinson, who had long lamented the "peaks and valleys" of military procurement, said, "We are in complete accord on this fundamental philosophy of a proper defense structure."[3] Vinson was so supportive of Wilson's testimony because two weeks earlier the secretary had spent the day with Vinson discussing national security. In that meeting, Uncle Carl informed him that the harsher defense cuts proposed by Secretary of the Treasury George Humphrey were unacceptable and warned against balancing the budget or cutting taxes at the expense of an adequate military force. The two leaders came to an agreement. Thus, to a large extent, Wilson's testimony on 26 January reiterated Vinson's own thinking.[4] When General Matthew B. Ridgeway objected to proposed cuts in army manpower, Vinson scheduled hearings to allow the army to

---

[2] Richard Bolling, *Power in the House* (New York: Dutton and Co., 1968) 192–201.

[3] *Congressional Record*, 84th Cong., 1st sess., 26 January 1955, 771–76.

[4] Frank Eleazer, "He controls 55¢ of your tax dollar," *Nation's Business*. 43 (December 1955): 32–33.

present its views. The hearings, however, failed to convince Vinson or the committee that the reduction of 173,000 men was not necessary. As always, Vinson had concern about the reductions in manpower, but he acquiesced in them because of the new policy of stability.[5] Several months later he told a Kiwanis Club audience in Macon that a "stable force" military program had been worked out. While expressing concern that tax cuts might jeopardize an adequate defense program, he praised President Eisenhower and "that remarkable American" Secretary of State John Foster Dulles, for "a magnificent job…in handling our foreign policy."[6]

As usual, Vinson's seniority brought Georgia a generous share of military spending. On 14 June 1955, Vinson's committee unanimously approved a $2.3 billion military public works authorization bill for bases around the globe. Out of the total, Georgia received $36,861,000 for construction at twelve military bases. Fort Benning, near Columbus, received over $10,000,000, the largest appropriation, but Vinson's district did quite well. The Marine Supply Center in Albany received $3,157,000 for cold storage facilities, utilities, and recreational facilities, and the Naval Ordnance Plant in Macon received $3,800,000 for a building and equipment.[7]

Vinson, who lived comfortably but was far from affluent, was delighted when his salary was increased from $15,000 to $22,500. He commented, "Well, if they are going to pay that kind of money in Congress, I think I'll make a career out of it."[8] He candidly wrote to Erwin Sibley that he thought he was worth the higher salary and hoped his constituents agreed with him.[9] While grappling with national issues

---

[5] *Atlanta Journal*, 6 February 1955, A10.

[6] "Military Pruning Disturbs Vinson," a 1955 newspaper clipping in Vinson Scrapbooks, book 1954–1956, on loan from Tillman Snead to Georgia College and State University, Milledgeville, GA.

[7] Ken Turner, "House Unit Backs Spending of 38 Million," *Atlanta Journal*, 14 June 1955, in Carl Vinson file, Atlanta Journal-Constitution Office.

[8] Eleazer, "He controls 55¢ of your tax dollar," 71.

[9] Carl Vinson to Erwin Sibley, 1 March 1955, Erwin Sibley Papers, 14 February–15 March 1955 folder, Special Collections, Ina Dillard Russell Library, Georgia College and State University, Milledgeville, GA.

and billion-dollar appropriations, Vinson maintained a keen interest in
local affairs. He continually sought improvements on the Vinson
Highway, which ran by his farm, and he exerted influence on the
development of the city of Milledgeville as well. Convinced that
Milledgeville needed more roads and bridges, he prodded local and state
officials to build them. A new bridge across the Central Railroad at the
end of Montgomery Street, he thought, would make a substantial
contribution to the town. When a new bridge over Fishing Creek was
completed, he expected it to relieve traffic congestion on Montgomery
Street, where his house was located. He told his friend Erwin Sibley that
he was trying to get a portion of the Vinson Highway widened with
sidewalks added. After that project was accomplished, he would try to
get a new bridge across Fishing Creek at Columbia Street or Clarke
Street and a new bridge across the Oconee River in the vicinity of Black
Springs as part of an east-west by-pass of Milledgeville. He knew these
projects would take years to complete, but as he told Sibley, "if you
don't make an effort you never succeed." Vinson was certain that
nothing would contribute more to the development of Milledgeville than
having good roads coming into it.[10]

Vinson had flown in an airplane only one time, back in 1949, and it
had not been a pleasant experience. When his flight from Washington to
Macon encountered what the air force called "mild turbulence," Vinson
belted himself tight into the seat, got a death grip on both arms, and held
on grimly until the plane landed. Upon alighting, he announced that the
flight was his last. Six years later, Secretary of Defense Wilson came to
Macon to inspect the Naval Ordnance plant there. Vinson showed him
around and explained why the plant was vital to the national security and
the welfare of Bibb County and how an outlay of $3,800,000 was needed
to safeguard the government's investment. The inspection tour took
longer than planned, and late in the day Vinson realized that he was not
going to make it to Athens in time to catch the train on which he had an
overnight reservation to Washington. Secretary Wilson pointed out that
his plush air force Convair was waiting at the airport to return him to the
capital. It would get there, he added, before Vinson's train could get out

---

[10] Ibid., 8 March 1955.

of Athens. Reluctantly, Vinson climbed aboard. "I took one look out the window," he reported later, "and couldn't see nothin' but clouds. I turned my head straight to the front and never looked out again." Three days later, when he had to return to Georgia, he went by train.[11]

Vinson made no concession to his advancing age and maintained the same busy schedule that he had followed for years. The Armed Services Committee continued its extraordinary workload, and Vinson dominated its proceedings with his usual flair. In May 1957 he wrote Erwin Sibley that he probably would not get home until 1 July because "we are very busy up here now." Although his committee had passed thirty bills, "more than any other committee in Congress," he was working on a $1.75 billion bill and had held hearings on it every day for three weeks. After it was taken care of, the House would consider the civil rights bill and a school bill, both of which he intended to vote against, and then he would have to present his public works bill to the House.[12] Eight months later he wrote the same correspondent, "I have all I can say grace over right now holding an investigation on the largest business in the world—THE DEPARTMENT OF DEFENSE."[13]

Vinson's iron hand, heavy gavel, and good humor were displayed when his committee took up a bill to let the government spend four million dollars as host to the Winter Olympic Games set for 1960 in Squaw Valley, California. Representative Clair Engle, in whose district the event would take place, waited his turn while Assistant Defense Secretary William H. Francis, Jr. took twenty minutes to say why the bill should be passed. Finally Vinson recognized Engle, who settled comfortably into the witness chair with the righteous air of a lawmaker ready to spend the next thirty-five or forty minutes speaking out in his constituents' behalf. "In view of the fine statement made by the secretary," Engle began, "I don't think there is much for me to add." Bang went the gavel. "Thank you very much, for being considerate of the

---

[11] Eleazer, "He controls 55¢ of your tax dollar," 70–71.

[12] Carl Vinson to Erwin Sibley, 24 May 1957, Erwin Sibley Papers, March–May 1957 folder.

[13] Ibid., 18 January 1958, January 1958 folder. Vinson's emphasis.

committee's time," Vinson interjected. Before Engle realized that his testimony was over, Vinson had called, "Next witness."[14]

With a keen eye for incipient rebellions in his committee, Vinson seemed to defuse them in the nick of time. He deflated one budding revolt by explaining blandly that he always informed the members about important decisions just as soon as he made them. Before anybody could figure out why this was not a satisfactory explanation, Vinson had banged the gavel and adjourned the meeting.[15] The secret to running a committee, he once told a younger congressional protégé, was "never let them all get mad at once. You lose control. It's all right if they get mad one at a time."[16]

In the mid-1950s Vinson was not able to concentrate exclusively on military affairs because the issue of civil rights had emerged, and it took much of his time and energy. Prior to this time, civil rights had not been a major issue in the South because those in power were so united in upholding the Jim Crow system that the opposing view was barely heard. For as long as anyone could remember, segregation had been the law of the land in Dixie, and white Southerners, for the most part, expected the existing system to continue indefinitely. Politicians differed only in the rhetoric they employed in reaffirming white supremacy and black inferiority in the segregated system. None called for fundamental change in the system. Politicians also agreed that Yankee politicians, unfamiliar with Southern racial mores, should keep their noses out of the issue altogether. Their meddling, so the argument went, would only complicate matters, engender strife, and actually harm race relations, which were gradually improving under enlightened Southern leadership. Periodic racial disturbances had little effect on this outlook, as they were dismissed as aberrations, usually incited by outside agitators.

Reared in the "black belt" of the rural South, Vinson naturally accepted the culture of his area. There is no evidence to indicate that he disagreed with the system in his early years or that he even gave it much thought. It appears that he simply accepted segregation as a normal part

---

[14] *Atlanta Journal,* 21 March 1958, 19; 18 April 1958, 15.

[15] Ibid., 25 April 1958, 23.

[16] Ibid., 18 April 1958, 15.

of life. Although public facilities in Georgia were segregated by race, Vinson had much contact with blacks throughout his life. Blacks performed much of the labor on his farm, and he, like most Southerners of his class, employed black cooks and domestic helpers. To his credit, he never resorted to the vile racial rhetoric used by many Georgia politicians, such as Tom Watson, Gene Talmadge, Herman Talmadge, and Marvin Griffin.

In his speech accepting the congressional nomination in 1948, a time when civil rights had become an issue in the national Democratic Party, he expressed concern that an effort was being made to enact by law an "alien and vicious Civil Rights Program." He described the civil rights issue as "the most important issue that has confronted the people of the South" in many decades. In Georgia, he declared, "We are trying to work out in our own way the advancement of all citizens and we are better able to solve our own problems *than outsiders*." Without going into specifics, he pledged that he, along with every senator and representative from Virginia to Texas, would do "every thing in their power" to defeat the civil rights program. "We will fight to the last ditch," he said.[17]

What is perhaps most noteworthy about this speech is that it is one of the few references Vinson made to civil rights during this era. Since he faced no political opposition in 1948, 1950, 1952, or 1954, he did not have to articulate his views on the subject. Even after the momentous *Brown v. Board of Education* decision in 1954, which aroused a paroxysm of defiance from many Southern politicians, Vinson said very little about the subject. His reticence, however, may have damaged him politically; it clearly motivated his opponent in the 1956 race. On 1 May 1955, almost exactly one year after the Brown decision was delivered by the Warren Court, and nearly a year before the next congressional campaign normally would begin, Carter Shepherd "Shep" Baldwin announced that he would oppose Vinson in 1956 for the Sixth District congressional seat. His announcement in the *Macon Telegraph*

---

[17] Vinson Acceptance Speech for Democratic nomination to the 81st Congress, Erwin Sibley Papers, Miscellaneous Speeches folder.

emphasized that he was running because Vinson had never come out against the Supreme Court's decision abolishing segregation.[18]

Shep Baldwin, fifty-eight years old, was a native of Madison, Georgia. A 1917 graduate of the University of Georgia, he had served in World War I. Following his discharge, he studied law at Mercer University and was graduated in 1921. He practiced law for a few years in Macon, then moved to Madison, and since 1942 had resided in Milledgeville. For twenty-two years he had served as solicitor general of the Ocmulgee Judicial Circuit. In making his announcement, the solicitor general emeritus declared that the ideals, customs, and heritages of the South were in "graver danger right now than they have been since the Civil War. Our present congressman is not talking the voice of the people of Middle Georgia," he asserted. Worried about things that were happening in the United States, Baldwin declared that "the voice of the South will be spoken in Congress one more time."[19]

Soon after Baldwin's announcement, Vinson became embroiled in a dispute to integrate the National Guard, which revealed his native cunning and mastery of the intricacies of the parliamentary rules. The House, having transformed itself into the Committee of the Whole,[20] was well on the way to approving an administration reserve program designed to produce a force of 2.9 million reservists in five years. The bill included tougher restrictions, such as requiring reservists to show up for weekly drills and summer encampments. It also funneled some reservists into national guard units. Difficulties for Vinson ensued when

---

[18] Erwin Sibley to Carl Vinson, 2 May 1955, Erwin Sibley Papers, 1–17 May 1955 folder.

[19] *Atlanta Journal*, 8 May 1955, D16.

[20] When Members are in regular session in the House Chamber, a large, ceremonial mace is first placed on a high pedestal at the right hand side of the Speaker's chair, denoting that the Speaker of the House is in charge. When certain bills are reported to the floor and brought up for debate, the Speaker relinquishes his seat, the mace is moved to a lower pedestal next to the desk of the Sergeant at Arms, and the body is converted into a committee designated as the Committee of the Whole House, or more familiarly as the Committee of the Whole. Some Member other than the Speaker then takes the chair, and debate proceeds with all of the House Members acting as committee members.

Representative Adam Clayton Powell of Harlem, one of three African Americans in the House, offered an amendment preventing the assignment of reservists to national guard units that practiced segregation. He had brought up the amendment so often that it had become known as the Powell amendment, but on this occasion the flamboyant minister, a spell-binding orator, was in top form and his amendment was adopted. The next day, Vinson tried to remove the Powell amendment with a hastily-drawn amendment of his own, but Powell was not to be denied. After his introductory remarks, the New York congressman began a peroration of dramatic, mesmerizing imagery, which transfixed not only his fellow representatives, but the press gallery and public gallery too:

> When George Washington's ragged troops of the Continental Army marched across the snows of Valley Forge, you will find the bleeding footprints of Negro men who marched with them in that Army. They were segregated, but their patriotism was not in doubt. And later, when Black Jack Pershing went after Pancho Villa in Mexico, Negroes rode in segregated artillery units by his side. Their patriotism was not questioned even thought they were Jim Crowed. When Teddy Roosevelt went up San Juan Hill, Negroes were by his side fighting and dying in the Spanish-American War. Call the roll of World War I and World War II. They were there. Second-class citizens, but dying the same as anyone else.

His rhetoric prevailed and Vinson's amendment was defeated 167 to 143.[21]

Making the best of a bad situation, Vinson moved that the "Committee do now rise." His motion passed, and the chairman banged his gavel and left his seat. Officials moved the ornate bronze mace back to the higher pedestal, the Speaker took his accustomed seat, the House of Representatives was back in session, and the Committee of the Whole, at Vinson's request, had been discharged. The defense bill was no longer

---

[21] *Congressional Record*, 84th Cong., 1st sess., 19 May 1955, 6573–657.

under discussion. It had been removed from the floor and was winging its way back to the Armed Services Committee, where it would rest on Vinson's desk until he decided what next to do with it. The Georgia Swamp Fox had once more won what had seemed like a losing battle.[22]

In striking a blow to prevent integration of the National Guard, Vinson told the *Atlanta Journal*:

> Georgians have long held sacred the right to operate their own schools. By the same token they have reserved to the governor, control of the National Guard.
>
> As long as I can prevent it, I shall not permit the passage of any federal legislation to change this pattern, much less abolish segregation.
>
> Operation of the National Guard is strictly a state matter, and so long as I am concerned it will remain so. Georgians may rest assured of that.[23]

The Armed Services Committee rewrote the bill, leaving out the National Guard clause. When the committee approved it by vote of 29 to 1, Vinson declared, "We're going to defeat the efforts of the NAACP to inject something extraneous and foreign into the bill. We're backing the President up 100 percent."[24] The bill became law when President Eisenhower signed it on 9 August 1955.[25]

As soon as Congress adjourned on 2 August 1955, Vinson returned to his Milledgeville farm. It had been a grueling session, and Vinson needed to get away from Washington. On the quiet rolling hills of River Ridge Plantation, away from the hectic pace of Capitol Hill, he could rest, clear his head, and "recharge his batteries." Rising early, as he always did, he spent his days inspecting every aspect of his farm

---

[22] Louis Stockstill to the author, 19 March 2003, Stockstill Papers, currently in author's possession.

[23] *Atlanta Journal*, 22 May 1955, B11; "Slap for an Iron Hand," *Newsweek* 46 (4 July 1955): 19.

[24] *Atlanta Journal*, 28 June 1955, 1.

[25] *New York Times*, 10 August 1955, L10; *Congressional Record*, 84th Cong., 1st sess., 9 August 1955, 13081.

operation. Since he had a competent overseer in Barnie Collins, things ran smoothly in his absence. Vinson made sure that they did by sending his overseer a steady stream of instructions from Washington through regular correspondence and an occasional telephone call. Once on the farm, he wanted to know every detail about his farm, just as he did about every bill his committee prepared. Confident of his own expertise in farming, he peppered Barnie with questions to determine if all his instructions had been carried out properly. Not content with an oral report, he walked over the entire farm, inspecting barns, fences, chickens, cattle, and fields. Observers marveled at his stamina. Walking was his one form of exercise, and he practiced it diligently, both in Washington and on the farm. He thought nothing of hiking five miles by himself. Oddly enough, he did not look like a Middle Georgia farmer; on the farm he wore dress pants and a white shirt, just as he did in Washington. His only concession to the rural environment was a pair of boots.

When Congress was not in session, Vinson habitually traveled throughout his district, attending local functions, giving a few speeches, listening to constituent complaints, and meeting with political supporters. Since he already had opposition for the next election, he made extra efforts to contact key individuals to ensure his reelection. Near the end of the congressional recess, just before the year ended, he purchased a new Ford. Even though he never drove, he still enjoyed riding in a new car.[26]

Back in Washington Vinson resumed his busy schedule, presiding over committee hearings and directing bills on the floor of the House, but the farm was never far from his thoughts. He tried to arrange his schedule so that he could return to Milledgeville for a few days at the end of January. He enjoyed good health and told Erwin Sibley that he "never felt better," but Molly suffered from a bad cold, and young Tillman had been sick for weeks with a cold, earache, and chicken pox. Finally, after two or three shots of penicillin, the youngster recovered and returned to school.[27]

---

[26] Carl Vinson to Erwin Sibley, 27 December 1955, Erwin Sibley Papers, September–December 1955 folder.

[27] Ibid., 14 January and 17 January 1956, January 1956 folder.

On 26 January 1956, Vinson introduced the following constitutional amendment in the House: "Notwithstanding any other provision of this Constitution, or any amendment thereto, the States of the United States have, and shall forever have, the right to manage their own internal affairs with respect to any matter not expressly forbidden by the Constitution." He declared that he was "shocked" by the Supreme Court decision of 17 May 1954 (*Brown v. Board of Education*), which, in effect, "overturned at one fell swoop by judicial fiat doctrines and principles of constitutional law which had become a part of our Constitution by repeated adjudication." From his lengthy experience in Congress, he knew that the states' rights doctrine was "not peculiar to the beliefs of the people of my State and my section." Having given "serious and mature consideration" to the problems then confronting the nation, he became convinced that the amendment was necessary. "This amendment," he argued, "states the law as it really exists today and simply reaffirms principles of constitutional government which are as old as the Constitution itself."[28]

Though Vinson sincerely believed in the states' rights doctrine and clearly objected to the judicial activism of the Warren Court, the timing of his amendment raises questions. If the Brown decision shocked him, why did he wait twenty months to respond to it? Throughout the South, numerous critics of the decision had immediately called for the impeachment of Chief Justice Earl Warren and had begun to look for ways to circumvent the Supreme Court ruling, but Vinson had remained silent. It would appear that Shep Baldwin's decision to challenge him with an extreme states' rights campaign prompted Vinson to act. Quite possibly, discussions with key people in the district during the congressional recess convinced him that he was politically vulnerable on the issue. Never one to take an opponent lightly, Vinson acted decisively to eliminate that possibility. Two days after introducing the amendment, he wrote Erwin Sibley that the amendment would be "one of the main issues in my campaign." He planned to get the amendment out of the

---

[28] *Congressional Record*, 84th Cong., 2d sess., 26 January 1956, 1392-93.

Judiciary Committee and have a full debate on it on the floor of the House.[29]

True to his word, on 24 April he delivered a forceful sixty-minute address in support of his amendment. He began his eloquent speech by extolling the wisdom of the founding fathers, who had created a Constitution that ensured freedom by dividing the power between the states and the federal government. They also had adopted the Tenth Amendment, which assigned undefined powers to the states. He quoted liberally from Dwight Eisenhower, the Republican platform of 1860, Franklin Roosevelt, and James Madison to show that the position he espoused was not new. On the contrary, it was the traditional interpretation of the Constitution that had been recognized for many, many years.

But on May 17, 1954, 168 years of precedent was shattered and abandoned to the sociological ideas of an alien who misled nine members of the United States Supreme Court into an attempt to set aside the principles of constitutional government so dearly bought, and so carefully preserved—principles which made us a great and federal union—principles which had protected us against the creation of an all-consuming, all-powerful, Federal Government.

For we know that the Federal Government, like any other uncontrollable growth, has an insatiable appetite, and will continue to expand at the slightest provocation until it has gnawed away at the very fibers which sustain it—namely, the States which gave this nation its very name—the United States of America. And, when that day happens, and we are fast approaching it, we will have lost the initiative and the greatness of America.

The power to make laws is vested in the Congress; the power to execute the laws is vested in the President; the power to interpret the laws is vested in the judiciary. No power is vested

---

[29] Carl Vinson to Erwin Sibley, 28 January 1956, Erwin Sibley Papers, January 1956 folder.

in the judiciary by the Constitution to make the laws—and any power so assumed is in direct violation of the separation of powers that constitute the very heart of our form of government. The Supreme Court may say what the law is; they may not say what the law should be. Only the Congress may write our Federal laws.[30]

Vinson was so pleased with his speech that he had 10,000 copies of it printed and distributed throughout his congressional district.[31]

While Vinson waged a futile battle with the Supreme Court, he steered major defense bills through his committee and the House of Representatives. On 1 February 1956, the House approved a $1.4 billion naval shipbuilding program that included construction of the first nuclear-driven surface vessel, a missile-launching cruiser. The program also called for six more atomic-powered submarines like the successful *Nautilus*, and a nuclear supercarrier. There was little debate on the Vinson measure, and the House approved it by vote of 358 to 3.[32] When a representative proposed naming the supercarrier for Vinson, the chairman squelched that idea immediately. "You only name ships after people who have passed from the scene of action," he said.[33] Vinson had become alarmed when he learned that 94 percent of the armed services contracts had been spent in direct negotiation with suppliers. The armed services, it seems, were still functioning under a Korean War emergency provision. On 20 February the House passed a Vinson bill by vote of 372 to 2 to restore competitive bidding.[34]

In protest against the Supreme Court decision, many states passed "interposition resolutions." When the Georgia General Assembly considered adopting such a measure, Vinson urged the members not to

---

[30] *Congressional Record*, 84th Cong., 2d sess., 24 April 1956, 6888–92.

[31] Carl Vinson to Erwin Sibley, 30 April 1956, Erwin Sibley Papers, April–May 1956 folder.

[32] *New York Times*, 2 February 1956, 11.

[33] "Vinson Squelches Idea Of Namesake Carrier," 30 March 1955, Carl Vinson file, Atlanta Journal-Constitution Office.

[34] *Macon Telegraph*, 19 December 1955, 1; *Atlanta Constitution,* 21 February 1956, 1.

adopt a "watered-down" resolution. In a letter to Governor Marvin Griffin he declared: "I hope that the Legislature in its resolution of interposition, which has my wholehearted support, will declare the Supreme Court decision of May 17, 1954, null and void and of no effect because the Supreme Court had no authority under the Constitution."[35] A few weeks later, however, when the Georgia Senate passed a resolution calling for the impeachment of Chief Justice Warren and Justices Black, Douglas, Reed, Frankfurter, and Clark for "high crimes and misdemeanors," Vinson refused to go along. He quickly responded that the decision on the school question does not constitute high crimes and misdemeanors on the part of the Supreme Court. Therefore, he would neither introduce nor vote for a resolution of impeachment.[36]

While Vinson campaigned for reelection in the spring and summer of 1956, another political campaign attracted much interest in Georgia. Former Governor Herman Talmadge had launched a determined effort to unseat Georgia's senior senator, Walter George. When Talmadge sought the support of Erwin Sibley, it put Vinson's closest friend in an awkward position. He wanted to help Talmadge, but he did not want to do anything that might jeopardize Vinson's campaign. Vinson suggested that he "write Talmadge and tell him that in view of the fact that you have Baldwin to contend with you can't take any interest in any campaign except that of mine." He added that although he had always been for Talmadge and had taken an active part in his campaigns, he did not intend to get involved in the senatorial race. "I will tote my own skillet," he wrote, "but there is no doubt that Shep [Baldwin] is going to try to ride Talmadge's coat tail."[37]

Vinson continued to make opposition to the Supreme Court decision and adoption of his constitutional amendment the centerpiece of his campaign. "We are witnessing a drastic and dangerous effort to concentrate power in the federal government," he declared in a speech to

---

[35] *Atlanta Journal*, 2 February 1956, 2.

[36] "Vinson Says He Won't Ask Impeachment," newspaper clipping in Vinson Scrapbooks, book 1954–1956.

[37] Carl Vinson to Erwin Sibley, 12 March 1956, Erwin Sibley Papers, March 1956 folder.

American Legion Post 74. The Supreme Court has taken upon itself the "illegal prerogative" of writing the laws of the states and they "have laughed at the intentions of the Founding Fathers." In that same speech, he also criticized the proposed civil rights bill that was passed by the House but died in the Senate. He said the bill would have set up a "commission on snooping." Such a commission, he said, would have been able to tell anyone whom he could employ and how to run his business and might even affect churches.[38]

To solidify his position as a champion of states' rights and constitutional government, Vinson introduced a bill to prohibit the Supreme Court from reviewing any decision that had been in effect for fifty years or more without specific permission from Congress. Since the bill, introduced on 14 June 1956, was retroactive to January 1954, it would nullify the Brown decision of 1954.[39] It fared no better than his proposed constitutional amendment, but it was useful for the campaign, which grew increasingly heated.

In a public statement, Baldwin declared that a turnover of the state's representatives in Washington would be beneficial, "since some of the incumbents have been in Washington so long that their usefulness has suffered from the association with the Yankees."[40] He charged that Vinson had been "supine" on the question of segregation. Now he was giving "lip service" to the question, the challenger acknowledged, but for two years after the Supreme Court's antisegregation decision the congressman "never opened his mouth about it." He had "pussyfooted" in fighting the South's battles in Congress and had been "an administration man" who had followed "the New Deal of Roosevelt, the Fair Deal of Truman and the free wheeling of Eisenhower." Baldwin

---

[38] Bill Tribble, "Vinson Strikes At Court Action," newspaper clipping in Vinson Scrapbooks, book 1956.

[39] *Congressional Record*, 84th Cong., 2d sess., 10427; "Vinson Joins Assault On Supreme Court," *Christian Century* 73 (27 June 1956): 765; Vinson form letter to constituents, 28 June 1956, Erwin Sibley Papers, 12–30 June 1956 folder.

[40] "Baldwin-Vinson Battle Develops," newspaper clipping in Vinson Scrapbooks, book 1954–1956.

insisted that if elected he would "stand up for states' rights and segregation" and uphold the South's position in Congress.[41]

Baldwin even challenged Vinson's "chief claim to fame," his role in bringing military installations to Georgia, charging that the congressman had neglected his own district in the placing of these military bases. Of the 20,000 jobs connected with military installations in Middle Georgia, Baldwin claimed that 52 percent of them were in the Third District, 44 percent were in Bibb County, and only 4 percent were in the other counties of the district.[42] Baldwin's charges seemed to make headway, and the press described the contest as a "battle of political veterans," a "battle between giants," and a battle of "political pros."[43]

Both men campaigned vigorously, and Vinson called in all his political IOUs to combat his determined challenger. In February 1956 he announced that the Milledgeville-Baldwin County Airport would receive a grant of $59,200 for construction of a runway and necessary lighting from the Civil Aeronautics Administration.[44] In a festive ceremony on 4 July the armory he had secured for Baldwin County was named the "Carl Vinson National Guard Armory."[45] Late in July he announced that a new army reserve armory would be built in Milledgeville during the current year at a cost of $97,000. He also said the army had agreed to take "immediate action" to build an armory in Cochran and additional armory facilities in Macon as soon as recruiting boosted manpower to required

---

[41] *Atlanta Journal*, 29 August 1956, 14.

[42] Ibid. The President of the United States once told Senator Herman Talmadge that "Carl Vinson and Dick Russell had so many military reservations in Georgia that if we got another one we'd have to double deck it." Andrew Sparks, "Carl Vinson Comes Home," *Atlanta Journal and Constitution Magazine*, 3 January 1965, 21.

[43] *Atlanta Journal*, 29 August 1956, 14; *Washington Evening Star*, 14 June 1956 and *Eatonton Messenger*, 12 May 1956, in Vinson Scrapbooks, book 1954–1956.

[44] *Union-Recorder*, 16 February 1956, 1.

[45] Ibid., 5 July 1956, 1.

strengths.[46] At the same time, he announced that Milledgeville would get a new post office building at a cost of $502,000.[47]

Despite the newspaper accounts of a close race, Vinson trounced Baldwin in the Democratic primary. He carried every county in the district and won the popular vote 44,183 to 11,679. Baldwin polled fewer popular votes than Vinson's last opponent, Harvey Roughton, had garnered ten years before.[48]

Although Vinson told the Democratic convention that formally nominated him that he would reintroduce his bill to wipe out the Supreme Court decision on school segregation, he never did.[49] With Baldwin disposed of so handily, he quickly lost interest in restricting the power of the Supreme Court. Despite the publicity that his proposed constitutional amendment and bill to limit the Court's power had received in Georgia, the integration issue was not his main concern in 1956. A glance at the index of the *Congressional Record* for the Eighty-fourth Congress, second session shows all of the bills, amendments, reports, and remarks Vinson made during the session. Of the 117 items listed, only 7 concern his proposed amendment and bill and 1 refers to remarks he made on the civil rights bill. As usual, the overwhelming majority of the references are to the armed services.[50] The index for the Eighty-fifth Congress, first session has one reference to his speech opposing the civil rights bill and no references to his proposed amendment and bill limiting the Supreme Court's authority.[51] Thus, his emphasis on upholding segregation and attacking the Supreme Court was largely a political maneuver designed to defuse the attacks of an extremist opponent. Once the political threat was removed, he dropped the issue and concentrated on his primary concerns—his constituents and

---

[46] *Atlanta Journal*, 20 July 1956, 24.

[47] *Union-Recorder*, 26 July 1956, 1.

[48] Georgia, Department of Archives and History, *Georgia Official and Statistical Register, 1955–1956*, 773.

[49] "Vinson Acceptance Slaps At Court," 20 September 1956, Carl Vinson file, Atlanta Journal-Constitution Office.

[50] *Congressional Record Index*, 84th Cong., 2d sess., 3 January–27 July 1956, 619–20.

[51] Ibid., 85th Cong., 1st sess., 3 January–30 August 1957, 805.

the armed forces. In February 1957, when the Georgia legislature again passed a resolution calling for the impeachment of several justices of the Supreme Court, Vinson responded emphatically: "I am not introducing a resolution of impeachment nor am I voting for a resolution of impeachment."[52]

With the longest tenure of anyone in the House of Representatives, except Sam Rayburn, Vinson received countless honors and awards during his final years of service. On 21 May 1957, at a special luncheon at the Pentagon hosted by Secretary of Defense Wilson and attended by members of the Joint Chiefs of Staff and the members of the Armed Services Committee of the House, the National Aeronautics Association presented Vinson the Elder Statesman of Aviation award. After the keynote address, Secretary Wilson presented Vinson an engraved scroll, which cited Vinson's "significant and enduring contributions over the years to the progress of aeronautics, and his demonstrated qualities of patriotism, integrity, and moral courage worthy of emulation." In thanking the group, Vinson stressed the "inventive genius of man," which in a short period of time had brought us into an age of rockets and missiles of such speeds as to "defy imagination." But, the seventy-three-year-old chairman added, "Who knows what vistas will yet be opened through the further genius of man in this great field of aviation?"[53]

As Vinson continued to gain seniority in the House, he experienced the problem that inevitably accompanied old age, namely, the loss of friends and loved ones. During his campaign for reelection, his brother Fred died after a long illness. Unmarried, he had worked for many years as an inspector for the Newport News Shipbuilding Company in Virginia. He died at the Veterans Administration Hospital in Dublin and was buried in Milledgeville, where so many of the Vinsons were interred. Although the Vinsons generally lived long lives, Fred died at age sixty-four.[54] Less than two years after Fred's death, Carl's older sister Harriett died after a short illness at age eighty-one. She was buried

---

[52] *Atlanta Journal*, 22 February 1957, 1.
[53] *Congressional Record*, 85th Cong., 1st sess., 22 May 1957, 7472–73.
[54] *Atlanta Journal*, 27 July 1956, 1; 28 July 1956, 6.

in Cordele next to her husband, J. W. Cannon, Sr.[55] Over the years he had seen much turnover on his committee, as members retired and died, and he had delivered numerous eulogies on the floor of the House for departed colleagues. On 5 August 1957, he gave another one. It was for his distinguished colleague Walter George, who had represented Georgia in the United States Senate from 1922 until 3 January 1957.[56]

On 5 October 1957 Americans were shocked by front-page stories in the newspapers that explained that the Soviets had launched the world's first artificial earth satellite. The satellite, called Sputnik, was 22 inches in diameter, weighed 184.3 pounds, whirled about the earth at a maximum height of 560 miles and at a speed of 18,000 miles an hour, circling the globe once every hour and 35 minutes. Almost all scientists agreed that the launching of Sputnik proved that the Russians were well ahead of the United States in building and controlling rockets. Twenty-nine days later, on 3 November, the Russians put up Sputnik II, a heavier satellite, weighing 1,120 pounds and orbiting as much as 1,056 miles away. Throughout America a sense of "alarm, exasperation, humiliation, and confusion mounted," observed historian Eric Goldman, for "the supremacy of American know-how had been bluntly challenged." Frantically trying to get a satellite into orbit to match the Russians, America suffered a series of humiliating failures. A wit wisecracked: "The American satellite ought to be called Civil Servant. It won't work and you can't fire it." It was not until 31 January 1958 that America successfully placed a 30.8-pound satellite in space.[57]

In the hysteria that followed the launching of Sputnik, critics demanded many reforms, including a renewed effort to unify the Joint Chiefs of Staff. Once again, Vinson became aroused and spoke out emphatically against such a move. He calmly pointed out that the Russian success resulted from "a simple matter of concentration of

---

[55] *Atlanta Constitution*, 28 May 1958, 27; "Funeral to be Held Today For Sister of Rep. Vinson," newspaper clipping in Vinson Scrapbooks, book May 1958–1960.

[56] *Congressional Record*, 85th Cong., 1st sess., 5 August 1957, 13608.

[57] Eric Goldman, *The Crucial Decade—And After: America, 1945–1960* (New York: Vintage Books, 1960) 307–12.

efforts." Had America started its program sooner or concentrated on it at an earlier date, "we would have launched the first earth-circling satellite," he asserted. Since America did not do this, alarmists placed the responsibility for failure on the Joint Chiefs of Staff system and called for its replacement by a super-Prussian-type supreme general staff. Vinson argued that giving a supreme staff the sole responsibility of planning and no responsibility for the execution of those plans was the "way to commit national suicide." The alarmists, he continued, also complain about "interservice rivalry," but "I have not seen demonstrated one single example of interservice rivalry with a deleterious effect upon our war efforts." Perhaps as a warning to those alarmists seeking legislative reforms, he closed his remarks with this statement: "I refuse to be stampeded into precipitous and dangerous changes merely because a Soviet-built satellite is circling the earth." Vinson rarely filled up the *Congressional Record* with the insertion of his own remarks, but he made an exception in this case. His expanded remarks on this subject ran to four columns of agate type. Clearly, he felt passionately about this issue.[58]

In general, Vinson had approved of Eisenhower's military policies and had worked harmoniously with his administration for five years. But maintaining separate military services under congressional control was a bedrock principle to Vinson, and he was not about to sacrifice it to the popular president, or anyone else. The president, with a new secretary of defense, Neil H. McElroy, as his chief spokesman, was equally determined to drastically overhaul the Joint Chiefs of Staff, concentrating more power in the chairman and in the secretary of defense. It was a battle of giants. Eisenhower would have been well advised to study the recent history of his predecessors who had challenged the venerable chairman of the House Armed Services Committee to see who had the most clout in such a contest.

After Admiral Arleigh Burke attacked the concept of a single chief of staff in a talk at the National Press Club, the White House imposed strict censorship on the armed services. The censorship was so stern that a top commander had to eliminate half of a speech he was scheduled to

---

[58] *Congressional Record*, 85th Cong., 2d sess., 8 January 1958, 127–9.

deliver because it defended the present law. When he objected, the assistant secretary of defense told him, "That law isn't going to be around here very much longer."[59]

Vinson responded by calling the Pentagon's "high brass" to testify before his committee. After the committee finished with the Defense Department chiefs, it summoned leaders from the army, the navy, and the air force. The purpose of the detailed questioning, the chairman explained, was to see just where U.S. defense is today with regard to manpower, money, military hardware and overall management. "We are going to squeeze this lemon dry for once," he promised. Having chaired committees for twenty-four years and conducted countless investigations, he assured one and all that "this is going to be a sure-enough squeezing investigation to get all the facts and be constructive and beneficial."[60]

When McElroy returned from a secret planning session on defense reorganization in Puerto Rico, he announced that there would be no big upheaval in the Defense Department and no single military chief.[61] On the basis of reports of the meeting he had received, Vinson felt otherwise. To counter the administration, Vinson, with the co-sponsorship of Representative Leslie Arends, the Republican whip and ranking minority member on the Armed Services Committee, introduced a bill that would prune away 14 of the 29 under secretaries and assistant secretaries and reduce the number of civilian employees in the office of the defense secretary from 2,400 to 600. The effect of the Vinson-Arends bill would be to give the three separate services greater autonomy and leave the secretary of defense with less power than he currently possessed.[62]

In a major address delivered in the House on 16 April, Vinson thoroughly denounced the president's reorganization plan as detrimental to the nation and to "Christian civilization." "The entire philosophy of

---

[59] *Macon Telegraph*, 27 January 1958, 4.

[60] "Carl Vinson of Georgia Puts Spotlight on Defense," *U.S. News & World Report* 44 (14 February 1958): 21.

[61] *Washington Post*, March 7, 1958, A-14; "Defense Shake-Up? Maybe, But Not for Joint Chiefs," *U.S. News & World Report* 44 (7 March 1958): 12.

[62] Ibid.; "The Pentagon: Checkmate?" *Newsweek* 51 (10 March 1958): 40.

the Pentagon reorganization proposal is greater military centralization and concentration of power," he declared. Rather than achieve large-scale efficiency, as its defenders claim, the actual result would be "a supreme Prussian-type general staff." He further stated that the plan, in essence, would eliminate three civilian secretaries and would enhance the power of the secretary of defense. Such a change, he concluded, was "an open invitation to the concept of the man on horseback." As for the budgeting aspects of the plan, the chairman said, "I know of no concept more dangerous to the security of the United States than that which the President recommends in his message with respect to the appropriation of funds."[63] When Vinson finished his hour-long speech, Republicans joined Democrats in standing up and applauding the congressional expert on military affairs, and not a word was said in rebuttal to his speech.[64]

Vinson had timed his speech well, for the next day President Eisenhower delivered a scheduled address to the American Society of Newspaper Editors and the International Press Institute. His speech was also broadcast coast to coast on television and radio. The president, in a fighting mood, urged Congress to pass his controversial plan quickly. Claiming that his critics were misinformed, he assured his listeners that his plan would not create a Prussian general staff or a "czar" that would "dominate our armed forces." Such charges, he said, were "nonsense." Under his plan, he maintained, "The Congress will keep, in every respect, its full constitutional authority over the appropriation of funds. But greater flexibility in defense spending will result in greater efficiency, more responsiveness to changing military requirements, and more economical management of major defense programs."[65]

The next week, Vinson had McElroy back before his committee for four days of questioning. There, the chairman sat in his high-backed chair and presided with his customary iron hand. With his shell-rimmed glasses teetering on the very brink of his prominent nose, he peered over rather than through them, and, as one observer noted, this gave him "the

---

[63] Carl Vinson, "President's Proposal Means 'Prussian-type General Staff,'" *U.S. News & World Report* 44 (25 April 1958): 80–81, 123.

[64] *Atlanta Journal*, 18 April 1958, 15.

[65] Ibid., 17 April 1958, 1.

appearance of a kindly grandpa sorrowfully studying the misdeed of a favorite grandson as he looked down on Defense Secretary Neil H. McElroy." As usual, he was both demanding and protective of the military. He smiled when a committee member forced McElroy to admit that congressional fears over the plan were not "nonsense," as the president had described them. Another committee member drew from McElroy the statement that he was willing to drop a minor part of the proposal. When the congressman continued to press the point, the chairman banged the gavel. "Didn't you hear the distinguished Sekkerterry?" he demanded. The scolded committeeman, once warned, turned beet red and changed the subject.[66]

The unsympathetic committee gave McElroy such a thorough drubbing that some observers concluded that the administration had made a quiet, well-ordered retreat from the president's position. Such reports incensed Eisenhower, who issued a statement declaring that there would be no compromises or retreat from the essentials of his plan.[67] Thus the antagonists had staked out their turf like two lions in the jungle preparing to battle for dominance of the pride. Despite the rhetoric, thoughtful observers predicted that eventually a compromise would be reached. That is exactly what happened. The House version of the bill, however, bore more of Vinson's influence than the president was willing to accept. At his insistence, the Republicans tried to add three amendments to the bill, but the Democratic majority in the House, led by Vinson, defeated them 211 to 192. The final bill, crafted largely by Vinson, passed the House 402 to 1.[68] The votes in the House showed that when it came to legislating military matters, a popular president, even a five-star general with an impeccable military record, was no match for the canny Georgia congressman.

---

[66] *Atlanta Constitution*, 25 April 1958, 2; Russell Baker, "Again Vinson Mounts the Ramparts," *New York Times Magazine*, 4 May 1958, 78; House, Committee on Armed Services, *Reorganization of the Department of Defense*, 85th Cong., 2d sess., 22 April–21 May 1958, Hearings No. 83, 5971–6174.

[67] *Atlanta Journal*, 27 April 1958, 1.

[68] *Atlanta Constitution*, 13 June 1958, 1, 8; "The Gentlemen From Georgia Vs. The President," *U.S. News & World Report* 44 (27 June 1958): 19; *Congressional Record*, 85th Cong., 2d sess., 12 June 1958, 11051.

Under White House pressure, the Senate version of the bill had restored some of the authority Eisenhower desired, and conferees from the two Armed Services Committees met to decide between the House and Senate versions. As described by reporter Louis Stockstill, the closed-door meeting was "vintage Vinson." With members of his committee in tow, Vinson arrived at the conference room a few minutes early. When the senators arrived, led by their chairman, Georgia Senator Richard B. Russell, Vinson did not wait for them to find seats. "Well now, weah all heah," he announced in his Middle Georgia drawl. "Now Senatuh Russell will be the Chai'man of this confe'ence. You sit heah, Senatuh." He motioned Russell to a seat and kept talking. "Now heah's what weah gonna do," Uncle Carl told the group, quickly outlining how the main Senate proposals were to be eliminated. "Aren't you even going to let us discuss it, Carl?" chuckled Senator Leverett Saltonstall of Massachusetts. "Well now, weah all busy men. We haven't got time fo' a lot of talk," Vinson replied. Discussion lasted for about fifteen minutes. Vinson then pulled out an already prepared statement explaining what the conference group had done. He turned to his chief committee counsel, Robert W. Smart, and said, "Bob, put Chai'man Russell's name on the statement with mine, and everywheah it says "I," take out "I" and put in "We." Senator Russell changed one word in the statement. The following day, both houses agreed to the conference report.[69]

The chagrined president learned—as his predecessors had learned—that more could be accomplished by working with the Old Operator than by working against him. Despite his setbacks, Eisenhower seemed satisfied with the result or at least convinced that he had gotten everything he could from Congress. By the time the reorganization issue had been resolved, he was again writing the chairman personal notes, addressed to "Dear Uncle Carl" and signed "D. E."[70]

---

[69] Louis R. Stockstill, "'Uncle Carl' Vinson: Backstage Boss of the Pentagon," *Army Navy Air Force Journal* 98 (18 February 1961): 1; *Congressional Record*, 85th Cong., 2d sess., 24 July 1958, 14900, 14963.

[70] Dwight Eisenhower to Carl Vinson, 28 July 1958, Vinson Scrapbooks, book August 1952–December 1954.

For the remainder of Eisenhower's term, Vinson conducted the routine armed services matters, dealt with constituent needs, and continued to challenge issues and practices he thought detrimental to the country. In March 1959 he became aroused when the Tennessee Valley Authority sought to expand its operation. Vinson, with the strong backing of the Georgia Power Company, questioned why the government-owned agency should expand into 25,000 square miles being served well by private utilities. He testified before the House Ways and Means Committee and secured passage of an amendment limiting T.V.A. to the area it served on 1 July 1957.[71] In April 1959 he demanded that Congress extend the Renegotiation Act permanently to protect taxpayers from profit-hungry defense contractors. In sharply worded testimony before the House Ways and Means Committee, he stated, "Without the Renegotiation Act, the sky would be the limit as far as profits are concerned." He was especially concerned by the action of seven large aircraft and missile firms seeking greater profits. "I have a very plain philosophy," Vinson said. "I do not believe in excessive profit because it is called an incentive profit."[72] In May he expressed concern about cost overruns in the construction of the Air Force Academy in Colorado Springs, Colorado.[73] In August he asked the navy for "full information" on the cancellation of its multimillion-dollar seaplane program. He wanted to know why, after several years of developmental work and the expenditure of $400,000,000 for the P6M SeaMaster, the navy had quietly canceled the project.[74] Early in 1960 Vinson, distressed over air force manuals linking some clergymen and churches with

---

[71] Statement of Carl Vinson of Georgia Before House Ways & Means Committee, 11 March 1959, Charles Bloch Papers, box 19, folder 91, Middle Georgia Regional Library, Macon, GA; Analysis of H. R. 3460, John Sibley Papers, Special Collections, Box 362, Robert W. Woodruff Library, Emory University, Atlanta, GA; *Atlanta Constitution*, 12 March 1959, 6; *Atlanta Journal*, 3 August 1959, 28.

[72] *Washington Daily News*, 28 April 1959, Vinson Scrapbooks, book May 1958–1960.

[73] *Congressional Record*, 86th Cong., 1st sess., 6 May 1959, 7532–33.

[74] *Atlanta Journal*, 30 August 1959, A6.

communism, ordered a full-scale investigation.[75] In April 1960 he called upon the Department of Defense in Washington to investigate charges of fraud in the sale of milk to army camps.[76] At the same time, his committee, responding to charges of lobbying and influence peddling in the military, approved a bill that would make it illegal for an officer to take a job selling to the armed forces within two years after the date he shed his uniform.[77]

During this same period, Vinson received several prestigious awards. On 6 March 1959, the Georgia Department of the American Legion bestowed Distinguished Service Awards on Vinson and Senator Richard Russell at a quail-and-grits supper at the Lafayette Hotel in Washington, DC.[78] On 11 September 1959, the American Political Science Association named Vinson, along with Senators Hubert Humphrey of Minnesota, John Williams of Delaware, and Kenneth Keating of New York, as the first recipients of their Congressional Distinguished Service Award. The two Democrats and two Republicans were honored at a luncheon ceremony at the Mayflower Hotel in Washington.[79] When Vinson received the Distinguished Citizen Award from the Veterans of Foreign Wars, he joined a select company. Previous recipients included statesmen he esteemed highly: Lyndon Johnson, Walter George, and Sam Rayburn. In accepting the award at the V.F.W.'s annual congressional dinner at the Sheraton-Park Hotel in Washington, DC on 6 February 1960, Vinson delivered a moving speech that reiterated many of the themes he had emphasized for years. Warning against succumbing to "the fatal disease of complacency," he pointed out that "a friendly smile does not necessarily imply the beginning of an everlasting friendship." Indeed, the hard facts of international life, he said, indicate that we must now be "eternally vigilant." America has troubles today, he asserted, because "for the last decade we have

---

[75] *Atlanta Constitution*, 19 February 1960, 6.

[76] *Atlanta Journal*, 9 April 1960, 2.

[77] Ibid., 6 April 1960, 8.

[78] Ibid., 6 March 1959, 5.

[79] Ibid., 11 September 1959, 44; *Congressional Record*, 86th Cong., 1st sess., 11 September 1959, 19085–86, 19180–81.

measured our military requirements in dollars and not in missiles, rockets, submarines, armor, planes, and men. We have worried about dollars when we should have worried about a more adequate defense." Vinson argued that genuine peace had not been achieved because "the Soviet Union's objective of world domination has not changed." Yet, in spite of the obvious threats, America's naval power had declined, the army had been reduced in size, the president had refused to spend the money Congress appropriated to increase the size of the Marine Corps, and the country faced a "missile gap," he lamented. Convinced that the American people, when given the "real, hard, clear facts," would willingly bear the burden of increased defense costs to "insure our survival and way of life," he called for a stabilized military manpower policy and a stabilized military establishment.[80]

One month later, in the same Sheraton-Park banquet room, the District of Columbia Council of the Navy League presented Vinson a scroll from the service secretaries, signed by the secretaries of defense, army, navy, and air force. He responded with a brief address. In a letter to Erwin Sibley he explained that he thoroughly enjoyed the meeting, especially the music of the Marine Band, and described it as "the nicest kind of an affair." Vinson confided to his friend, who had attended the V.F.W. dinner but was unable to attend this one, that this would be his last "social" affair for the year. About two or three a year, he wrote, was his limit. "When night comes," he added, "I like to go to bed undisturbed from social activities. That is the reason I like to live in the country, for then you are out of touch and not worried about being invited any where."[81] On 4 May 1960, the Navy League of the United States bestowed upon Vinson its highest award, the Robert M. Thompson

---

[80] Address of Carl Vinson Before Veterans of Foreign Wars," Vinson Scrapbooks, book May 1958–1960; *Congressional Record*, 86th Cong., 2d sess., 10 February 1960, 2377–78.

[81] Carl Vinson to Erwin Sibley, 24 February 1960 and 7 March 1960, Erwin Sibley Papers, February–March 1960 folder; *Congressional Record*, 86th Cong., 2d sess., 7 March 1960, 4827–28.

Award for inspirational civilian leadership. Since the ceremony was held in Anaheim, California, it was awarded to him in absentia.[82]

Till Snead drove Vinson to Georgia on 24 June 1960, so that he could give a speech to the Veterans' Legion Post in Macon and participate in the cornerstone laying exercises of the Milledgeville Post Office building. Vinson hoped that Congress would adjourn by 4 July so that it would not be necessary for him to return to Washington.[83] Unfortunately, the second session of the Eighty-sixth Congress was an unusually long one, and Congress did not adjourn until 1 September. As always, Vinson was eager to get back to his farm. In addition, the presidential campaign was underway, and Vinson always actively supported the Democratic slate. But this election was special. A new personality had emerged within the Democratic ranks, a candidate who had created quite a stir nationally and had favorably impressed the old chairman. Vinson wanted to do all he could to help the young senator from Massachusetts, John F. Kennedy, become the next president.

---

[82] *Congressional Record Appendix*, 86th Cong., 2d sess., 5 May 1960, A3853.

[83] Carl Vinson to Erwin Sibley, 17 June 1960, Erwin Sibley Papers, June–August 1960 folder.

13

The Kennedy Years

I am confident that not only will representative
government survive, and continue to enhance the
inalienable rights of man, but eventually our democratic
way of life shall prevail throughout the world.

Carl Vinson, 1962

When John Kennedy first arrived in the House of Representatives in
1947, the Georgia patriarch, at the request of his nephew Ed Vinson,
took the young congressman from Massachusetts under his wing.
Kennedy got an office near Vinson's in the Old House Office Building,
and the two Democrats got to know and respect each other.[1] After six
years in the House, Kennedy advanced to the Senate by defeating Henry
Cabot Lodge in 1952. Although Kennedy's record in the House was
undistinguished, Vinson followed his career with interest, for he
discerned qualities of leadership in the slender young Bostonian. In 1960
Vinson, like most Southerners, backed his friend Lyndon Johnson for the
presidency, but he was not terribly disappointed when the Texan lost the
nomination to Kennedy on the first ballot. Indeed, after Kennedy picked
Johnson for the vice presidential nomination, Vinson became an

---

[1] Ed and Betty Vinson, interview with the author, Atlanta, GA, 7 August
2001; Neil MacNeil, *Forge of Democracy: The House of Representatives* (New
York: David McKay Company, Inc., 1963) 259–60.

enthusiastic supporter of the Democratic ticket. At the Democratic convention in Macon, he heartily endorsed the nominees:

> I am thoroughly convinced from personal association with them that in these two men we have the experience, the maturity, the determination, the wisdom, the knowledge, the vitality and the imagination so vital to the decision-making process that will not only assure our survival as a free nation, but will assure our leadership and progress in the ever-continuing quest for a better life.
>
> In these great Democrats, we have a combined and blended ability that will permit our nation to regain her position as the leader of the free world....
>
> By next November, a large majority of the American people will all recognize in Jack Kennedy those qualities of leadership, ability and determination that augur well for the nation over the next four years.
>
> And back of Jack Kennedy will be the greatest Senate Majority Leader of our time, Lyndon B. Johnson.[2]

During the campaign, Vinson welcomed Senator Kennedy to Warm Springs, where the presidential candidate delivered a speech to a responsive crowd at the Little White House. Vinson also greeted Senator Johnson in Macon, where the vice presidential nominee commemorated Law Day at Mercer University. Vinson's support of the Democratic ticket was exceptional, for he was the only member of Georgia's congressional delegation who actively campaigned for the Democratic nominees.[3]

For the inauguration, Vinson had the honor of serving as Speaker pro tem for the "Day" and led the House members to the platform. He sat through the whole ceremony and thought the president made a great

---

[2] Carl Vinson to Harry Truman, October 11, 1960, Erwin Sibley Papers, September–November 1960 folder, Special Collections, Ina Dillard Russell Library, Georgia College and State University, Milledgeville, GA.

[3] Ibid.

speech. Captivated by the Kennedy mystique, he afterwards wrote Erwin Sibley that he "was very close to Kennedy's mother and about ten feet away from him."[4]

After eight years of Republican rule, Vinson was delighted to have a Democrat in the White House and large Democratic majorities in both houses. Party identifications, however, were misleading. Of the 261 Democrats in the House, 99 were from Southern states, and most of them were conservatives who often voted with the 174 Republicans. This meant that conservative-leaning members now constituted a majority of the House, and they were hostile to most of the liberal legislative program candidate Kennedy had pledged to enact. Even before the election, when liberals were in the majority, very little progressive legislation had been passed. The rump session of Congress, which met for three weeks in August during the presidential campaign, failed to pass a single piece of pending legislation related to the Democratic platform. The Rules Committee killed the school bill, House conferees killed a Senate-passed minimum wage bill bearing Kennedy's name, and the Senate rejected a healthcare bill. That session taught Kennedy a sobering lesson—he had to break the back of the Rules Committee, a committee that exercised broad discretionary power in deciding what legislation could go the House floor for a vote by the representatives.[5]

Democrats ostensibly controlled the Rules Committee, holding eight of the twelve seats, but two of the Democrats—Howard Smith of Virginia and William Colmer of Mississippi—were arch-conservatives, opposed in principle to the Kennedy welfare and economic programs. By voting with the Republican members, they could block legislation, for no major bill could be sent to the House floor for action without a clear majority vote in the Rules Committee. "Judge" Smith, as the seventy-eight-year-old chairman was called, set the committee's agenda, determined which bills would be called up for discussion, and decided

---

[4] Carl Vinson to Erwin Sibley, 23 January 1961, Erwin Sibley Papers, January 1961 folder.

[5] Richard Bolling, *Power in the House* (New York: Dutton & Co., 1968) 205–206

when the committee would meet. Consequently, he and his conservative colleagues could thwart almost any legislation they chose.[6]

After meeting with the president-elect in Palm Springs, Speaker Rayburn initiated a plan to alter the Rules Committee. There were two ways to strip Judge Smith of his arbitrary power. One approach was to purge Representative Colmer from the committee for disloyalty, since he had opposed Kennedy's election as president, and replace him with a more liberal Democrat. The other approach was to enlarge the committee. Rayburn met with Smith for two hours on 1 January 1961, and suggested that the Rules Committee be enlarged by three members. When Smith rejected that offer, Rayburn then announced that Colmer would be purged for disloyalty. Vinson and other senior party members were disturbed by this decision. Anxious to preserve the seniority system in the House, Vinson became a mediator between the two camps and tried to work out an accommodation. When Smith refused to compromise at all, Vinson realized the conservatives had lost control of the Rules Committee. Acting to change the terms of surrender, he called a caucus of Southern conservatives on 10 January. He told the assembly that the fight to keep the Rules Committee in the hands of conservatives had been lost, as they could not defeat Rayburn's plan to purge Colmer. He urged the members to settle the quarrel by going back to Rayburn's original terms of enlarging the Rules Committee's membership. That alone, he argued, would save Colmer and a breach in the seniority system. For the next three weeks, both sides waged a furious battle, using all the political clout they could muster. Vinson worked indefatigably to keep wavering members in the Rayburn camp. Finally, eleven days after Kennedy's inauguration, the Rules Committee was enlarged by a vote of 217 to 212. Vinson had brought enough Southern Democrats to Rayburn's side to produce this narrow victory. The vote did not mean that the Kennedy domestic program would be adopted, but it did mean that it would be debated on the floor of the House.[7]

------

[6] MacNeil, *Forge of Democracy*, 412–13.

[7] Ibid., 412–37; D. B. Hardeman and Donald C. Bacon, *Rayburn, A Biography* (Austin: Texas Monthly Press, 1987) 452–65; Carl Vinson to Erwin Sibley, 2 February 1961, Erwin Sibley Papers, February 1961 folder.

Regarded as the second in command of the conservative Southern representatives behind Judge Smith, Vinson surprised observers by strongly endorsing the reform. He did it out of loyalty to the Democratic Party and admiration for President Kennedy. "It was a fight we just *had to win*," he explained to Erwin Sibley two days after the vote. When later asked about his stand on the Rules Committee fight, he commented: "Now, the way I looked at that proposal, we weren't voting to pack the Rules Committee. It was already packed, and I was in favor of unpacking it."[8] To a constituent who had criticized his role in the Rules Committee fight, Vinson replied, "We need have no fear that Kennedy will sponsor leftwing legislation," for "he is essentially a conservative, thoughtful, but at the same time progressive leader."[9] The chairman expected a busy but productive session because "we have a great man in the White House!! He is going to do something and I feel he will make the greatest record since the days of Woodrow Wilson."[10]

Courting Vinson had been a high priority of the Kennedy administration, for as one representative told Larry O'Brien, the president's congressional liaison chief, "Vinson is the absolute key to the whole session of Congress." The effort paid substantial dividends, as Vinson became an enthusiastic supporter of the Kennedy program. Indeed he voted for every one of Kennedy's major bills, and his support helped swing other Southern representatives behind the president's legislative program.[11] The president wisely, in view of his tenuous political position, did not ask for civil rights legislation during the first two years of his term. At an age when most people become more conservative, Vinson became more liberal, and his votes stood out in stark contrast to the votes of his Georgia colleagues. In October 1961 the liberal Americans for Democratic Action gave Vinson a rating of 87 out of a possible 100. The next highest rating among Georgia congressmen

---

[8] Rowland Evans, Jr., "The Sixth Sense of Carl Vinson," *Reporter* 26 (12 April 1962): 30.

[9] *Atlanta Constitution*, 10 February 1961, 1.

[10] Carl Vinson to Erwin Sibley, 2 February 1961, Erwin Sibley Papers, February 1961 folder.

[11] MacNeil, *Forge of Democracy*, 256–66.

was Phil Landrum's 40. Both Senator Russell and Senator Talmadge earned a 10 on the A.D.A. rating.[12] A *Redbook* magazine poll conducted early in 1962 among members of the House placed Vinson as the third most influential member, behind Howard Smith, chairman of the Rules Committee, and Wilbur Mills, chairman of the Ways and Means Committee—all Southerners.[13]

Congress rejected many of Kennedy's proposals, including bills for mass transit, education assistance, job training, and a proposed Department of Housing and Urban Development. But the Kennedy administration did secure passage of the Peace Corps, the Trade Expansion Act, a 4.9-billion-dollar comprehensive housing bill, an increase in the minimum wage, and several antirecession bills.[14] Vinson's support of these measures was crucial, and without it the Kennedy legislative record would have been meager indeed.

As always, Vinson's primary interest was defense, and the new secretary of defense, Robert McNamara, a forty-four-year-old former president of Ford Motor Company, was solicitous of Vinson. In December 1960, before he was sworn in, the secretary met with both Senator Russell and Vinson. At issue was a new Department of Defense reorganization plan prepared by Senator Stuart Symington of Missouri, a former secretary of the air force. For many years Vinson had consistently opposed efforts to abolish the Departments of the Army, Navy, and Air Force and establish a single chief of staff, and he emphatically opposed the Symington plan. He told McNamara it would create a "colossus of chaos" and might seriously disrupt the whole defense set up. McNamara listened patiently to Vinson's arguments and after the meeting told reporters, "I will undertake no major reorganization of the Defense Department in the near future." McNamara made a favorable first impression on the venerable chairman, who was serving in Congress before the new secretary had been born. Vinson said the nation was "fortunate" to have the "young, brilliant" McNamara in the Pentagon and

---

[12] *Atlanta Journal*, 5 October 1961, 7.
[13] Ibid., 18 January 1962, 14. The poll named Georgia's Richard Russell as the most influential senator.
[14] Bolling, *Power in the House*, 211–13.

predicted that "he'll make the best Defense Secretary the country has had."[15]

McNamara did not reorganize the Pentagon, but he imposed his personal style of leadership upon it. "I believe that a leader should lead," he remarked shortly after his appointment as secretary of defense. A few weeks later, Vinson observed his new type of leadership firsthand when McNamara testified before the Armed Services Committee:

Vinson: "Mr. Secretary, you use the President's famous statement in his inaugural address: 'Only when our arms are sufficient beyond doubt can we be certain beyond doubt that they will never be employed.' How much is enough, when it boils down? Now will you be in a position to advise the President that we have a sufficiency beyond a doubt?"

McNamara: "Yes, sir. That is the objective of our studies. As I stated earlier, we expect to complete them at the time scheduled—that is, the end of the month."

Vinson: "You will be in a position to tell the committee, then, from your study, what we need in the field of missiles, aircraft, and vessels?"

McNamara: "Yes, sir."

Vinson (incredulously): "You will be able to tell us what we need?"

McNamara (quietly confident): "Yes, sir."

Representative Leon Gavin of Pennsylvania (breaking in, also incredulously): "And hardware?"

McNamara: "Yes, sir."

McNamara's thrice repeated "Yes, sir" was startling to Vinson because no previous secretary of defense had ever been able to answer his question—"How much is enough, when it boils down?"—with any real conviction or assurance.[16]

---

[15] *Atlanta Constitution*, 21 December 1960, 1, 7; *Atlanta Journal*, 29 December 1960, 14.

[16] Stewart Alsop, *The Center: People and Power in Political Washington* (New York: Harper & Row Publishers, 1968) 133–34.

When Atlanta civic leaders, led by attorney Robert B. Troutman, Jr., honored Vinson and Russell with an Armistice Day dinner at the Dinkler Plaza Hotel in Atlanta, it was fitting that McNamara was the featured speaker. Governor Ernest Vandiver introduced McNamara, and Senator Herman Talmadge served as master of ceremonies for the festive dinner attended by 1,300 guests from throughout the state. In paying tribute to the guests of honor, Secretary McNamara described himself as "the newest pupil in the Russell-Vinson school for secretaries of defense."[17] In his brief remarks, Vinson described McNamara as "a man of genius" who had brought incisive leadership to our defense forces.[18] The only negative aspect of the gala occasion was the presence of N.A.A.C.P. picketers, protesting the appearance of a cabinet member at a segregated hotel, and picketers from three segregationist organizations carrying signs demanding the impeachment of President Kennedy.[19]

Vinson's great admiration for McNamara and Kennedy did not prevent him from speaking out emphatically against administration policies he deemed unwise. On 7 March 1962 he issued a press release declaring, "I simply don't like the idea of Congress being thought of as a kindly old uncle who complains but who finally, as everyone expects, gives in and raises his hand in blessing, and then rocks in his chair for another year, glancing down the avenue once in a while wondering whether he's done the right thing." What had aroused the chairman's ire was the administration's failure to spend money appropriated by Congress, specifically $525,000,000 for manned bombers and $400,000,000 for development of the B-70. For years he had been concerned that the executive branch was usurping powers granted by the Constitution to Congress, and he was convinced that Congress should be "an active participant in the direction of policy" and "a partner in the achievement of the ends sought by our Government." He also believed,

---

[17] *Atlanta Journal and Constitution*, 12 November 1961, 1, 20.

[18] Vinson speech, Vinson Scrapbooks, book May 1958–1960, on loan from Tillman Snead to Georgia College and State University, Milledgeville, GA.

[19] *Atlanta Journal and Constitution*, 12 November 1961, 20; *Atlanta Constitution*, 13 November 1961, 4.

in contrast to the administration, that the country should continue to build manned bombers. The House Armed Services Committee agreed with the chairman, and it unanimously adopted a $13 billion military procurement authorization bill which added $491,000,000 for the RS-70 bomber (formerly the B-70). Instead of recommending the additional amounts, as it had in the past, the committee stipulated that the secretary of the air force would be "directed to utilize" the money to permit a production start on the plane as a full weapons system.[20]

Five days earlier, in a speech to the Reserve Officers Association, Vinson had warned against the trend of consolidation that McNamara had set in motion in the Pentagon. "I know of no surer threat to the security of our nation," he declared, "than to adopt the ill-considered proposal that the four services be merged into one service, or that the three military departments be fused into one conglomerate department, or that all military thinking be directed toward one strategic concept." Such a step, he concluded, would create "a hodgepodge of confusion that would make us easy prey for any aggressor."[21]

Neither McNamara nor Kennedy wanted the supersonic RS 70, which they believed would be obsolete by the time it was in production, but they were reluctant to antagonize Vinson. With the chairman so aroused, McNamara quietly set about mending his fences on Capitol Hill. He met privately with Vinson to talk over their impasse.[22] A few days later, as opposition to Vinson mounted in the House, President Kennedy met with Vinson. As they strolled through the White House rose garden, the president said, "Uncle Carl, this kind of language and my ignoring it will only hurt us and the country. Let me write you a letter that will get us both off this limb." Without a word, Vinson reached into his briefcase and pulled out a draft of a letter. The president laughed. "That's why you

---

[20] Press Release, 7 March 1962, Vinson Scrapbooks, book February–March 1962; *New York Times*, 8 March 1962, 1, 10.

[21] *Congressional Record*, 87th Cong., 2d sess., 5 March 1962, 3391–93. For a series of letters Vinson and McNamara had exchanged on the subject of reorganization, see "Vinson-McNamara Exchange Letters On Changes," *Army Navy Air Force Journal* 98 (10 June 1961): 1, 24, 27.

[22] "Uncle Carl Gets Mad," *Time* 79 (16 March 1962): 16–17; *Atlanta Constitution*, 10 March 1962, 4.

got the name 'Swamp Fox,'" he said. McNamara and presidential special counsel Ted Sorensen polished the Vinson draft and sent the finished product to Vinson's office that evening. Uncle Carl liked it. The next morning he read the letters from Kennedy and McNamara promising a thorough study of the RS 70 to the Armed Services Committee. He then moved to strike the language "directing" the secretary of the air force to spend $491,000,000 in the fiscal year 1963 for the RS-70. The committee accepted the change, and a few hours later the House followed suit and approved the defense bill 403 to 0. Claiming victory in the dispute, Vinson said, "We had to raise a good hot rumpus, and we got our point across." Most observers, however, recognized that for one of the few times in his lengthy career Uncle Carl was striking his colors—although with honor. For the good of the country, he had acceded to the power of a commander in chief he did not wish to further embarrass.[23]

Despite this setback, Vinson continued to agitate for construction of manned bombers and to criticize McNamara's efforts to centralize Pentagon authority as a means of eliminating waste. Yet, he steadfastly defended McNamara and continued to assert that he was the best defense secretary the nation had ever had. As for the criticism McNamara received, Vinson explained that "Anyone who makes decisions is bound to have people disagree with him."[24]

Vinson and Sam Rayburn, the two longest-serving members of the House, occasionally discussed the possibility of retirement. The last time Vinson mentioned the subject to the Speaker, Rayburn replied, "Now, Carl, you're not going to do any such thing. We're both going to stay

---

[23] *Congressional Record*, 87th Cong., 2d sess., 21 March 1962, 4692–97; Mary McGrory, "The Verdict Went to McNamara But the Praise Went to Vinson," n. d. Atlanta Journal-Constitution Office; *New York Times*, 26 March 1962, L12; Katherine Johnsen, "Restudy of RS-70 Is Ordered; Vinson-McNamara Clash Averted," *Aviation Week and Space Technology* 76 (26 March 1962): 17–18; "The Admiral Strikes His Colors," *Time* 79 (30 March 1962): 15–16; "'Swamp Fox' Letter," *Newsweek* 59 (2 April 1962): 23–24; Theodore C. Sorensen, *Kennedy* (New York: Harper & Row, Publishers, 1965) 347–48.

[24] *Atlanta Journal*, 24 March 1962, 1; *Atlanta Constitution*, 16 August 1962, 45; *Atlanta Journal*, 25 February 1963, 1, 6; *Atlanta Journal*, 14 March 1963, 13; *Atlanta Constitution*, 22 March 1963, 4.

right here until we die."[25] Mr. Sam was half right. Suffering from cancer, he went home to Bonham, Texas, in July 1961. He died there on 16 November, coincidentally the same date on which Vinson's beloved wife had died eleven years earlier. An enormous gathering of the nation's leaders, including the president, the vice president and 128 members of Congress, attended the funeral at Bonham's First Baptist Church.[26] Overcoming his aversion to airplanes, Vinson flew from Warner Robins to Texas to pay respects to his oldest friend in the House. They had served together for forty-seven years. Describing Rayburn as "the most outstanding statesman of this age and generation," a visibly shaken Vinson added: "No one in the House can fill his shoes."[27]

The death of Rayburn made Vinson the senior member of the House, having served eight years longer than his closest competitors, Clarence Cannon, Emanuel Celler, and John Taber. Early in 1962 he announced that he was going to ask his constituents "to send me back for one more term at least, so I can round out 50 consecutive years in Congress." His announcement meant that those politicians in the Sixth District, anxiously waiting in the wings for him to retire so they could run for his seat, would have to wait at least two more years. As was his custom, Vinson left his farm and returned to Washington before Christmas to get ready for the second session of Congress. "We have a great deal to do," he said, "so I come back to get things moving."[28]

As Vinson had noted, no one could fill the shoes of Sam Rayburn, the short, bald Texan who had been Speaker longer than anyone in history, but when Congress assembled, the Democrats chose lanky, white-haired John McCormack of Massachusetts as his successor. Vinson, who swore in McCormack, was pleased with the choice of the

---

[25] Louis R. Stockstill, "'Uncle Carl' Vinson: Backstage Boss of the Pentagon," *Army Navy Air Force Journal* 98 (18 February 1961): 28.

[26] Hardeman and Bacon, *Rayburn*, 472–74.

[27] *Atlanta Journal*, 16 November 1961, 1; 20 November 1961, Vinson Scrapbooks, book April 1961–January 1962.

[28] Cecil Holland, "Senior Member of the House," *Washington Star*, 7 January 1962, Charles J. Bloch Papers, Box 25, folder 112, Middle Georgia Regional Library, Macon, GA.

experienced majority leader and worked well with him.[29] A week later, he delivered a short but heartfelt tribute to the late Speaker.[30] He also announced that he would move to have the third House office building, scheduled to be completed in 1964 at a cost of $80,000,000, named for Rayburn.[31] On 15 January he sent Erwin Sibley a photograph taken when he administered the oath to McCormack and told him "I hold my first Committee hearing tomorrow and from now until late summer it will be a constant grind."[32]

Staying busy was nothing new, for Vinson had always been so, but during the Kennedy years he was extremely active on Capitol Hill and at home too. Even when approaching his eighth decade, he remained so vigorous and energetic that he seemed to exhaust those around him. Sometimes he became engulfed in his own maelstrom. On one occasion in March 1961, after meeting individually with Secretary of Defense McNamara, Secretary of Labor Arthur Goldberg, Attorney General Robert Kennedy, former Secretary of the Army Robert Stevens, a sub-cabinet officer and several lesser luminaries, he opened a textile discussion with a hundred House colleagues, herded a major bill to passage on the floor of the House, and dispatched his routine chores. Near the end of the day, he walked to the Senate to confer with the vice president on a critical foreign policy problem. As he returned from the Senate, he encountered a friend who, upon learning all that he had done that day, asked him what he had eaten for lunch. The chairman, looking nonplussed, replied, "Why, I forgot to eat."[33]

On 26 July 1960, Till and Molly Snead had a second son. They named him Carl William Snead, and his namesake could not have been prouder. As Till and Molly were Vinson's surrogate children, young Tillman and Carl became his "grandchildren." He doted on them in

---

[29] *Congressional Record*, 87th Cong., 2d sess., 10 January 1962, 6.

[30] Ibid., 18 January 1962, 488.

[31] *Atlanta Journal*, 11 January 1962, 4.

[32] Carl Vinson to Erwin Sibley, 15 January 1962, Erwin Sibley Papers, January 1962 folder.

[33] *Congressional Record Appendix*, 87th Cong. 2d Sess, 26 January 1962, A-574; Lou Stockstill to the author, 31 March 2003, Stockstill Papers, currently in author's possession.

typical grandfatherly fashion. The gruff chairman, whose icy stare and blunt questions terrified generals and admirals, was as gentle as a lamb at home, where politics was never mentioned and family matters took priority over everything else. How military leaders would have marveled to see the feared chairman romping about the house playing "cops and robbers" with Tillman. By the Kennedy years, Tillman had reached an age when Vinson could take him to movies and ball games and watch "shoot-'em-ups" on television together. Vinson enjoyed spending time with the youngster and made a point of attending his school functions. Sometimes this produced embarrassing situations. When Tillman was eight, Vinson made an appointment with the secretary of defense, completely forgetting about his promise to watch Tillman in a Christmas school play the same day. When he remembered at the last moment, he canceled the meeting with the cabinet member to honor his promise to Tillman. No one ever told the secretary of defense he had been outranked by a third grader. On Saturday mornings, when there was no urgent House or committee business, the chairman and Tillman sometimes spent hours in the imposing two-story Armed Services Committee chambers. Young Tillman, occupying Vinson's throne-like seat, gaveled imaginary meetings to order. Vinson, sitting attentively below in the big witness chair, where men such as Admiral King and General Eisenhower had listened to his own sage council, answered questions put to him by "Chairman Snead."[34]

President Kennedy, grateful for Vinson's assistance, invited Tillman and his "grandpa" to the White House for a social visit in July 1961. The president showed Tillman around the White House and chatted with him about school and his favorite sports. After a while, Tillman later told a friend, "The President talked to Grandpa about foreign affairs and all that jazz."[35] During the summer of 1963, when the chubby brown-haired youngster was twelve years old, Vinson got him a job in the Speaker's office. He rode to Capitol Hill with his father and "grandpa," did odd

---

[34] Stockstill, "Backstage Boss," 24; Tillman and Karen Snead, interview with the author, Dale City, VA, 8 June 2001.

[35] "Tillman Takes The 'Backstage Boss' Of The Pentagon To The White House," *Army Navy Air Force Journal* 98 (29 July 1961): 27.

jobs in Vinson's office until 9 a. m., and then worked two hours daily as a messenger for Speaker McCormack. He worked until school started in September, when he entered the eighth grade at Georgetown Prep.[36]

Vinson treated his secretaries and the staff of the Armed Services Committee as his family. Although the workload was onerous, often requiring extra hours on Saturdays, the staff loved him and stayed with him for many years. One of his first secretaries, Edna Lytle, worked for him for thirty years and retired. Her successor, Marguerite Phillips, had nearly equaled that mark when she retired. James "Jimmy" Deakins, served for many years as a clerk for the House Armed Services Committee. A "jack of all trades," he was a "walking biographer" of congressmen, senators, and presidents (past and present) who gave countless "guided tours" of Capitol Hill at the request of Congressman Vinson. Several attorneys, such as Russ Blandford, Bryce Harlow, Bob Smart, and Frank Slatinshek, had long tenures on the Armed Services Committee. Oneta Stockstill, who began working as a secretary in 1954 and ultimately became the first woman named to the professional staff of the committee, recalled that even though he was a stickler for detail and the workload was overwhelming, "the staff just adored him." He respected the staff and "treated them like they were his children." He was nosy about the staff's personal life (in a nice way) and sometimes acted as a matchmaker. Having decided that two young singles on the staff were meant for each other, he told Mary Ellen Williams how to attract Charles "Duke" Ducander. "Get him over and fix him a good meal," he advised. "Now you are both Southern, so fix him some fried chicken, mashed potatoes with gravy and biscuits. After dinner you get him on the couch and get him all loved-up. When he gets real hot, send him home." He offered so much advice that Bob Smart finally told him to back off. His intuition was correct, however, as Mary Ellen and Duke did get married.[37]

Vinson was a man of extraordinary discipline, as friends and family members attest. He organized his day's activities and followed his

---

[36] *Atlanta Constitution*, 30 June 1963, 19.

[37] Lou and Neta Stockstill, interview with the author, Indiatlantic, FL, 21 June 2001.

schedule relentlessly. He arose at 5:10, left the house by 6:00, and arrived at work at 7:00. In the evening supper was served at 5:30 and he went to bed at 9:00.[38] Rarely did he deviate from this schedule. Always punctual, he was adamant about others being on time. He was disciplined in his language and emotions as well as his time. When Lou Stockstill once remarked that he had never seen him mad, Vinson replied, "You can't afford to get mad."[39] When really provoked by someone, the worst invective he used was "He's full of prunes."[40] The only recorded account of Vinson ever losing his temper came many years before when he was trying to secure a right of way through Alice Lawrence's property in Milledgeville so that a bridge could be built over the Oconee River. He thought he had completed all the arrangements when she called him up and accused him of stealing her land. Even though Alice was known to be eccentric, if not mentally unbalanced, Vinson lost his temper when she accused him of being a thief. "Alice," he thundered, "I can assure you one damn thing, today and every day. I'll never darken your door again. I'll see you in hell before I will do anything for you."[41]

Since Vinson was so busy, he developed a very effective way of ending a discussion or an interview. He simply stood up, shook hands, and thanked the person for coming. When he did this, it was clear that the meeting was over. The staff had seen Vinson do this many times, and chief counsel Bob Smart decided to have some fun with this trait. Major General Fred Weyand had been serving in Berlin when the army notified him that he was going to be named chief of legislative liaison. When he returned to Washington, he went to see the vice chief of staff and told him that he did not have any experience with legislative liaison and wondered if he would be given a refresher course before he took on the new responsibilities. The vice chief said, "Fred, you don't need to worry about that. It is going to be like on-the-job training, and you will get your training as you go along." General Weyand then went to see Bob Smart

---

[38] Tillman and Karen Snead, interview with the author.

[39] Lou and Neta Stockstill, interview with the author.

[40] Ed and Betty Vinson, interview with the author.

[41] Eugene Ellis, interview with Emmett Hall and the author, Milledgeville, GA, 7 December 2001.

and told him exactly what he had told the vice chief; namely, that he did not have much experience in these affairs and did not know much about them. But he did know that the one thing he had to do immediately was to make a courtesy call on Chairman Vinson. He asked Bob to give him some hints as to what he should do during this courtesy call. "Fred," Bob assured him, "just go in and introduce yourself and tell him a little bit about your background. He's not going to want to know a lot. When you are finished, the chairman might ask you something or he might not, but when he stands up, holds out his hand and says, 'Thank you for coming in, General,' you will know your time is up." With this sage advice under his belt, Fred went in to see the chairman. As soon as he entered, Vinson stood up. Fred held out his hand and said, "Mr. Chairman, I am Major General Fred Weyand, the new chief of army legislative liaison." After getting that much out, he heaved a sigh of relief, whereupon Vinson said, "Thank you very much for coming in, General." Fred staggered outside and there stood Bob Smart with a stopwatch. "God damn, Fred, that was terrific," Bob said. "Six seconds is a new record!"[42]

The Armed Services Committee was a demanding mistress, and Vinson served her faithfully as chairman for a longer period than anyone in history. Serving in Congress was an all-consuming job for him, and aside from his family and his farm, he had few other interests. He had no hobbies and showed scant interest in art, music or drama. For relaxation and diversion, he attended movies occasionally and read omnivorously. A student of the Bible, he read it several times. He also read *Ben Hur* and *Les Misérables* more than once. He loved reading histories, biographies, and the novels of Zane Gray and Louis L'Amour. Neither television nor sports interested him particularly, although he did watch "Saturday Night Fights" and "Gunsmoke" when he lived in Chevy Chase, and in retirement watched Walter Cronkite on weekdays and the Atlanta Falcons on Sundays. He attended some sporting events and watched other television programs primarily to spend time with Tillman. He also attended the traditional army-navy football game whenever the president

---

[42] Lou and Neta Stockstill, interview with the author.

invited him, for he considered that a command performance, comparable to an invitation to the White House.[43]

Despite the increasingly partisan nature of Congress, the Armed Services Committee remained strictly nonpartisan. When a young representative from Florida ignored that longstanding policy and made a very partisan remark about constructing a base in Ohio, several committee members including the chairman chastised him severely. The naïve congressman, a decorated combat veteran of World War II was so upset by the reprimands that he left the committee meeting in tears.[44] Nonpartisanship, however, did not prevent Vinson from aiding committee members get reelected. Congressman Victor Eugene Wickersham of Oklahoma, who faced a tough reelection fight, told Vinson that he had a problem out in his district that needed to be examined. He asked the chairman to create a subcommittee to go out and examine the problem. It was apparent to Vinson and everyone else that he simply wanted to chair a subcommittee in his district for the publicity it would generate that would help him get reelected. The chairman looked at him and said, "All right, Mr. Wickersham, we are going to send a committee out there and it will go all over your district and get you reelected."[45]

The combination of extraordinary political clout coupled with numerous idiosyncrasies made Vinson irresistible to reporters. While he was pleased to see his public activities covered in articles in newspapers and periodicals, he nevertheless remained a private person who was very reticent about discussing his personal life. Lou Stockstill, who knew Vinson well, finally got the chairman's permission to write an article about him by promising that the work would be mostly about Tillman Snead. Based on extensive research in Washington and Milledgeville, the article appeared in the *Army Navy Air Force Journal* in February 1961. Although it mentioned Tillman and included his picture, the emphasis

---

[43] Ibid.; Tillman and Karen Snead, interview with the author; Sam Nunn, interview with the author, Atlanta, GA, 4 April 2001; Henry Jennings, telephone interview with the author, Gainesville, GA, 22 August 2001.

[44] Lou and Neta Stockstill, interview with the author.

[45] Ibid.

was on Vinson, and it captured his personality better than any previous work. The article was reprinted in the *Congressional Record* and reprinted in a condensed version in *Reader's Digest*.[46] Following its publication, *Army Navy Air Force Journal* and *Reader's Digest* jointly hosted a luncheon in Vinson's honor in the chamber of the Capitol building where the Supreme Court had held sway from 1860 to 1935. A vast assemblage of military and political leaders attended. Vinson praised the author by stating, "It takes genius to commit the story of a crusty old man like myself into something readable."[47]

Since Vinson was newsworthy and the most accessible of congressmen, he developed warm friendships with several reporters and enjoyed conversing with them on an individual basis. But for some reason, he adamantly refused to have news conferences. The only news conference he ever held came after the U-2 incident in 1960. Since the wife of captured U-2 pilot Francis Gary Powers was from Milledgeville, the press harangued him about the subject so much that he finally relented and held a press conference. It was the only one of its kind. At the appointed time, a dozen newsmen assembled in his office. He explained to them that he had called this press conference to talk about the U-2 incident and proceeded to ask a question he anticipated they would ask. After giving his answer, he read from a prepared list a second question they might want to ask. He answered it and proceeded to the third question on his list. After he had asked and answered all the questions on his list, he announced that the press conference was over. Frank Eleazar, an experienced United Press reporter and a native Georgian, said to him, "Mr. Chairman, aren't you even going to let us ask a question?" Vinson replied, "I've already answered all your questions."[48]

---

[46] Ibid.; Stockstill, "Backstage Boss," 1, 22–28; *Congressional Record,* 87th Cong., 1st sess., 21 February 1961, 2482–85; *Reader's Digest* 78 (March 1961): 128–32.

[47] *Atlanta Journal and Constitution*, 26 February 1961, 38.

[48] Lou and Neta Stockstill, interview with the author; Bill Surface, "Carl Vinson: A Half Century in Congress," *Family Weekly* (19 July 1964): 13.

During the remainder of Vinson's tenure in Congress, he received a profusion of honors and awards. Macon, the largest town in his Georgia district, proclaimed 7 April 1961, "Carl Vinson Day." The Chamber of Commerce had tried for years to honor Vinson, but he had always rebuffed their efforts. Finally, their persistence paid off, as the ceremony honoring him was a part of the annual Chamber of Commerce meeting. After his speech, which emphasized the accomplishment of the Kennedy administration, the Chamber of Commerce presented him with a new Cadillac.[49] Upon returning to Washington, he wrote Erwin Sibley that it was "the most comfortable trip I have made back through the country."[50]

The Georgia General Assembly proclaimed 9 February 1962, "Carl Vinson Appreciation Day." At the Russell-Vinson Appreciation Dinner the previous November, Vinson had received an oil portrait. He took this occasion to present his portrait to the governor, who was to have it hung in the Capitol building.[51] Douglas Kiker, then the *Atlanta Journal's* Washington correspondent, covered the event and made some pertinent observations about Vinson:

> Just about everything about Mr. Vinson—his appearance, his manner—is greatly deceiving.
>
> Walking down the long corridor of the Old House Office Building, he looks like some kindly old gentleman on his way to his daily checkers game. But the fact is, he is on his way to an Armed Services hearing which concerns the little matter of how best to spend $50 billion in defense of this nation and the rest of the free world.
>
> Drop in his office, as I do about three times a week, for a chat. He'll impress you as an easy-going, homespun type of man

---

[49] *Macon Telegraph*, 19 March 1961, 1; 2 April 1961, 21; *Atlanta Journal*, 8 April 1961, 1, 2, 19; Carl Vinson, Speech before Chamber of Commerce, Macon, GA, 7 April 1961, Vinson Scrapbooks, book 7 April 1961.

[50] Carl Vinson to Erwin Sibley, 12 April 1961, Erwin Sibley Papers, April–May 1961 folder.

[51] *Atlanta Constitution*, 10 February 1962, 3.

who wasn't doing a thing until you dropped in, except enjoying a cigar....

His activity is constant. Between breakfast and lunch he's apt to meet with two or three major administration officials, a half-dozen military leaders, and an uncounted number of other lesser luminaries on a variety of subjects that range from a new super-secret anti-anti-anti-missile to a new post office for Milledgeville.

He's got a dry, delicious wit and his bluntness is legend in this town. By all laws of nature and politics he ought by now to have grown into a grumpy, unresponsive man who is against everything. Instead, his thinking is young, dynamic and progressive in character. His is an amazing capacity to respond to change. Mr. Vinson lives in the present, not in the past.[52]

Less than a month after being honored by the Georgia General Assembly, Vinson received the "Minuteman of 1962" award from the Reserve Officers Association of the United States in a ceremony at the Sheraton-Park Hotel in Washington, DC. The award was given annually to the citizen who has contributed most to national security. Speaker of the House John McCormack introduced Vinson, whose speech emphasized the importance of the reserves and the need to keep the three services separate. It also emphatically seconded President Kennedy's call for a resumption of nuclear testing.[53] On 2 June the University of Georgia named him an "Honorary Alumnus," and on 4 June Mercer University granted him an honorary doctorate of humane letters.[54] On 14 June Speaker McCormack was the main speaker at a ceremony where the Boy Scouts of America bestowed upon Vinson and Senator Carl Hayden

---

[52] Douglas Kiker, "Georgia Assembly to Honor Him, The Patriarch of Congress," *Atlanta Journal and Constitution*, 4 February 1962, B7

[53] *Congressional Record*, 87th Cong., 2d sess., 5 March 1962, 3391–93; *Atlanta Constitution*, 3 March 1962, 1.

[54] John Sibley to Carl Vinson, 21 May 1962, John Sibley Papers, box 362, Robert W. Woodruff Library, Emory University, Atlanta, GA; *Union-Recorder*, 24 May 1962, 1.

of Arizona the Silver Buffalo award, scouting's highest award for distinguished service to boyhood.[55]

In April 1962 President Kennedy summoned Vinson, along with nineteen other members of Congress and fifty members of the Washington diplomatic corps, to accompany him to Norfolk, Virginia, to inspect a nuclear submarine, the nuclear carrier *Enterprise*, and other ships of the fleet. Vinson, whose aversion to flying was well-known, must have accepted the invitation with serious misgivings, for it involved not only flying in a jet from Washington to Norfolk but also flying in a helicopter over the fleet. He had never before been in a helicopter, and he had not inspected a naval vessel since 1917, but to him, a presidential invitation required obedience. He survived the ordeal, which included viewing combat demonstrations from the command cruiser *Northampton* and the *Enterprise* and spending the night on the *Northampton*. After returning home safely, he reported, "It was a great experience." He added, however, that on his next trip to Milledgeville, he would go, as usual, by train or by car.[56] Six months later, Vinson had another experience in a jet. President Kennedy sent his new jet plane, which he had not yet used, to Dobbins Air Force Base near Atlanta to transport Vinson, Senator Russell, and Senator J. William Fulbright of Arkansas, to Washington for a White House conference on the Cuban missile crisis.[57]

In the midst of this busy year, Vinson learned that he had opposition again for his Sixth District seat. Joe Briley's friends and supporters tried to convince the thirty-six-year-old lawyer from Dublin not to challenge Vinson, but they failed. Briley, who had never held elective office, campaigned vigorously, depicting himself as a young conservative and his opponent as an old liberal. He contended that since President Kennedy took office, Vinson had deserted the rest of the Georgia delegation in the House and "betrayed our traditional conservative

[55] *Congressional Record*, 87the Cong., 2d sess., 15 June 1962, 10705–706.

[56] *Atlanta Constitution*, 13 April 1962, 31; 17 April 1962, Atlanta Journal-Constitution Office; *Atlanta Journal*, 14 April 1962, 1; 15 April 1962, 2; John Kennedy to Carl Vinson, 15 March 1962, Snead Family Papers, Dale City, VA.

[57] *Atlanta Constitution*, 23 October 1962, 7.

stand."[58] Confident of victory, Vinson spent very little time campaigning. From the beginning, political observers said Briley did not have a chance, and they were right. As usual, Vinson won the Democratic primary by the overwhelming margin of 58,519 to 9,563 and carried all of the district's sixteen counties.[59]

More honors came Vinson's way in 1963. On 13 March he received the American Legion award for most distinguished service to the United States. At the Legion Congressional Banquet he received a plaque which read:

In appreciation of long and exemplary service to the American public and for his vast contributions to the country's defense policies for nearly five decades:

The American Legion proudly honors Congressman Carl Vinson, dean of the House, father of the two-ocean Navy, elder statesman of aviation, champion of the belief that a nation can maintain peace only if its defenses are strong; who holds that our beloved country and its safety comes ahead of any party, who has never shown any willingness to compromise his basic beliefs as they relate to the safety of America.

We confer upon him the American Legion award for most distinguished service to the United States of America.[60]

On 16 July Vinson completed 48 years, 8 months, and 13 days as a House member, breaking the longevity mark of his friend, the late Sam Rayburn. The political and military leaders went to extreme lengths honoring the dean of the House that day. His day began, as usual, with his early arrival at his office. It ended amid the drums and flourishes of a colorful Marine Corps parade, topped off with Secretary of the Navy Fred Korth presenting him the navy's highest civilian honor, the Distinguished Public Service Award. Not to be left out, Secretary of the

[58] *Atlanta Journal and Constitution*, 10 September 1962, 2.
[59] Georgia, Department of Archives and History, *Georgia Official and Statistical Register, 1961–1962*, 1486; *Union-Recorder*, 10 May 1962, B2.
[60] *Atlanta Journal*, 14 March 1963, 10.

Air Force Eugene M. Zuckert and General Curtis LeMay dropped in unannounced at the banquet and presented Vinson a silver and wood plaque. Just before the navy reception, Vinson, accompanied by Till and Molly Snead and Tillman III, visited the White House, where President Kennedy presented the congressman a spike and foot-long board, relics from the first United States Navy ship, the frigate *Constellation.* During the day his office received 3,000 telegrams of congratulations.[61] In the House thirty-five members spoke in tribute to him, and another twenty-five placed tributes in the *Congressional Record,* covering a total of thirty-five pages. Numerous tributes also were delivered in the Senate, led by Vice President Lyndon Johnson, who had served on Vinson's committee for twelve years.[62] When asked how he felt about the job, the seventy-nine-year-old Georgian replied, "Just like the day before. Plenty of work to do."[63]

For Vinson, there was always much work to do. In the Eighty-seventh Congress, his committee had met 125 times and reported 94 bills, and all but one of the bills passed the House. The hectic pace continued in the Eighty-eighth Congress.[64] Early in April he wrote Erwin Sibley that he had passed the only two major bills the House had passed this session and hoped to get two more bills enacted before the end of the month. Six weeks later he wrote the same correspondent that he had so much committee work that he had declined an invitation from the president to visit the Air Force Academy in Colorado Springs, Colorado. "I have never been as busy in all my life," he complained.[65] Besides all his duties in Washington, he also was supervising the operation of his farm, arranging for more roads and bridges to be built in Milledgeville, trying to sell his house in Milledgeville for $30,000 so that he could live

---

[61] Ibid., 17 July 1963, 1, 12; *Atlanta Constitution,* 17 July 1963, 1, "Congressman Vinson's Happy, Busy Day," *Army Navy Air Force Journal and Register* 100 (27 July 1963): 18.

[62] *Congressional Record,* 88th Cong., 1st sess., 16 July 1963, 12003–18, 12630–31, 12680–97, 12772.

[63] *Atlanta Journal,* 17 July 1963, 1, 12.

[64] Ibid., 12 March 1963, 5.

[65] Carl Vinson to Erwin Sibley, 2 April 1963, 23 May 1963, Erwin Sibley Papers, April and May 1963 folders.

in the country, and occasionally making speeches. He gave a speech at the Georgia State College for Women in Milledgeville on 24 April and dedicated a bridge in Milledgeville on 3 July and a post office in Sparta on 4 July. He wrote Erwin Sibley, "This will wind up all my speaking activities for this year, as I do not intend to make any more."[66]

President Kennedy, fearing the loss of Southern congressional support, had avoided civil rights for the first two years of his administration, but in June 1963 he issued a ringing call for legislation to combat the worst abuses of the Jim Crow system. He not only sought to speed up school desegregation, but also wanted a bill to ensure the voting rights of African Americans and a bill to outlaw discrimination in privately owned public accommodations. Within the Georgia congressional delegation, only freshman Representative Charles Weltner of Atlanta expressed any sympathy for the president's proposals. All of the other members emphatically opposed the message. Vinson, the strongest Kennedy supporter within the delegation, could find nothing good in the president's message. "The entire message is based on the concept that minorities have rights that supersede their obligations," he said. "Perhaps it is time for us to consider the rights of majorities, since we have been constantly told about our obligations. Perhaps it is time that minorities should be made more fully aware of their obligations as American citizens."[67]

While the Kennedy civil rights program was slowly proceeding through Congress, Vinson took issue with a Defense Department order that could put segregated communities or businesses "off limits" to military personnel. Acting on the recommendations of the Gesell Report, a study on the effects of racial discrimination on members of the armed forces, Secretary McNamara issued the order that allowed military commanders, with approval of the secretary of the service involved, to declare "off limits" adjacent communities or businesses practicing "relentless discrimination" against servicemen and their families. Before issuing the order, McNamara met with Vinson, who vigorously protested

[66] Ibid.; Carl Vinson to Erwin Sibley, 29 April, 28 May, 10 June, 12 June 1963, Erwin Sibley Papers, April, May, June 1963 folders.
[67] *Atlanta Journal*, 20 June 1963, 1.

the measure, arguing that "the military should not be used to bring about social reforms."[68] Convinced that the Department of Defense order was a direct invasion into local affairs, he introduced a bill to nullify it. His bill would make it a court-martial offense for any base commander to seek to "direct or control in any way the manner in which a member of the armed forces lives off military bases." Also, any officer who directs, implements or requests the use of an off-limits sanction "because of race, color or religion" would be subject to court-martial, under his bill. "My bill," the chairman added, "keeps the military where it belongs—in the business of defending our nation. Let the Congress, the courts, the States, and the people worry about social reform."[69] His measure gained the support of the *Atlanta Journal* but not the *Atlanta Constitution*.[70] Rowing against the tide of public opinion, Vinson made little headway in restricting the armed services' social policies.

For a number of years the chairman had contemplated retirement, and late in 1963 he finally made the decision to end his congressional career. Although he already held the record for longevity in the House, all signs indicated that he could serve additional terms if he ran, and many encouraged him to do so. But he chose to retire at this time for several reasons. As he surveyed the political landscape, he believed the executive branch was in the hands of a very capable leader, a man of destiny, who very likely would be reelected to a second term in 1964. Moreover, President Kennedy could rely on the mature judgment and experience of Vice President Lyndon Johnson, a man Vinson had trained. He was confident that the military would be well served by the House Armed Services Committee, which had several experienced, capable leaders, such as Mendel Rivers of South Carolina and Edward Hébert of Louisiana. They could carry on the work without him. Finally, after observing several members of Congress who were aged, infirm, and practically senile, he told his nephew Ed Vinson that he wanted to leave

---

[68] Ibid., 19 August 1963, 2.

[69] "Georgia's Vinson: Battling The Pentagon," *U.S. News & World Report* 55 (30 September 1963): 16.

[70] *Atlanta Constitution,* 25 September 1963, 4; *Atlanta Journal,* 12 September 1963, 32.

before he reached that condition.[71] Besides the reasons for relinquishing his seat, there was also the lure of living fulltime on his Georgia farm, an attraction that became irresistible after sixty years of public service.

Curious newsmen constantly pestered him about his plans, as did aspiring politicians in the Sixth District who wished to succeed him. Governor Carl Sanders, in the midst of the daunting task of reapportioning Georgia's congressional districts, also eagerly awaited his decision because preserving the Sixth District intact was complicating his job.[72] Resisting such pressures, Vinson kept everyone in suspense until he was ready to make the announcement. On his eightieth birthday, 18 November 1963, he announced that he would not be a candidate for reelection to the Eighty-ninth Congress. In identical letters to the chairman and the secretary of the Democratic Executive Committee, Sixth Congressional District of Georgia, he stated:

> When my present term expires on January 3rd, 1965, I will be in my 81st year, and will have served fifty years consecutively in the Congress.
>
> Notwithstanding the fact that I am blessed with good health I desire, at the end of the 88th Congress, to be relieved of all official responsibility in my remaining years. At that time I will with pride, hand back to the people of the District their commission, with the sincere hope that I have rendered to the District, the State and the Nation the full measure of my ability and devotion.[73]

In reading the announcement to visitors in his office, he added, "I plan to keep busy. I'm not going to rust out. I'm going to wear out."[74]

---

[71] Ed and Betty Vinson, interview with the author; Jerome Doolittle, "The Gentleman From Georgia Goes Home," *Saturday Evening Post* 237 (5 December 1964): 26.

[72] Carl Sanders, interview with the author, Atlanta, GA, 23 August 2001.

[73] Carl Vinson to Erwin Sibley, 18 November 1963, Erwin Sibley Papers, November–December 1963 folder; Carl Vinson to Charles J. Bloch, 18 November 1963, Charles Bloch Papers, Box 28, folder 132.

[74] *Atlanta Constitution*, 19 November 1963, 1.

His birthday began with meetings with Secretary of the Army Cyrus Vance, members of the Joint Chiefs of Staff, and three other callers on official business before 9:00 a. m. He was honored with numerous tributes and a standing ovation in the House and with a luncheon attended by Secretary of Defense McNamara, Speaker of the House McCormack, the Georgia congressional delegation, other congressional leaders, and several longtime friends from Georgia. Officials in Washington and Georgia as well as the national press saluted him as a great leader and an extraordinary statesman.[75] In an editorial lauding his half-century of service, the *New York Times* stated, "Mr. Vinson, who has exercised his talents, his wisdom and his patriotism to the benefit of the United States for so many years, has set an example to other veteran legislators of how to retire gracefully before one has outlived one's usefulness."[76]

Three days after making his announcement to retire, he wrote Erwin Sibley that since President Kennedy had invited him to accompany him to the army-navy football game in Philadelphia on 30November, "I will have to go."[77] The next day, 22 November, Vinson was in the Armed Services Committee Meeting Room munching sandwiches with Ed Vinson, when Till Snead came in. With deep concern and sorrow etched in his face, he said, "Mr. Chairman, I have terrible news. The president has just been shot."[78]

---

[75] Ibid., 3; *Atlanta Journal*, 18 November 1963, 1, 8; *Congressional Record*, 88th Cong., 1st sess., 18 November 1963, 22018–21.

[76] *New York Times*, 19 November 1963, 40.

[77] Carl Vinson to Erwin Sibley, 21 November 1963, Erwin Sibley Papers, November–December 1963 folder.

[78] Ed and Betty Vinson, interview with the author.

14

Retirement

I know of nothing that can give a man a greater feeling of pride than to know that he has done his job well.

Carl Vinson, 1966

Two days after the death of President Kennedy, Vinson issued the following statement:

> The tears of the free world flow unashamedly for the tragedy that has befallen the people of America. Our President is dead, the victim of the bullets of a mad assassin.
>
> Our loss cannot be measured in words. John F. Kennedy was a much-loved President. His brilliant mind, his dedication to the cause of freedom, his love for his fellowmen, his goals for the betterment of America, his understanding of the problems of his fellow citizens, his ambitions for a better life for free men everywhere are stilled. But the accomplishments he leaves behind will take their place in the annals of history.
>
> John F. Kennedy was, and remains, a man of destiny. He died in the service of his nation—prematurely and tragically—leaving behind a shocked and mourning family, a stunned nation and a saddened world.
>
> Had he lived, the nation would have had the continued benefit of his wisdom, his foresight, his humanity, his

understanding, his vigor and stamina and his incomparable leadership.

All has now been ended for this great and good man. He now belongs to the ages. But the good he has accomplished will live on. His memory will remain as an inspiration for every American.[1]

Vinson served as a member of the official delegation to represent the House at the funeral of the president, and a decision he had made years before had a significant impact upon the funeral procession, viewed by millions throughout the world. The dignity and historic simplicity of the funeral cortege existed only because of Vinson. In 1957, as an economy measure, the Pentagon had tried to dispense with horse-drawn funeral caissons for military leaders. When the measure came before the House Armed Services Committee, the chairman objected strenuously. "We would be wrong in destroying a tiny symbol that gives proper recognition to the great men of the past, the present and the future who will, one day, rest in final glory in Arlington Cemetery," he declared. Admittedly, using a sleek black hearse was cheaper than maintaining seventeen horses at Ft. Myer for funerals, but Vinson insisted on the traditional ceremony. "In a $38 billion budget there must be some better way of saving a few thousand dollars a year than at the incalculable cost of destroying the traditions of the past," he insisted in a public letter. While a horse-drawn funeral entourage might seem incongruous in an age of supersonic speed, Vinson "hoped that the pace of modern living might at least be retarded for our honored dead." It was. Stung by Vinson's opposition, Secretary of the Army Wilber M. Brucker abruptly cancelled the plan to eliminate the horses.[2]

For Vinson, the only redeeming aspect of the tragic death of President Kennedy was that Lyndon Johnson would succeed him. He had

---

[1] *Atlanta Journal and Constitution*, 24 November 1963, 47.

[2] *Atlanta Journal*, 26 November 1963, 16; "Caisson Correspondence Holds Horses' Fate," *Army Navy Air Force Journal* 94 (16 February 1957): 3; "The Caisson And Cost Effectiveness," *Army Navy Air Force Journal* 101 (7 December 1963): 11.

known Johnson since the early 1930s, when the young Texan was an administrative assistant to Congressman Richard Kleberg of Texas. When Johnson entered Congress in June 1937, he was assigned to the Naval Affairs Committee, and Chairman Vinson was immediately impressed by the young congressman's energy, drive, and capacity for work. Vinson utilized his capabilities by placing him on a number of subcommittees and sending him on innumerable inspection visits to various military installations throughout the country. Johnson, in turn, supported all of Vinson's efforts to strengthen the navy and played a major role in enacting the draft extension in 1941, a bill that passed the House by one vote. Like Vinson, Johnson was a loyal Democrat, possessed a keen analytical mind, read constantly, and always demonstrated a desire for more knowledge. Both could be ruthless in extracting information from witnesses, staff members, and others. A warm friendship, which lasted for the rest of their lives, developed between the two legislators. Vinson never tired of praising the accomplishments of his protégé, and Johnson often remarked that he was a graduate of "Vinson College" and claimed that everything he learned about politics he learned at the knee of Vinson.[3] Although Vinson had been very close to President Kennedy and was deeply saddened by his death, he confided to a friend that "I have been closer to Lyndon than any other man that I have served with except probably Speaker Rayburn and Speaker McCormack."[4] Confident that Johnson would be an outstanding president, he told the same correspondent, "We have a great pilot to guide the ship of state through these troubled waters."[5]

When Johnson, already sworn in as president, returned from Dallas, Vinson met with him and promised him his full support. Vinson was one of the three Democrats chosen by the Speaker to escort President Johnson into the House for his inaugural address. In an emotional speech interrupted many times with loud applause, the new president pledged to

---

[3] Transcript, Carl Vinson Oral History interview, 24 May 1970, by Frank Deaver, LBJ Library, Austin, TX.
[4] Carl Vinson to Charles Bloch, 27 November 1963, Charles J. Bloch Papers, Box 28, folder 132, Middle Georgia Regional Library, Macon, GA.
[5] Ibid., 2 December 1963.

carry out the slain president's program. The loudest applause came when Johnson said, "Let us put an end to the teaching and preaching of hate and evil and violence." In contrast to Georgia's senators, Russell and Talmadge, who expressed concern over Johnson's support of a civil rights bill, Vinson described the address as "a dynamic message which should make every American proud." Having no reservations about Johnson's leadership, he urged Democrats to get behind him, support him, and elect him to a full term in 1964.[6]

In Dublin, Georgia, a Superior Court judge started a draft movement to encourage Vinson to serve a twenty-sixth term, arguing that with the death of President Kennedy, Vinson's experienced leadership was needed to guide the nation at this critical time. President Johnson also asked him to serve another term and help him with his program. Vinson squelched the effort immediately. In both public and private statements, he emphatically said that he had reached his decision to retire after careful consideration and would not reconsider it.[7]

When Congress reconvened on 7 January 1964, Vinson, as usual, was organized and raring to go. He had already paid his income tax, for, as he explained to Erwin Sibley, "I never want much in front of me, I want it all behind me. As a Frontiersman, I must look to the front and keep blazing away." Expecting a busy session, he scheduled hearings for the next week and hoped to get his main bills passed before he returned to Georgia for the Easter recess.[8]

With minimal opposition he guided several military bills through the Armed Services Committee and the House. H. R. 9637, which provided almost $17 billion for the Defense Department in fiscal year 1965, was the largest separate fund authorization ever enacted by

---

[6] Carl Vinson to Erwin Sibley, 29 November 1963, Erwin Sibley Papers, November–December folder, Special Collections, Ina Dillard Russell Library, Georgia College and State University, Milledgeville, GA; *Atlanta Journal,* 28 November 1963, A22; *Atlanta Constitution*, 30 November 1963, 4.

[7] Carl Vinson to Erwin Sibley, 29 November 1963, Erwin Sibley Papers, November–December 1963 folder; *Atlanta Constitution*, 29 November 1963, 3; 30 November 1963, 8; 6 December 1963, 16.

[8] Carl Vinson to Erwin Sibley, 7 January 1964, Erwin Sibley Papers, January–February 1964 folder.

Congress. It authorized over 2,700 aircraft, 35,000 missiles, 53 new ships, and 7 ship conversions. To commemorate the last such bill Vinson would handle, President Johnson held a special signing ceremony at the White House on 20 March. With Vinson at his side, the president signed the bill and extolled the chairman.

> This bill represents still another tribute to the wisdom and the dedication of Carl Vinson.
> This bill marks one of the final official acts of patriotism from a man whose entire life has been an exercise in patriotism.
> He has given 50 years to the Congress.
> No man in the history of this Republic knows more about the posture of our defense—or has done more to improve it.
> I love him as a man—I respect him as a public servant.[9]

For most of his fifty years in Congress, Vinson had labored in relative obscurity, and few outside of Washington were aware of his contributions. The lack of publicity came about because he refused to "toot his own horn." Unlike most members of Congress, he rarely issued press releases and almost never held press conferences. But in his last years, he was deluged with awards, including the nation's highest honors. It seemed as if the nation, suddenly realizing what a treasure it was about to lose, attempted to make up for any previous failures to accord him proper recognition. In 1963 countless honors had been bestowed upon him, and the parade of awards continued in 1964. Modest by nature, he was somewhat embarrassed by the tributes and the grandiloquent accolades that accompanied them. He usually responded that he was unworthy of the award and had only done his duty. Yet he was proud of his record and gratified to be honored by his peers, especially those in the government and in the military who were most familiar with his contributions.

---

[9] Remarks made by the President, 20 March 1964, Vinson Scrapbooks, book December 1963–May 1964, on loan from Tillman Snead to Georgia College and State University, Milledgeville, GA.

On 22 January Governor Carl Sanders of Georgia and 600
government, political, civic, and business leaders massed at the Dinkler
Plaza Hotel in Atlanta to award Vinson the Georgia Medal for
Distinguished Public Service. He was the third recipient of this
prestigious award, following Arthur J. Moore, retired Bishop of the
Methodist Church, and John A. Sibley, Atlanta banker and civic leader
and brother of Vinson's closest friend, Erwin Sibley. Mercer University
president Rufus Harris, after summarizing the highlights of Vinson's
career, presented the medal and a magnificent scroll to Vinson. He
accepted the award "with a deep sense of humility" and delivered an
acceptance speech that was interrupted more than a dozen times with
applause. Earlier that day, the Georgia General Assembly had
unanimously adopted a resolution asking him to reconsider his decision
to retire. When informed of the legislature's action, he responded, "No,
I'm not going to reconsider. When a man reaches 80 years old and 50
years in Congress, it's time to go home."[10]

Two months later, the Georgia State Chamber of Commerce
honored Vinson at their annual congressional dinner. Since he usually
attended the annual affair, he was surprised when the chamber presented
him a silver platter in recognition of his half century of service in the
House. He accepted the award, said "Thank you very much," and sat
down. The crowd of several hundred, which included both Georgia
senators, seven of the ten Georgia representatives in the House, staff
members, and chamber of commerce members and their wives, who
came to Washington for the occasion, gave the venerable chairman a
standing ovation.[11]

A week later, he received the Air Force Academy's highest annual
award, the Thomas D. White National Defense Award for 1964. The
award was presented annually to the person who had contributed "most
significantly to the national defense and security of the United States."
The air force, well aware of Vinson's aversion to traveling long
distances, wisely held the ceremony in the Pentagon office of the

---

[10] *Congressional Record*, 88th Cong., 2d sess., 27 January 1964, 1159–61;
Atlanta Constitution, 23 January 1964, 1, 11.

[11] *Atlanta Journal*, 29 April 1964, 37.

secretary of the air force rather than at the Air Force Academy in Colorado Springs, Colorado.[12]

The chairman, still busy with his congressional duties and plans for retirement, was not eager to make another major speech. But when President Johnson personally urged him, "as an old friend," to deliver the commencement address at Annapolis on 3 June 1964, "to give this graduating class and the Nation the benefit of your wisdom and sage advice," he could not refuse.[13] Since Vinson had been the navy's best friend in Congress for many years, it was only fitting that he deliver the principal address at the graduation exercises at the United States Naval Academy. With the help of several members of his staff, he spent much time composing his thoughts. His speech, titled "The Navy of the Future," touched on topics dear to his heart: maintaining a national defense that can destroy any enemy or combination of enemies, maintaining the separate identities of the four branches of the military, and maintaining supremacy over the oceans of the world. While acknowledging the goal of "universal reduction in the capability of nations to destroy one another," he warned of the dangers of unilateral disarmament. Until universal peace is fully attained, he believed that "readiness for war is the sentinel of peace in this threatened world."

He then directed his attention to the fantastic advances of technology. The chairman may have been eighty years old and still advocating the same old principles he had followed for many years, but his thinking was not old. Indeed he was remarkably receptive to using new technology which, he felt, would soon multiply the power of the navy in myriad and unforeseeable ways. He understood that national security could be ensured only by utilizing the latest technology. His speech specifically identified several technological innovations which subsequently transformed America's national defense:

Today, we verge upon aircraft which can take off and land vertically, yet fly horizontally at high speed.

---

[12] *Atlanta Constitution*, 8 May 1964, 15.
[13] Letter, Lyndon Johnson to Carl Vinson, 31 March 1964, "Carl Vinson file," WHCF, Name File, LBJ Library.

We are close to the development of beams of light which can transmit energy with pin-point accuracy.

Research and development are fast perfecting a navigational system which at all times will instantly and accurately fix the position of a ship or an aircraft.

And the day is near when long-distance radar will peer around the curve of the earth.

I do not doubt that during your careers we will perfect a method of detecting submarines, regardless of their depth.

Engineering officers are already expert in methods of using oil and nuclear power to develop steam. But the engineering officers of tomorrow will surely develop more direct methods of applying nuclear power to propulsion systems.[14]

In view of the technological advances, he urged the navy to convert to nuclear power as quickly as it becomes militarily advantageous and to modernize the entire fleet promptly. The speech, one of the best concise statements of his beliefs, received much coverage in the press and was reprinted in the *Congressional Record* and in *Shipmate*, the publication of the U.S. Naval Academy Alumni Association.[15]

Three weeks after delivering the commencement address at Annapolis, the chairman was feted by the National Guard Association and the Georgia National Guard at a Washington dinner with 135 guests, including the secretary of the army, the secretary of the air force, former Georgia Governor Ernest Vandiver, and Georgia Adjutant General George J. Hearn. The National Guard Association presented Vinson a bronze plate to go on a specially built desk to be placed in the Mary Vinson Memorial Library in Milledgeville. Ironically, Vinson at first objected to naming the library for his late wife. After he had secured a new post office for Milledgeville, the old post office was converted into a library, and local leaders insisted on naming it the Mary Vinson

---

[14] Carl Vinson, "The Navy of the Future," *Shipmate* 27 (June–July 1964): 8–9, 11.

[15] Ibid.; *Congressional Record*, 88th Cong., 2d sess., 4 June 1964, 12778–79.

Memorial Library. Overcoming his initial objections, Vinson soon became a staunch supporter of the library. He accepted the gift with much appreciation. The Georgia National Guard then honored Vinson with its highest decoration, the Distinctive Service Medal. The citation praised him for his support of the armed forces in general and for the National Guard in particular. It also lauded him for "never wavering under pressures when his farsighted and highly accurate decisions were questioned."[16]

Two days later, the armed services, which Uncle Carl had watched over with a fatherly eye for half a century, bestowed high tributes on him and paid him a formal farewell in a gala ceremony at Fort Leslie J. McNair in Washington. Accompanied by Secretary of Defense Robert McNamara and General Maxwell Taylor, the guest of honor arrived at the parade ground in a limousine escorted by the stately horses used at Arlington National Cemetery that he had saved back in 1957. While awaiting Vinson's arrival, the Air Force Pipe Band, the Army's Old Guard Fife and Drum Corps, and the Marine Drum and Bugle Corps had marched smartly up and the down the sunlit field, filling the air with music, including bright, rollicking Dixie music for the Georgia honoree. Following a seventeen-gun salute, five groups of massed troops marched on the field, as the navy band played service tunes. Standing in a jeep with Defense Secretary McNamara, Vinson inspected the command. Following the playing of the National Anthem, each of the three secretaries of the armed services presented its flag to Vinson as a memento of his long service and help to them. It was the first time the flags of the three armed services had ever been presented to an individual. After Vinson returned to the reviewing stand, Deputy Secretary of Defense Cyrus Vance read a citation bestowing the Distinguished Service Medal on him. It was the first time the award, the top decoration for civilians, had been conferred upon a member of Congress. McNamara then pinned the medal on Vinson's lapel and thanked him for "the burden he has carried so well, so long, and so far."

---

[16]*Atlanta Journal*, 25 June 1964, 32; Carl Vinson to Erwin Sibley, 13 February 1961, Erwin Sibley Papers, February 1961 folder; *Union-Recorder*, 12 September 1963, 1.

"Carl Vinson is a great man," the secretary told the audience. "He leaves us wiser than he found us." After all the bands had played, all the troops had marched by, and all the speeches were made, Vinson was the guest of honor at a reception given by McNamara, the service secretaries, and the Joint Chiefs of Staff. Among those attending the reception honoring Vinson was aged General of the Army Omar Bradley, who rarely attended public functions. The evening culminated with the presentation to Vinson of a huge memory book, containing all of the speeches as well as letters of tribute from military men, high and low, from all over the world. The first letter in the book was from President Johnson, who said, "No hero ever returned from battle in greater triumph."[17]

The marines, not to be left out, honored Vinson the next week with a special full-dress parade and review at the marine barracks in Washington. Members of both Armed Services Committees as well as ranking marine and naval officers attended the event.[18]

During the 4 July recess, Vinson paid a visit to the Warner Robins Air Force Base, an important base employing 15,000 that he had helped secure for the Sixth District. He was especially interested in seeing the hospital and the site for a new fifty-bed facility. For many years he had used his influence on behalf of Warner Robins, and he had sponsored the latest capital improvement project in the House. In an interview a few months later, he explained to *Atlanta Journal* reporter Margaret Shannon how the base happened to be located there. In World War II, he related, Macon and Atlanta were competing for a proposed airfield. Atlanta seemed to have the airport cinched when a group of Macon businessmen bought 3,500 acres in neighboring Houston County and offered it as a site. Vinson then went to see Assistant Secretary of War for Air Robert A. Lovett and insisted on a study to determine which site would be more economical from a construction standpoint. When Vinson's site won by a million dollars, he told the secretary the taxpayers did not want to waste

---

[17] *Atlanta Journal*, 27 June 1964, 1; *Atlanta Constitution*, 27 June 1964, 1, 5; "Armed Services Salute Chairman Vinson," *Journal of the Armed Forces* 101 (11 July 1964): 20–21.

[18] *Atlanta Journal*, 2 July 1964, 2; *Atlanta Constitution*, 2 July 1964, 14.

a million dollars. Secretary Lovett said, "But you don't have any houses there." Vinson asked how many he needed, and Lovett replied, "2,500."

Vinson quickly called his group and urged them to get the banks of Macon to underwrite the construction of 2,500 houses at Warner Robins, a community that then had one store. When they agreed, Vinson went back to Lovett and told him that he had the houses. Lovett questioned whether the Federal Housing Authority would guarantee them, so Vinson got in a taxi, went to the F.H.A. and presented the proposition to them. When the F.H.A. agreed to the proposal, Vinson got back in the taxi, with an F.H.A. official in tow, and went back to Secretary Lovett's office. Since Vinson had met all his objections, a surprised Lovett said, "You've got yourself an airfield."[19]

Upon assuming the presidency, Lyndon Johnson had pledged to implement the Kennedy program, which had been stymied in Congress. He carried out his promise with dispatch. Capitalizing on the emotional impact of Kennedy's tragic death and utilizing his own persuasive arm-twisting tactics on Congress, he succeeded in enacting Kennedy's domestic agenda. Johnson exercised the forceful and dynamic executive leadership that Vinson expected of him, and the chairman supported him loyally on all measures except civil rights. Although not nearly as vocal in his opposition to the civil rights bill as Senator Russell, who led the opposition in the Senate, Vinson nonetheless thought the measure was unwise and voted against it. When Congress overcame the impassioned opposition of Southerners and enacted the Civil Rights Act of 1964, Vinson urged compliance with the law. "The bill has been enacted now and we must live under the law," he said. "We are a nation of law and our strength lies in the law."[20]

When Vinson returned to Georgia again in early August, he apparently had overcome his fear of flying. He wrote Erwin Sibley that he planned to travel by jet. "It is too slow to travel by train," he stated.

---

[19] *Atlanta Constitution*, 4 July 1964, Atlanta Journal-Constitution Office; *Atlanta Journal and Constitution*, 4 October 1964, 47.

[20] *Atlanta Journal*, 21 July 1964, 42.

"In my old age, I must move fast!"[21] By the time he arrived in Georgia the presidential campaign was well underway. The South, long the bastion of Democratic support, had cooled to the Democratic team of Lyndon Johnson and liberal Minnesota Senator Hubert Humphrey largely because of civil rights. Many traditional Democrats rallied behind the conservative Republican nominee, Barry Goldwater, who was one of the six senators who voted against the Civil Rights Act. In Georgia, most of the public officials, all of whom were Democrats, either backed Goldwater or remained conspicuously silent during the campaign. Vinson was not among them. At the Democratic convention in Atlantic City, he had escorted the president to the convention podium for his acceptance speech, and he emphatically endorsed the Johnson-Humphrey ticket. He urged other Democrats to do the same. But aside from Governor Carl Sanders, who vigorously campaigned for the Democrats, the only other prominent Georgia Democrats who joined him in backing the Democratic ticket were State Highway Director Jim Gillis and Representative Phil Landrum.[22]

In dedicating a new post office building in Dublin, Vinson declared that "to risk the consequences of a Goldwater Administration is the height of folly for the South, as it is for the entire Nation." After enumerating the economic advantages a Democratic administration would bring to the South, he attempted to justify the president's support of civil rights to a skeptical audience. "Lyndon Johnson, as a Southerner, espoused the cause of the South; Lyndon Johnson, as president, had no other choice but to reflect the will of the majority of the Nation." Moreover, he continued, Barry Goldwater has "repeatedly identified himself with proponents for civil rights" and currently is a member of the N.A.A.C.P. If the South supports Goldwater and opposes Johnson, he

---

[21] Carl Vinson to Erwin Sibley, 24 July 1964, Erwin Sibley Papers, July–August 1964 folder.

[22] *Atlanta Constitution*, 11 August 1964, 4, 10; 1 September 1964, 4; James F. Cook, *Carl Sanders: Spokesman of the New South* (Macon GA: Mercer University Press, 1993) 209–12.

concluded, it would be rewarding a political enemy, punishing an old friend, and cutting off its own nose to spite its face.[23]

The Georgia Swamp Fox mischievously stirred up the politics of Middle Georgia when he suggested that if Goldwater were elected, Warner Robins Air Force Base would be closed. Goldwater, a major general in the air force reserve, quickly issued a statement refuting his charge. After Congress adjourned, Vinson did all that he could to keep Georgia in the Democratic column, but his effort failed. For the first time since 1868, Georgia voted for a Republican presidential candidate. Nationally, Johnson won by a landslide, but in Georgia he carried only 46 percent of the vote. Vinson was not even able to keep Baldwin County in the Democratic column, as it went for Goldwater by vote of 3,422 to 2,742. [24]

As his last session of Congress drew to a close, the chairman received more honors. On 19 August at 11:00 a. m., he gaveled his noisy committee to order in the big, ornate, red-carpeted House Armed Services Committee Hearing Room, as he had done countless times. The stated agenda called for a group photograph. After a dozen photos were taken, Mendel Rivers, who would succeed Vinson as chairman the next session, reached across Vinson and picked up his gavel. "Since we are living in the days of coups," he told Vinson, "it's just as well for me to take this gavel now so I can get accustomed to it." In a more serious vein, he talked about Vinson's leaving and how he had been accused of running the committee as a tyrant, a monarch, and a dictator. "You have done one thing," Rivers conceded. "You have sown in the hearts of the members of this committee seeds of love and affection that have grown and matured and will last as long as the sun and life itself. We will never forget our association with you."

Rivers then pounded the gavel and ordered staffers to bring out a "small token" for Vinson. Laboriously they lugged in and placed on the witness table a box the size of a desk. Rivers directed Vinson to open it. With his pocket knife Uncle Carl slit the top. He pulled out the padding

---

[23] *Union-Recorder*, 13 August 1964, 1.

[24] Ibid., 5 November 1964, 1; *Atlanta Journal and Constitution*, 4 October 1964, 4; *Atlanta Constitution*, 4 November 1964, 1, 11.

and discovered a smaller box. He opened it and discovered yet another box. It contained a spittoon engraved with the names of the committee members and a note. The note explained that the spittoon could be placed next to a color television set that soon would be delivered to his farm in Milledgeville. Already engraved, for later installation on the top of the television, was a brass plaque praising Vinson for his "50 years of outstanding leadership and dedication to the nation." After thanking the committee members, Uncle Carl commended Rivers' vigorous style. He said Mendel definitely seemed to be learning the job.[25]

In a ceremony in the East Room of the White House on 14 September, President Johnson awarded the Presidential Medal of Freedom, the highest governmental honor the president can award civilians, to thirty individuals. "Their lives and their work have made freedom stronger for all of us in our time," the president intoned. Three of the medals were awarded with special distinction. They went to former Secretary of State Dean Acheson, broadcaster Edward R. Murrow, and Representative Carl Vinson. Vinson's citation read: "Master legislative captain, helmsman and navigator, his fixed star has always been the national interest."[26]

The second day of October 1964 was scheduled to be the last day of the Eighty-eighth Congress, the last day Carl Vinson would answer a quorum call and roll call in the House. The retiring congressman followed his usual routine. Out of bed at 5:45, he was in his Capitol Hill office by 7:00, going over his mail. At eight he went to the House side of the Capitol building for his unvarying breakfast of fresh orange juice, oatmeal, dry toast and coffee. At 8:30 he was back in his office, where staff members were arriving and phones had begun to ring. He passed the morning with routine congressional business and showed up in the House chamber briefly when the session began at noon. Just after 2:00, having had his usual cup of the House restaurant's bean soup for lunch, he settled down in his customary seat in the seventh row back to listen to debate on a bill setting up new salary scales for congressional employees. Vinson used the same seat because there was a spittoon under the seat in

---

[25] *Atlanta Constitution*, 20 August 1964, 5.
[26] Ibid., 15 September 1964, 5, 6.

front. Inserting a "chaw" of tobacco, he chatted amiably with his Georgia colleagues Elliott Hagan and Robert Stephens.

They were still talking when Speaker McCormack left the podium for the microphone below. After extolling Vinson and highlighting his career, the Speaker offered a resolution commending Vinson "for his incomparable record as a legislator, his manifold contributions to the strength of our country, and unimpeachable devotion to the public interest…. As he retires…he carries with him the love, respect and admiration of his colleagues and the gratitude of the Nation." The House shouted unanimous approval. The resolution, which had been prepared by the Georgia delegation, McCormack, and others, was the first such resolution ever passed by the House, so far as the Speaker could discover.[27]

The Speaker had opened the floodgates. He was followed by Charles Halleck of Indiana, Carl Albert of Oklahoma, Hale Boggs of Louisiana, Robert Stephens of Georgia, Mendel Rivers of South Carolina, and a host of others—all expressing their deep admiration and affection for their retiring colleague. After all the accolades had been delivered, the chairman came to the microphone for the last time, wearing in his buttonhole the rosette of the Distinguished Service Medal President Johnson had given him. With his glasses perched halfway down his big nose, the slight, bald man had, according to one observer, the look of an aging hawk. "Quite literally," Vinson said, "my service started with the Springfield rifle and is ending with the Polaris submarine and the intercontinental ballistic missile." He thanked the members with a short speech and sat down. Before leaving, he learned that the Congress would have to go into brief session again the next day. The session began at 11:00, an hour earlier than normal. In his usual seat, Vinson was chatting with old friends Representative William Bates of Massachusetts and former Congressman Paul Kilday of Texas when a vote was taken on extending a federal aid-to-education program to the District of Columbia. The Democratic leadership favored the measure; conservatives of both

[27] *Congressional Record*, 88th Cong., 2d sess., 2 October 1964, 23702–703; Jerome Doolittle, "The Gentleman From Georgia Goes Home," *Saturday Evening Post* 237 (5 December 1964): 26–27.

parties opposed it. At five minutes before noon the clerk finally got to
Vinson's name. The chairman rose slightly and cried, "Aye." After
voting, he went to the cloakroom, picked up his cane, and went home. It
was the last roll-call vote in his fifty-year career, and it was, typically,
the vote of a loyal party man.[28]

After campaigning for Johnson, being feted in Milledgeville with
Carl Vinson Day on his eighty-first birthday, dedicating a $4 million post
office in Macon, and taking care of business on his farm, Vinson
returned to Washington to clean out his office. Deciding what to do with
files accumulated over half a century was a perplexing question. From
his earliest days in Congress, Vinson had documented his career by
keeping newspaper articles and selected correspondence in scrapbooks,
which he first placed in the Mary Vinson Memorial Library and later
bequeathed to Tillman Snead, III. The University of Georgia was eager
to house his official papers, and in 1962 Dr. O. C. Aderhold, the
president of the university, had raised that issue with Vinson. Aderhold
assured him that any correspondence that he did not want published
could be sealed off for whatever period of time he designated. As soon as
Vinson announced that he was retiring, the University's Director of
Libraries traveled to Washington and discussed the matter with him. The
librarian explained that the university could preserve his papers safely
and make them available for scholars.[29] John Sibley encouraged his old
friend to place his papers at the University of Georgia, which has "proper
physical facilities and trained personnel to care for and preserve these
papers for posterity."[30] Unfortunately, after giving the matter much
thought, Vinson rejected the offer. Molly Snead later told Dr. Larry
Elowitz, Vinson Professor at Georgia College, that he destroyed his
papers because he feared that they might reveal national secrets and

---

[28] Doolittle, "The Gentleman From Georgia Goes Home," 27–28.

[29] O. C. Aderhold to John Sibley, 13 December 1963, John Sibley Papers,
Box 362, Special Collections Department, Robert W. Woodruff Library, Emory
University, Atlanta, GA.

[30] John Sibley to Carl Vinson, 16 December 1963, John Sibley Papers, Box
362.

embarrass friends and colleagues.[31] Till Snead told his son Tillman that he assisted Vinson in trashing the papers in his office before he retired.[32]

Vinson craftily let word pass around that he would remain in Washington until the opening day of the Eighty-ninth Congress. That was a ruse because he did not want any teary goodbyes. He could have flown home in a plush air force jet, but that was not his way. Without any fanfare, Till Snead drove him to Union Station on Christmas Day 1964. The old chairman sent Snead home to be with his family, carried his own two suitcases, and boarded the 3:10 train for Georgia. Except for a couple of newspapermen, nobody was on hand for the final leave-taking of a congressional legend.[33]

One day, shortly before Vinson retired, Till Snead was driving him around Washington. In a moment of reflection the chairman said, "Till, when I get on that train and ride home from Washington for the last time, none of these people, these admirals and generals, are going to care a thing about me."[34] He seemed to believe that it was only the position of chairman of the House Armed Services Committee that they respected, and not him personally. His analysis was wrong. The military and political leaders in Washington did not forget him. For several years after he retired, Mendel Rivers, Edward Hébert, Senator Margaret Chase Smith, another graduate of "Vinson College," and many executive officials kept in touch with him, sought his advice from time to time, and occasionally traveled to his Baldwin County farm to visit him. In the 1970s President Richard Nixon often sought his advice. But no one in Washington was more solicitous of Vinson than President Johnson, who

---

[31] Larry Elowitz, telephone interview with the author, Milledgeville, GA, 6 January 2003.

[32] Tillman and Karen Snead, interview with the author, Dale City, VA, 8 June 2001.

[33] *Atlanta Constitution*, 26 December 1964, 3; *Union-Recorder*, 17 November 1964; Andrew Sparks, "Carl Vinson Comes Home," *Atlanta Journal and Constitution Magazine*, 3 January 1965, 8–9, 21–22.

[34] Tillman and Karen Snead, interview with the author.

corresponded regularly and made sure his mentor received proper recognition.[35]

When the president learned that Vinson was returning to Washington to receive an award from the American Veterans of World War II on Saturday, 3 April, he saw an opportunity to honor his old friend. Johnson had a car and driver waiting when Vinson arrived by train on Friday morning. The limousine carried him to President Johnson's office. The president then escorted Vinson to the new Rayburn House Office Building. There assembled were Secretary of Defense McNamara and top military and civilian leaders of the Pentagon, together with past and present members of the House Armed Services Committee and Democratic and Republican leaders of the House who wanted to pay proper respect to the chairman. He had foiled their efforts when he slipped out of town alone the previous Christmas, but with the assistance of the president, they had him this time and there was no escape. Also in attendance at the invitation of the president was Reverend Billy Graham, Vinson's favorite preacher, who gave the invocation. Johnson led Vinson into the twenty-eight-foot-high walnut-paneled hearing room of the Armed Services Committee and announced that the room henceforth would be called the "Carl Vinson Room." After Johnson dedicated a plaque to Vinson, the group gave the guest of honor "The Treatment." Beaming at the adulation heaped on him, Vinson said he didn't really deserve it. All he did was his duty.[36]

The president announced that Vinson would be his guest at the White House for the week end and proceeded to regale the group for twenty minutes with his own experiences in "Vinson College." As a subcommittee chairman, Johnson related that he once got into a big controversy with Secretary of the Navy James Forrestal over the naval oil reserves. His subcommittee demanded some papers that the secretary

---

[35] Lou and Neta Stockstill, interview with the author, Indiatlantic, FL, 21 June 2001; Roger Vinson Sheffield, interview with the author, Jekyll Island, GA, 22 November 2001.

[36] *Atlanta Constitution*, 3 April 1965, 1, 5; 5 April 1965, 4; Louis R. Stockstill, "'Uncle Carl' Couldn't Be There," *Journal of the Armed Forces* 102 (10 April 1965): 31.

refused to provide. Johnson said he worked up quite a head of steam about the matter and drafted a stiff letter threatening to subpoena the records and air the issue in public. Chairman Vinson endorsed the letter, but told Johnson he wanted to keep it on his desk overnight. The next morning, Vinson called Johnson before he was out of bed and told him to get down to his office. When he arrived, the chairman said, "Here are the papers you wanted." They were spread out in array on the chairman's desk. Johnson was dumbfounded. "Where did you get them," he asked? Vinson explained: "I just stopped off at the Secretary's office at 7 o'clock this morning on the way to work and picked them up." The wise old chairman added, "There are all kinds of ways of doing these things."[37]

That evening President and Mrs. Johnson held a full-dress reception for Vinson at the White House. Arranged at the last minute, some 200 guests—including all of the House leadership—attended. As the president quickly moved from room to room shaking every hand, the guest of honor stood with Lady Bird in a two-person reception line in the Blue Room, looking unimpressed but pleased by all the music and glitter.[38] Vinson had a wonderful time in Washington, but he had to get back to Georgia because his sister Mabel was in critical condition. The widow of Charles Stone of Griffin, Mabel had been in poor health for six years. She survived this crisis, but died six months later.[39]

When Governor Sanders and the legislature reapportioned the congressional districts, they obliterated Vinson's old Sixth District and placed Baldwin County in Robert Stephens' Tenth District. Representative Stephens graciously allowed Vinson the use of his office in the Milledgeville Post Office Building. Regimented even in retirement, Vinson habitually went to the office each morning and kept Stephens' secretary, Mrs. Clyde Peddy, busy with his correspondence.

---

[37] Ibid.; Lou and Neta Stockstill, interview with the author; Remarks at the Dedication of the Carl Vinson Hearing Room, 2 April 1965, Public Papers, LBJ Library.

[38] *Atlanta Constitution*, 5 April 1965, 4.

[39] *Atlanta Journal and Constitution*, 31 October 1965, 52; Carl Vinson to Neta Stockstill, 8 April, 5 November, 1965, Lou and Neta Stockstill Papers, notebook 1, in author's possession.

Each afternoon he worked on his farm. Among his favorite correspondents were Lou and Neta Stockstill. As the executive secretary to the Armed Services Committee, Neta knew everything the Committee did, and she kept him informed of its actions. Lou, a knowledgeable and experienced journalist, apprised him of other congressional activities. Both had attended the Vinson reception at the White House. Vinson relied on them not only for information but also for favors. He had to know if the plaque for the Vinson Room would be placed on the door or inside the room. Several letters passed between them on the subject. Finally, after Neta sent him photographs of the room, Vinson declared, "It is a magnificent door, and the way the Architect fixed up the plaque designating it the CARL VINSON ROOM is superb."[40] After Neta had thoughtfully sent him pictures of the room dedication, he requested that she get pictures of his reception at the White House. He asked both of them to have his Freedom Medal framed and mentioned the subject in at least seven letters. Pleased with the result, he paid them $56.50 for the framing and hung the medal in his office. Clearly retirement had not diminished his persistence and thoroughness.[41]

Unlike most politicians, Vinson did not actively participate in church affairs and had never belonged to a civic club.[42] But in retirement he remained busy nonetheless. Besides his farm and correspondence, he continued to be actively involved in the development of Milledgeville and the surrounding area, especially the Mary Vinson Library. After he retired, he led a drive to raise money for the library, something he was unwilling to do while still in office.[43] He also had more time to work on the industrial, educational, and financial development of Georgia. Lockheed of Georgia, in Marietta, was then the greatest industrial

---

[40] Carl Vinson to Neta Stockstill, 28 September 1965, Stockstill Papers, notebook 1.

[41] Stockstill Papers, notebook 1.

[42] Why Vinson did not attend church remains a mystery. Without exception, family members and close friends agree that he believed in the Christian doctrine and practiced its tenets, but Vinson never explained to them why he did not attend services.

[43] Carl Vinson to Erwin Sibley, 4 November 1964, Erwin Sibley Papers, September–December 1964 folder.

enterprise in the state, employing 20,000. "Except for you," his friend John Sibley wrote him, "Georgia could not now be enjoying the prosperity that this company is bringing to the state. We want to keep that prosperity from moving to the West Coast or to some other place where it should not be."[44] Sibley urged Vinson to tour the Lockheed plant with him, which he did on 23 April 1965.[45]

Although Vinson had much to do in Milledgeville, he missed the Sneads, who had been his "family" for so many years. He telephoned Tillman and Molly frequently, urging them to move to Milledgeville and live in his house on Montgomery Street. At first, they rejected his overtures because they were happily settled in their Primrose Street home, which was newly redecorated, with a brand new kitchen that Molly dearly loved. Moreover, all four of the Sneads had many friends and good neighbors that they were reluctant to leave, and Tillman was happy attending Georgetown Prep. But, after only a few months of separation, they decided to move in order to reunite the family.[46]

Vinson was so pleased when he learned that the Snead family had decided to move to Georgia that he told everybody he saw in Milledgeville, "My family is coming home."[47] Till, Molly, Tillman, and Carl had barely arrived in Georgia, when Molly had a physical crisis. She had to have emergency aortic aneurysm surgery. The surgery was performed at the Methodist Hospital in Houston, Texas, by Dr. Michael DeBakey, a renowned specialist, who also did a carotid endarterectomy. Although Molly survived the complicated surgeries, she remained hospitalized for weeks. When she was strong enough to travel, Till, who had been with her in Houston throughout the ordeal, took her to Macon, where they stayed with family while she recuperated. While their parents were away, Carl stayed with his grandmother and aunt in Macon, and Tillman lived with Vinson at the farm. When the school year began on 8

---

[44] John A. Sibley to Carl Vinson, 12 April 1965, John Sibley Papers, box 362.

[45] Carl Vinson to John Sibley, 16 April 1965, John Sibley to Carl Vinson, 7 May 1965, John Sibley Papers, box 362.

[46] Karen Snead to the author, 16 May 2003.

[47] Tillman and Karen Snead, interview with the author.

September, fourteen-year-old Tillman entered the tenth grade at Georgia Military College. He lived by himself in a room at the Baldwin Hotel near the Georgia Military College campus during the week and spent the weekends with Vinson at the farm until the family was reunited. In the meantime, Vinson was busy modernizing his house at 421 Montgomery Street for the Sneads. By the end of September 1965, all of the work had been completed, and the Sneads moved in. The house had been air conditioned, re-carpeted, and a new stove and refrigerator had been installed. Molly had recovered as well as could be expected but still was unable to do much, so Mrs. Ruby Nelson, a young, dignified woman of proud carriage, was hired as a full-time maid to ease her workload.[48] In January Vinson wrote Neta Stockstill that the Sneads were doing well and "have the old house looking very pretty and have just about settled down to enjoy living in Milledgeville."[49]

Uncle Carl continued to live in his farmhouse, but he went to town nearly every day and spent much time with the Sneads. He ate supper with them every night Monday through Friday, but fixed his own meals on Saturdays and Sundays. Young Tillman remembers that either he or his father would drive to the farm and bring Vinson to supper, which he wanted served promptly at 5:30. For supper he always wore a suit and suspenders. In fact, the only time he did not wear a suit was at night when he watered the plants in his yard. For that chore, he took off his coat and tie. After supper, he went out on the porch and cut a plug of tobacco. When he had finished his chew, he went in the house and announced that he was ready to go. He spoke with such authority that everybody automatically did what he said without question. He timed his leaving so that he could watch the news with Walter Cronkite, one of the few television programs he watched regularly.[50]

On Saturday, 8 January 1966 a portrait of Mary Vinson was presented to the Mary Vinson Memorial Library. The portrait, done by

---

[48] Carl Vinson to Neta Stockstill, 13 July, 24 September, 29 September 1965, Stockstill Papers, notebook 1; Tillman and Karen Snead to the author, 9 April 2003.

[49] Ibid., 24 January 1966.

[50] Tillman and Karen Snead, interview with the author.

Orlando Lagman of Washington, DC., had been commissioned by the
Naval Reserve Association. The mayor of Milledgeville attended the
ceremony, as did seventy-five members of the Naval Reserve
Association, including its president who came all the way from Seattle,
Washington. Mrs. Aurelia Lawrence Herndon, a close personal friend of
Mrs. Vinson, had the honor of unveiling the portrait. Vinson was pleased
with the portrait and described the ceremony as "a great affair for which
I shall always be most grateful."[51]

When Vinson received an honorary doctor of laws degree from
Emory University in Atlanta on 25 January 1965, he may have assumed
that that was the last major honor he would ever receive.[52] If so, he was
mistaken, for more honors were in store for him. In June 1966 he
received a letter informing him that the Association of Graduates of the
United States Military Academy had selected him to receive the
prestigious Sylvanus Thayer Medal. The letter explained that the award
had been presented each year since 1958 to a citizen whose record of
service to his country, accomplishments in the national interest, and
manner of achievement exemplify outstanding devotion to the principles
expressed in the motto of West Point: "Duty, Honor, Country." Among
the previous recipients were Harvard president Dr. James B. Conant,
General of the Army Douglas MacArthur, and President Dwight D.
Eisenhower. This was the first time the award had been granted to a
legislator.[53]

When the eighty-two-year-old Vinson arrived at West Point for the
ceremony on 10 September he was greeted by Lou and Neta Stockstill,
Sam Nunn, and other family members. Dignitaries attending the
ceremony included Mendel Rivers, chairman of the House Armed
Services Committee; General Earle G. Wheeler, chairman of the Joint
Chiefs of Staff; and Stanley R. Resor, secretary of the army. About 500
graduates also were on hand to review the 3,000 cadets. In his speech

---

[51] *Union-Recorder*, 13 January 1966, 1; Carl Vinson to Neta Stockstill, 24
January 1966, Stockstill Papers, notebook 1.

[52] *Atlanta Constitution*, 26 January 1965, 3.

[53] C. V. R. Schuyler to Carl Vinson, 7 June 1966, Vinson Scrapbooks,
book 1963–1965.

delivered in the cadet dining room, the old chairman observed that the true test of any man is "to be able to combine humility with pride, to be wisely aggressive without being dogmatic, to be firm without being stubborn, to be capable of making decisions without being rash, to accept criticism without resenting it, to be compassionate without being weak, to inspire others and at the same time be inspired by others, and to be loyal not only to those whom he serves but to those who serve under him." The congressman himself had met all of the tests he presented to the cadets.[54]

Vinson had thoroughly enjoyed the honor as well as the pleasure of seeing old friends. He described the event as "the zenith of my life." He also enjoyed spending Sunday with Mendel and Mrs. Rivers in their beautiful home in Washington. Although Vinson had displayed remarkable stamina for an octogenarian, the trip, no matter how pleasant, had been a strain on him. "The event at West Point closed my book of public life," he wrote Neta Stockstill. "I am not going to accept any more invitations or receive any more awards."[55]

Despite his resolve, Vinson could not prevent more honors from coming his way. Three months later, the highest mountain in Antarctica, a 16,860-foot peak scaled by a ten-member team, was named Vinson Massif in his honor.[56] In July 1967 the sixty-four counties of Central Georgia held a rally and dinner in the Carl Vinson Armory in Milledgeville. Governor Lester Maddox, Senator Herman Talmadge, and State Party Chairman James Gray, the principal speakers at the $25-a-plate dinner, lavished praise upon Vinson, the guest of honor. Vinson, who brought Till, Molly, his "grandsons," and his secretary Mrs. Clyde Peddy to the affair, thoroughly enjoyed the evening. He later wrote Neta

---

[54] *Atlanta Journal and Constitution*, 11 September 1966, 24; Louis Stockstill, "The Nation Is Grateful," *Journal of the Armed Forces* 104 (17 September 1966): 13; Vinson Speech, 10 September 1966, Vinson Scrapbooks, book 1963–1965.

[55] Carl Vinson to Neta Stockstill, 14 September 1966, Stockstill Papers, notebook 1; Lou Stockstill, telephone interview with the author, Indiatlantic, FL, 9 January 2003.

[56] *Atlanta Journal*, 26 December 1966, A13.

Stockstill that it was a "successful rally" and showed that "WE DEMOCRATS are on the ball down here!"[57]

On 3 January 1968 Governor Maddox, Mendel Rivers, and other dignitaries came to Milledgeville for the groundbreaking ceremony for the $870,000, 150-bed Georgia War Veterans Home to be named for Vinson. Taking a page from Lyndon Johnson's book, Chairman Rivers said, "Everything I know or everything I have learned in Washington about the military operation of our nation, I learned at the feet of Carl Vinson."[58]

On 2 March 1968 President Johnson came to Marietta, Georgia, to view the roll-out of the Lockheed C-5A "Galaxy," described as the world's largest airplane. The president led a standing ovation for Vinson when he introduced the congressman to the crowd. Then, in the text of his speech, Johnson, acknowledging Vinson as "my dear, beloved former chairman," said:

> Since Franklin D. Roosevelt, four Presidents have kept America's course firm. All of these four Presidents have been supported every step of the way by two great sons of Georgia—Dick Russell and Carl Vinson.
>
> Senator Talmadge and the other members of the Georgia delegation, Chairman Rivers and the other members of the Armed Services Committee, Senator Monroney and the other members of the Senate, have all contributed valiantly and generously to our achievement.
>
> But the lead horses—the ones that we all saluted, the ones we all listened to, the ones we all asked for permission to speak—there sits one of them (Carl Vinson) and the other one is thinking of us today (Dick Russell).[59]

---

[57] Clyde Peddy to Neta Stockstill, 7 July 1967, Carl Vinson to Neta Stockstill, 27 July 1967, Stockstill Papers, notebook 1.

[58] *Atlanta Journal*, 4 January 1968; *Veteran's Bulletin* (January 1968), Erwin Sibley Papers, newspaper clipping file.

[59] Susan Landrum, "Carl Vinson: A Study in Military Preparedness" (master's thesis, Emory University, 1968) 203–204.

Vinson maintained his regular schedule of activities, going to the office in the mornings, socializing with friends in Milledgeville, and working on the farm in the afternoon. He wrote Lou Stockstill that he was "getting along nicely and keeping very busy on the farm." He had a "splendid vegetable garden" in 1967, and Molly had canned and frozen quite a supply of vegetables for winter use.[60] Curious about activities on Capitol Hill, he insisted that Lou and Neta Stockstill keep him fully informed of the details of the Armed Service Committee. From time to time they sent him reports of bills being discussed. On the whole, he was quite pleased by the performance of his old committee. "I have been keeping up with the bills that have been reported by the Committee," he wrote Neta Stockstill in August 1967, "and I am proud of the outstanding manner the Armed Services Committee has met its responsibilities."[61]

An avid reader all his life, Vinson experienced vision problems, which necessitated cataract surgery on 20 March 1968. Despite some complications that kept him hospitalized at the Macon Hospital for two weeks, the surgery was successful. A month after the surgery, he wrote, "I am getting along fine and am able to see out of that eye, even without glasses, and when I get my new glasses next week I know I will be able to see as well as ever." Until he had fully recovered, he stayed in town with the Sneads, for he realized, "I still have to be very careful."[62]

In the presidential campaign of 1968, Vinson supported the Democratic ticket of Hubert Humphrey and Edmund Muskie with his usual enthusiasm. He served as honorary chairman of the Citizens for Humphrey-Muskie in Georgia, but made no campaign speeches.[63] On 30 October, as the election was reaching its final stage, Till Snead drove Vinson, Molly, and young Carl to McLean, Virginia, for the dedication of the laying of the cornerstone of Vinson Hall, a retirement home for

---

[60] Carl Vinson to Louis Stockstill, 10 July 1967, Stockstill Papers, notebook 1.

[61] Carl Vinson to Neta Stockstill, 11 August 1967, Stockstill Papers, notebook 1.

[62] Ibid., 17 April 1968; *Atlanta Constitution*, 21 March 1968, 9; *Union-Recorder*, 28 March 1968, 1, 11 April 1968, 1.

[63] *Atlanta Constitution*, 15 October 1968, 8.

widows of navy, marine corps, and coast guard personnel. Seeing the desperate need for such a home in the Washington, DC area, a blue ribbon commission of active and retired military leaders had raised funds for the $5.5 million structure. The project had been in the works for several years, and Vinson, who had supported it in Congress, was proud to have his name attached to it.[64]

Vinson had barely returned home when President Johnson summoned him to Washington again. This time he, along with Molly and young Carl, flew from Warner Robins to Andrews Air Force Base, where a limousine met them and carried them to the Mayflower Hotel. Vinson arrived in Washington on Saturday, 16 November, rested on Sunday, and went to the White House on Monday afternoon. There, President and Mrs. Johnson had gathered 130 top military officials and members of Congress for a nostalgic party to celebrate Carl Vinson's eighty-fifth birthday. Standing at the podium in the White House state dining room, the president presented Vinson a silver cup from "Lady Bird and Lyndon Johnson," which the chief executive said with a grin could be used "for eggnog, mint juleps—or pencils on your desk." "I'll find plenty of use for it," Vinson replied.

For the occasion, the White House chef produced a huge three-layer cake decorated with four stars and two anchors and an inscription, "Happy Birthday, Admiral." The eight candles on the cake were blown out by eight-year-old Carl William Snead. In thanking the "selected guests" for coming, President Johnson stated:

> For half a century, this great and good man graced the Congress of the United States. Through our birth pangs as a global power, through two terrible World Wars, through isolationism and a cold war, through the momentous first years of the atomic age, he stood like a towering rock, lending his voice and his vision to the cause of national responsibility. His voice was not always heeded, but his vision was never faulty.

---

[64] *Atlanta Journal*, 2 November 1968, Atlanta Journal-Constitution Office; *Congressional Record*, 88th Cong., 2d sess., 28 September 1964, 23010–11; Carl Vinson to Neta Stockstill, 22 October 1968, Stockstill Papers, notebook 1.

And if the Congress is, as I believe it is, the combined product of those who have served in it since it was founded, then Carl Vinson will surely go down in history as one of those who added more honor to that body than he took from it. He belongs with the Clays, the Websters, the Calhouns, and the Rayburns as a legislative giant. And he is a living legend in Georgia, the State he represented so ably and well.

On a more personal note, I think everyone here knows the debt that I owe to Carl Vinson. He was my Chairman, my tutor, and my friend. And in more recent times, he has advised me, he has bolstered me, and he has stood by me when it was not always the most popular thing to do. Now I could go on and on, singing his praises, but if there is anything I learned from Carl Vinson, it is brevity.

So, with your leave, Mr. Chairman, I'll just make one more point. Power and greatness seldom carry with them the guarantee of affection. But Carl Vinson was the exception. For more than 30 years, he was not only one of the most powerful men in Washington, but one of the most beloved men as well. And we are here today to prove it. Happy birthday, Carl, and God bless you. Maybe we can all make a pilgrimage to Milledgeville 5 years from now to celebrate your 90th birthday. Or maybe we'll rent D. C. Stadium and really do it up right.[65]

The kindly old man had enjoyed many birthday parties, but never anything like this one. He was overwhelmed with emotion.

---

[65] Remarks at a Party Marking the 85th Birthday of Former Representative Carl Vinson, 18 November 1968, Public Papers, LBJ Library; *Atlanta Constitution*, 19 November 1968, 1.

15

The Last Years

*It's not so important how long a man lives but what
he does with his time.*

Carl Vinson, 1964

During his last years in Congress and his first years in retirement, Vinson
had received a profusion of political, military, and Georgia honors, and
more awards kept coming. A month after his wonderful eighty-fifth
birthday party at the White House, he was at the Navy Supply Corps
School in Athens, Georgia, for the dedication of Carl Vinson Park. Since
Vinson had been responsible for securing funds to establish the first
permanent home for the navy's school for training newly commissioned
supply corps officers, the navy dedicated the thirty existing and forty-two
planned housing units to him. A large granite marker identified the
housing area as Carl Vinson Park. Mendel Rivers, Vinson's successor as
chairman of the House Armed Services Committee, was the principal
speaker, and Admiral Thomas H. Moorer, chief of Naval Operations, and
Representative Robert Stephens of the Tenth District were featured
guests.[1]

The following April, Mendel Rivers was back in Georgia to
dedicate the Carl Vinson Building, a 150-bed facility at the Georgia State
War Veterans Home in Milledgeville. In addition to Rivers, several other
members of Congress, several members of the Georgia legislature, and

---

[1] *Atlanta Constitution*, 20 December 1968, 3.

Governor Lester Maddox participated in the ceremony. Visibly moved by the praise lavished upon him, Vinson wiped away a tear when he received a standing ovation from the 500 guests in attendance.[2]

Although retired for several years, Vinson continued to give the Armed Services Committee the benefit of his advice and counsel. He advised Rivers not to abolish the draft law and by all means to "lay down a very strong shipbuilding program." After learning that Rivers had included $2,900,000 for the supply school in Athens, he wrote Neta Stockstill that Mendel is "making an outstanding record."[3] Convinced that Rivers had done an excellent job as chairman, he grieved when his friend died on 28 December 1970. Despite his age and physical limitations, Vinson traveled to South Carolina to attend the funeral, the largest one he had ever attended.[4]

Edward Hébert of Louisiana succeeded Rivers as chairman, and Vinson enjoyed the same cordial relationship with him that he had had with Rivers. Having known Hébert for many years, Vinson assured Neta Stockstill that "Working with Eddie is going to be a genuine pleasure." By May, Vinson had concluded that Hébert "is making a great chairman." Again, in August he wrote, "Eddie is making an outstanding chairman."[5] Vinson wanted to attend the unveiling of Hébert's portrait in the Armed Services Committee Hearing Room, but his physical condition prevented him from making the trip. "Time," he wrote Hébert, "is exacting its toll of my physical and mental health." He explained to his friend that his infirmities were increasing daily. He had completely lost the hearing in his left ear and could barely hear telephone conversations in his right ear, even with "boosters" installed in the telephone. He continued: "My locomotion is so sluggish I drag my feet and wobble from side to side with fear and apprehension constantly in my mind of falling. My vision is such that I cannot read the fine print of

---

[2] Ibid., 30 April 1969, 11; *Union-Recorder*, 1 May 1969, 1.
[3] Carl Vinson to Neta Stockstill, 8 January 1969, 23 July 1969, Stockstill Papers, notebook 2, in author's possession.
[4] Ibid., 5 January 1971.
[5] Ibid., 15 March 1971, 17 May 1971, 6 August 1971.

the newspapers even with a powerful hand-glass. And to cap the climax of my physical deterioration, my arteries are becoming sluggish."[6]

Taking a keen interest in Vinson Hall in McLean, Virginia, Vinson first offered the retirement home several books on World War II, including the fifteen volumes of Samuel Eliot Morison's *History of the United States Naval Operations in World War II*, as well as a complete set of *Harvard Classics*, and Emerson's *Essays*. Then he decided to donate all of his Navy and Marine Corps plaques and awards to the retirement home, providing they would be properly displayed. Although it took more than two years, a dozen letters, and numerous visits to the home by Lou and Neta Stockstill, Tillman Snead, and others, the plaques, at last, were suitably displayed there. The ones Vinson Hall could not use were given to the Mary Vinson Library in Milledgeville.[7]

In typically grandfatherly fashion, Vinson enjoyed the company of his "grandsons." Tillman had spent much time with him and was a great help in working on the farm. In the summer of 1971, when Tillman secured a one-month position at the House of Representatives Post Office, his mother and younger brother accompanied him to Washington and spent a few days with friends there. Vinson made arrangements for Carl to tour the Capitol, the Bureau of Engraving, and the Smithsonian. He particularly wanted him to see Lindbergh's plane, the moon exhibits, and Theodore Roosevelt's collection of wild animals. The Sneads had a pleasant experience in Washington, and the highlight of the trip—according to Vinson—was a visit to Vinson Hall. Young Carl had earned a trophy for playing a fourteen-game baseball schedule that summer, and for his eleventh birthday on 26 July 1971, Vinson gave him a motorbike so that he could ride over the fields at the farm. Because of the turmoil caused by integration at the public school in Milledgeville, his parents decided to send Carl to a private school in Eatonton twenty-

---

[6] Carl Vinson to F. Edward Hébert, 26 July 1971, Stockstill Papers, notebook 2.

[7] Carl Vinson to Neta Stockstill, 20 May, 23 July, 6 August, 4 September, 15 September 1969, 8 June 1970, 26 January, 8 February, 15 March, 17 May, 6 August, 27 August, 14 September, 30 September 1971, Stockstill Papers, notebook 2.

five miles away the next year, where they believed he would receive a better education. Vinson supported their decision, wanting what was best for Carl.[8]

During the summer of 1971, a crew from the University of Georgia filmed and recorded Vinson at his office, on the farm, and in the Mary Vinson Memorial Library for a documentary of his career to be shown on Georgia Public Television. Vinson traveled to Athens early in October to review all the finished portions and fill in whatever was needed to complete the program. That same evening, Vinson and Representative Jack Flynt received the Blue Key award at a dinner in Athens. Representative Wilbur Mills was the featured speaker. The film, which was the first in a series on the lives of prominent Georgians, was shown on public television on 3 April 1972. Vinson sent a copy of it to the House Armed Services Committee, which delayed a scheduled closed door hearing on Vietnam so that the members could view it.[9]

As 1972 began Vinson wrote Neta Stockstill that he was still "feeling fine and in good physical condition" for a person of his age. But, since he could no longer walk all over his farm as he once could, he had decided to sell his cattle and get completely out of the business. When he informed Lou and Neta Stockstill that he was getting out of the "ranching" business, they wondered what he would get into next. "We know you won't be idle!"[10] Their assumption was correct, as Vinson was extremely active throughout 1972. On 11 March Chairman Eddie Hébert and three staff members of the Armed Services Committee visited him at the farm. They literally "dropped in" on him, as they arrived in a helicopter that landed in his pasture. After a "session" at the farm, they lunched with Molly in town and returned to the farm for another "session." Before his guests departed for Warner Robins and Washington, Vinson had the opportunity to express his views on many current issues, including draft dodgers living in Canada and Europe.

---

[8] Ibid., 6 August 1971; 27 August 1971.

[9] Ibid., 29 March 1972, notebook 3; *Atlanta Constitution*, 17 August 1972, A23; *Union-Recorder*, 30 March 1972, 1.

[10] Carl Vinson to Neta Stockstill, 1 February 1972, Neta Stockstill to Carl Vinson, 16 February 1972, Stockstill Papers, notebook 3.

Opposed to amnesty, he believed that instead of bringing them back, "We should thank ourselves that such type people are not in our country." The old chairman thoroughly enjoyed the visit with his friends.[11] Apparently Vinson had urged Hébert to be more forceful, because a few days after the visit, Neta Stockstill wrote him that Hébert had taken his advice. "He summarily adjourned a Committee meeting yesterday because the army had not supplied the committee with certain information we had requested. That will put all the services on notice."[12]

The next week, Vinson entertained Michael West, a history student from Ohio State University, who was doing research for a master's thesis on Vinson's stewardship of the Naval Affairs Committee. Vinson cooperated fully and urged him to consult Lou and Neta Stockstill as well as staff members of the Armed Services Committee. West continued his research, and in 1980 completed an excellent dissertation titled "Laying the Legislative Foundation: The House Naval Affairs Committee and the Construction of the Treaty Navy, 1926–1934."[13]

Early in 1972 Tillman Snead announced his engagement to Karen Bodkin, a vivacious brunette from Jacksonville, Florida. Karen was a junior at Georgia College in Milledgeville, and Tillman was completing his senior year there. Since Tillman was scheduled to receive his degree on 3 June, the wedding was planned for 11 June.[14] Before Tillman and Karen announced their plans, Vinson had already decided that they should be married. When they drove to the farm and informed Vinson that they were engaged, he responded, "Wonderful. The sooner you two get married the better." After the marriage, Vinson asked Karen what her

---

[11] Carl Vinson to Neta Stockstill, 25 February 1972, 15 March 1972, Stockstill Papers, notebook 3.

[12] Neta Stockstill to Carl Vinson, 17 March 1972, Stockstill Papers, notebook 3. Hébert, along with the secretary of the navy and the chief of naval operations, also "dropped in" again on 21 November 1972 as a belated birthday surprise for Vinson's eighty-ninth birthday. *Union-Recorder,* 22 November 1972.

[13] Carl Vinson to Neta Stockstill, 22 March 1972, Stockstill Papers, notebook 3.

[14] *Union-Recorder*, 23 March 1972, 9; Tillman and Karen Snead interview with the author, Dale City VA, 8 June 2001.

favorite bush was. She told him that she loved gardenias. A week later, he invited the newlyweds to his farm. As soon as they passed the gorgeous crepe myrtles that lined his drive, they noticed that he had planted ten mature gardenias in front of his house, a thoughtful gesture that Karen much appreciated.[15]

While Molly was getting her house in order and tending to the details of the wedding, Vinson radically altered the appearance of his farm house. He installed Old English oak paneling on all his walls and re-carpeted the entire house. The den and the hall received a rich burgundy carpet, and the rest of the house was carpeted in green. He later air conditioned the house, but rarely allowed the temperature to fall below seventy-five degrees. He improved the house so that when Tillman occupied it, "He will be able to enjoy it as much as I will in my old age."[16]

Karen's family came to Milledgeville and made a favorable impression on Vinson, who took everyone to the Country Club for dinner so that Molly would not have to cook on Easter Sunday. Mrs. Peddy and several local families had teas and bridal parties for Karen. Although reared in the Protestant faith, Karen converted to the Roman Catholic faith of her husband. The wedding took place in the Sacred Heart Catholic Church, in Milledgeville, and a reception followed at Till and Molly's home. After the wedding and honeymoon, Tillman and Karen moved into a small house in Milledgeville. Three weeks after his marriage, Tillman received his draft notice ordering him to report for his induction physical in August. Until beginning his two-year military obligation, he helped Vinson on the farm. After Tillman departed for Fort Jackson, he called Karen and told her that the first thing the army did was what Delilah did to Samson. Vinson, no fan of long hair, remarked, "Even if it was shaved, it would be an improvement."[17]

---

[15] Tillman and Karen Snead, interview with the author.

[16] Carl Vinson to Neta Stockstill, 22 March 1972, 4 April 1972, Stockstill Papers, notebook 3.

[17] Ibid., 4 April 1972, 28 August 1972, 5 October 1972; *Union-Recorder*, 4 May 1972, 9; 18 May 1972, 9; 25 May 1972, 12–13; 1 June 1972, 10; 22 June 1972, 7; Tillman Snead to the author, 9 April 2003.

Uncle Carl was quite impressed with Karen. Shortly after meeting her, he wrote Neta Stockstill, "She is a charming young lady and we are most pleased to have her in the family." Six months later, he commented, "She is a lovely young girl and is making Tillman a fine wife."[18] The feeling was mutual, and Karen's affection for Vinson increased over the years. Upon first meeting Tillman's "grandpa," she found him to be a "genteel, well-spoken, well-mannered, kind, stately" gentleman with a "uniquely charming Southern accent." Over time, she learned that he was "confident; grounded; knew right from wrong and always stuck to the right; loved solitude and a good book; loved nature; loved a good meal; loved the Sneads; rarely talked about the past, only the present and the future; and never boasted or bragged about any of his accomplishments."[19]

Although not demonstrative by nature, Vinson had deep affection for all of his family and thoroughly enjoyed family gatherings at Thanksgiving. But he had special interest in, and affection for, two of his nephews—Sam Nunn and Wilbur Vinson, Jr. One excelled in the political arena and the other had an outstanding career in the military—occupations that Vinson was keenly interested in. After earning an undergraduate degree and a law degree from Emory University, Nunn worked for a year as a special counsel for the House Armed Services Committee. A native of Houston County, he practiced law in Perry and Warner Robins and followed his father's footsteps by entering the Georgia legislature in 1969. After serving two terms, he decided to run for a seat in the United States Senate in 1972. Following the death of Senator Russell on 21 January 1971, Governor Jimmy Carter had appointed David Gambrell, an Atlanta lawyer with no previous political experience, to succeed him. Gambrell sought election to the unexpired portion of Russell's term and to a full six-year term, as did former Governor Ernest Vandiver, extreme segregationist J. B. Stoner, flamboyant civil rights activist Hosea Williams, and ten other candidates. With little name recognition, Nunn was a decided underdog in a field of

---

[18] Carl Vinson to Neta Stockstill, 4 April 1972, 28 August 1972, Stockstill Papers, notebook 3.

[19] Karen Snead to the author, 16 May 2003.

fifteen. Vinson told him he was a "damn fool" to run for the Senate. He thought Nunn should first run for a seat in the House, but Nunn had concluded that local conditions militated against his making a successful race for the House.[20]

Despite any reservations he may have had about the outcome, Vinson backed his great-nephew with enthusiasm. Vinson was among the 1,500 supporters at Perry on 15 March when Nunn officially announced his candidacy. The local community raised $50,000 for Nunn, and Vinson personally contributed $500.[21] Vinson was not able to travel around the state campaigning for Nunn, but his contacts and selected telephone calls proved invaluable. Many political observers were surprised when Nunn edged out Vandiver for second place behind Gambrell in the 8 August primary election. Gambrell won 31.4 percent of the vote to Nunn's 23.1 percent, but in the run-off three weeks later, Nunn defeated the incumbent Senator, carrying 54 percent of the vote.[22]

Although Nunn still faced a Republican opponent, Fletcher Thompson, in November, he was so confident of victory that he went to Washington to lobby for a seat on the Senate Armed Services Committee. Since Vinson still knew many of the key senators, he, along with Tillman Snead, accompanied his great-nephew. When their overnight train arrived at Union Station, a big black limousine awaited them, along with several television reporters. Vinson and Snead gladly accepted the ride arranged by some of Nunn's well-meaning friends, but candidate Nunn, fearing political fall-out from riding in a limousine, waved goodbye and jogged to the Capitol. Nunn and Vinson called on Senators John Stennis of Mississippi, Robert Byrd of West Virginia, Russell Long of Louisiana, Herman Talmadge of Georgia, and Representative Hébert, chairman of the House Armed Services

---

[20] Georgia, Department of Archives and History, *Georgia Official and Statistical Register, 1971–1972*, 1617–40; Sam Nunn, interview with the author, Atlanta, GA, 4 April 2001; Robert Jennings, Sr., telephone interview with the author, Gainesville, GA, 23 August 2001.

[21] Carl Vinson to Neta Stockstill, 22 March 1972, Stockstill Papers, notebook 3.

[22] *Georgia Official and Statistical Register, 1971–1972*, 1617–40, 1738–45; Sam Nunn, interview with the author.

Committee. After spending two pleasant nights in Washington, Vinson and Tillman Snead returned home by train, while Nunn remained in Washington a few more days to strengthen his contacts.[23] Until the November general election, Vinson devoted his time and energy to Nunn's campaign, even traveling to Augusta on his behalf. "I don't know how long I can hold out," he wrote Neta Stockstill, "but I hope the results will be beneficial to him." Uncle Carl was so delighted when his great-nephew trounced Thompson and secured the desired seat on the Senate Armed Services Committee that he made plans to attend the swearing in ceremony. He later canceled his reservation, explaining, "When a man is as old as I am he should curtail all travel which is not absolutely necessary, and stay out of the cold weather, snow and rain."[24]

Carl Vinson's younger brother, Wilbur, had had a successful career in the army and saw extensive combat in both world wars. Ending his service with the rank of colonel, he retired to an Atlanta home designed by famed architect Neel Reid. His son, Wilbur Jr., known as "Vin," followed in his father's footsteps. After graduation from West Point in 1945, he married Margaret Ann Benedict, the daughter of General Jay Benedict, who had served as superintendent of West Point from 1938 through 1940. They had four children, two boys and two girls. An officer of exceptional ability, Vin rose through the ranks quickly. In the Korean War he served with the field artillery of the First Cavalry Division. He earned a master's degree in mechanical engineering at the University of Southern California in 1962 and was graduated from the National War College in Washington in 1966. In Vietnam he was a battalion commander and deputy commander of artillery with the First Air Cavalry Division.[25]

---

[23] Sam Nunn, interview with the author; Neta Stockstill to Carl Vinson,. 30 August 1972, Carl Vinson to Neta Stockstill, 21 September 1972, Stockstill Papers, notebook 3; Tillman Snead to the author, 9 April 2003.

[24] *Georgia Official and Statistical Register,. 1971–1972*, 1844–45; Carl Vinson to Neta Stockstill, 21 September, 13 December 1972, Stockstill Papers, notebook 3.

[25] Ed and Betty Vinson, interview with the author, Atlanta, GA, 7 August 2001; Margaret Benedict Vinson Hallgren, telephone interview with the author, Alexandria, VA, 23 January 2003; *Washington Post*, 2 April 1979, C4.

When Vin's son, John, was a student at the University of Virginia, Uncle Carl used his influence with Representative Hébert to get him a summer job in 1971 and in 1972. With his usual thoroughness, Vinson wrote Neta Stockstill numerous letters to make sure that John was suitably placed.[26] In August 1972 Vin, then a brigadier general, drove his family, including his mother and father, to Milledgeville to visit Uncle Carl. Over lunch at the Holiday Inn, they discussed the documentary film on the life of Vinson, which they had recently viewed. John thanked Uncle Carl for the summer job and told him how much he had enjoyed working at the House Post Office.[27] On 22 December Vinson began seeking another three-month job for John at the House Post Office for the summer of 1973. In his next letter to Neta Stockstill, on 4 January 1973, he added that John's sister, Meg, a freshman at the University of Virginia, also was looking for a summer job. In each of his next four letters to Neta, he inquired about the status of their jobs.[28] His efforts proved unnecessary, however, for General Vinson received command of the U.S. Army Southern European Task Force headquartered in Vicenza, Italy, and an element of NATO. He left for Italy on 1 April with Margaret and the two younger children; John and Meg joined them when the spring semester ended.[29] "I have two fine nephews—General Vinson and Senator Nunn," Vinson wrote, and he was extremely proud of both of them.[30]

As Vinson expected, Nunn became an exceptional political leader, serving twenty-four years in the Senate. Vin's career, on the other hand, came to an early tragic end. After completing his tour in Italy, he became deputy chief of staff for Combat Developments at the U.S. Army Training and Doctrine Command at Ft. Monroe, Virginia. In 1977 he was transferred to the Pentagon as assistant deputy chief of staff for Army Research, Development and Acquisition. At a conference in Australia in

---

[26] Carl Vinson to Neta Stockstill, 15 March, 22 March, 29 March, 4 April, 30 May, 30 June, 14 August, 28 August 1972, Stockstill Papers, notebook 3.

[27] Ibid., 28 August 1972.

[28] Ibid., 22 December 1972, 4 January, 8 January, 17 January, 31 January, 8 February 1973.

[29] Ibid., 22 February 1973.

[30] Ibid., 12 April 1973.

October 1978, he began to experience physical problems. A few weeks later, when he had his annual physical examination at Walter Reed Hospital, the doctors discovered that he had leukemia. With periodic treatments, he was able to remain on duty until early in 1979. On 28 March, the distinguished career of the major general ended. He died at age fifty-four and was buried in Arlington Cemetery. His military decorations included the Silver Star, the Bronze Star, and the Legion of Merit with Oak Leaf Clusters. He was awarded the Distinguished Service Medal posthumously.[31]

Retirement did not diminish Vinson's concern about national defense, and for many years he continued to express his views, both privately and publicly, to the House Armed Services Committee. A consistent hawk on Vietnam, he believed that once American troops had been committed, the country should do whatever was necessary to achieve a victory.[32] Reports that permissiveness had made inroads in the navy upset him so much that he pointedly advised Chairman Hébert to "return the Navy back to strict military discipline—no long hair, no beards, neat appearance of personnel, saluting officers, and not a slip-shod manner in which respect of discipline seems to be bogged down."[33] Convinced that only strength produces peace, he frequently urged the committee to maintain a strong national defense and to make sure the U.S. Navy was equal to the combined navies of the world.[34] When Vinson learned from newspaper accounts that Representative Otis Pike, a member of the Armed Services Committee, had opposed the sale of government land in Hawaii, he backed him completely. "I think he is absolutely right in not selling any government land at any time."[35] When the energy crisis of 1973 prompted some politicians to demand that the Naval Oil Reserve at Elk Hills, California, be opened for civilian use, he

---

[31] Ed and Betty Vinson, interview with the author; Margaret Hallgren, telephone interview with the author; *Washington Post*, 2 April 1979, C4.

[32] *Union-Recorder*, 6 January 1966, 1; *Atlanta Constitution*, 11 May 1972, A13.

[33] Carl Vinson to Neta Stockstill, 13 December 1972, Stockstill Papers, notebook 3.

[34] Ibid, 13 December 1972, 8 February 1973.

[35] Ibid., 12 April 1973.

told the committee to keep "the Navy oil in the ground at Elk Hills."
When the demand persisted, he wrote Neta Stockstill, "Don't you and
Eddie let the Committee open up Elk Hills. There's no justification to do
so. When Congress declares a declaration of war, then that is time to
open it up, but not during this energy crisis."[36]

The same topic came up when Lou Stockstill interviewed Vinson in
Milledgeville in 1974 for an article for *Air Force Magazine*. The former
chairman, then ninety years old and retired for a decade, stated:

> The Administration wanted to start pumping this oil. They
> wanted to pump out more than we took out during all of WW
> II—as much as 200,000 barrels a day, compared with 64,000
> barrels a day that we used during the war.
>
> Of course, it's up to Congress to decide this issue. But,
> personally, I opposed it and will continue to oppose it. And I
> hope and trust that the Congress will insist on keeping this oil
> right where it is—in the ground.
>
> These reserves were set aside for defense need in wartime.
> If we allow this oil to be used for every kind of emergency, we
> run a grave risk of eventually having no backup supply in some
> future time of national danger.[37]

In that same interview, Vinson praised the work of the Armed
Services Committee since his retirement, opposed a general amnesty for
those who had fled the country or refused to serve in the military, and
expressed doubts about the effectiveness of an all-volunteer armed
services. He also doubted that the Strategic Arms Limitation effort would
produce a significant reduction in military expenses. To make America
less dependent upon foreign nations for energy, he advocated a "new, all-
out effort" utilizing "the magnificent brainpower that is now being
drained out of the space program" in a special task force charged with
finding new answers to our energy needs. The results, he predicted,

---

[36] Ibid., 21 September 1973, 16 January 1974.
[37] Louis R. Stockstill, "The View From Milledgeville, Georgia," *Air Force Magazine* 57 (August 1974): 76.

might amaze us. "Every potential means of improving our energy resources must be thoroughly explored and exploited," he insisted, "not only for the benefit of the military but for the benefit of every citizen of the nation." When asked what advice he had for new members of the Armed Services Committee, he responded: "Never allow geographic concerns, or narrow constituent concerns, or private or political or vested interests, or any such interests to influence your vote on issues of national security. Your main concern, always, must be the welfare of the United States of America."[38]

At Vinson's eighty-fifth birthday party at the White House, President Johnson had invited all of the guests "to join Mrs. Johnson and me at the LBJ Ranch when Carl Vinson reaches his 90th year." From time to time Vinson and Johnson alluded to the planned party, and both men eagerly looked forward to it. When Johnson died on 22 January 1973, some of Vinson's friends in Washington and Georgia stepped in to carry out the late president's wishes. It so happened that Vinson's ninetieth birthday coincided with the one hundredth birthday of the Mercer School of Law, an institution Vinson had been closely associated with since earning a law degree there in 1902. Mercer had awarded Vinson two honorary doctorates, and in 1970 bestowed on him its Distinguished Alumni Award. For his part, Vinson had arranged for Lyndon Johnson to speak at the Mercer Law Day celebration in 1960 and had chaired Mercer's $42.5 million fund drive in 1971.[39] Dr. Rufus Harris, president of Mercer, seeing an opportunity to celebrate the law school centennial with the ninetieth birthday of the institution's most famous alumnus, appointed a committee of distinguished men to organize a joint affair. The results exceeded Harris's expectations and fulfilled Lyndon Johnson's wish of honoring his friend.

On 18 November 1973, the Willingham Chapel of Mercer University was filled to capacity with invited distinguished guests. Seated in the audience with Vinson's relatives and closest friends,

---

[38] Ibid., 72–77.

[39] *Union-Recorder*, 7 May 1970, 1; *The Mercerian* (January 1972) in Carl Vinson File, Georgia Military College, Milledgeville GA; *Atlanta Journal,* 15 November 1973, A21–22.

including Lou and Neta Stockstill, were selected dignitaries from Washington and Georgia. Seated on stage with Vinson, President Harris, and the Dean of the Law School, were Congressman Phil Landrum, Senator Herman Talmadge, Governor Jimmy Carter, and President Richard Nixon.[40] Never before had such an esteemed gathering of political leaders ever assembled in Macon, Georgia. Vinson thanked President Nixon "for redeeming Lyndon Johnson's promise made five years ago—that of giving an old friend a presidential send-off into the tenth decade of his life." After citing the accomplishments of the Walter George School of Law, the lifelong Democrat ended his speech with the following tributes to the Republican president:

> Our President, who honors us all with his presence at this ceremony today, has done as much as any man alive over the past several years to educate all Americans in the paramount necessity of keeping his country second to none in our national defense.
>
> He had also provided strong leadership in opening a new era of negotiation and a new hope for lasting peace among the great powers.
>
> He had the vision it took to visit Peking and Moscow, and the stature it took to look those Communist leaders square in the eye when he got there.
>
> He had the backbone it took to lead America out of the Vietnam War not with disgrace but with honor, and to bring our prisoners of war safely home.
>
> At the same time, he is a President who knows that peace does not mean weakness.
>
> He has stood firm against the pressures to cut our strategic weapons or our troop strength overseas without mutually negotiated cuts on the other side.

---

[40] "Joint Celebration, November 18, 1973," *The Mercerian* (Winter 1974), Carl Vinson File, Special Collections, Mercer University, Macon, GA.

He has insisted that Congress must never send any President to the conference table as head of the second strongest power in the world.[41]

President Nixon closed his remarks with an announcement that shocked everyone, including Vinson. A monument must be built to this man, the president declared, nodding toward Vinson. "Next to his country, and next to his State of Georgia, Carl Vinson loved the Navy most," he continued. "As you know, we have just begun to develop nuclear carriers. The first one was named the *Eisenhower*; the second was named the *Nimitz*, after the great Naval Commander of World War II; the third is just beginning and it will be named the *Carl Vinson*."[42] The president added that he made the announcement with the approval of the chairmen of both the House and Senate Armed Services Committees. After the speech, the president and Secretary of the Navy John Warner presented Vinson a model of the nuclear carrier to be named after him.[43] It was a surprising and fitting tribute to a man often called "the Admiral." Rarely had the navy named a ship for a civilian, and never before had it named a ship for a living person. When receiving tributes, Vinson had become accustomed to saying, "This is the greatest honor ever bestowed upon me." This time, it would be true. "Having the new nuclear-powered aircraft carrier bear my name," he wrote Neta Stockstill, "is the highest honor any living person could have bestowed upon him."[44] On matters of national defense, Vinson had always insisted on bipartisanship. Appropriately, his greatest honor came on his ninetieth birthday from a Republican president.

---

[41] Carl Vinson Address at Mercer, 18 November 1973, Vinson Scrapbooks, book 1973, on loan from Tillman Snead to Georgia College and State University, Milledgeville GA.

[42] "The President's Remarks at Mercer University, November 18, 1973," *Presidential Documents: Richard Nixon, 1973*, 1357–59, Vinson Scrapbooks, book 1973.

[43] "Joint Celebration," *The Mercerian*, 4.

[44] Carl Vinson to Louis Stockstill, 1 December 1973, Stockstill Papers, notebook 3.

A few days after the ceremony, Lou Stockstill wrote Vinson that a number of guests who had not seen him in a long time "expressed amazement that you are still so vigorous and strong, and still so much like the Carl Vinson they always knew."[45] Vinson also appeared vigorous and strong the following September, when he attended the ceremony at Georgia College establishing the Carl Vinson Professorship of Political Science and Public Administration. After laudatory remarks by Congressmen Phil Landrum, Robert Stephens, and W. W. "Bill" Stuckey, University System Chancellor George Simpson turned to Vinson and said, "We are all honored that you will come on campus often as an honorary professor." Vinson walked to the lectern with a firm step. In an unwavering voice he said, "I hope this chair will inspire students to enter a public service career. We are a nation governed by laws, but enactment is just the first step in the government process. The laws must be faithfully executed and when challenged, interpreted. I hope this chair will produce many highly motivated public servants."[46]

Although Vinson enjoyed good health, Molly did not. Some years before, she had undergone surgery in Houston, Texas, for an aortic aneurysm and carotid surgery on the right side of her neck. Ten years later, a similar problem developed on the left side of her neck. When the condition became so critical that her eyesight was impaired, she could delay the surgery no longer. It was performed at St. Joseph's Hospital in Atlanta in April 1974, by a surgeon who had studied under Dr. Michael DeBakey, the famed doctor who had done her earlier surgery in Texas. She came through the operation without any complications. While Molly was hospitalized, Karen, who was then working in Washington, took time off to look after Till and Carl.[47] Molly recovered quickly and resumed her regular routine, but the next summer she was hospitalized

---

[45] Louis Stockstill to Carl Vinson, 27 November 1973, Vinson Scrapbooks, book 1973.

[46] *Atlanta Constitution*, 27 September 1974, A8.

[47] Carl Vinson to Neta Stockstill, 9 April 1974, 15 April 1974, Stockstill Papers, notebook 3.

for a week for gallbladder surgery. Vinson, who worried about her, was happy to report that she came through the surgery "with flying colors."[48]

Ten years after retirement and then in his nineties, Vinson continued to care for his extended family by helping members get employment in Washington. Karen obtained a full-time clerical job with the House Armed Services Committee, great-nephew John Vinson, then a student in law school, received a summer job in the office of Senator Henry "Scoop" Jackson, another graduate of "Vinson College," and "grandson" Carl worked as a page in Congressman Landrum's office.[49] Vinson missed his "grandsons" and made a point of talking to Carl, Tillman, and Karen every Friday night. He continued to live by himself on the farm and spent much of his time outdoors. On good days he could ramble about the rolling hills. He took pride in his yard and made sure the grass was cut properly, the shrubs pruned, and an abundant supply of flowers was in bloom throughout the growing season. The ravages of age, however, were taking their toll. In July 1975 he spent one night in the local hospital but recovered quickly. He looked forward with great anticipation to traveling to Newport News for the keel-laying ceremony for the *Carl Vinson* scheduled for 11 October 1975. By mid-August he had prepared a fifteen-minute speech, but he would not be able to deliver it. A circulatory impairment prevented him from getting about. Unable to talk properly and often losing his balance, he entered the Baldwin County Hospital. His doctor reported that he had a circulatory problem and "early" pneumonia. He expected that Vinson would be hospitalized for a week. Vinson, who had brought a rocking chair from home, sat in it to watch the World Series. He remained mentally sharp and regretted not being able to make the trip to Newport News. Vinson's condition, it turns out, was more serious than a circulation problem—he had suffered a stroke. After two weeks in the Milledgeville hospital, he was transferred to the military hospital at Warner Robins Air Force Base for further treatment and convalescence. The therapy program strengthened him enough so that he could return to Milledgeville, where Molly and Till could look after him. They converted a room on the first floor of their

---

[48] Ibid., 9 July 1975.
[49] Ibid., 16 January 1974, 9 April 1974, 15 April 1974, 5 May 1975.

ante-bellum home into a bedroom equipped with hospital furniture for him to use.[50]

He continued to improve gradually, but remained bedridden through January. Molly Snead, the tough navy nurse who had cared for Mary Vinson during her last years, refused to allow Vinson to remain bedridden. Determined that he would recover, she hired attendants who gave him round-the-clock care, while she personally took charge of his therapy. At first, he was unwilling to respond to her constant attempts to put him back on his feet. But the feeble old congressman, who had successfully battled admirals, generals, congressmen, and even presidents for half a century, was no match for the resolute Molly. She pushed and prodded him and made him get up and walk. Essentially, she forced him to recover. On 7 April 1976 he dictated a letter to his dear friends Lou and Neta Stockstill, who had retired and moved to Florida. He thanked them for sending him "delicious Florida oranges," informed them that Eddie Hébert, Robert Stephens, and Phil Landrum were retiring from Congress, and described his physical condition. "I am getting along as well as can be expected," he wrote. "I've made good progress, slowly, and am now able to walk about some with my canes. On pretty days I walk in the yard and sit in the sun. I even rode down to the farm a few days ago." That was his last letter to the Stockstills, but they would visit him again and Lou was to play an interesting role in the final stages of the aircraft carrier construction.[51]

Vinson had missed the keel-laying ceremony for the *Carl Vinson*, but he desperately wanted to attend the launching of the ship. The ceremony was set for 15 March 1980, at Newport News, where the enormous vessel was being constructed. At the time of the launching, the C V N 70 (the official name of the *Carl Vinson*) was only two-thirds complete, but the steel hull was finished and the major machinery had

[50] Tillman and Karen Snead, interview with the author; *Atlanta Journal*, 12 October 1975, C8; 23 October 1975, A6, 28 October 1975, A12.

[51] Carl Vinson to Lou and Neta Stockstill, 27 January 1976, 7 April 1976, Stockstill Papers, notebook 3; Tillman and Karen Snead, interview with the author; Alice Andrews, interview with Emmett Hall and the author, Milledgeville, GA, 7 December 2001.

been installed. When finished, the *Carl Vinson* would measure 1,092 feet from bow to stern, nearly as long as the Empire State Building is tall; the distance from its keel to the top of its mast would equal the height of a 24-story high-rise; and from port to starboard, its 4.5-acre flight deck would stretch over 256 feet. Powered by 2 nuclear reactors, the 93,000-ton vessel would reach speeds in excess of 30 knots.[52]

Under Molly's demanding care, Vinson made a surprising recovery from the stroke that had paralyzed his left side. In fact, his recovery was so successful that his mental and physical faculties were nearly the same as before the stroke. With the use of metal canes, he was able to get around, and his mind remained keen and alert. Ruby Nelson, who cooked and cleaned for Vinson and the Sneads for sixteen years, recalled that he liked to spend his early afternoons in the backyard visiting with friends and then take a nap before supper.[53] Floride Moore Gardner, a longtime friend and neighbor, remembered that he enjoyed sitting in the sun at Chester Hodges's service station near his home chatting with folks.[54] A few days before the launching ceremony, he talked with a visiting reporter from the *Atlanta Constitution* for half an hour in the parlor of the Snead home. "I feel fine," he told Frederick Allen, but "I have all the ailments that a man should have when he's the age I am." With his wits still firmly about him, he declined to make any statement about the forthcoming launch, noting, "When a man has reached my age, going on 97, he should be seen and not heard." He did add, however, that "I sent invitations to all of my family and found out that I had 68 kin-people."[55]

After his arrival at Newport News for the ceremony, the old congressman was again in his element, chatting with friends, congressional colleagues, admirals, and other dignitaries. The ceremony was conducted without a hitch. Senator Sam Nunn delivered the

---

[52] Program of the Launching of CVN 70, 15 March 1980, John Sibley Papers, Box 362, Special Collections, Robert W. Woodruff Library, Emory University, Atlanta, GA.

[53] Ruby Nelson, telephone interview with the author, Milledgeville GA, 8 November 2001.

[54] Floride Moore Gardner, telephone interview with the author, Milledgeville, GA, 8 November 2001.

[55] *Atlanta Constitution*, 13 March 1980, C1.

principal address and Molly Snead had the honor of christening the vessel. When asked about her thoughts on christening the world's most powerful nuclear-powered aircraft carrier, she said she would be thinking what a fitting monument it is for a man who has done so much for America. Vinson dismissed such grand thoughts. "All Molly will be thinking about is that champagne might splash on her dress."[56] Retired banker John Sibley, Vinson's ninety-two-year-old lifetime friend, wrote that the christening and launching of the *Carl Vinson* "was the greatest tribute that I have ever seen paid to any public official in my lifetime." Vinson's brother Wilbur observed that "Every feature of the ceremony was perfect, including the manner in which you greeted your many friends."[57]

Chest pains forced the ninety-six-year-old congressman to enter the intensive care unit at the Baldwin County Hospital on 11 August 1980. Tests showed that he had suffered a mild heart attack. Although he remained mentally alert and rested comfortably, he was not discharged until 2 September. Upon releasing him, his private physician, Dr. James Baugh, remarked that it was most unusual for a person of his age to survive a heart attack, but he had recovered nicely. "I think it is a credit to his robust health that he has had over the years."[58]

On 18 November 1980, two-hundred local citizens held a party in the reception hall of the Exchange Bank for the ninety-seventh birthday of Milledgeville's most famous resident. A huge chocolate cake trimmed

---

[56] "Program of the Launching of the CVN 70." In addition to having the honor of christening the *Carl Vinson,* Molly also had two planes named for her. Captain Richard Martin, the first commander of the *Carl Vinson*, had a fixed wing plane on the carrier named "Miss Molly" and had it flown to the Milledgeville-Baldwin County Airport so that Molly could see it. In 1989, the captain of the *Carl Vinson* honored her by naming one of the F-14 Tomcats after her. "Miss Molly" was painted on the side of the plane and a logo of a World War II Navy nurse was painted on its nose. This was the first F-14 on the carrier to have a non-military symbol painted on it. Tillman Snead to the author, 9 April 2003.

[57] John A. Sibley to Carl Vinson, 17 March 1980, John Sibley Papers, box 362.

[58] *Atlanta Constitution*, 12 August 1980, A1; *Atlanta Journal*, 4 September 1980, A23.

in red and blue and adorned with the emblem of the *USS Carl Vinson* dominated the center table. White frosting displayed the number 97. Slowly with a cane in each hand, the honoree rose from his seat, approached the cake, bent low over the sixteen candles, and blew. His friends and acquaintances applauded as the orange flames turned into tiny trails of gray smoke. His chore completed, Vinson smiled broadly as the group sang "Happy Birthday." Long known as "the admiral," Vinson accepted a cap bearing the title "Admiral" from Captain Richard L. Martin, the commander of the *Carl Vinson*, who declared, "You are the First Admiral of the Navy." Later, when the captain returned to say goodbye, Vinson responded in a loud voice, "I'll see you in two years," alluding to the commissioning of the *Carl Vinson*, tentatively set for March of 1982.[59]

At Vinson's suggestion, Lou Stockstill had agreed to assist the navy in the design of a special "distinguished visitors room" aboard the *Carl Vinson*. Stockstill's suggested design concept was adopted, and in May 1981 he traveled to Washington to meet with officials of the firm that had been engaged to execute the plan. As he and Neta headed back home to Florida, they stopped off in Milledgeville for what was to be their final visit with the aging congressman. They were amazed at how strong he looked and sounded, but they were also concerned about the noticeable discoloration of his arms and legs, which they assumed was due to a circulatory problem. Nevertheless, the three old friends had an enjoyable visit. Vinson insisted that Neta sit beside him on the couch and he patted her affectionately. When he had to get up to take one of the short walks that Molly demanded of him, he told Neta, "Now don't you move until I come back." Although essentially uncomplaining, the old man remarked, "Longevity isn't what it's cracked up to be." The next day the Stockstills started for home, unaware that Vinson would enter the Baldwin County Hospital two days later.[60]

In his last years, Vinson had two remaining goals: he hoped to live to be 100, and he wanted to see the ship named for him go into the water. Even when he went to the hospital for the last time in May 1981, he said

[59] *Macon Telegraph*, 19 November 1980, B1.
[60] Louis Stockstill to the author, 23 February 2003, Stockstill Papers.

to Molly, who had been a member of his family for more than three decades, "I know I'm slipping, Molly, but if I can, I just want to live to see that ship go into the water." He rested comfortably in the hospital for two weeks, suffering very little pain. When his condition deteriorated, the doctors—against the wishes of the Sneads and Vinson himself—put him on a pulmonary ventilation machine. It assisted his breathing for two days. At 5:00 a.m. on 1 June 1981, his heart stopped beating.[61]

Throughout his life, Vinson had made a point of always being thoroughly prepared for events, so it was not surprising that he had left careful instructions for his funeral. He wanted a simple funeral and wrote down detailed arrangements for it three years before his death. For the 3:00 p.m. funeral on 3 June, the First United Methodist Church of Milledgeville was filled with flowers even though the family had requested that in lieu of flowers memorials be sent to the Carl Vinson Professorship Fund at Georgia College, to Georgia Military College, or the Mary Vinson Memorial Library, all in Milledgeville. The brown brick church was filled to capacity. Among the mourners sitting in the pews were Georgia's Governor George Busbee, Lieutenant Governor Zell Miller, and both United States Senators Sam Nunn and Mack Mattingly, as well as former Senator Herman Talmadge and former Governor Lester Maddox. Outside, an overflow crowd stood in the sweltering heat and listened to the service over loudspeakers. Pastor of the church, the Reverend Julian Brackman, compared Vinson's death to the falling of a giant tree in the forest. "We shall miss you, Mister Carl," he said, "but we have not come to mourn so much as to celebrate your long and productive life." Former Congressman Phil Landrum delivered the eulogy for his old friend and colleague. He interrupted his prepared

---

[61] *Atlanta Constitution*, 2 June 1981, A1, A4, A6,C1; *New York Times,* 2 June 1981, B10; *Washington Star*, 1 June 1981, A1, B4; Tillman and Karen Snead, interview with the author. Less than two months after Vinson's death, Till Snead died on 25 July 1981. Molly later was stricken with Alzheimer's disease and spent the last four years of her life in Virginia, three years under the care of Tillman and Karen Snead in Dale City and one year in an Alzheimer's care facility in Woodstock. She died on 23 December 1992, in Dale City VA, and was buried next to her husband in Westview Cemetery in Milledgeville.

speech to read a letter from Ronald Reagan in which the president thanked "our Creator for the magnificent life" of Vinson.[62]

After the service, the funeral procession of military units, family, dignitaries, friends, onlookers, and journalists marched several blocks to the Memory Hill Cemetery. Farmers, uncomfortable in Sunday suits, came by to say goodbye to a good neighbor. College students in cut-offs and T-shirts were there to watch the burial of a man they knew only from history books. At the cemetery, they all gathered around the wrought-iron fence that surrounded the Vinson plot. Military pallbearers, representing all the services, stood beside the flag-draped coffin. Vinson had named ten Georgia friends as honorary pallbearers. They ranged from Barnie Collins, his old farmer friend and overseer, to Malcolm Moore, the Vinson Professor at Georgia College. Near the canopied gravesite, a naval ceremonial platoon from Charleston, South Carolina, stood on one side. Next to the platoon, fresh-faced cadets from Georgia Military College, which Vinson had attended, stood at attention in their creased gray uniforms. Also nearby were Captain Richard L. Martin of the *USS Carl Vinson* and Commander Steve Jones, the engineering officer for the ship. At the conclusion of the service, a military band played "America the Beautiful." Some Cub Scouts gave two-fingered salutes. Wilbur Vinson, the eighty-seven-year-old brother of the deceased, put his straw hat down and saluted, too. The honor guard ceremoniously took the American flag off the coffin, folded it, and gave it to Molly Snead. The haunting sounds of "Taps" drifted over the tombstones as Vinson's body was lowered in the red Georgia clay until it rested peacefully under a leafy dogwood tree beside the body of his beloved wife.[63]

"Mr. Vinson always told me he just wanted a simple country funeral," said Barnie Collins, who had worked on Vinson's farm for more than thirty years. As the old farmer looked at the uniformed honor guards and the crowds, he added, "But I'm real proud they added the military and all. It's more fitting."[64]

---

[62] *Atlanta Constitution*, 4 June 1981, A1, C1, C4.

[63] Ibid.

[64] Ibid.

Of the countless obituaries written about Vinson, the one by Otis Pike, a former Democratic congressman from New York, came closest to capturing the essence of the man:

When I was first sworn in as a member of Congress on January 3, 1961, a representative from Georgia named Carl Vinson also raised his right hand and took the same oath to uphold the Constitution and defend the nation from all enemies, foreign and domestic. The representative from Georgia, however, had done it 23 times before, starting when Woodrow Wilson was president.

By the time he had retired, he had taken the oath 25 times and served 50 years, longer than any other man had ever served in the House, in the history of the nation. Last Monday, in Milledgeville, Georgia, he died.

Three different obituaries in three different papers failed to describe the man I had known. They talked about his nicknames: "The Swamp Fox," for his ability to guide legislation through the House, and "Admiral" Vinson, for his dominant role in enlarging the United States Navy, first as chairman of the Naval Affairs Committee, then as chairman of the Armed Services Committee. Newspaper stuff, written by one and copied by others.

He was called, not merely by the members of his own committee, but by all of the rest of the House, simply, "Mr. Chairman."…I served on that committee under that chairman for four years. Admirals and generals loved him, for he gave them almost everything they wanted. He gave them recognition, respect, power, prestige and money. Especially money…

The obituaries perpetuated the myth that he ruled the Armed Services Committee "with an iron hand" or "like a potentate" and that junior members were not allowed to speak. Everyone who asked got his turn—he was impatient only with speakers who had nothing to say. One of the great sports congressmen enjoy is casting the blame on other people when things go wrong. Then, the chairman had no patience….

He was courtly, gentlemanly, humorous, tough and honest.

Above all, he brought to and left in Washington a great surplus of integrity for an institution too often criticized for having none.[65]

In an article written fifteen years earlier, when Vinson received the Sylvanus Thayer Award, Lou Stockstill accurately summarized his friend's impact. "Carl Vinson's contributions to his nation, to the cause of national security, to the growth and development of the individual Armed Forces and to the men and women who wear their country's uniform will never be surpassed. And they must never be forgotten."[66]

---

[65] *Atlanta Journal and Constitution*, 7 June 1981, C1.

[66] Louis Stockstill, "The Nation Is Grateful," *Journal of the Armed Forces* 104 (17 September 1966): 13.

Sources Cited

Manuscripts and Archival Holdings

Charles J. Bloch Papers. Middle Georgia Archives. Middle Georgia Regional Library, Macon, GA.

Tom Watson Brown Private Papers. Marietta, GA.

Emmett Hall Private Scrapbook. Atlanta, GA.

Thomas W. Hardwick Papers. Richard B. Russell Library for Political Research and Studies, University of Georgia Libraries, Athens, GA.

Lyndon Baines Johnson Papers. Public Papers, Oral History of Carl Vinson by Frank Deaver, WIICF Carl Vinson. LBJ Library, Austin, TX.

Ernest King Papers. Manuscript Division, Library of Congress.

Laura Vinson Northrop. Private Vinson Genealogy Files, Atlanta, GA.

Franklin D. Roosevelt Papers. PPF 5901 Carl Vinson. Franklin D. Roosevelt Library, Hyde Park, NY.

John A. Sibley Correspondence. Special Collections Department, Robert W. Woodruff Library, Emory University, Atlanta, GA.

U. Erwin Sibley Papers. Special Collections, Ina Dillard Russell Library, Georgia College and State University, Milledgeville, GA.

Snead Family Papers. Dale City, VA.

Louis and Oneta Stockstill Papers. Currently in the author's possession.

Carl Vinson File. Special Collections. Georgia Military College, Milledgeville, GA.

Carl Vinson File. Special Collections. Jack Tarver Library, Mercer University, Macon, GA.

Vinson Scrapbooks, 27 vols. Owned by Tillman Snead. Currently on loan to Georgia College and State University, Archives of Georgia Education, Milledgeville, GA.

Federal Government Documents

Biographical Directory of the American Congress, 1774–1971.
Washington: Government Printing Office, 1971.

Congressional Record. 63rd Cong.–88th Cong. Washington:
Government Printing Office, 1914–1965.

Historical Statistics of the United States, Colonial Times to 1957.
Washington: Government Printing Office, 1960.

*Tributes in the House of Representatives to Carl Vinson, Representative
from Georgia, October 2, 1964.* Washington: Government Printing
Office, 1965.

U.S. House Committee on Armed Services. *Investigation of the B-36
Bomber Program.* 81st Cong., 2d sess. H. Rept. 1470. Washington:
Government Printing Office, 1950.

———. *Reorganization of the Department of Defense.* 85th Cong., 2d
sess. Hearing 83. Washington: Government Printing Office, 1958.

———. *Unification and Strategy.* 81st Cong. 2d sess. H. Doc. 600.
Washington: Government Printing Office, 1950.

U.S. House Committee on Naval Affairs. *To Encourage Development of
Aviation.* 69th Congress, 1st session. H. Rept. 1396. Washington:
Government Printing Office, 1926.

———.*To Establish the Composition of the United States Navy.* 73rd
Congress, 2nd session. H. Rept. 335. Washington: Government
Printing Office, 1934.

———. *To Establish the Composition of the U.S. Navy, To Authorize the
Construction of Certain Naval Vessels, and for Other Purposes.* 75th
Cong., 3rd sess. Hearings on H. R. 9218. Washington: Government
Printing Office, 1938.

———. *To Further Expedite the National Defense Program....* 77th
Cong., 1st sess. Hearings on H. R. 4139. Washington: Government
Printing Office, 1941.

———. *Investigation of the Naval Defense Program.* 77th Cong., 2d
sess., 7 vols. Hearings Pursuant to H. Res. 162. Washington:
Government Printing Office, 1942.

————. *Investigation of the Naval Defense Program, Preliminary Report*. 77th Cong., 2d sess. H. Rept. 1634. Washington: Government Printing Office, 1942.

————. *Investigation of the Naval Defense Program, Supplemental Report*. 77th Cong., 2d sess. H. Rept. 2371. Washington: Government Printing Office, 1942.

————. *Investigation of the Progress of the War Effort*. 78th Cong., 1st sess. Hearings Pursuant to H. Res. 30. Washington: Government Printing Office, 1943.

————. *Investigation into Status of Naval Defense Program*. 77th Cong., 1st sess. Hearing 17. Washington: Government Printing Office, 1941.

————. *To Permit the Performance of Essential Labor on Naval Contracts Without Regard to Laws and Contracts Limiting Hours of Employment, to Limit the Profits on Naval Contracts, and for Other Purposes*. 77th Cong., 2d sess. Hearings on H. R. 6790. Washington: Government Printing Office, 1942.

————. *Prohibiting the Payment of Contingent Fees for Services in Connection with the Procurement of Naval Contracts, Requiring Certain Warranties in Naval Contracts*. 77th Cong., 2d sess. H. Rept. 2356. Washington: Government Printing Office, 1942.

————. *Report on Need of Additional Naval Bases to Defend the Coasts of the United States, its Territories, and Possessions*. 76th Cong., 1st sess. H. Doc. 65. Washington: Government Printing Office, 1939.

U.S. House Conference Committee. Conference Report to Accompany H. R. 6604. 73rd Congress, 2nd Session. H. Rept. 1024. Washington: Government Printing Office, 1934.

U.S. House District of Columbia Committee. *Appointment of Recorder of Deeds, District of Columbia*. 64th Cong., 1st sess. H. Rept. 170. Washington: Government Printing Office, 1916.

————. *Inquiry Into the Cost of Living in the District of Columbia*. 64th Cong., 1st sess. H. Rept. 310. Washington: Government Printing Office, 1916.

————. *Salaries of Police Officers in the District of Columbia*. 64th Congress. Ast Session. H. Rept. 1061.

U.S. House Pensions Committee. *Granting Pensions....* 63rd Cong., 3rd
 sess. H. Rept. 1307. Washington: Government Printing Office, 1915.
U.S. Senate Committee on Military Affairs. *Aircraft in National Defense.*
 69th Cong., 1st sess. S. Doc. 18. Report of the board, appointed by
 the President of the United States on September 12, 1925, to make a
 study of the best means of developing and applying aircraft in
 National Defense. Washington: Government Printing Office, 1925.

State and County Government Documents
Baldwin County, Georgia. *Deed Book.* Milledgeville GA.
Georgia. Department of Archives and History. *Georgia Official and
 Statistical Register.* 1911–1972.
Georgia. General Assembly. *Journal of the House.* 1909–1911.

Unpublished Interviews by Author
Andrews, Alice with Emmett Hall. Milledgeville GA, 7 December 2001.
Ellis, Eugene with Emmett Hall. Milledgeville GA, 7 December 2001.
Elowitz, Larry. Telephone interview. Milledgeville GA, 6 January 2003.
Gardner, Floride Moore. Telephone interview. Milledgeville GA, 8
 November 2001.
Hall, Emmett. Cedartown GA, 6 March 2001.
———. Jekyll Island GA, 22 November 2001.
———. Milledgeville GA, 7 December 2001.
Hallgren, Margaret Benedict Vinson. Telephone interview. Alexandria
 VA, 23 January 2003.
Hood, Elizabeth Pollard. Telephone interview. Corpus Christi TX, 16
 October 2000.
———. Griffin GA, 26 November 2001.
Jennings, Henry. Telephone interview. Gainesville GA, 22 August 2001.
Jennings, Robert. Telephone interview. Gainesville GA, 23 August 2001.
Kinnett, Patricia Pollard. Jekyll Island, GA, 22 November 2001.
McMillan, Joe and Carol (with Emmett Hall). Milledgeville GA, 7
 December 2001.
Nelson, Ruby. Telephone interview. Milledgeville GA, 8 November
 2001.

Nunn, Sam. Atlanta GA, 4 April 2001.

Pollard, Mary Ann. Jekyll Island GA, 22 November 2001.

Sanders, Carl. Atlanta GA, 23 August 2001.

Sheffield, Roger Vinson. Jekyll Island GA, 22 November 2001.

Snead, Tillman and Karen. Dale City VA, 8 June 2001.

Stockstill, Louis and Oneta. Indiatlantic FL, 21 June 2001.

Stockstill, Louis. Telephone interview. Indiatlantic FL, 9 and 15 January 2003.

Vinson, Ed and Betty. Atlanta GA, 7 August 2001.

Newspapers

Atlanta Constitution

Atlanta Journal

Augusta Chronicle

Macon Telegraph

Milledgeville News

New York Times

Union-Recorder (Milledgeville)

Washington Post

Books

Abbazia, Patrick. *Mr. Roosevelt's Navy: The Private War of the U.S. Atlantic Fleet, 1939–1942*. Annapolis: Naval Institute Press, 1975.

Adler, Selig. *The Isolationist Impulse*. Westport CT: Greenwood Press, 1957.

———. *The Uncertain Giant, 1921–1941: American Foreign Policy Between the Wars*. New York: Macmillan, 1965.

Alsop, Stewart. *The Center: People and Power in Political Washington*. New York: Harper & Row, Publishers, 1968.

Anderson, William. *The Wild Man from Sugar Creek*. Baton Rouge: Louisiana State University Press, 1975.

Bacon, Donald C. et al., editors. *The Encyclopedia of the United States Congress*. 4 volumes. New York: Simon & Schuster, 1995.

Bailey, Thomas A. *A Diplomatic History of the American People*. 10th edition. Englewood Cliffs NJ: Prentice-Hall, Inc., 1980.

Bolling, Richard. *Power in the House: A History of the Leadership of the House of Representatives*. New York: E. P. Dutton & Co., 1968.

Bonner, James C. *Milledgeville: Georgia's Antebellum Capital*. Athens: University of Georgia Press, 1978.

Brown, Walter J. *J. J. Brown and Thomas E. Watson: Georgia Politics, 1912–1928*. n. p.: Walter J. Brown, 1988.

Buell, Thomas B. *Master of Sea Power: A Biography of Fleet Admiral Ernest J. King*. Boston: Little, Brown and Company, 1980.

Cantril, Hadley and Mildred Strunk, editors. *Public Opinion, 1935–1946*. Princeton: Princeton University Press, 1951.

Caraley, Demetrios. *The Politics of Military Unification*. New York: Columbia University Press, 1966.

Caro, Robert A. *Master of the Senate*. New York: Alfred A. Knopf, 2002.

———. *The Path to Power*. New York: Alfred A. Knopf, 1982.

Cole, Wayne S. *America First: The Battle Against Intervention, 1940–1941*. New York: Octagon Books, 1971.

———. *Roosevelt & the Isolationists, 1932–45*. Lincoln: University of Nebraska Press, 1983.

———. *Senator Gerald P. Nye and American Foreign Relations*. Minneapolis: University of Minnesota Press, 1962.

Coleman, Kenneth, editor. *A History of Georgia*. Athens: University of Georgia Press, 1977.

Connery, Robert H. *The Navy and the Industrial Mobilization in World War II*. Princeton: Princeton University Press, 1951.

Cook, Anna Maria Green. *History of Baldwin County Georgia*. Anderson SC: Keys-Hearn Printing Co., 1925.

Cook, James F. *Carl Sanders: Spokesman of the New South*. Macon GA: Mercer University Press, 1993.

———. *The Governors of Georgia, 1754–1995*. Macon GA: Mercer University Press, 1995.

Crowley, James B. *Japan's Quest for Autonomy: National Security and Foreign Policy, 1930–1938*. Princeton: Princeton University Press, 1966.

Dallek, Robert. *Franklin D. Roosevelt and American Foreign Policy, 1932–1945*. New York: Oxford University Press, 1979.

————. *Lone Star Rising: Lyndon Johnson and His Times, 1908–1960*. New York: Oxford University Press, 1991.

Davis, B. Vincent. *The Admirals Lobby*. Chapel Hill: University of North Carolina Press, 1967.

Davis, George T. *A Navy Second to None: The Development of Modern American Naval Policy*. New York: Harcourt, Brace and Company, 1940.

————. *Postwar Defense Policy and the U.S. Navy, 1943–1946*. Chapel Hill: University of North Carolina Press, 1966.

Divine, Robert A. *The Illusion of Neutrality*. Chicago: University of Chicago Press, 1962.

Engelbrecht, H. C. and F. C. Hanighen. *Merchants of Death: A Study of the International Armament Industry*. New York: Dodd, Mead & Company, 1934.

Ferrell, Robert H. *American Diplomacy in the Great Depression: Hoover-Stimson Foreign Policy, 1929–1933*. New Haven: Yale University Press, 1957.

————. *Harry S. Truman, A Life*. Columbia: University of Missouri Press, 1994.

————. *Peace in Their Time: The Origins of the Kellogg–Briand Pact*. New Haven: Yale University Press, 1952.

Frank, Judith Waldrop. *Washington By Night*. Washington: Starwood Publishing, Inc., 1992.

Goldman, Eric F. *The Crucial Decade–And After: America, 1945–1960*. New York: Vintage Books, 1960.

Goodhart, Philip. *Fifty Ships That Saved the World: The Foundation of the Anglo–American Alliance*. Garden City NY: Doubleday and Company, 1965.

Hardeman, D. B. and Donald C. Bacon. *Rayburn, A Biography*. Austin: Texas Monthly Press, 1987.

Harris, Ted Carlton. *Jeannette Rankin: Suffragist, First Woman Elected to Congress and Pacifist*. New York: Arno Press, 1982.

Hood, Elizabeth Pollard. *Lest We Forget: The Ancestors and Descendants of Edward Story Vinson and Annie Adela Morris Vinson*. Columbia SC: McDonald Printing, n. d.

Hoyt, Edwin P. *U-Boats Offshore*. New York: Stein and Day Publishers, 1978.

Hurley, Alfred F. *Billy Mitchell, Crusader for Air Power*. New York: Franklin Watts, Inc., 1974.

Kimball, Warren F. *The Most Unsordid Act, Lend-Lease, 1939–1941*. Baltimore: Johns Hopkins Press, 1969.

Koginos, Manny T. *The Panay Incident: Prelude to War*. Lafayette IN: Purdue University Studies, 1967.

Leahy, William D. *I Was There*. New York: McGraw-Hill Book Company, 1950.

Leuchtenburg, William E. *Franklin D. Roosevelt and the New Deal*. New York: Harper & Row, Publishers, 1963.

Levine, Robert H. *The Politics of American Naval Rearmament, 1930–1938*. New York: Garland Publishing, Inc., 1988.

Liddell Hart, B. H. *History of the Second World War*. New York: G. P. Putnam's Sons, 1970.

Link, Arthur S. *American Epoch*. New York: Alfred A. Knopf, 1967.

MacNeil, Neil. *Forge of Democracy: The House of Representatives*. New York: David McKay Company, Inc., 1963.

Members of Congress Since 1789. Washington: Congressional Quarterly Inc., 1977.

Millis, Walter. *Arms and the State*. New York: The Twentieth Century Fund, 1958.

————. editor. *The Forrestal Diaries*. New York: The Viking Press, 1951.

————. *Road to War: America, 1914–1917*. Boston: Houghton Mifflin Company, 1935.

Mooney, Booth. *Roosevelt and Rayburn: A Political Partnership*. Philadelphia: Lippincott, 1971.

Morison, Samuel Eliot. *The Two-Ocean War*. Boston: Little, Brown and Company, 1963.

Murdock, Myrtle Cheney. *Your Uncle Sam in Washington*. Washington: Monumental Press, 1948.

O'Connor, Raymond G. *Perilous Equilibrium: The United States and the London Naval Conference of 1930*. Lawrence: University of Kansas Press, 1962.

Pelz, Stephen E. *Race to Pearl Harbor: The Failure of the Second London Naval Conference and the Onset of World War II.* Cambridge: Harvard University Press, 1974.

Ragow, Arnold A. *James Forrestal: A Study of Personality, Politics, and Policy.* New York: The Macmillan Company, 1963.

Rappaport, Armin. *The Navy League of the United States.* Detroit: Wayne State University Press, 1962.

Reynolds, David. *From Munich to Pearl Harbor.* Chicago: Ivan R. Dee, 2001.

Rosenman, Samuel I. editor. *The Public Papers and Addresses of Franklin D. Roosevelt.* 13 volumes. New York: Random House, Macmillan, Harper, 1938–1950.

Seldes, George. *Iron, Blood and Profits: An Exposure of the World-wide Munitions Racket.* New York: Harper & Brothers, 1934.

Sherwood, Robert E. *Roosevelt and Hopkins: An Intimate History.* New York: Harper & Brothers Publishers, 1948.

Sorensen, Theodore C. *Kennedy.* New York: Harper & Row, Publishers, 1965.

Stein, Harold. editor. *American Civil-Military Decisions.* Tuscaloosa: University of Alabama Press, 1963.

Steinberg, Alfred. *Sam Johnson's Boy.* New York: Macmillan Company, 1968.

———. *Sam Rayburn: A Biography.* New York: Hawthorn Books, 1975.

Stimson, Henry L. and McGeorge Bundy. *On Active Service in Peace and War.* New York: Harper & Brothers, 1947.

Sulzberger, C. L. *World War II.* New York: McGraw-Hill Book Company, 1970.

Tansill, Charles C. *America Goes to War.* Boston: Little, Brown and Company, 1938.

Timmons, Bascom N. *Garner of Texas, A Personal History.* New York: Harper & Brothers Publishers, 1948.

Truman, Harry S. *Memoirs.* 2 volumes. Garden City NY: Doubleday & Company, Inc., 1955–1956.

Turnbull, Archibald D. and Clifford L. Lord. *History of United States Naval Aviation.* New York: Arno Press, 1972.

Vinson, John Chalmers. *William E. Borah and the Outlawry of War.* Athens: University of Georgia Press, 1957.

Weinstein, Allen and Frank Otto Gatell. *Freedom and Crisis.* 3rd edition. 2 volumes. New York: Random House, 1981.

Periodicals

Adams, Hancock. "Uncle Sam's New Naval Plan." *National Republic* 19 (March 1932): 5–7.

"'The Admiral.'" *Newsweek* 27 (3 June 1946): 30.

"The Admiral Strikes His Colors." *Time* 79 (30 March 1962): 15–16.

"Air Marshal Vinson." *Newsweek* 33 (28 March 1949): 18–19.

Albion, Robert Greenhalgh. "The Naval Affairs Committees, 1816–1947." *Proceedings of the United States Naval Institute* 78 (1952): 1226–37.

"Armed Services Salute Chairman Vinson." *Journal of the Armed Forces* 101 (11 July 1964): 20–21.

"Arms and Men." *Fortune* 9 (March 1934): 53–57, 113.

Baker, Russell. "Again Vinson Mounts the Ramparts." *New York Times Magazine.* 4 May 1958, 13, 78.

"Building a Navy Second to None." *United States News* 9 (14 February 1941): 13.

"Caisson Correspondence Holds Horses' Fate." *Army Navy Air Force Journal* 94 (16 February 1957): 3.

"The Caisson And Cost Effectiveness." *Army Navy Air Force Journal* 101 (7 December 1963): 11.

Capper, Arthur. "Let Us Keep Out of Foreign Wars." *Vital Speeches of the Day* 7 (1941): 293–96.

"Carl Vinson, Friend of the Navy and of Air Force Expansion." *U.S. News & World Report* 26 (17 June 1949): 34–37.

"Carl Vinson of Georgia Puts Spotlight on Defense." *U.S. News & World Report* 44 (14 February 1958): 21.

"The Congress." *Time* 39 (26 January 1942): 14.

"The Congress." *Time* 40 (27 July 1942): 14.

"The Congress." *Time* 59 (17 March 1952): 18–19.

"Congressman Vinson's Happy, Busy Day." *Army Navy Air Force Journal and Register* 100 (27 July 1963): 18–19.

"Defense Shake-Up? Maybe, But Not for Joint Chiefs." *U.S. News & World Report* 44 (7 March 1958): 12.

Doolittle, Jerome. "The Gentleman From Georgia Goes Home." *Saturday Evening Post* 237 (5 December 1964): 26–28.

Eleazer, Frank. "He controls 55¢ of your tax dollar." *Nations's Business* 43 (December 1955): 32–33, 64–71.

Elliott, Charles F. "The Genesis of the Modern U.S. Navy." *U.S. Naval Institute Proceedings* 92 (March 1966): 62–69.

Evans, Rowland Jr. "The Sixth Sense of Carl Vinson." *Reporter* 26 (12 April 1962): 25–30.

"Fifty-Year Man." *Newsweek* 64 (28 December 1964): 20–21.

Fischer, Louis. "Keeping America Out of War." *Nation* 144 (27 March 1937): 347–49.

"The Gentleman From Georgia Vs. The President." *U.S. News & World Report* 44 (27 June 1958): 19.

"Georgia's Vinson: Battling the Pentagon." *U.S. News & World Report* 55 (30 September 1963): 16.

Halsey, W. F. interview. "Why the Navy Wants Big Carriers." *U.S. News & World Report* 26 (20 May 1949): 24–28.

Hutcheson, Carl F. "Alumnus Writes of Vinson and Watson." *The Mercerian* 45 (December 1958): 4.

Janeway, Eliot. "The Man Who Owns the Navy." *Saturday Evening Post* 218 (15 December 1945): 17, 101–102.

Johnsen, Katherine. "Restudy of RS–70 Is Ordered; Vinson–McNamara Clash Averted." *Aviation Week and Space Technology* 76 (26 March 1962): 17–18.

"Meet the Author." *Time* 54 (5 September 1949): 14.

"More Than Half a Billion Asked for Naval Increase." *Literary Digest* 112 (23 January 1932): 8.

"Navy: House Launches Bill for Construction up to the Limit." *Newsweek* 3 (3 February 1934): 11.

"New Draft: Winners and Losers." *U.S. News & World Report* 30 (8 June 1951): 26.

Packard, Vance. "Uncle Carl." *American Magazine* 149 (April 1950): 30–31, 120–23.

"The Pentagon: Checkmate?" *Newsweek* 51 (10 March 1958): 40.

"Probe's View of Arms Profits Raises Cry for Drastic Curbs." *Newsweek* 19 (2 February 1942): 38, 40.

Reed, Ralph. "'Fighting the Devil with Fire': Carl Vinson's Victory over Tom Watson in the 1918 Tenth District Democratic Primary." *Georgia Historical Quarterly* 67 (Winter 1983): 451–79.

Scott, Walter. "Personality Parade." *Parade Magazine.* In *Atlanta Journal-Constitution.* 13 January 2002, 2.

Seibold, Louis. *Universal Services.* 8 January 1932. http://www.cvn70.navy.mil/vinson/vinson9.htm.

"Shaping New-Style Campaign: Opposition to Major Changes." *U.S. News & World Report* 21 (18 October 1946): 27–28.

"Slap for an Iron Hand." *Newsweek* 46 (4 July 1955): 19.

Smith, Beverly. "He Makes the Generals Listen." *Saturday Evening Post* 223 (10 March 1951): 20–21, 134–38.

Sparks, Andrew. "Carl Vinson Comes Home." *Atlanta Journal and Constitution Magazine.* 3 January 1965, 8–9, 21–22.

Stockstill, Louis R. "The Nation Is Grateful." *Journal of the Armed Forces* 104 (17 September 1966): 13.

———. "'Uncle Carl' Couldn't Be There." *Journal of the Armed Forces* 102 (10 April 1965): 31.

———. "'Uncle Carl' Vinson: Backstage Boss of the Pentagon." *Army Navy Air Force Journal* 98 (18 February 1961): 1, 22–28.

———. "'Uncle Carl' Vinson: Backstage Boss of the Pentagon." *Reader's Digest* 78 (March 1961): 128–32.

———. "The View From Milledgeville, Georgia." *Air Force Magazine* 57 (August 1974): 72–79.

Surface, Bill. "Carl Vinson: A Half Century in Congress." *Family Weekly.* 19 July 1964, 12–13.

"'Swamp Fox' Letter." *Newsweek* 59 (2 April 1962): 23–24.

"Tillman Takes The 'Backstage Boss' of the Pentagon To the White House." *Army Navy Air Force Journal* 98 (29 July 1961): 27.

"Uncle Carl Gets Mad." *Time* 79 (16 March 1962): 16–17.

"Vast U.S. Navy Program Is Put Under Congressional Microscope." *Newsweek* 15 (22 January 1940): 11–14.

Vinson, Carl. "The Aircraft Program Passes in Review." *National Aeronautics* 19 (March 1941): 7–8.

————. "The Battle of the Atlantic." *Collier's* 110 (31 October 1942): 18–20.

————. "For a 'West Point' of the Air." *New York Times Magazine*. 22 June 1952, 13, 35.

————. "Legislation to Curb Strikes in Defense Industry." *Congressional Digest* 20 (April 1941): 110–13.

————. "The Navy of the Future." *Shipmate* 27 (June–July 1964): 8–9, 11.

————. "President's Proposal Means 'Prussian-Type General Staff.'" *U.S. News & World Report* 44 (25 April 1958): 80–81, 123.

"Vinson Joins Assault on Supreme Court." *Christian Century* 73 (27 June 1956): 765.

"Vinson-McNamara Exchange Letters On Changes." *Army Navy Air Force Journal* 98 (10 June 1961): 1, 24, 27.

Walter, John C. "Congressman Carl Vinson and Franklin Roosevelt: Naval Preparedness and the Coming of World War II, 1932–1940." *Georgia Historical Quarterly* 64 (Fall 1980): 294–305.

White, William S. "Carl Vinson Has Been Unified, Too." *New York Times Magazine*. 10 September 1950, 12, 42, 44.

Whittle, Inge. "Milledgeville: Georgia's Capital, 1807–1868." *Teaching Georgia's Government* 24 (Summer 2001): 1–2, 7.

"Why Air Force Wants B-36." *U.S. News & World Report* 26 (17 June 1949): 18–19.

"Why Bigger Draft Is Coming: An Interview with Carl Vinson." *U S. News & World Report* 29 (27 October 1950): 40–46.

Films

Carl Vinson: A Great Georgian. Athens:University of Georgia, Georgia Center for Continuing Education, 1972.

Dissertations and Theses

Berg, Meredith William. "The United States and the Breakdown of Naval Limitation, 1934–1939." Ph.D. dissertation, Tulane University, 1966.

Cashin, Edward L. "Thomas E. Watson and the Catholic Layman's Association of Georgia." Ph.D. dissertation, Fordham University, 1962.

Coode, Thomas H. "Georgia Congressmen and the New Deal, 1933–1938." Ph.D. dissertation, University of Georgia, 1966.

Enders, Calvin W. "The Vinson Navy." Ph.D. dissertation, Michigan State University, 1970.

Landrum, Susan. "Carl Vinson: A Study in Military Preparedness." Master's thesis, Emory University, 1968.

West, Michael A. "Laying the Legislative Foundation: The House Naval Affairs Committee and the Construction of the Treaty Navy, 1926–1934." Ph.D. dissertation, Ohio State University, 1980.

Index